Arts 3

Stages of Theater
The Dramatic Criticism of Stanley Kauffmann, 1951-2006

Stanley Kauffmann, 1968, as photographed in New York by Jerzy Kosiński.

Stages of Theater
The Dramatic Criticism of Stanley Kauffmann, 1951-2006

James R. Russo

© Individual author and College Publications 2023
All rights reserved.

ISBN 978-1-84890-429-3

College Publications
Scientific Director: Dov Gabbay
Managing Director: Jane Spurr

http://www.collegepublications.co.uk

Cover art: "Rhythmic Spaces" (1906-28), as designed and drawn by Adolphe Appia.

Stanley Kauffmann, 1968, as photographed by Jerzy Kosiński.

Cover produced by Laraine Welch

All rights reserved. No part of this publication may be reproduced, stored in a retrieval system or transmitted in any form, or by any means, electronic, mechanical, photocopying, recording or otherwise without prior permission, in writing, from the publisher.

TABLE OF CONTENTS:
Stages of Theater: The Dramatic Criticism of Stanley Kauffmann, 1951-2006

Acknowledgements

Chronology
Introduction

PRODUCTION REVIEWS

1. *After the Fall*, by Arthur Miller. *Wilson Library Bulletin*, May 1965.

2. *Malcolm*, by Edward Albee. *New York Times*, Jan. 12, 1966.

3. *The Condemned of Altona*, by Jean-Paul Sartre. *New York Times*, Feb. 4, 1966.

4. *Winterset*, by Maxwell Anderson. *New York Times*, Feb. 10, 1966.

5. *Phaedra*, by Jean Racine. *New York Times*, Feb. 11, 1966.

6. *Philadelphia, Here I Come!*, by Brian Friel. *New York Times*, Feb. 17, 1966.

7. *Where's Daddy?*, by William Inge. *New York Times*, March 3, 1966.

8. *Serjeant Musgrave's Dance*, by John Arden. *New York Times*, March 20, 1966.

9. *The Caucasian Chalk Circle*, by Bertolt Brecht. *New York Times*, March 25, 1966.

10. "Six Short Plays from La Mama." *New York Times*, April 12 & 13, 1966.

11. *The Skin of Our Teeth*, by Thornton Wilder. *New York Times*, June 2, 1966.

12. *The Dance of Death*, by August Strindberg. *New York Times*, June 3, 1966.

13. *The Kitchen*, by Arnold Wesker. *New York Times*, June 14, 1966.

14. *All's Well That Ends Well*, by William Shakespeare. *New York Times*, June 17, 1966.

15. *Hello and Goodbye*, by Athol Fugard. *New Republic*, Oct. 11, 1969.

16. *The Three Sisters*, by Anton Chekhov. *New Republic*, March 21, 1970.

17. *Lemon Sky*, by Lanford Wilson. *New Republic*, June 13, 1970.

18. *Old Times*, by Harold Pinter. *New Republic*, Jan. 18, 1971.

19. *Slag*, by David Hare. *New Republic*, March 13, 1971.

20. *Follies*, by Stephen Sondheim. *New Republic*, May 8, 1971.

21. *The Master Builder*, by Henrik Ibsen. *New Republic*, Nov. 6, 1971.

22. *Narrow Road to the Deep North*, by Edward Bond. *New Republic*, Feb. 5, 1972.

23. *The Beggar's Opera*, by John Gay. *New Republic*, April 29, 1972.

24. *Medea*, by Euripides. *New Republic*, June 24, 1972.

25. *And They Put Handcuffs on Flowers*, by Fernando Arrabal. *New Republic*, June 24, 1972.

26. *Enemies*, by Maxim Gorky. *New Republic*, Dec. 16, 1972.

27. *Outcry*, by Tennessee Williams. *New Republic*, March 24, 1973.

28. *The Orphan*, by David Rabe. *New Republic*, May 26, 1973.

29. *The Widowing of Mrs. Holroyd*, by D. H. Lawrence. *New Republic*, Dec. 15, 1973.

30. *What the Wine-Sellers Buy*, by Ron Milner. *New Republic*, March 9, 1974.

31. *Short Eyes*, by Miguel Piñero. *New Republic*, April 20, 1974.

32. *In Praise of Love*, by Terence Rattigan. *New Republic*, Jan. 4-11, 1975.

33. *God's Favorite*, by Neil Simon. *New Republic*, Feb. 22, 1975.

34. *The Mound Builders*, by Lanford Wilson. *New Republic*, March 1, 1975.

35. *The Misanthrope*, by Molière. *New Republic*, April 12, 1975.

36. *A Fable*, by Jean-Claude van Itallie. *New Republic*, Nov. 8, 1975.

37. *Trelawny of the "Wells"'*, by Arthur Wing Pinero. *New Republic*, Nov. 8, 1975.

38. *Ice Age*, by Tankred Dorst. *New Republic*, Dec. 20, 1975.

39. *Rich and Famous*, by John Guare. *New Republic*, March 13, 1976.

40. *Boy Meets Girl*, by Bella and Sam Spewack, & *Secret Service*, by William Gillette. *New Republic*, May 8, 1976.

41. *The Runner Stumbles*, by Milan Stitt. *New Republic*, June 12, 1976.

42. *A Texas Trilogy*, by Preston Jones. *New Republic*, Oct. 23, 1976.

43. *Sly Fox*, by Larry Gelbart. *New Republic*, Jan. 15, 1977.

44. *Anna Christie*, by Eugene O'Neill. *New Republic*, May 7, 1977.

45. *Otherwise Engaged*, by Simon Gray. *New Republic*, June 26, 1977.

46. *Antony and Cleopatra*, by William Shakespeare, & *All for Love*, by John Dryden. *New Republic*, Sept. 24, 1977.

47. *The Dybbuk*, by S. Ansky. *New Republic*, Jan. 14, 1978.

48. *Fefu and Her Friends*, by María Irene Fornés. *New Republic*, Feb. 25, 1978.

49. *A Prayer for My Daughter*, by Thomas Babe. *New Republic*, Feb. 25, 1978.

50. *A History of the American Film*, by Christopher Durang. *New Republic*, April 22, 1978.

51. *Ballroom*, by Michael Bennett. *New Republic*, Jan. 27, 1979.

52. *The Bacchae*, by Euripides. *Saturday Review*, Nov. 1980.

53. *Coming Attractions*, by Ted Tally. *Saturday Review*, March 1981.

54. *Key Exchange*, by Kevin Wade. *Saturday Review*, Sept. 1981.

55. *Crimes of the Heart*, by Beth Henley. *Saturday Review*, Jan. 1982.

56. *The Dining Room*, by A. R. Gurney. *Saturday Review*, May 1982.

57. *A Soldier's Play*, by Charles Fuller, & *Colored People's Time*, by Leslie Lee. *Saturday Review*, June 1982.

58. *La Cage aux Folles*, by Harvey Fierstein. *Saturday Review*, Nov.-Dec. 1983.

59. *Einstein on the Beach*, by Robert Wilson. *Saturday Review*, March-April 1985.

60. *Strange Interlude*, by Eugene O'Neill. *Saturday Review*, June 1985.

61. *Chicago*, by John Kander, Fred Ebb, and Bob Fosse. *Slant Magazine*, Nov. 26, 1996.

62. *The Resistible Rise of Arturo Ui*, by Bertolt Brecht. *Theater*, Fall 2003.

THEATER FEATURES

1. "The Trail of the Splendid Gypsy: On Edmund Kean." *Horizon*, March 1962.

2. "An Invitation to Some Comic Authors." *New York Times*, Jan. 16, 1966.

3. "Sartre's Theater and Ours." *New York Times*, Feb. 13, 1966.

4. "Brecht—In Theory and Fact." *New York Times*, April 10, 1966.

5. "An Alternative Theater: Off-Off Broadway." *New York Times*, May 1, 1966.

6. "Bored But Very Vital: Chekhov's Theater." *New York Times*, May 15, 1966.

7. "A Life in the Theatre: Harley Granville-Barker." *Horizon*, Autumn 1975.

8. "Theatre As You Like It: A Round of Applause for Repertory." *Horizon*, Autumn 1976.

9. "Why We Need Broadway: Some Notes." *Performing Arts Journal*, May-Sept. 1985.

10. "George Bernard Shaw: Twentieth-Century Victorian." *Performing Arts Journal*, May 1986.

11. "Howard Brenton: A British Firebrand, Lost in Translation." *New York Times*, April 23, 2006.

12. "Our Debts to the Duke: A Note on the Duke of Saxe-Meiningen." HotReview.org, Aug. 2006.

RECORDED DRAMA

1. *The Lady's Not for Burning*, by Christopher Fry. *Saturday Review*, Dec. 29, 1951.

2. *Hedda Gabler*, by Henrik Ibsen. *Saturday Review*, April 26, 1952.

3. *The Importance of Being Earnest*, by Oscar Wilde. *Saturday Review*, Aug. 29, 1953.

4. *Romeo and Juliet*, by William Shakespeare. *Saturday Review*, Nov. 28, 1953.

THEATER AND FILM

1. "End of an Inferiority Complex: Theater vs. Film." *Theatre Arts*, Sept. 1962.

2. "To Be Taken as Directed: Some Plays (Not Movies)." *New York Times*, May 22, 1966.

3. "Gabriel Blew His Horn: On Bernard Shaw and Gabriel Pascal." *Theater*, Spring-Fall 1997.

4. "Shakespearean Projections, or the Bard on Screen." *Theater*, Winter 2002.

BOOK REVIEWS

1. *A History of American Acting*, Garff B. Wilson. *New York Times*, July 24, 1966.

2. *Melodrama Unveiled: American Theater and Culture, 1800-1850*, by David Grimsted. *New Republic*, Sept. 28, 1968.

3. *More Theatres*, by Max Beerbohm. *New Republic*, Nov. 8, 1969.

4. *Bernard Shaw: A Reassessment*, by Colin Wilson. *New Republic*, Nov. 22, 1969.

5. *Notes on a Cowardly Lion: The Biography of Bert Lahr*, by John Lahr. *New Republic*, Dec. 20, 1969.

6. *The Autobiography of Joseph Jefferson*. *New Republic*, May 6, 1972.

7. *McGraw-Hill Encyclopedia of World Drama* and Others. *New Republic*, Oct. 21, 1972.

8. *The Letters of Anton Chekhov*, translated by Avrahm Yarmolinsky, Simon Karlinsky, & Michael Henry Heim. *Saturday Review*, July 17, 1973.

9. *Theatres: An Architectural and Cultural History*, by Simon Tidworth. *New Republic*, Sept. 29, 1973.

10. *The Federal Theatre, 1935-1939: Plays, Relief, and Politics*, by Jane DeHart Mathews. *American Scholar*, Winter 1967-1968; & *Stage Left*, by Jay Williams. *New York Times* "Book Review," March 10, 1974.

11. *The Last Days of Mankind*, by Karl Kraus. *New Republic*, May 4, 1974.

12. *Black Theater USA: 45 Plays by Black Americans, 1847-1974,* edited by James V. Hatch. *New Republic*, June 22, 1974.

13. *Meyerhold: The Art of Conscious Theater*, by Marjorie L. Hoover. *New Republic*, Jan. 25, 1975.

14. *The Theatrical Event*, by David Cole. *New Republic*, Aug. 16-23, 1975.

15. *"The Ride Across Lake Constance" and Other Plays*, by Peter Handke. *New Republic*, Nov. 20, 1976.

16. *Wilhelm Meister's Apprenticeship*, by Johann Wolfgang von Goethe. *New Republic*, Aug. 26-Sept. 2, 1978.

17. *The House of Barrymore*, by Margot Peters. *New Republic*, Jan. 28, 1991.

18. *Tragic Muse: Rachel of the Comédie-Française*, by Rachel M. Brownstein. *Salmagundi*, Fall 1993.

Postscript

Bibliography
Index

Acknowledgements

All of the material in *Stages of Theater: The Dramatic Criticism of Stanley Kauffmann, 1951-2006*, by Stanley Kauffmann, originally appeared in the following places: *New Republic, Saturday Review, New York Times, Salmagundi, Horizon, Wilson Library Bulletin, Theatre Arts, Performing Arts Journal, Theater, Slant, American Scholar*, and *Hot Review*. Permission to reprint this material came from all of these publications, as well as Stanley Kauffmann himself, who during his long career always copyrighted his articles, reviews, and essays in his own name rather than the name of the journal or newspaper in which they first appeared.

My deep gratitude goes out to the late Mr. Kauffmann and his wife, Laura, for their valuable support of and assistance on this project during the final years of their lives.

Chronology: Stanley Jules Kauffmann

Born 24 April 1916 in New York City, the son of Joseph H. Kauffmann, a dentist, and Jeanette (Steiner) Kauffmann; one sibling, a sister, who predeceased him

Died 9 October 2013 in New York City

Educated in the public schools of New York City (including DeWitt Clinton High School in the Bronx) and in the College of Fine Arts at New York University (B.F.A. in drama, 1935)

Married 5 February 1943, to Laura (Cohen) Kauffmann (deceased, 2012); no children

Positions

Actor-Stage Manager, Washington Square Players, New York, 1931-1941
Writer, producer, and director of a weekly radio serial for the Mutual Broadcasting Company, 1945-1946
Associate Editor, Bantam Books, 1949-1952
Editor-in-Chief, Ballantine Books, 1952-1956
Consulting Editor, Ballantine Books, 1957-1958
Editor, Alfred A. Knopf, 1959-1960
Film Critic, *New Republic*, 1958-1965, 1967-2013
Freelance Book Reviewer & Cultural Commentator, 1961-2013, for such publications as *Horizon*, *Commentary*, *Salmagundi*, *Yale Review*, *Kenyon Review*, *Theater*, and the *American Scholar*
Freelance Book Reviewer & Cultural Commentator, 1961-2013
Drama Critic, WNET-TV, New York, 1963-1965
Host, "The Art of Film," WNET-TV, New York, 1963-1967
Drama Critic, *New York Times*, 1966
Associate Literary Editor, *New Republic*, 1966-1967
Theater Critic, *New Republic*, 1969-1979
Professor of Drama, Yale University, 1967-1973, 1977-1986
Distinguished Professor of English, York College, City University of New York, 1973-1976
Visiting Professor of Drama, City University of New York Graduate Center, 1976-1992
Theater Critic, *Saturday Review*, 1979-1985

Distinguished Visiting Professor of Theater and Film, Adelphi University, 1992-1996

Visiting Professor of Drama, Hunter College, City University of New York, 1993-2006

Awards and Distinctions

Emmy for "The Art of Film," WNET-TV, New York, 1963-1964

Honorary Fellow, Morse College, Yale University, 1964-2013

Ford Foundation Fellow for Study Abroad, 1964 and 1971

Member, National Society of Film Critics, 1966-1971

Juror, National Book Awards, 1969, 1975

George Jean Nathan Award for Dramatic Criticism, 1972-1973

Member, Theater Advisory Panel, National Endowment for the Arts, 1972-1976

Member, Theater Advisory Panel, New York State Council on the Arts, 1977

Rockefeller Fellow, 1978

Guggenheim Fellow, 1979-1980

George Polk Award for Film Criticism, 1982

Edwin Booth Award for Significant Impact on Theater and Performance in New York, 1986

Travel Grant from the Japan Foundation for Interest in and of Support of Japanese Films, 1986

Birmingham Film Festival Prize for Lifetime Achievement, 1986

Fellow, New York Institute for the Humanities, 1995

Outstanding Teacher Award, Association for Theatre in Higher Education, 1995

Telluride Film Festival Award for Criticism, 1999

"Film Culture: Past and Present," Symposium in Honor of Stanley Kauffmann, sponsored by the Center for the Humanities at the City University of New York Graduate Center, 2002

Featured in the documentary film *For the Love of Movies: The Story of American Film Criticism*, 2009

Introduction: "Person of the Drama: Stanley Kauffmann as Theater Critic"

Although best known for his film criticism, Stanley Kauffmann (1916-2013) was also a frontline drama critic for a time, for the *New York Times* and the *Saturday Review*, among other publications; and some remarks on this role of his—among his others as a playwright, novelist, trade-house editor, book reviewer, and professor—are in order.

But, before discussing Kauffmann's work as a drama critic, I want to point out the difference between criticism and reviewing where the theater is concerned. Such a distinction is snobbish, if you will, indecorous, perhaps quixotic. But it seems to me that we are never going to get out of the miasma of deceit, self-pity, and wishful thinking that emanates from the theater in the United States as it does from no other medium, unless we begin to accept the distinctions that operate in actuality between actors and stars, dramas and hits, art and artisanship—and critics and reviewers.

Perhaps the greatest irony in a situation bursting with ironies is the reiterated idea that the *critics* are killing the theater. Now we all know that when theater people or members of the public refer to the "critics," they almost always mean the New York reviewers. It is certainly true that the critics—those persons whom the dictionary describes as "skilled in judging the qualities or merits of some class of things, especially of literary or artistic work"—have long harbored murderous thoughts about the condition of American drama, but their ineffectuality as public executioners is legendary. The reviewers, by contrast, come close to being the most loyal and effective allies the commercial theater could possibly desire. (They are killing the *non*-commercial theater.) But not close enough, it would seem, for this "marriage" constitutes the case of an absolute desire encountering a relative compliance.

As a corollary of its demand for constructive criticism the theater insists on absolute loyalty, and clearly receives a very high degree of it from reviewers, who are all "theater lovers" to one or another extent. And that brings us to our second irony. For "loyalty in a critic," George Bernard Shaw wrote in 1932 in *Our Theatres in the Nineties*, "is corruption" (Vol. 3, 177). This richly disturbing remark comes near the heart of so much that is wrong in the relationship between the stage and those who write about it from seats of power or places of romantic yearning. From the true critics the theater generally gets what can only be interpreted as gross infidelity, the reason being—as Shaw and every other major observer of drama make abundantly clear, and as our own sense of what is civilized should tell us—that critics cannot give their loyalty to people and institutions, since they owe it to something a great deal more permanent.

They owe it, of course, to truth and dramatic art. Once they sacrifice truth to human beings or art to institutions, they are corrupt, unless, as is so frequently the case, they never had any capacity for determining truth or any knowledge of dramatic art in the first place; for such persons, corruption is clearly too grandiose a condition. But some reviewers, at least, are people of ordinarily developed taste and a little intellectual maturity, and it is among them that corruption—in the sense not of venality or outright malfeasance but of the abandonment of a higher to a lower good—operates continually and in the name of that very loyalty which is worn like a badge of honor.

The point about reviewers is that they exist, consciously or not, to keep Broadway functioning within staked-out grounds. They preserve it as the arena for theatrical enterprises that may neither rise above an upper limit determined by a line stretching between the imaginations of Lillian Hellman, William Inge, and Richard Rodgers, nor sink beneath a lower one marked out by the inventiveness and sense of life of Norman Krasna, Harry Kurnitz, and Garson Kanin. (These are names from Broadway's supposed Golden Age; they have changed, but nothing else has.) Whatever creeps into the spaces north or south of this Central Park of the imagination is adventitious, arbitrary, and hermetic; if it is good, if it is art, if it is *Waiting for Godot* (1953), its presence on the Street may confidently be ascribed to someone's idea of a joke that just might pay off. (Beckett's masterpiece was billed in advertisements as "the laugh riot of two continents.")

Outside the theater's hothouse, not part of its clubbiness, its opening-night ceremonies, or its cabalisms, unconsulted about the honors it awards itself every year, and owing no more devotion to it than the literary critic owes to publishers or the art critic to galleries, the serious critic of drama like Stanley Kauffmann is left free—to do what? *To judge.* "There is one and only one justification for the trade of drama criticism," George Jean Nathan wrote, "and that is to criticize drama and not merely apologize for it" (64). Shaw went further:

> A critic is most certainly not in the position of a co-respondent in a divorce case: he is in no way bound to perjure himself to shield the reputation of the profession he criticizes. Far from being the instigator of its crimes and the partner of its guilty joys, he is the policeman of dramatic art; and it is his express business to denounce its delinquencies. (*The Drama Observed*, 969)

It is this idea of the critic as policeman that infuriates theater people to the limit of their anarchistic temperaments.

Go through the three volumes of Shaw's criticism, or police blotter, covering as many London seasons, and you will find that not once in any sequence of fifteen to twenty reviews was he anything but indignant at what he was called upon to see. Without pity in *Our Theatres in the Nineties*, he excoriated that theater, which sounds so much like our own, with its "dull routine of boom, bankruptcy, and boredom" (Vol. 2, 68), its performers' "eternal clamor for really artistic work and their ignominious collapse when they are taken at their word by Ibsen or anyone else" (Vol. 2, 76), its lugubrious spectacle of the drama as it "loses its hold on life" (Vol. 3, 181). Only when, once or twice a year, something came along that actually had a hold on life did Shaw's critiques turn enthusiastic and positive. But not "constructive"; you do not patronize or act generously toward artistic achievement—you identify it.

For if critics are not the makers of dramatic art, they are the persons most able to say what it is, and at the same time to establish the conditions under which it may flourish or at least gain a foothold. By being negative or *destructive*, if you will, toward everything else, they can help dramatic art to outlast the ephemera described as "smash" and "riot" and "socko," as "haunting," "riveting," and "stunning." And they will do their championing nearly always in the teeth of the coiners of these inimitable if vacuous terms. To the handful of great journalist-critics the English-speaking stage has had—Shaw, Max Beerbohm, Nathan, and Stark Young; Eric Bentley, Richard Gilman, Robert Brustein, and finally Stanley Kauffmann—we owe most of our knowledge of the permanent drama of our time, and in most cases we owe even the opportunity to read or see it.

When, for instance, the London reviewers were doing their best to drive Ibsen back to the depraved Continent (*Ghosts*, in 1882, was "unutterably offensive," "revoltingly suggestive and blasphemous," "a dirty act done publicly" [cited in Archer, 209]), it was Shaw, along with William Archer, who fought brilliantly and implacably to keep open the door to a resurrected drama. Later, Nathan helped Eugene O'Neill past the roadblock of those newspapermen who characteristically admired his "power" while being terrified of his thematic and technical innovations. And, in the 1950s, the truly heroic work of Eric Bentley—both in introducing us to the most vital contemporary as well nineteenth-century European plays and in promulgating standards for a potentially mature American theater—is a monument to the critical spirit at its untiring best. When, for example, Jack Gelber's *The Connection* was savaged by the daily newspapers in 1959, it was salvaged through the combined support of Bentley and other magazine critics, just as, three years earlier, these intellectual critics had rehabilitated the American reputation of *Waiting for Godot* after its disastrous reception at the hands of such reviewers as Walter Kerr. (The process used to work the other way, too: in 1958, Archibald MacLeish's *J.B.* was more accurately evaluated by the weekly critics after the *New York Times* had called it "one of the most memorable works of the century" [Atkinson, A2].)

If the history of the modern theater, then, is one of mutual suspicion between playwrights and their audiences—or between playwrights and the audience's stand-in, the reviewer—the history of the postmodern theater in the United States is one of quick rewards and instant media replay. In this arena, serious writers fight not poverty and neglect but the fickleness of a culture that picks them up and discards them before they have had sufficient time to develop properly. Like any jaded culture, America's hungers not for experience but for novelty, while an army of media commentators labors ceaselessly to identify something new. In such an atmosphere, where unorthodoxy becomes a new orthodoxy and fashion the arbiter of taste, the function of the vanguard artist, sacrificing popularity for the sake of penetrating uncharted ground, is radically changed. The emblematic avant-garde figure is no longer the expatriate playwright, exiled from nation, home, and church, but rather Julie Taymor—catapulted from the lofts of the Open Theater and the Chelsea Theater Center (where she began) to the Broadway stage, where, through *The Lion King* (1997), she peddled visual emptiness and dramatic pabulum, in the guise of experimental technique, to fat cats and wide-eyed tourists at $100 at throw.

One of the causes of this condition can be found in the peculiar relationship between the American playgoer and the American theater critic, for never before has a handful of reviewers possessed so much power and lacked so much authority. The mediocrity of newspaper, radio, and television reviewing throughout the country is nothing new—it is the inevitable result, first, of the need for haste, and, second, of choosing reviewers from the ranks of journalism (from the sports page, say, or from what used to be known as the "women's department") rather than from literary or professional training grounds. What is new, and most depressing, is the scarcity of decent critics *anywhere*. It is almost as if the theater had been abandoned by men and women of intelligence and taste, only to be delivered over wholesale to the publicists and the proselytizers.

Among them was Clive Barnes of the *New York Times*. It was always difficult to take seriously the judgments of a man, like Barnes, who could speak in nothing but superlatives—who, in the course of a single year, said that five or six different actors were giving the most brilliant performances of their careers, called eight or nine resident companies one of the finest in the country, announced four or five plays to be the best of this or any other season, compared a young writer who had just completed his first play with the mature Chekhov, and identified Stacy Keach as the finest American Hamlet since Barrymore, though Barnes was too young to have seen Barrymore's performance. Barnes's use of hyperbole, with its promiscuous display of the word *best*, exposed not the splendors of the theater season but rather its bankruptcy, for it suggested that his need to identify works of merit or interest had far outrun the theater's capacity to create them.

Obviously, no theater can benefit in the long run from fake approval, partly because the critic becomes discredited, partly because the spectator grows disenchanted, partly because the theater practitioner begins to lose faith in his or her craft. The very rare work with serious aspirations thus gets lost in the general atmosphere of praise—either because it is ignored or unappreciated, or more likely because it is acclaimed in the same way as everything else. When the inspired and the routine are treated exactly alike, the act of criticism comes to seem arbitrary and capricious; when the corrective impulse is abandoned, the whole construct of standards breaks down. A serious *literary* artist can always hope for an understanding review or two in the midst of the general incomprehension, and anyway, regardless of reviews, his or her book continues to exist for future generations to discover. But the theater artist writes on air, and preserves his or her work only in the memories of those who see it. In the present critical atmosphere, even those memories are tainted. The marriage that must exist in any art form between the mind that creates and the mind that judges has for the most part dissolved in the theater, with the result that the art form itself is in danger of losing its purpose and direction.

I'm speaking only about the United States, of course. In London, Rome, Paris, and Berlin, critics like Stanley Kauffmann are likely to be found writing for leading newspapers, rather then being relegated to the back pages of weekly, monthly, or even quarterly intellectual magazines. This is one of the reasons Kauffmann's theater criticism should be of interest to international readers, especially European ones: he is a public intellectual who writes for the educated reader from any country, not an arcane academic who preaches to a highly specialized and limited audience of fellow scholars; he writes like a citizen of the world rather than as a parochial American. Not only do Kauffmann's urbane style and wide knowledge of all the arts, past and present, tell us of his global outlook; so too do his choices of plays or productions about which to write. Witness this short, diverse list from *Stages of Theater*: *The Dramatic Criticism of Stanley Kauffmann, 1951-2006*: *Phaedra*, by Jean Racine; *The Caucasian Chalk Circle*, by Bertolt Brecht; *The Dance of Death*, by August Strindberg; *Hello and Goodbye*, by

Athol Fugard; *The Three Sisters*, by Anton Chekhov; *Old Times*, by Harold Pinter; *The Master Builder*, by Henrik Ibsen; *And They Put Handcuffs on Flowers*, by Fernando Arrabal; *Antony and Cleopatra*, by William Shakespeare; *The Dybbuk*, by S. Ansky; *The Bacchae*, by Euripides; and *After the Fall*, by Arthur Miller.

Kauffmann was dismissed from the *New York Times* in 1966 after only eight months and relegated to the back pages of intellectual magazines because, in his own words,

> the theater has always resisted serious criticism and tolerates it only when it is relatively powerless. A chief component of this condition is the attitude of much of its audience, who would probably be happier with a one-to-four-star rating service plus a brief synopsis. The theater's view of the matter is supported by most newspaper publishers and editors, whose standard in criticism is not quality but readability. The writer who can supply bright, readable copy, and supply it quickly, is an acceptable critic. (*New American Review*, 36)

The reasons for this journalistic development can be found in the history of American theater criticism, which has outlines that, not surprisingly, correspond to large socio-cultural movements.

To wit: as American society became less dependent on the theater for diversion (with the advent of film, radio, and the automobile), as the middle class turned into the pseudo-aristocracy, as new wealth gave more people a leisure that had once been restricted to a few, including the leisure to be elegantly bored, there arose a tribe of critics whose principal qualifications were urbanity, wit, and fundamental non-commitment to the theater. In the United States a chief haven for that kind of critic has been the *New Yorker*, which, from its outset as well as from its very insignia, has always had a strong streak of Anglophilia—promulgated over the years by such (unidentical) critics as Alexander Woollcott, Wolcott Gibbs, Brendan Gill, and Robert Benchley.

A quite different kind of reviewing also arose in America, out of the same root social causes. Newspaper and mass-magazine reviewing in the first half of the twentieth century was, understandably, in the hands of representatives of this new middle class, men and women who represented both the appetite for boredom and an equivalent appetite for cultural acquisition at a level that imposed no strain. Mr. Average Person filled the job to the average person's satisfaction, his or her virtue being that he or she knew just as little as the common spectator, and sometimes even less. But where American cultural and intellectual life had been relatively homogeneous in the nineteenth century, it was now dividing into major and minor elements—again, for a complex of social reasons.

One of the minority elements found its critical voice around the turn of the century, approximately, with the "arrival" of James Gibbon Huneker and the now-forgotten Percival Pollard. The theme of this "adversary" criticism was that American culture was provincial, puritanical, and benighted, and that mass-media criticism was banal when not together dumb. Huneker, who criticized several arts, developed these ideas about the theater specifically, and his themes, even when unspoken, persisted through the first five decades of the twentieth century—usually in magazines of oppositional stance with theater critics like Joseph Wood Krutch as well as the aforementioned Young, Nathan, and Bentley.

This schizoid situation, between popular reviewing and intellectual criticism, altered after the Second World War, again in response to social change. Higher education became democratized, culture "exploded," and the middle class became aesthetically radicalized—very strictly within the limits of middle-class values (themselves now somewhat circumscribed by television) but still with a lot of innocuous daring. The result is that today we live in a critical situation in which the vocabulary and stance (if not the literary style) of the mass-medium reviewer are very different from his or her predecessor's and much more like those the adversary critic. The dividing line is no longer a line; only the ends of the spectrum are clearly defined. But what is forgotten in the new joy about the "improvement" of mass-circulation reviewing is, fundamentally, that the critical spectrum still exists.

Furthermore, no one collects one man's mass-circulation theater reviews in a book, as Stanley Kauffmann collected his selective dramatic criticism for the educated reader. However, unlike Kauffmann's collections of film criticism, which, among other uses, serve as guides to movies that are "revived" in theaters, on television, and in VHS or DVD format, his collections of theater criticism have no precisely parallel use. When one of the plays discussed is revived, the new production must in some way alter it. For this very reason, collections of theater criticism like Stanley Kauffmann's have, I think, a special importance that more than compensates for their lack of "utility." In a sense, one part of the past—like the "unknown" plays of Shaw that Kauffmann has treated both in his criticism and in an interview published in *Shaw* in 1987—would not exist without these them. Collections of performance criticism, then, are books of *witness*. Surely, like other critics, performance critics can help to illuminate works, can test, revise, and extend criteria, can capture qualities and pose questions (if not posit answers). But the unique reward of performance criticism is in its immediacy and the distillation of that immediacy, in the salvaging for posterity of pertinences.

Those pertinences, for Kauffmann, always included acting (as well as directing and design), just as they did in his film criticism. But the pertinences also included the play as a piece of literature; and, in his combining of telling performance criticism with keen dramatic evaluation, Kauffmann had to know he was emulating his acknowledged hero, George Bernard Shaw. As Kauffmann himself wrote of the arrival of Shaw the critic, in an essay in *Yale/Theatre* later adapted for inclusion in his first collection of theater criticism, *Persons of the Drama* (1976):

> Through the nineteenth century, English-language criticism concentrated on acting and was often good on the subject; it was weak on new scripts. This fitted a theater that was strong on acting, particularly of old plays, and whose new plays were patterned to a pietistic society. There was bound to be a change because of changes in social attitudes, literary standards, and consequent theater ambitions. The change is first importantly apparent in the criticism of George Bernard Shaw. (*Yale/Theatre*, 11)

Only a few theater critics are worth reading; still fewer are worth reading twice. That Stanley Kauffmann, along with Shaw, belongs in the second group is evidenced in *Theater Criticisms* (his second such collection, from 1983) by some eighty reviews and a handful of essays spanning the seasons between *Travesties* (1975) and *'night, Mother* (1983). As it happens, these two plays, as plays, were deliriously received by most critics, while Kauffmann had grave reservations about their dramatic art. He had grave reservations about many of the productions, playwrights, and performers applauded by his colleagues. But Kauffmann was no mere naysayer. He had reasons for his nays; he presented them with clarity; and he tried to create a critical environment in which good things in the theater could get recognized at the expense of what was bad. Discussing *Travesties*, for example, he showed how its playwright, Tom Stoppard, "plunges into promising situations and then breaks their promises, too short-winded to fulfill them artistically and intellectually" (14). Marsha Norman's *'night, Mother*, he wrote, is "a stunt" (174), and his analysis of the play's plot and characters leads inescapably to his conclusion that "if the play were true—to Norman's characters as she wants us to think of them—it wouldn't exist" (176).

Stanley Kauffmann's value as a drama critic resides in his values as a critic generally. For him, the drama should be something other than a repetitive theatrical game designed to comfort the bourgeoisie; it must be an art that renews itself as serious playwrights in every age reinvent their chosen form. Kauffmann admired all such writers, who know that art is not a complement to life but an increment; that drama is not psychology, sociology, philosophy, or political theory; and that the only new content is new form. He was thus always attentive, in his articles and reviews, to the manner in which plays are made, but he was never concerned with form as embroidery or decoration. Instead, dramatic forms for him were forms of new knowledge, a mutual freeing of the self—the audience's as well as the author's—from artistic and cultural conventions that limit our sense of possibility.

Kauffmann's chief interest was always in discovering how new ways of presenting drama and unfolding consciousness aid in revealing character, transmitting ideas, and in general increasing the potential for capturing a sense of "felt life" on stage. Like Eric Bentley, he wisely saw the playwright as thinker—a shaper of modern consciousness—*and* as showman. The best playwrights, Kauffmann regularly suggests in *Persons of the Drama*, *Theater Criticisms*, and the essay collection *About the Theater* (2010), are the ones who can turns ideas and problems, moral conundrums and philosophical complexities, into engaging theater. Yet even these fine dramatists, with the exception of Shakespeare, have never held the kind of central position in educated minds that the authors of fiction and poetry have. This must have something to do with the relative difficulty of seeing good performances of great plays, with the trouble most readers have in imagining how a dramatic text would sound and look on the stage (if not in their mind's eye), with (for English-speaking readers) a mistrust of translations that have often well deserved the mistrust they engender. And, I suppose, there is a larger suspicion that drama is an impure medium: commercially exploitable, subject to the vanity or stupidity of actors, unlikely to come off in the theater at all. One goes to a play expecting disappointment, and one usually finds just that.

Despite Kauffmann's recurrent disappointment with the productions he saw over the years, his collected theater reviews have a genuine charm that comes, paradoxically, from their suggestion that the author did not entirely believe his own doomsday judgment on American theater and drama. So much so that, after decades of going to the theater, he still expected excellence (as in an intermittent review of the kind he published in the May 2002 issue of *Performing Arts Journal*: on the New York production of Shaw's *Major Barbara* [1905] at the Roundabout), and he was brilliant at explaining why he had or had not found it. That he stopped writing regular theater criticism in 1985, while he continued as a film critic, deserves some comment, however. For theater criticism once attracted a number of writers of the caliber of Stanley Kauffmann: not only the aforementioned Bentley, Brustein, and Gilman, but also Susan Sontag, Mary McCarthy, Kenneth Tynan, and John Simon—writers, in short, who could be expected to analyze a play or production intelligently, and to correct the misjudgments of the daily press. Today, this kind of corrective has practically disappeared, as the dissenting critics have departed, retired, or shifted to other fields like music. Most intellectual journals, on their side, have long since stopped carrying theater chronicles.

Moreover, John Simon's own virtually single-handed crusade, in *New York* magazine, to preserve high standards became vitiated by his uncontrolled savagery, his excessively punning style, his peculiar prejudices, his personal attacks on the physical appearance of actors, his obsessive campaign against real or imagined homosexuality on the stage, and, lastly, his turning of his critical fury into its own mode of performance for the amusement of television talk-show audiences eager to see the bad guy in person. Simon's "progress" (which finally ended in 2005, though he, too, continued to write film criticism—for the *National Review*) may suggest why so many other serious authors, like Stanley Kauffmann, have abandoned the writing of all but occasional theater criticism, for it shows what may happen to a person of intelligence and discrimination when he or she observes too long the execrable products of the American theatrical scene (unmitigated, as in the case of film, by international imports in sufficient number and quality).

After all, it was Max Beerbohm, a similarly high-minded critic, who wrote the following words back in 1904—partly in indictment of himself: "A critic who wants the drama to be infinitely better than it is can hardly avoid the pitfall of supposing it to be rather worse than it is. Finding that it rises nowhere near to his standards, he imagines that it must be in a state of motionless prostration in the nethermost depths" (110). To counteract this tendency in himself, Beerbohm (like Shaw), when faced with an evening of despicable entertainment, went home and devised a substitute entertainment of his own, loosely disguised as a review. See in Beerbohm's *Around Theatres* (1924), for example, the little theatrical event this critic stages as his lead into a review of Victor Hugo's *Ruy Blas* (1838) in dismal English translation. Stanley Kauffmann himself, it is true, lacks such playfulness—some would say triviality—but that may be because the American theater itself is almost wholly one of play, of child's play, even when it is ostensibly trying to be serious. And such a theater at one time required, I think, the stern but stimulating contempt, the acerbic yet arousing intolerance, of a Stanley Kauffmann.

Initially backing up Kauffmann in his ire were the seminal essays of Francis Fergusson as well as Eric Bentley, comprising the academic artillery being fired (chiefly from Columbia) at the philistines in Sardi's and Shubert Alley, at the entrenched establishment of Lincoln Center and the Actors' Studio, and at the new breed of barbarians storming south of 14th Street past the Living Theater and toward other assorted dead ends. It is not too far-fetched to suggest that not only Bentley but also Fergusson, and later Robert Brustein and Stanley Kauffmann (themselves having moved, like Bentley, to the academy—in their case Yale—in the 1960s), represented an authentic revolution in the modern theater away from the championing of realism of the poetic as well as prosaic variety, toward an appreciation of a still (at the time) undetermined fusion of the ironic and the absurd. With tragedy in tatters and comedy in confusion, these modern critics turned to irony as the only link between the form or formality of theater and the flux of history. Chekhov, Pirandello, Brecht, and Beckett are neither tragedians nor comedians but ironists, and a genuinely ironic sensibility is something unheard of on Broadway. Hence, even on the infrequent occasions of revivals of Chekhov, Pirandello, Brecht, and Beckett, the ironies of their plays are swallowed up by the slobbering sentimentality of a realistic stage tradition; and it took an "ironic" critic like Kauffmann or Brustein to point this out.

In this constantly contentious period of cultural history, Fergusson functioned as a remote Hegelian influence on the revolutionaries, Bentley played Marx as he translated Brecht, and Brustein was Lenin arriving at the Finland Station on the New Haven Railroad (which would eventually take him from Yale to Harvard). On the other side, Walter Kerr turned into the Kerensky of the revolution by betraying his academic origins to consort with the hated bourgeoisie, while the drama critics of the *Village Voice* (among them Gordon Rogoff and later Richard Gilman) became the left-wing revisionists of Off-Off Broadway. Stanley Kauffmann himself wound up playing Trotsky with a tortured ambivalence that robbed him of nothing except professional stamina. (Exclusively as a drama critic, that is; apart from his eighteen years as a drama-and-film critic and his more than fifty years as a film critic, Kauffmann spent only the aforementioned eight months at the *New York Times*, compared with George Jean Nathan's half a century or longer on the critical firing line).

Stages of Theater attempts to document, if not Stanley Kauffmann's longevity as a drama critic, then his range and perspicacity as one. This volume is designed to complement Kauffmann's earlier anthologies *Persons of the Drama* and *Theater Criticisms*. (His *About the Theater*, again, is a collection of essays, not production reviews.) No reviews of key productions have been excluded from *Stages of Theater*, but no reviews from previous collections have been re-included here, either. Contained in this volume are reviews of productions of such notable plays as *Serjeant Musgrave's Dance, Strange Interlude, The Skin of Our Teeth, All's Well That Ends Well, Medea, Hedda Gabler, The Beggar's Opera, The Misanthrope, The Importance of Being Earnest, Romeo and Juliet*, and *The Resistible Rise of Arturo Ui*; discussions concerning dramatists such as Shaw, Albee, Racine, Bond, Sartre, Gorky, Handke, and Tennessee Williams; a section containing reviews of audio recordings of staged readings of classic plays; a selection of pieces on one of Kauffmann's favorite subjects, the relationship between theater and film; and, lastly, a section containing reviews of books on the history of American acting, the Federal Theatre Project, Vsevolod Meyerhold, theater architecture, the Barrymores, and the *Comédie Française*, among other subjects.

I would like now to provide some notes on lesser-known dramatists, particularly American ones, whose work is treated in *Stages of Theater*. Before doing so, I should like to explain why Kauffmann's writings on these lesser-known and, in some cases, lesser dramatists have been included in this volume. My explanation is simple: *most* of what is done in the theater is lesser—mediocre or worse. Even so, the mediocre or worse is as much a part of the theater critic's subject as the good or better. Shaw himself wrote one of his best reviews about a long-since forgotten item called, of all things, *The Chili Widow*. Every critic grapples continually with *Chili Widows*. Such plays need to be identified and at least generically understood, both as a matter of clear vision and because every critic either has a touch of John the Baptist in him or her or that critic ought to quit. Critics ought to live in hope that true art is continually en route—and does in fact occasionally appear. Part of this proselytizing function is to make sure that false messiahs, peddlers, and charlatans are shown as such. But hope—non-delusionary, non-inflationary, non-self-aggrandizing *hope*—is the core of the critic's being: hope that good work will recurrently arrive; hope that (partly by identifying trash) he or she may help it to arrive; hope that the critic may have the excitement and privilege of helping to connect such good work with a good audience.

Look, then, through the index of the collected writings of any theater critic you admire, and note how many *Chili Widows* are listed, how few of the plays he or she discusses are ones that you have seen or would want to see or read. But the critic hoped and persisted; through hoping and persisting, even when the theater was bad, created a *literature*. The theater critic, like other critics, creates a literature about an art, a literature that has both art and the critic's life as its subject matter. If a purpose of art is to explore and distill one's existence, which art is greater: Edmund Wilson's criticism or Edmund Wilson's novels, plays, and poems? Or, to separate the functions in different people, who would hesitate to choose Robert Brustein's theater criticism over Robert Anderson's plays? When we read fine criticism in any field, that of Lionel Trilling and Northrop Frye, say, of Edgar Wind and Herbert Read, we often lose all sense of reading *criticism* and simply have a sense of *reading*. We are simply enjoying a kind of literature.

So the theater, finally, is a subject. That is why the critic writes and why the reader, even the one who rarely goes to the theater, reads. The theater is a complex, significant, reflective, implicative *subject*. The consumer-guide motive for, or function of, reviewing is quite secondary—though, like any human being, the critic naturally likes to see his or her enthusiasms prosper. Much more important, more central to the critic's being than any box-office influence he or she may have, is the realization that this person works in a concurrent plane to the theater, not a congruent plane. That is, the critic exists in a kind of para-reality to the theater's reality. His or her criticism is a body of work obviously related to, yet still distinct from, what the theater does; possibly influential, possibly not, criticism in the end is no more closely connected to the theater than is political science to the current elections. The critic knows that, on the one hand, there is the theater, with good and bad productions, and, on the other hand, there is criticism, which ought to be good about both good and bad productions.

Life is the playwright's subject, and the playwright ought to be good about its good and bad people; the theater is the critic's subject, and the critic ought to be good about its good and bad plays.

Some of the plays treated in *Stages of Theater: The Dramatic Criticism of Stanley Kauffmann, 1951-2006*—plays good, less than good, and bad—were written by the Americans Lanford Wilson (1937-2011), a kind of poor man's Tennessee Williams, and Beth Henley (b. 1952), a kind of poor woman's Eudora Welty or Flannery O'Connor; by David Rabe (b. 1940), best known for his loose trilogy of plays about the Vietnam experience, *Sticks and Bones* (1969), *The Basic Training of Pavlo Hummel* (1971), and *Streamers* (1976); by Ron Milner (1938-2004), whose *What the Wine-Sellers Buy* was, in 1974, the first play by an African-American produced by Joseph Papp at the New York Shakespeare Festival in Lincoln Center, where Thomas Babe (1941-2000) himself became Papp's most prolific playwright; by Charles Fuller (b. 1939) and Leslie Lee (1935-2014), two black writers once associated with Manhattan's Negro Ensemble Company; by Miguel Piñero (1946-1988), co-founder of the Nuyorican (or New York-Puerto Rican) Poets Café and a leading member of the Nuyorican literary movement; by A. R. Gurney (b. 1930), Milan Stitt (1941-2009), Christopher Durang (b. 1949), and Ted Tally (b. 1952), all of whom studied, and in some cases taught, at the Yale School of Drama; by Larry Gelbart (1928-2009) and Kevin Wade (b. 1954), each of whom became better known for his work on films (Gelbart, *Tootsie* [1982]; Wade, *Working Girl* [1988]); and by Preston Jones (1936-79), who spent the majority of his career in the employ of Texas's Dallas Theater Center, performing many different roles including actor, stage manager, director, and playwright.

Most of the non-Americans Stanley Kauffmann discusses in *Stages of Theater* are classic dramatists or are otherwise well known, but a few require some identification. S. Ansky (a.k.a. Shloyme Zanvl Rappoport [1863-1920]), for example, was a Russian Jewish author, playwright, folklorist, polemicist, and cultural-political activist. Fernando Arrabal (b. 1932) is a Spanish playwright, screenwriter, film director, novelist, and poet who was born in Melilla, Spain, but settled in France in 1955. And Tankred Dorst (b. 1925) is a German playwright whose farces, parables, one-act plays, and adaptations are inspired by the Absurdist drama of Eugène Ionesco and Samuel Beckett. Such other figures as the British actor Edmund Kean (1787-1833); the English actor, director, playwright, manager, critic, and theorist Harley Granville-Barker (1877-1946); the Hungarian producer and director Gabriel Pascal (1894-1954); the Austrian writer and journalist Karl Kraus (1874-1936); the German director Georg II, Duke of Saxe-Meiningen (1826-1914); and the English dramatist Christopher Fry (1907-2005) are all important figures in the history of the theater and therefore duly placed in historical context by Kauffmann, but, because they may be unfamiliar to younger readers, they merit at least initial mention here.

In *Stages of Theater*, as in his previous collections of dramatic criticism, Stanley Kauffmann regularly comments not only on the above writers, directors, and producers, but also on the revolution, or crisis, in dramatic criticism—a situation created these days, in part, by the advent of the Internet, where anyone can publish dramatic criticism, at any time, in a blog or other form of web page, on a media platform, etc. Is the quality of dramatic criticism therefore now declining, since anybody can upload his or her theater reviews, without editorial control (of the kind with which print critics such as Kauffmann always had to contend) or careful vetting, to the Internet? Are the blogosphere and social networking sites just the virtual equivalent of "talk" or chatter where the theater is concerned—a pullulating buzz of artists promoting shows, audience members offering their opinions, badly written reviews by amateurs, and friends promoting friends? Or will dramatic criticism ultimately be enriched by such democratic, "immediate," often highly personal practice online, and will the print critic at the same time slowly disappear, even as print journalism itself is dying?

Indeed, have digital reviewing and even the uploading of entire productions to YouTube begun to impact the very way in which we see theater? Moreover, how do younger students of theater feel about these matters? How, especially, do those youthful theatergoers feel who do not know the work of print critics like Kauffmann, yet might learn, from an acquaintance with his theater reviews, about something currently in short supply—critical standards and aesthetic values, historical perspective and social discernment, careful writing and close reading? These are legitimate questions that, naturally, only began to be asked toward the end of Stanley Kauffmann's lifetime; such questions were inconceivable during his tenure as a drama critic in the mid-twentieth century, when print journalism was still king and the media landscape had not yet burgeoned to its present, inordinate—and sometimes overwhelming—size.

Kauffmann nonetheless comments in *Stages of Theater* on such subjects of continuing relevance, in the Age of the Internet (also known as the Information Age, the Computer Age, the Digital Era, or the New Media Epoch), as the function of criticism, the qualifications of a critic, the influence or power of critics, newspaper reviewing versus magazine criticism versus academic scholarship, critical theory as opposed to critical practice, performance *study* in contrast with play analysis, and the arts criticism of the New York "school." Other topics routinely touched on in this new book include the relationship between theater and film, particularly the difference between stage and screen acting and the combining of both in the careers of performers such as Laurence Olivier and Al Pacino; Shaw, criticism, and theater (a kind of leitmotif that weaves its way through much of Kauffmann's writing); various national theaters along with the best works to come out of them; the phenomena of theater festivals and radio plays (and their nearest relative, audio recordings of drama); Broadway, Off-Broadway, Off-Off Broadway, and regional theater in the United States; and the issue of government subsidy for the arts in general.

In sum, Stanley Kauffmann was, and is, the critic many of us aspire to be—in print or online—as well as the champion of criticism in an art form, theater, more hostile to it than any other with the possible exception of film. Particularly impressive is the extent to which his criticism reveals not only an application to drama of the highest standards, but also a love of good art in any form—theatrical, cinematic, or literary. Speaking to this love, I would like to close with these words, written by Lionel Trilling about a great artist, F. Scott Fitzgerald, but equally applicable to Stanley Kauffmann, the *critic* as artist: "We feel of him, as we cannot feel of all moralists, that he did not attach himself to the good because this attachment would sanction his fierceness toward the bad—his first impulse was to love the good" (245).

Works Cited

Archer, William. "*Ghosts* and Gibberings" (1891). In Egan, Michael, ed. *Henrik Ibsen: The Critical Heritage*. 1972. London: Routledge, 1999. 209-214.

Atkinson, Brooks. "MacLeish's *J.B.*: Verse Drama Given Premiere at ANTA." *New York Times* (December 12, 1958): A2.

Beerbohm, Max. *Last Theatres, 1904-1910*. Ed. Rupert Hart-Davis. London: MacGibbon, 1970.

Kauffmann, Stanley. "Drama on the *Times*." *New American Review*, no. 1 (September 1967): 30-49.

----------. "Theater and Drama Criticism: Some Notes." *Yale/Theatre*, 4.2 (Spring 1973): 8-16.

----------. *Persons of the Drama: Theater Criticism and Comment*. New York: Harper & Row, 1976.

----------. *Theater Criticisms*. New York: Performing Arts Journal Publications, 1983.

Nathan, George Jean. *The Morning After the First Night*. New York: Alfred A. Knopf, 1938.

Shaw, Bernard. *Our Theatres in the Nineties*. Vol. 2. 1932. London: Constable, 1954.

----------. *Our Theatres in the Nineties*. Vol. 3. 1932. London: Constable, 1954.

----------. *The Drama Observed*. Vol. III: 1897-1911. Ed. Bernard Dukore. University Park: Penn State University Press, 1993.

Trilling, Lionel. "F. Scott Fitzgerald." In Trilling's *The Liberal Imagination: Essays on Literature and Society*. 1951. New York: New York Review of Books, 2008. 243-254.

PRODUCTION REVIEWS

After the Fall, by Arthur Miller. *Wilson Library Bulletin*, May 1965.

Arthur Miller's play *After the Fall*, which was the first production of the Lincoln Center Repertory Company in New York in 1964 (with which production I shall not be concerned here), is a stream-of-consciousness work that, despite the author's punctilious denials, is plainly autobiographical. The hero, Quentin (who has been made a lawyer), has a crisis of conscience caused by a congressional committee investigating (communist) subversion. He leaves his wife for a second wife who is a highly neurotic, popular sex idol; when she commits suicide, he marries a European woman.

There was much debate in the press about the propriety of Miller's writing here about his second wife, Marilyn Monroe, so lately dead by her own hand. Much more to the artistic point would have been debate about almost every other subject touched in the play, for the portrait of Maggie (as she is called) is the most vital element in the work. Her character is not realized in dynamic purpose, it is merely telescoped biography; but her dialogue has a ring of authenticity that at least gives it veracity, a sting and immediacy that the other characters lack.

An American curse, it has often been noted, is the lust for bigness, and this is nowhere more apparent than in the arts. And, in the arts, it is nowhere more apparent than in an artist who is desperate for material. If a writer is searching for a subject and can find nothing within the scope of personal experience or of human observation and interest to move him, he can always fall back on what can be called "spiritual navigation," or the Big Questions (such as "Where is Western man going and why?"). It seems fair to assume that this has been true of Miller, who has been silent for years. A true heir of Strindberg might well have written fiercely on his marriage to "Maggie" and, by concentrating on that relationship, would have permitted our whole era to filter in, as it must. But Miller, more grandiose and less perceptive, has felt compelled to be "large," to produce a play that confronts all the great subjects of the recent American past and the present, almost as if he had drawn up a checklist and ticked off the items one by one. The congressional investigation menace, the scars of the concentration camp on the Western world, the resultant anomie and ultimate quest for hope that are central issues—these are all mentioned rather than explored and are bound together with dialogue that is most of the time laboriously figurative. What is worse, it is less a drama of contemporary dilemmas than of the hero's search for exoneration for every aspect of his private and public action and inaction.

The structure of *After the Fall* resembles that of *Death of a Salesman* in that there is a free time-flow. As memories come into Quentin's head, relevant characters appear. This is a serviceable technique and was highly effective in the earlier play because the juxtapositions were meaningful. Here the motifs that recur—for example, a crisis when he was a child, a scene with his brother—have no relation to what is happening "now," no bearing on it, and the method is merely used, not used to a purpose. It reminds us clumsily of the earlier occasion when he used it well, as also do the family quarrels, which are reminiscent of both *Death of a Salesman* and *All My Sons*.

Certain enforced relationships (such as Maggie's suicide and the concentration camps) only emphasize the straining for universality, the conscious attempt to write an Everyman of the mid-twentieth century. But Miller has created neither a protagonist capable of tragedy nor a credible symbolic character. Little skillful moments (like the scene when the father hears of the wife's death), numerous pungent lines of Maggie's (which, one feels, Miller has remembered from life) do not compensate for the play's philosophic and artistic failure. Miller has tried in *After the Fall*, then, to embrace the cosmos by agonizing blatantly about contemporary themes, instead of distilling the *effect* of these themes into a microcosm where very little needs explicitly to be stated or argued. The difference, finally, is that between surface garrulousness and a subsurface of echoing silences, between a poetaster's verbiage and succinct metaphor. After the fall, indeed.

Malcolm, by Edward Albee. *New York Times*, January 12, 1966.

Malcolm, Edward Albee's dramatization of James Purdy's novel, which opened last night at the Schubert, is an exquisite production. The triumphs are those of the setting and lighting and costume designers, of some of the actors, and of the director. Mr. Albee's contribution—predictably literate and occasionally amusing—is not, in its own terms, up to the level of their work.

The story, which is a fantasy of the corruption of innocence, concerns a fourteen- or fifteen-year-old boy, well-dressed and well-spoken, who—when we meet him—has been sitting daily on a bench in front of a hotel in a nameless American city. He is observed by an elderly astrologer named Cox, who speaks to Malcolm one day and learns that the boy is waiting for his father, who has disappeared. Cox seizes psychological dominance over him and sends him on a series of visits, ostensibly to integrate him into the world but which ultimately destroy him.

Malcolm visits a December-May couple (she is a young former prostitute, he is an ancient who claims to be 192), a middle-aged couple (he is ludicrously rich, she is attended by four lovers in white suits), a hip couple (an author and a painter), and a blond pop singer, who takes the youth as her latest husband and kills him with drink and sex. All of these characters know one another. They are further linked within the play because two of the principal actors—who play Cox and the prostitute—are also used to play other roles. At the end, all of them gather around Malcolm's deathbed, mourning what they have lost.

The proper, abstract atmosphere is set beautifully by William Ritman's stage design, almost Japanese in its spare, rectangular purity. There are three treadmills on different levels that bring in people and furniture in tableau style; other scenic elements descend and ascend—panels and translucent scrims. From our first view of it, Ritman's setting, as much as anything that happens or is said, creates the play's rarefied world, and is discreetly aided by Tharon Musser's lightning. Willa Kim's costumes themselves are superb—caricatures, such as the yellow boudoir overalls for the singer, and inventions, such as the two-tone stockings for a streetwalker. William Flanagan's music is unobtrusive; when we feel that there ought to be music, it is present, and apt enough.

In the title role is Matthew Cowles, a pleasant and appealing young man who has listened attentively to his director and has obeyed intelligently. However, he shows little sign of innate talent. John Heffernan, the ancient, is as excellently wrinkled in performance as he is in dress. As several prostitutes, Estelle Parsons, remembered for her touching titular role in *Mrs. Dally Has a Lover* Off-Broadway, shows again her fine serio-comic gifts. Henderson Forsythe, so impressive Off-Broadway last year in Harold Pinter's *A Slight Ache*, does his best here with Cox, a character too nebulous to be played satisfactorily. Alice Drummond and Donald Hotton, for their part, are vivid as the artists, and Jennifer West, in the relatively easy role of the blond bombshell, makes the most of it.

The outstanding performance is by Ruth White as the wealthy woman with the four young men. White is one of the reasons for anger when American actors are uniformly downgraded. I have never seen her give anything less than an extraordinary performance, and here she is first-class. Her sharp understanding, her subtle design of inflection, her phrasing of gesture and speech, provide pleasures beyond their primary purpose as part of a scene. She takes a bare line like "Dear God, I have suffered so much," and by lightly placing each word on a descending scale and ending on a rich mocking contralto note, she doubles us up with laughter. She has the essential comic gift: she can comment on the character she plays, at the same time that she gives it credibility.

Alan Schneider, who directed Albee's last two plays, has never served his author better. His evident sympathy with the play has heightened his imagination and refined his sense of composition. The moments when interest sags—almost all of them when Malcolm, the catalyst, is absent—are not curable by him.

So to Albee's play. The changes from Purdy's novel (too lengthy to examine here), plus the basic fact that Albee chose it, make the result discussable as his own work. Like *Tiny Alice*—this may have been the attraction of the novel—*Malcolm* is a religious allegory. But, unlike most allegorical plays, it is not a consistent dramatization of oblique references to our lives; it is a series of options, which we can take or not. Does Cox represent Satan or is he a messenger of the devious Divine Will? Does Malcolm's missing father represent God turned away from the world or God choosing to sacrifice another son to inform and save some sinners? And so on. These questions might be stimulating except for one lack: we are never convinced that Albee himself knows the answers or—which is worse—that he cares.

The structure in this work is more organic than it was in *Tiny Alice*, but the net effect is the same arty hugger-mugger—almost a superciliousness that permits the viewer to supply meanings if he chooses or else to be content with his ignorance. Albee complained, with *Tiny Alice*, that people asked questions of it and would not merely let the play occur to them. He complains of those critics who judge a play's matter and do not restrict themselves to its manner. Both of these statements tend to a view, much in vogue, that art consists principally of style, of encounter between us and the figurative surface of a work. This view reduces ideas to decoration, character to pageant symbol, and theme to a conveyor belt for effects. It is to shrink art to no more than sensual response—one kind or another of "happening." To some of us, this modish view is nihilistic, not progressive. It can be seen as theory of the socially eccentric, using their undoubted gifts to attack vindictively the main body of society through its culture.

The dispute is not academic; it centers on the seat of the pants. *Malcolm* frequently makes us wriggle with boredom. We know, as we watch, that Albee has wit, imagination, and a rare sense of theatricality; we also know that his play is never truly engaging or moving. It gets tedious to be treated as tolerated guests at an aesthetic charade where we must not presume to ask for such a philistine element as meaning. One does not insist on conventional plot or suspense; many good modern plays live without them. But here there is not even enjoyable ambiguity. And the only theme that really comes through clearly—as it also did in *Who's Afraid of Virginia Woolf?* and *Tiny Alice*—is of woman as destroyer. After all the various taintings of Malcolm's innocence—in which women are involved—he is at last killed by a girl, through her use of him in bed.

The holy innocent is a perennially vital theme, whether religious as in *Parsifal* or comic as in *Candide*—a means of articulating what is continually being found and lost in the world and in each of us. But Albee's play is more pretentious than pertinent, is fashionably disdainful of communication, is shiny with an artistic veneer that may cover as much vacancy as depth. *Malcolm* disintegrates into some more or less effective moments; it does not sustain mystery.

Unquestionably, Edward Albee is an eminent talent in our theater. Also unquestionably, his eminence is due in some measure to the present flatness of the surrounding countryside.

The Condemned of Altona, by Jean-Paul Sartre. *New York Times*, February 4, 1966.

The production of Jean-Paul Sartre's *The Condemned of Altona*, which opened last night at the Vivian Beaumont, is the most interesting that has so far been presented by the Lincoln Center Repertory Company under either of its managements. But it must be added that this is true largely for negative reasons.

To comment only on the Herbert Blau-Jules Irving regime, its first two productions, *Danton's Death* and *The Country Wife*, were far beyond the company's present competence. Sartre's play, though serious and important, is more accessible to the abilities of Blau and his company. And—a crucial point— he has brought in an actor (George Coulouris) who fills a leading role admirably and whose work underscores the weaknesses of the permanent group.

Sartre's play is an allegory of our lives. It is set in Germany in 1959, but it could be set in France after the Algerian war or in Mississippi today. *The Condemned of Altona* examines guilt: to determine where it begins, where it pertains, where (and if) it ends. The theme is no diluted Tolstoyan patter that "we are all responsible." This drama attempts to reconcile the life of conscience, of moral passion, with the simple fact that if any crime is pursued to its logical source, the criminal is not alone. There is always a reason, social or psychological or historical, behind every immoral act that leads back to another reason, and then back to others—away from the criminal himself. But, Sartre asks, if this is true, how are we to judge, as we must? How are we to know what good is? How are we to make life better, more bearable?

The dramatic image that Sartre has chosen for his theme is striking. A German family of shipbuilders named Gerlach—obviously suggested by Krupp or Thyssen—live in their gloomy mansion in Altona, a Hamburg suburb. Old Gerlach learns that he has cancer of the throat and six months to live. He summons a council of his family: Leni, his daughter; Werner, his son; and Johanna, his daughter-in-law. He makes Werner swear to continue living in this house. Gerlach's older son, Franz, supposedly dead, has imprisoned himself—for thirteen years—in his room upstairs. The father wants to be sure that Franz, his favorite, is cared for.

Franz had served in the army on the Russian front, having joined because of his father's involvement with the Nazis and some trouble because of his own protests. In the course of the war Franz found, not only that he could fight, but also that he could torture and murder. After his return through devastated Germany, he locked himself in his room to punish and purify himself. The only other person permitted to enter is his sister, Leni, who takes care of him. Passionate about her brother, Leni has fed his fantasies by keeping the truth from him for thirteen years. She feeds his dream of suffering and understanding, his tape-recorded orations that he is leaving for the thirtieth century. There has been incest between them, relatively passive on his part, ravenous in her.

Old Gerlach wants to see his son before he dies. He uses his daughter-in-law, Johanna, as an agent to penetrate the locked room and persuade Franz, who has not even heard from Leni about his father's cancer. Johanna and Franz are attracted to each other at once, in an encounter of two scourged and scourging souls. Through her (and through Leni's jealousy of her) he learns about his father and about German recovery. To Johanna he makes full confession of his crimes so that she can accept him, horror and all. But she cannot do so. As a result, he is stripped of delusion and hope. Evil is not any one man's sole doing, but no one man is therefore exonerated for partaking of it. The punishment that Franz had given himself is no longer enough.

Franz leaves his room and meets his father again, in a stiff but emotional reunion. The dying old man and the son with no future then go off in an automobile to suicide together. Johanna and Werner are freed from this house, which is as free as they can be. Leni goes up to Franz's room, to replace him as prisoner. (This is the weakest action in the play, with a sheerly romantic motive—lorn love—as against the deeper motive of most actions.) The curtain comes down, after we know that Franz and his father are dead, on an empty stage, as Franz's voice addresses the future: explaining, confessing, warning.

The Condemned of Altona has two chief defects. First, as in most of his plays, Sartre tends to push valid drama to extremes of action and contrast, close to melodrama. It is the defect of a nearly humorless mind, and thus sometimes almost makes us giggle (as in some of Franz's behavior). Second are the impediments of realism. In the first act, out of the realistic characters and matter, a poetic mode begins to soar. This frequently bogs down later in conformity to realistic-cum-naturalistic drama: in details of flirtation between Franz and Johanna, in a marital quarrel between her and Werner. The play never quite shakes free of mere verisimilitude. Yet there is in it an overriding sense of the confrontation of giant subjects by a fine mind—a faulty but nevertheless spacious imagination.

George Coulouris is excellent as old Gerlach. This English actor, who has not been seen on the American stage in years, was always an effective performer and has improved tremendously. The essence of the improvement is simplification. There is no superfluous gesture or movement; he allows his presence and his concentration to work for him. With scalpel speech and agile phrasing, he cuts Gerlach out of granite.

Tom Rosqui, as Franz, gives a vital and caustic performance. But in vain. He is utterly miscast—doomed to failure because of Blau's putting him in the role in the first place. The essentially romantic Franz, with whom women fall in love, a figure capable of self-damnation, is simply not in Rosqui's spectrum. In the wretched film version of *The Condemned of Altona* a few years ago, Maximilian Schell ranted as Franz but had the requisite Byronic quality. If there is no one in the Lincoln Center company who is right for the part, why wasn't an actor brought in, as Coulouris was? Must the audience be deprived for the sake of the repertory principle?

Priscilla Pointer is also miscast as Leni, even more hurtfully to the play. Her performance is a three-act excursion in strain. Carolyn Coates, for her part, is adequate as Johanna. She has a good voice, grace, dignity. But the fire of the instinctive anarchist—anarchic through moral vision—is quite beyond her. Edward Winter, as Werner, himself is flavorless, perhaps deliberately.

The keynote of Blau's direction is intelligence. He quickly convinces us that he understands this play and can project its ideas. What we are less convinced about is his emotional force, his sheerly theatrical perception and style. In short, although this production adds to our respect for Blau's mind and purpose, it does not much lessen our doubts about him as an artist.

Justin O'Brien's adaptation (necessarily condensed) must be noted. As he did for the production of Albert Camus's *Caligula* in 1960, O'Brien has provided live English, immensely superior to the English in the published version that is, in two senses, unspeakable.

The settings by Robin Wagner are effective: a Teutonic hall and a room for Franz that is like the interior of his head. I question only the gaunt fire-escape stairs in the council room, which hardly fit with the Biedermeier furnishings.

Much of this production of *The Condemned of Altona*, and admittedly much of the play, sags beneath the high level of its intent. But some of it, especially George Coulouris's scenes, is rich with dynastic tragedy. The dynasty, of course, is our own.

Winterset, by Maxwell Anderson. *New York Times*, February 10, 1966.

Maxwell Anderson's verse play *Winterset*, first produced in 1935, was revived last night at the Jan Hus Theater on East 74th Street. All during the production, a line of King Lear's kept running through my head: "You do me wrong to take me out o' the grave."

I can at least claim consistency in my opinion of Anderson's play. It has not faded for me; I thought it poor when I saw it thirty-one years ago. It is a work by a man who very much wanted to achieve poetic tragedy but whose main qualification was earnestness. *Winterset* makes the sophomoric error of taking poetic ambition as an excuse for language unrelated to character, and for manipulation of action to provide chances for spoken arias.

The story is related to the Sacco-Vanzetti case. (An incidental irony is that recent writings give a dubious color to the underdog sympathy in this case.) The son of a wrongfully executed man has been hazily wandering around the

United States—although he is characterized as a single-minded, purposeful demon of revenge. On a thin hint he crosses the country to find the witness who could clear his father's name. The place is a tenement under an East River bridge.

The boy accidentally meets a girl in the street there, and, with Instant Ecstasy, they fall deathlessly in love. She turns out to be the sister of the witness he is seeking. The judge in the trial, now demented, accidentally wanders 300 miles to the same street. The man who shelters him accidentally turns out to be the witness's father.

The true criminal, though doomed to death by disease, wants to insure that those who know the facts are silenced. He accidentally blurts out these very facts to his enemy, the boy. The "tragic" ending finds the boy trapped in an alley under the bridge with the girl. The criminal is waiting to kill him when he goes up the dark street.

The flimsiness of this catastrophe is underscored by memory of the happy ending in the film version. As I recall, the hopelessly trapped hero of the movie wheels out a barrel-organ that he knows is stored in a nearby shed, and plays it, thus irritating the police, who have previously objected to it. The police come, and take him and the girl—safely—to jail. A mark of this tragedy's lack of conviction is that I kept wondering why the hero in this production wasn't as bright as the one in the motion picture.

For some years there were people who maintained that the best way to get great modern drama is to apply old poetic forms and formalities to contemporary materials. *Winterset*, once hailed as an outstanding example, now suggests that the idea was always musty, that new times need new modes. Indeed, the play's language strains so hard to reach old tragic strophe that it makes the listener almost physically uncomfortable. Yeats said that rhetoric is the will trying to do the work of the imagination. *Winterset* is all rhetoric.

When we are not bothered by the plodding verse, we are assaulted by the flaws in structure. Scraps of action are hastily hammered into platforms from which the characters can spout. For instance, the girl's father sees her murdered. Instead of reacting as even tragic fathers have been known to do, he says at one, "It lacked only this." He then promptly goes into a little ode meant to serve this drama as the final chorus serves *Oedipus the King*. One can at least say that, like the concluding choral ode in *Oedipus*, this final speech is on the level of the play that precedes it.

In the large cast there are one-and-a-fraction good performances. Lester Rawlins, as the criminal, is substantial, malevolent, with nicely controlled ugliness. Joseph Hindy, the hero, brings on stage with him some hints of freshness and interest. These are quickly dissipated by insufficient technique: his voice keeps trailing into stagy diminuendos, and his movement confuses gawkiness with impulse. But there is some promise in him. The others range from the newest kind of amateur self-expression to the oldest kind of barnstorming rotundity, with no touch of truth anywhere along the line.

Amnon Kabatchnik directed, employing both a fog machine and a wind machine. A cloud of fog opens and closes the play. The additional fog is superfluous.

Phaedra, by Jean Racine. *New York Times*, February 11, 1966.

A lovely production of a great play, Racine's *Phaedra*, opened last night at the Off-Broadway Greenwich Mews Theater. It is the best performance of a classic French tragedy that I have ever seen.

This production is its director's triumph. More than coincidentally, it arrives while the *Comédie Française* is in New York City. For the director of this English-language production is a member of the *Comédie*: Paul-Emile Deiber, who has been with that company for twenty-two years. (He will appear in Feydeau and Montherlant plays at the City Center and has directed the new production of Corneille's *The Cid* that will be seen there.) From the first moment of *Phaedra*, there is an assurance that directorial knowledge and talent are producing the right style. Deiber knew, as classicists must, that such a style depends not on trickery or splashy effects, but entirely on what the actors do with the lines. They do admirably.

This tragedy was written at the end of a thirteen-year burst of creativity during which Racine produced all but two of his twelve major plays. *Phaedra* uses the same ancient myth that was the base of Euripides' *Hippolytus*: the story of the love of a passionate queen for her stepson; his revulsion; his vengeance; and the destruction that results from his vengeance. Unfailingly gripping though the story is, the quintessence of French neoclassic theater is not merely to wring our withers. It wants to abstract and purify emotion, to preserve it in timeless form.

Such an aim is different from that of subjective art, of which we see a great deal more nowadays, whose aim is immediacy. In a sense, the classic aim is more sophisticated because to the validity of its feeling it adds a graceful consciousness of the art itself. Thus it provides a double reward that we do not get so often from the romantic or realistic: a pleasure in the telling that is simultaneous with the effect of what is being told.

The elevation of the timeless in this *Phaedra* is accomplished quickly and surely. I do not derogate when I say that I did not expect a performance in this grand, broad line from an American cast: the classic style is not in our native tradition. But, under a knowledgeable director, these actors have achieved it admirably. The virtues of this style are largeness without pomposity, height without chill. The performance works itself out in arched balletic patterns, never false and never vernacular. Gesture is simple; voices are well orchestrated and modulated by Deiber's sensitive ear.

In a cast so small, every actor is crucial; but the production nevertheless depends on the title role. Beatrice Straight, as Phaedra, is fine. Always a handsome figure on stage, here she is every inch a queen. The classic vein is especially happy for Straight, who has not always been entirely comfortable in contemporary roles. Phaedra fits her well. Her good voice sometimes loses a bit of resonance in the *piano* passages, but this is a spirited classic performance of which she and we can be proud.

To complement Straight's work, Michael Durrell's Hippolytus is sustained at a heroic level. His declaration of love to Aricia is particularly well done. As Aricia, Anne Draper has beautiful dignity and charm. Mildred Dunnock, in the role of Phaedra's nurse, outdoes her own high standards with a performance of stature and rich feeling. Sam Haigler Henry, as Hippolytus's servant, delivers the narrative of offstage death—the classic set-piece in a classic play—with good color. And James Pritchett's Theseus is competent.

The new translation by William Packard, in rhymed couplets, has muscular life. Sometimes the first word of the rhyme predicts the second a little too obviously, and the language as a whole is not on the level of Robert Lowell's recent translation of *Phaedra*, but this version is clear and theatrically useful. To house it, Geri Davis has provided an arrangement of columns in perspective that is in the requisite neoclassic tradition. And, with equal aptness, Sylvia Kalegi's costumes are simple yet sumptuous.

This production is sponsored by the Institute for Advanced Studies in Theater Arts (IASTA), which was founded in 1958 to allow American actors to benefit from the art of foreign directors, who are brought to the United States especially for that purpose. The Institute has done twenty-two previous productions, directed by artists from Europe and Asia, all of which have been presented here privately to professional audiences. *Phaedra* is the first IASTA production to be shown publicly, and if it is an index, we have all been grievously deprived.

Eric Bentley refers to Racine's play as "perhaps the most civilized great tragedy ever written." It is being played at the Greenwich Mews in an appropriately civilized production. Honor and congratulation to all its participants.

Philadelphia, Here I Come!, by Brian Friel. *New York Times*, February 17, 1966.

"This is a great country for export," a man said to me once in Galway, "and what we export is young men." That is the theme of Brian Friel's play *Philadelphia, Here I Come!*, which opened last night at the Helen Hayes Theater—the familiar tale of youth setting out in the world, and in this case an Irish youth leaving a tiny village that has grown tinier.

Young Gar O'Donnell is off to Philadelphia in the morning (as still another song has it), away from his father's brown house behind his father's dull shop, away from the girl he didn't marry, away from the lads with whom he lied about the trollops whom they never touched. In fact, Gar is leaving the lovely fiction of his youth for the beginning of some reality, and the trouble with Friel's play is that this fiction, for all the good feeling beneath it, has come off a well-rubbed shelf.

The agony of youthful frustration is familiar, and even the Irish version (through Frank O'Connor, Edna O'Brien, and a flock of lovely others) is familiar by now, too. What Friel has to offer is not new insight but novelty, which is not so novel at that: the idea of having his hero played by two actors. There is a public Gar, whom everyone sees, and a private Gar, seen only by the other one—a source of dialogues when alone, and of impudent comment when the public Gar is in company.

Through this not-quite-novel novelty of view, we see the last night at home before Gar's departure. There are scenes of reminiscence: when he lacked the gumption to speak up for his girl, when his "American" aunt and uncle visited their old village and asked him to come live with them in Philly and be their filial love—with air conditioning and the promise of a job. There are scenes of the ritual and rote in the O'Donnell household: the tea, the schoolteacher's visit on the way to the pub, the canon's nightly call for supper and checkers, the affectionate nagging of the old housekeeper (played with gnarled love by Mairin D. O'Sullivan).

The texture of Gar's repetitious life, then, is well woven. We know all the reasons why he wants to break out of this webby humdrum, all the fragments and snips of American jive and TV and film that have formed a transparent mosaic across his vision, and all the reasons deeper than reason that at last tug at him when he must go. All this Friel has made recognizable and believable. But all this is also a little flat.

Which is to say that *Philadelphia, Here I Come!*, as a dramatic event, moves along mostly in one plane of intensity and progress, and as a lyric of poignancy, it lacks edge. Only toward the end, there is one scene like a microphotograph of the familiar, scrutinizing so closely that the familiar becomes new. At two o'clock on that last morning, when the widowed father and his son cannot sleep and meet in the parlor, they try to reach across the long-frozen feelings between them, casting back and forth a thin filament of memory. But it snaps. They never embrace or exchange a really affectionate word. The awareness of that schism, unbridgeable, between the two, who see it, hate it, yet cannot even speak of it, is Friel's sharpest barb of the evening.

That scene is well played by Eamon Kelly, the dour, lantern-jawed father, and by both embodiments of his son, Patrick Bedford, the public one, and Donal Donnelly, the other. (Donnelly will be remembered as the appealing Irish lodger in the film of Ann Jellicoe's play *The Knack*.) In the rest of the production Kelly has little to do except paint the surface of his character, and the two Gars have to spend all their talent—of which they have plenty—on keeping their private one-man vaudeville duo brightly lit. Hilton Edwards' direction of them, and of *Philadelphia, Here I Come!* as a whole, is workmanlike, but it is a disappointment after the brilliant work of his that has been seen here. Lloyd Burlingame's setting, for its part, is, as it should be, depressingly decent.

At the last, despite the good work of most of the actors and the better work of some, it is the dramatist Brian Friel who lets us down. Not by trickery or fakery but simply by naïveté in art. There is considerable pleasantness, little poetry, and insufficient power in his play. His Ballybeg (or "Little Town") household is drawn honestly enough, but it comes trailing a long line of novels and plays that deal with the same material: with Billy-Liar youths dreaming fantasies in drab bedrooms, mocking the clichés around them and finally feeling the ties that underlie even dislike.

Forty or fifty years earlier we might all, figuratively speaking, have been bowled over by Friel's candor and this theatrical devices. He has his own countrymen to blame, as well as a lot of other authors, if we now think his play is like his hero: amiable and appealing enough, but finally unexciting.

Where's Daddy?, by William Inge. *New York Times*, March 3, 1966.

Hiram Sherman is in *Where's Daddy?*, which opened last night at the Billy Rose Theatre, and this is a comfort. Sherman is, in the happiest sense, a personality actor. This is only to say that his professional competence and authority ease the quality of his personality into the audience's cockles like a good wine on the palate: dry, tasteful, warming. No play that gives him the opportunity to sit and talk for a while can be all bad.

Not quite, but it's a narrow squeak. William Inge's new comedy very nearly is all bad: a scoopful of modern themes shoveled into an old-fashioned domestic-comedy container. Once more, dear friends, once more into the breach between the generations. This is still another play about a young couple misunderstood by their elders, a bride and a bridegroom who live by enlightenment, modern freedom, and non-sentiment. And yet once more, those kids—who had the right stuff in them all along—see the error of their ways at the end.

The boy and the girl have married after she became pregnant because he wants to do the right thing by the child. But he can't face the prospect of actually being a parent; and she understands. He will finance her but leave her, and at his behest she will put the child up for adoption when it is born. This may seem a far-fetched premise on which to start a play, but to think so is to be a dullard. If this kind of play doesn't start with a far-out premise, it can't very well end up dead conventional center. A play can't begin with the states of mind with which it finishes, can it? We all know this, as we listen to the outrageous statements in Act I, and we nod comfortably, recognizing that in the end those kids will prove true-blue under those crazy modern ideas.

The comedy plods along for its first forty-five minutes through this exposition of material, which we know is being set up merely to be demolished. In that time, it is enlivened—to a degree—only by a visit from the girl's Massachusetts mother (Betty Field and her homey back-fence voice). Then there is the first spark of genuine interest, because Hiram Sherman enters—a spark both because of him and because of the character he plays. He is the boy's former guardian, who raised him from the age of fifteen when he found the orphaned lad in a queer bar. Sherman is a Brooklyn teacher who makes very few bones about the fact that he is a homosexual and who is, without over-advertisement, obviously a man of honor, taste, and humor. We like the character as such, but in fact he makes the play worse because he uncovers a possibility that is never developed, let alone fulfilled.

For one fast moment, there is a suspicion that William Inge has deliberately lulled us into thinking that this is a conventional comedy about hip marriage and that he has planned to surprise us by slyly infiltrating a serious theme into all the deceptive coziness. But that is to credit Inge with more ingenuity of design and more ambition than this play ever reveals. The complexities of Sherman's character are only more elements thrown in to stuff out the full-evening bag that the author has to fill. *Where's Daddy?* simply plods and wriggles along. Field comes back in the second act. So does Sherman. So does the errant young husband. And when the boy finally holds his baby in his arms—well, even a hipster has a heart, right?

There are two further attempts at modishness. Ben Edwards' commonplace set of a New York walk-up apartment is framed with a proscenium covered with boxes from cartoon strips. This shows an awareness of Pop Art. The newlyweds' neighbors across the hall are blacks. This is Pop Pertinence. However, there is a bonus in this last item because the pair are played by Robert Hooks and Barbara Ann Teer, who provide some much needed vitality.

The pregnant young wife is played by Barbara Dana without distinction. The vacillating husband is Beau Bridges, who has a bright, affable sheepdog look and plays his emotional scenes with good feeling. If he will clarify his speech (even the television commercial actor he plays would have to speak clearly), he may turn out to be a useful performer. Harold Clurman has directed these actors, and this play, apparently under the impression that people who live in apartments, together with their guests, rarely sit down; further, that they do a good deal of their conversing virtually toe to toe.

Inge's comedy itself cannot even clearly be called a failure because it is hard to say what it has failed at. Perhaps it is an attempt to show that the schism between the generations is superficial: the oldsters really envy while they disapprove, and the youngsters in the long run are not going to say no to 5,000 years of civilization. But there is more that is interesting on this subject in the solicitor Maitland's one scene with his daughter in John Osborne's *Inadmissible Evidence* than in all of *Where's Daddy?*.

Serjeant Musgrave's Dance, by John Arden. *New York Times*, March 20, 1966.

John Arden, the English dramatist who was born in 1930, studied architecture at Cambridge and Edinburgh, but he began writing plays as a schoolboy. He was practicing as an architect when he was given his first professional play production—a Sunday night performance by the English Stage Company of *The Waters of Babylon* in 1957. He has written copiously in the nine years since, and his plays have drawn at the least serious criticism and sometimes high praise. His recent play, *Armstrong's Last Good Night*, is now in the repertory of the British National Theatre. *Live Like Pigs*, a highly interesting yet unsatisfying work, was produced Off-Broadway last season. *The Waters of Babylon*, equally interesting yet unsatisfying, was given three Monday night performances this winter by the New Theater Workshop.

That group's parent body, the Establishment Theater Company, has now presented Arden's best-known play, *Serjeant Musgrave's Dance*, at the Theater de Lys. *Musgrave* was first presented by the English Stage Company in 1959 and has recently been revived for their repertory in a quite different production. The play was given its American premiere by the San Francisco Actors' Workshop in 1961. The Arena Theater's own production, in Washington, D.C., opened this past Thursday.

Set approximately a century ago, the drama tells the story of Musgrave and three of his troopers, who return from a British colonial outpost with the skeleton of a fellow soldier who was killed there. These four are sick of war. Under Musgrave's rigorous command, they are seemingly on a recruiting trip but are in fact taking the skeleton back to the dead man's home town to rouse the townspeople against war. It is a colliery town, and the pitmen there are on strike. This particular conflict makes a figuratively stormy sea for the small expedition of soldiers to sail on. And the expedition—which is more of a gesture than a mission and which is nebulous even as gesture—fails.

It is known that Arden was moved to write *Serjeant Musgrave's Dance* by the events involving the British on Cyprus about ten years ago. By transposing his drama to the nineteenth century, his intent was to give it metaphorical strength, enlarging it into timelessness and freeing it of the bonds of petty familiar fact. (As for the "dance" in the title, it is Musgrave's purpose to let God's word "dance on this earth." Later, he incarnates the idea by dancing as he exhorts a crowd.) *Musgrave* certainly confirms that Arden is in the front rank of his generation of dramatists, English or otherwise.

The play begins at a level of intensity (which is really a synonym for power of selection) that is immediately gripping; and we respond with pleasure to the imaginative demands it makes on us. The central image—of the soldiers returning with the crated skeleton—is itself a Brechtian stroke of theatrical fire. That image is not fully disclosed at once, but the hints hold us as the play proceeds. Again like Brecht, Arden blends his dialogue with ballads. Sometimes the language is a bit distended, but generally it is deeply, affectingly English—a laconic yet rich rural diction, which has the feeling of the lovely English pastoral darkened by social change and the worst in the human heart.

But exactly because it is quickly apparent that Arden is an exceptional dramatist, the disappointments in his play are keen. Control of the central image is dissipated: tensions slacken; the theme is unclear and unresolved, even somewhat arbitrarily tied up. To be sure, the dramatist is concerned with human ambiguity, not with artificially pure rights and wrongs, but the ambiguous conclusion, as designed, is simply not credible. Concerning that ambiguity, Herbert Blau, who directed the American premiere, has written: "The first production of *Serjeant Musgrave's Dance* in London actually led to charges that this pacifist drama was urging a bloody revolution. Arden denies it; examined closely, the play isn't sure." In the end, then, *Musgrave*, together with his other plays seen in the United States, shows John Arden to be that familiar twentieth-century figure: the artist whose undeniable high talent is manifested in a series of faulty works.

Yet some of us who had long thought this play flawed (it was published in the U.S. four years ago) were nevertheless happy to learn that it was to be produced here. What is disheartening to Arden enthusiasts is that the production is inadequate. The settings and music are fine. Stuart Burge, the director, has envisioned graphic patterns of stage movement. But he has peopled his patterns with a spotty cast of actors. Some of the acting is poor, much is merely passable, and little of it is really good. John Colicos, as Musgrave, conveys the quality of the man's drive and of his being driven—by religious zeal; but his emotional crises tend to rise to the surface of the character rather than to penetrate. It is easy to imagine a production of the play that would be more ironic, heroic, taut, and pathetic—one that would make us less aware of the play's faults by more fully exploiting its virtues.

This raises a different but relevant matter. I have been told by readers that an article like this one, which discusses flaws equally with merits, is an instance of equivocation, and as such discourages the production of serious plays in what is obviously a tough time for serious work. To me, such a response brings a considerable whiff of the arguments of the 1930s, when we were enjoined to support proletarian plays, no matter what we thought of them, because at least their hearts were in the right place and, furthermore, they had to compete with floods of trash that were being produced all around them.

The conditions for serious work in the New York theater—on or off Broadway—are very, very grim, it's true. There can be nothing but sympathy for the impulse behind readers' response, as reported above. Further, there is truth in what Edward Albee said in a recent interview: "It is the responsibility of critics to judge a play not only on how well it succeeds in its intention but also on how important that intention is." But the harshness of current theatrical conditions and the truths of Albee's statement are not a license for distortion of opinion, however well-meaning.

That is to say, *Serjeant Musgrave's Dance* may be more significant than (for instance) Neil Simon's *Barefoot in the Park*, but the direction of *Barefoot* by Mike Nichols was superior to the direction of *Musgrave* by Stuart Burge. In just deference to the Albee rule, we cannot call Nichols a better director than Burge until he tackles something as difficult as *Musgrave*; but, glad as I am that *Musgrave* was done, I wish that Burge had done it better.

As I have noted, I do not think a play needs to be perfect in order to be produced: I looked forward eagerly to seeing *Serjeant Musgrave's Dance*. If the play were satisfactorily performed, I could urge that, because of its extraordinary merits, it ought to be seen despite its defects. As it is, I think the intelligent theatergoer will be both interested in, and disappointed by, the current New York production. To report otherwise would be a disservice to that theatergoer. (I omit ringing statements about critical integrity.) Those who think that theatrical prospects can be improved by glossing over defects in serious plays and productions—well, I don't know what they are thinking.

The Caucasian Chalk Circle, by Bertolt Brecht. *New York Times*, March 25, 1966.

A doubly pleasant occasion: one of the best of Bertolt Brecht's plays has at last reached New York (twenty-two years after it was written). And in presenting it, the Lincoln Center Repertory Company has given us its best production to date, and a good production by any standards.

The Caucasian Chalk Circle, which opened last night at the Vivian Beaumont, seems a kind of busman's holiday for Brecht. It is a diversion from his activist political plays into the arena of theatrical high-jinks, with plentiful opportunities for pageantry, music, horseplay, and sheer heart-tugging. Indeed, this is a big, conscious, melodramatic *show*, complete with infant waif, estranged lovers, Eliza-effects like an escape across a rickety bridge, and a happy ending without the deliberate fakery of Macheath's rescue in *The Threepenny Opera*. Yet this work is founded on a view of life as a pitched social battle between the rulers and the ruled, and it has a utilitarian purpose.

The body of the three-hour play/production follows a prologue about collective farmers in a Caucasian village in the Soviet Union at the end of the Second World War. Two groups of farmers lay claim to a valley. The dispute is in fact settled quickly, but to drive home the idea (the utilitarian point, in this case), a play is performed before the reconciled groups: to prove that anything—a valley, a baby—belongs morally to the person or persons who will do best by it.

The play-within-the-play is set in the very same locality 700 years earlier. In one of the wars of princes, a governor's infant is abandoned and later rescued by a kitchen maid named Grusha, who takes him with her on various risky journeys, all of which are interesting and some of which are funny. At the end of the war, the child is found by soldiers and re-claimed by the governor's widow. But Grusha, who has reared him for several years, wants to keep the boy.

So the case comes to trial. That trial is held before a judge named Azdak, but before the trial proceeds, we backtrack to learn how this wily, good-hearted scoundrel—out of Shakespeare and Rabelais—became a judge in the first place. In the trial itself, Azdak uses a version of King Solomon's old device: he determines which of the contesting women is willing to harm the child by pulling it out of a chalk circle.

Jules Irving has directed *The Caucasian Chalk Circle* (happily, from Eric Bentley's translation, the standard one for this play, as his others are for so much of Brecht)—the third director whose work has been seen with the Lincoln Center company and, on the basis of this season, the one with the most truly theatrical gifts. This is a circus-like show and is played as such, yet the broad character touches and the bitter flavors are well used. Movement swirls; the riotous colors of peasants like Brueghel's are splashed in; the interplay among the narrator (the Storyteller), the onstage musicians, and the action itself is well-balanced. And for the first time, we feel that the resources of the Vivian Beaumont Theater—revolving stages and so on—are dominated by the director, instead of dominating him.

The costumes are gorgeous when need be (some of the actors wear resplendent Persian rugs like gowns), and are fine peasant stuff otherwise. All the upper-class characters and their attendants wear masks, slightly outsized and grotesque. These and the costumes themselves are by James Hart Stearns, and all are excellent. Stearns also did the settings, which suggest a continuity between the ancient and modern Caucasus in their rough textures, but is it too literal-minded to ask about corrugated iron roofs in 1200 A.D.? Richard Nelson's lighting of those settings is purposely stagy but sometimes, I think, distractingly so. Morton Subotnick's music, for its part, is flavorless, the least rewarding aspect of the production.

The prime performance is by Robert Symonds as Azdak. Which is as it ought to be, because Azdak is a dream-part, sly, pragmatic, brusquely idealistic, and loaded with punchlines. Some believe that the part is a Brecht self-portrait: an ironic realist whose principles come second only to his peasant's instinct for survival. Symonds—wiry, slippery, sharp—is first-class in the role.

Elizabeth Huddle plays Grusha adequately, although she has not quite enough voice for her songs. Her chief asset is her sturdy, snub-nosed, rose-cheeked effect, which is very likable. Brock Peters, the Storyteller, conducts himself with the dignity of a veteran village ballad-singer. Ray Fry, whose Sir Jasper Fidget was the best thing in Wycherley's *The Country Wife*, has a cameo turn here as a besotted monk. In the otherwise enormous cast, many of whom double and triple, one can note the valuable addition to the company of Earl Montgomery and Murvyn Vye, the good work of Michael Granger in a couple of parts, and Edward Winter's decently dignified soldier-fiancé of Grusha.

And hands themselves should be mentioned, though adversely. This is a play in which a disguised nobleman is recognized by his soft white hands. But most of the peasants in the cast—ancient and modern—have noblemen's hands. Boris Tumarin, supposedly a grizzled dairy farmer, goes so far as to use his own very white hands like a ladies' hairdresser.

Nonetheless, perhaps the Lincoln Center company looks best, up to now, in this play because it requires neither the high style of Wycherley nor the high acting virtuosity of the Büchner and Sartre plays (*Danton's Death* and *The*

Condemned of Altona) that preceded it. But, even it is if for negative reasons, the result is positive. Lincoln Center's production of *The Caucasian Chalk Circle* achieves much of what Brecht presumably intended: a good show, charming and thoroughly theatrical, yet firmly based on an undeceived view of the world.

"Six Short Plays from La Mama." *New York Times*, **April 12 & 13, 1966.**

The Café La Mama is a downtown experimental theater club open to members and to membership, which serves uninteresting coffee and often serves interesting plays. Six of those plays have recently been performed in Copenhagen and Paris by a troupe of five young actors. The troupe is now presenting them—as "Six From La Mama"—at the Off-Broadway Martinique in two bills of three plays each.

The first bill, which opened last night, begins with *Thank You, Miss Victoria*, a monologue by William Hoffman. A rich and sybaritic young man is forced to go to work for his stockbroker father. On his first morning he amuses himself by telephoning in answer to a thinly disguised advertisement—in a girlie magazine—by a sadistic woman looking for a slave. The supercilious youth makes the call as a gag after a telephone bet with a friend. But in the course of the long conversation with the woman, of which we hear one side, he finds himself carried away into conviction, into discovery about himself. As exegesis of a passage in Krafft-Ebing, the play shows some craft that does not ebb, but the transition from gaga to absorption is played with insufficient power by Michael Warren Powell.

This Is the Rill Speaking is by Lanford Wilson, who recently had a double bill of one-act plays produced at the Theater East. The present play is an album of souvenirs from a small-town boyhood—sketches of different families, of adolescent encounters and escapades—with the author presumably as a character. The material is clearly seen and tenderly recalled, but it is overly familiar—snippets of *Our Town* spiced with sexual candor. A special difficulty with autobiographical material of youth is that it often poises the perceptions of the author against the lesser perceptions of the other characters; he sees more about them than they saw in themselves and him. But the author sometimes forgets that this experience is now put before an audience whose perceptions may at least equal his own.

In this multi-charactered play, each of the company has several roles, slipping from one into another and back again without costume or make-up change. The ladies, Jacque Lynn Colton and Marie-Claire Charba, play at the level of good acting students. A tousle-haired youth named Victor Lipari supplies some nice bucolic flavor, and touches of authenticity come from Kevin O'Connor.

The major contribution here is by the director, Tom O'Horgan, who staged all the plays in both bills. O'Horgan shows a fundamental directorial gift: the ability to see in a script the physical unfolding that will articulate its essences and rhythms. He also has some understanding of acting and can evoke the best from his players, whatever their respective abilities. *This Is the Rill Speaking* is limited by the limitations of its cast, and, additionally, there is in Mr. O'Horgan's work more evidence of talent growing than grown; but the talent is there.

The third play, *Birdbath*, by Leonard Melfi, starts and continues for some time as a good exercise in realistic snobbery-pathos. A Greenwich Village poet works in a cafeteria as a cashier. A bus girl—timid, virginal, unbright—is attracted to him and innocently but romantically goes to his room with him. He does not entice her; he doesn't begin to grow amorous until after he has had some drinks. Their conversation makes acceptable comedy out of their differences in background and experience.

Then, suddenly, after the girl, too, has had some drinks, she delivers a staggering confession. This shatters the little play, because nothing in her behavior or character has given us the slightest hint that she is capable of the act she admits. At least, if she *had* done it, her subsequent behavior would have been much different, we feel. The surprise seems the author's attempt to give his play a strong finish. Fifty years ago, the artifice would have been merely some sort of mechanical plot twist; here it is a psychological revelation, but it is equally a theatrical twist.

As the young man, Kevin O'Connor is again authentic, with a relaxed and forceful stage presence. One may say that O'Horgan, through the agency of Marie-Claire Charba, gives a reasonably effective performance in *Birdbath* as the girl. Charba seems to be doing adequately what she has been coached in, but a sense of personal force is missing.

The net of these three plays is some disappointment, not only because each play has shortcomings, but also because one expects work that is more adventurous in concept and method from the playwrights of an experimental theater. Here the principal difference from a conventional bill of little-theater one-act plays is in some frank language and some sexual reference. Even Hoffman's play is simply a "take" on a familiar sort of short play. But (there is no point in being coy about this) I have already seen the second bill of three plays (I saw the last preview), which open tonight, and, in general, I found them more rewarding. There are two interesting plays in this bill, and they share certain characteristics.

War, by Jean-Claude van Itallie, concerns two actors, young and old, and the dream figure of a girl. The young man, bearded and hip, visits his friend, who is a survivor from an old-fashioned theater of large gesture and gilt crowns. Their period differences merge in fantasy-games that they have evidently played before, including various "roles" that they flow in and out of. Together, too, they summon up the figure of a girl in late Victorian dress toward whom they both behave like young sons.

This is not plotted or schematically symbolic work; it is an exercise in pathetic imagination. The pleasure it provides is chiefly in the way the two men play together, without affectation and with a conviction that sustains the play's delicate fabric. The two actors are nicely performed by Michael Warren Powell (the older) and Kevin O'Connor. (Mari-Claire Charba is the dream figure.) What is missing, however, is some kind of resolution, in an appropriate vein. Even an unfettered imagist poem—which this play resembles—provides a sense of realization. Here, although it is very pleasant while we watch, it is unsatisfying when it is finished. This despite the evocativeness of the stark title, *War*, which suggests the battle, not between generations, but of all generations against cold fact and the passage of time.

Chicago, by Sam Shepard, the best play on both bills, is a fantasy-comedy about a young man in a bathtub. At first he looks naked, but he rises to reveal jeans and sneakers, which are probably concessions to convention and rough floors. As he sits in his tub, singing, soliloquizing, following the darting of his daydreams in rhyme, reason, and unreason, we learn that the girl who lives with him has got a job and is leaving that day. She passes through several times. So do friends, who breakfast with her before she goes. For the most part, the young man remains in the tub.

What gives the play its delights is Shepard's ability to follow fast after the ephemeral half-thought that is usually unspoken, and Kevin O'Connor's ability to speak it, sing it, savor it, and hasten over it. The pair of them, aided by Tom O'Horgan's sensitive direction, provide a bright patch of truthful nonsense. The ending—in which the hero's private world is breached by other people and by his acknowledgment of the audience—seems to me to hurt the play. Nevertheless, this is a free-flowing, salty, and touching little rhapsody on a small incident seen through the prism of fancy.

The third play, *The Recluse*, by Paul Foster, which deals with a demented old lady who lives in a crowded attic, is a tedious attempt at an old game: the Gothic grotesque. The scripts by van Itallie and Shepard, by contrast, may be called anti-plays. They exist in contrast to the theater as usually practiced—not as attacks on it but (one may say) as relief from it. These authors are simply *playing*—following the fantasies of their characters as they bubble out of an initial situation. Surely one function of an experimental theater is to make such playing possible, and here it has been amusingly and affectingly done.

Besides presenting these two promising plays by van Itallie and Shepard, La Mama's double bill promotes two exceptionally promising acting talents. Kevin O'Connor, the principal actor, and Tom O'Horgan, the director, are both admirably at home with the realities of the stage and the intangibles of volatile imagination.

The Skin of Our Teeth, by Thornton Wilder. *New York Times*, June 2, 1966.

The Minneapolis Theater Company has begun its new season at the Tyrone Guthrie Theater with a crackling production of Thornton Wilder's *The Skin of Our Teeth*. Douglas Campbell, who directed, has an estimable company and a beautifully usable stage; and he devours theatrical opportunities the way Joan Sutherland devours coloratura passages. The result, which opened last night, is the best staged production of the play that I have ever seen.

The Guthrie Theater has a thrust, or open, stage, surrounded by the audience on three sides and no proscenium or curtain. Some plays seem to resent this kind of production. The Wilder play thrives on it, excepting perhaps the ends of acts, which were written with a descending curtain in mind. Tanya Moiseiwitsch and Carolyn Parker have provided clever skeleton settings for the occasion (in addition to good costumes). Campbell makes clever use of these settings, with a beginning that bursts the play open in an amusing explosion of movement. In visual terms, the show never lags thereafter.

Campbell is not, like some open-stagers, a lopsided director. Besides his acute sense of movement and picture, he has ears and a sensibility for acting. He has helped Ruth Nelson, for example, to a performance of Mrs. Antrobus that is very easily the best of the three I have seen (two of them on Broadway). She is matriarchal without being maudlin, and (which is as rare in art as in life) she reveals a human being under the mother. Nelson misses no nuance of reality that the part offers, and in one moment—when she mourns her murdered son Abel—she touches true elegy.

That admirable actress Nancy Wickwire plays Sabina with wit and impeccable technique. If Wickwire is not the slinkiest serpent who ever roiled an Eden, she has the wherewithal in her voice and personality to make much longer-lasting trouble. As Antrobus, the heir of the scrambled ages, we get Lee Richardson, a thoroughly competent actor though not an exceptional force. As the Antrobus children, Ellen Geer and Len Cariou serve their various turns. Ed Flanders, for his part, is a humorously resigned stage manager. Among the leading actors, only Evie McElroy, the fortune-teller, is weak. She lacks the growl and bite of the quiet horror behind her perception of the future.

As for the play itself, it now seems a venerable war horse. In 1942 people walked out on it because they considered it too bizarre and experimental. Surely those same people, or their equivalents, must feel quite cuddly with it today. (Change—particularly artistic change—gallops quicker and quicker.) In purely theatrical terms, *The Skin of Our Teeth* is still a going enterprise, most of the time. Its ingenuity sometimes sinks into cuteness, and it is not built cumulatively—after an act ends, the play has to build all over again. But one thing is undeniably true of it: criticism comes second, impact is first. Later, we find ourselves asking what, after all, there was to it. At the moment—in many of its moments—it chills and moves us.

The second act is the weakest, when we are held neither by the novelty of discovering the play's method nor the holocaust aftereffects at the end. And in the second act the facile and irrelevant device of the play's awareness of being a play—with interruptions, missed cues, etc.—is at its most coy. Moreover, residually *The Skin of Our Teeth* seems thin because it never really explores its title: why or how mankind gets through by the skin of its teeth and whether we can really take comfort (as the author seems to) in this fact. The play wrings poignancy out of man's follies and persistences but generally from a relatively complacent view. When the crux of a large matter begins to be confronted, as in Antrobus's last speech, Wilder tends to write his way out of it with charming dialogue that has a hint of sleight of hand.

Yet, as a glittery carousel of human history, an airy advertisement on the theme of the human tragedy, *The Skin of Our Teeth* can still whirl and entertain. Campbell and his theatrical clan have played knowingly to its strengths, and those strengths have never looked stronger.

The Dance of Death, by August Strindberg. *New York Times*, June 3, 1966.

As the second offering in its three-play summer repertory, the Tyrone Guthrie Theater is giving the first professional production—in its entirety—of a towering modern drama. August Strindberg's *The Dance of Death*, written in 1901, is in two parts. Part I, which runs about two hours and is often performed alone, is in itself a masterwork. Part II, which runs about ninety minutes, carries this drama of a tormented marriage to its conclusion.

The production by the Minnesota Theater Company, which opened last night, deals well, if not overwhelmingly, with the play, though there are important shortcomings in the performance. Still, it is always interesting, sometimes stronger than that; and often—as Strindberg intended—it is sardonically funny.

Part I is an instance in the modern theater of an author's encompassing a tremendous range with a small cast. (*Long Day's Journey into Night* is another such instance; O'Neill was a Strindberg devotee.) There are, in effect, only three characters. Edgar, an army captain, commands an island fortress off the Swedish coast. He and his wife, Alice, have lived for twenty-five years in acrid love-hate. Her cousin, Kurt, who has been abroad for fifteen years, arrives to direct the quarantine station on the island. That quarantine station is the brooding symbol of the play, for the married couple are diseased with afflictions and frustration. They live together by killing each other a little bit each day, and they rely on this war to keep themselves alive. Neither has the life he or she wanted, but now it seems impossible to leave the other person—who made that life what it must continue to be.

Kurt is at first neutral between them. Then he almost becomes Alice's lover out of revulsion at Edgar's behavior, but she soon repels him by her own brutality toward Edgar. Edgar and Alice must survive together—until one of them dies. All of this poisonous, inescapable horror grows from the depth and truth of these three interlocked characters.

In Part II, Strindberg brings in three more characters: the daughter of Edgar and Alice; Kurt's son, who loves the girl; and a lieutenant who is his rival. This second part relies less on dynamics of character and more on contrivances of plot, as Edgar maneuvers for vengeance on his wife and Kurt. He injures them both, but the daughter, whom he has hoped to use in a grand vindictive coup, is instead the cause of his final defeat. Part II of *The Dance of Death* is intense drama, made before our eyes. But Part I itself is a great work, one that—like many other great works—hardly seems to have been made at all. It simply exists.

The new translation by Norman Ginsbury, in supple and responsive English, has been directed by the artistic director of the Guthrie Theater, Douglas Campbell. Inevitably, then, there are excellences. As he showed in his production of *The Skin of Our Teeth*, Campbell's apposite invention and his phrasing of movement and dialogue are fine. He makes Part I completely at home on the open stage: a circular viscous blob dropped down amid us with three creatures trapped in it. But in Part II the effort to accommodate Strindberg's play to this theater is evident. More important, the whole production never really closes with the demons in this drama, never quite breaks the skin. There are comprehension and clarity, and we are shown vistas of hell; but we never quite enter and feel the heat.

This is largely because Campbell has not got from two of his three crucial players the performances that are needed. As the wife, Nancy Wickwire acts with finesse. She has a good theater voice, and in this long role she never tires herself or us. But the net effect is that she is explicating the part, not harrowing us. We never quite believe that she is looking up from the bottom of a pit dug by twenty-five years of mutual malevolence and dependence.

Paul Ballantyne, as Kurt, is adequate at best. In his person he lacks appeal, and in his acting he seems to carry a Plexiglas plate (like a car in a showroom window) through which we can see how the engine works. The play is made and the evening sustained, however, by Robert Pastene as Edgar. Playing quietly but mordantly, he portrays the captain as a wry, mad, clever egocentric, amused at the torment he has helped to make, sometimes even amused at its effect on himself. Pastene convinces us that this man is absolutely alone in the midst of his home, of his life: segregated by the hate he has engendered and by his own bitterness resulting from that segregation. He has snared himself along with his wife. At the last we feel, for this chill monster, a measure of monstrous pity.

In Part II the pair of possible lovers are played pleasantly by Patricia Elliott and Robert Jackson. As an index of social evolution, if not sexual revolution, it seems relevant to note that Jackson is black. He and Elliott, along with the other performers, are unobtrusively helped by Lewis Brown's settings and costumes and Herbert Pilhofer's atonal music. They contribute, finally, to a performance that is a fascinating journey through the play, rather than a soul-shaking experience.

The Kitchen, by Arnold Wesker. *New York Times*, June 14, 1966.

Sometimes the physical limitations of the theater are an advantage over films. The film version of Arnold Wesker's *The Kitchen*, seen in the U.S. five years ago, burned with the fever of "backstage" life in a large restaurant during rush hours. But, subconsciously, we knew that it was all contrived in bits and pieces made over a period of weeks and then assembled in a cutting room. By contrast, on the stage of the Off-Broadway New 81st Street Theater, where Wesker's play opened last night, the fever is created before our eyes, all at one time and in one place. It is the sort of effect that is much more impressive when immediate; and it is the evening's chief achievement.

Jack Gelber, best known as a dramatist (*The Connection*), has directed. With twenty-nine actors—an enormous cast these days for a non-musical, on or off Broadway—he has neatly choreographed this kitchen frenzy, counterpointing little groups of waitresses and choruses of cooks and drudges, together with the owner moving through occasionally with smiling, resigned fretfulness. This is the kind of naturalistic direction—of a large cast bustling about in a lot of small parts—at which George S. Kaufman and Elmer Rice excelled in productions of their own plays. The technique might be called "Mobile Mosaic," and Gelber has revived it with professional dispatch. Wisely, he has made all the food that the actors handle imaginary, merely pantomimed. This spares us the distraction of watching for accidents, and it heightens the ballet effect.

Rip Torn plays the leading role, a likable German cook who loves a married waitress, pregnant by him. She dallies about getting a divorce and agreeing to bear his child; in his depression, a chance insult sends him berserk, chopping and smashing. Torn, who has frequently been typed as a Southern sadist, gives the part an excitable, desperately warmhearted quality, with the playfulness of a frustrated man objecting to the world by clinging to shreds of childishness. This is a good performance, by any standard, and it is complemented by acute acting from Conrad Bain, a sour butcher; John Kramer, another German; Morris Erby, a hot-tempered (Caribbean?) cook; Peter DeAnda, his friend; and Peter Rogan, an Irish newcomer.

The author, Arnold Wesker, is a British socialist who has gone on, after this first work (1960), to write a succession of plays that comment pungently on

English society—particularly in regard to the working class and to general class structures. (*Chips with Everything*, produced in New York in 1963, made its comment through the medium of the Royal Air Force.) *The Kitchen*, in the current production, has been taken out of England and placed nowhere precisely: so we get a mixture of British and American locutions, "bloody" along with "70,000 bucks."

The play reminds us vividly that there are hot little concealed horrors just out of eyeshot all along the edges of our comfortable lives. But after this elemental service, which a brief documentary would do better, Wesker's play falters; and its quieter moments become sentimental. With his multi-national cast, the playwright wants us, of course, to take the kitchen as the world-in-little. These are the conditions of capitalist life and labor, he implies. ("When the world is filled with kitchens," one man says, "you get pigs.") After the all the culinary running-amok, the owner asks the German what in the world he wants. Doesn't he have food, a job, good wages? "What is there more?" the boss asks bewilderedly.

But, in the end, this seems a bankrupt attempt to portray the bankruptcy of materialist society. What are the socialist Wesker's hopes for the German cook and his friends? If the play is an indictment of the callous capitalist world, what does Wesker think the kitchens of Soviet restaurants are like at mealtimes? Or, if that is a repugnant question to a democratic socialist, what then would it be like in Wesker's personal New Jerusalem? If these workers knew that they were not to be cast out into the alley when they were old, would that make the work any less fiendish during rush hours?

This early play of Wesker's, then, is essentially pointless. It looks with youthful, blurry sympathy at a grim phenomenon, presumably suggesting that we ought to Do Something about it. But *The Kitchen* has no grip on the true nature of the phenomenon, nor does it even explore the grimness itself in anything more than superficial terms. It does, however, have some theatrical aptness. It provides the chance for some busy naturalistic stage pyrotechnics, and Jack Gelber has used that chance dexterously.

All's Well That Ends Well, by William Shakespeare. *New York Times*, June 17, 1966.

Joseph Papp presses on. Under his administrative direction, the New York Shakespeare Festival opened its twelfth season on Wednesday night, and the open-air Delacorte Theater in Central Park was packed to welcome it. Under Papp's artistic direction, the company played *All's Well That Ends Well*, giving this play its New York professional premiere. The production will run through July 2nd and will be followed by *Measure for Measure* on July 6th and by *Richard III* on August 3rd. Admission—as who does not know?—is free.

All's Well That Ends Well is one of Shakespeare's later works, taken from an English version of a Boccaccio story and set in France. Helena, the orphaned daughter of a physician, falls in love with Bertram, a young nobleman. She cures the sick King of France with one of her dead father's medicines, and in return the king offers her anything she wishes. She wishes Bertram. As ordered, Bertram reluctantly weds but refuses to bed. She then follows him to the wars and tricks him into consummation. When he finds out that the girl in the boudoir was his wife, he falls in love with her. (Freudians, to your stations!)

No review of a production of this play is complete, it seems, without a reference to the fact that Bernard Shaw thought Helena the first Ibsenite heroine. She is a wife larger-spirited than her husband, a lady doctor (of a kind) who pursues her goal in defiance of at least some conventions. So this is a difficult role—not in technical demands but in the qualities it needs. Helena's aggressiveness, if she is to hold us, has to be encompassed in a girl of commanding poise, some humor, and a capacity for love that is wiser than the beloved.

Barbara Barrie seems to have faced the role, recognized its difficulties, and decided to accompany it, rather than to play it. She gives us the curious double image of moving next to the part, offering a modern vernacular comment on it as she goes along. This provides some moderately cute moments, but it does not provide a Helena. Barrie gets little help from her Bertram, Richard Jordan, who is not ready for the role.

The highlight of the evening is the performance by J. D. Cannon of Parolles, the hero's pseudo-soldierly companion. Cannon has a rich but not fruity voice, a lithe presence that takes the stage like a theater cat, a sure actor's imagination and the skills to back it. His smilingly self-knowledgeable blowhard is a real, yet not literal, creation.

As Lavatch, a jester, Charles Durning promises well, somewhat in the vein of Hiram Sherman's Shakespearean clowns. But he does not fulfill the line spoken of him (one of the keenest in the play): "A shrewd knave, and an unhappy." In small roles Paul Hecht, light and dry, and Robert Ronan, airily composed, made me want to see more of them.

Ming Cho Lee has provided a graceful two-story façade as background. For reasons unknown, Theoni V. Aldredge has dressed the play (well) in costumes of the *Traviata* era. Lafew, a top-hatted lord played by Staats Cotsworth, looked so much like the elder Germont that at any moment I expected "Di provenza il mar" from Verdi's opera.

The play itself is ungainly in story and structure, though some of the lines are Shakespeare at his best. ("The air of Paradise did fan the house / And angels offic'd all.") But there is not enough language like that, the characters and atmosphere are not sufficiently taking, to compensate—as in *The Winter's Tale*—for the stilted story.

Still, I am glad I had the chance to see this play. It is easy to conceive of direction more sensitive to its romance and comedy than Joseph Papp's, and more exciting in conceptual design. But the movement on his open stage is at the mercy of the microphone locations, and at least his work represents persevering devotion. Although we are not often deeply involved with what is happening on stage in this production of *All's Well That Ends Well*, much of the time passes pleasantly under the stars—and the helicopters.

Hello and Goodbye, by Athol Fugard. *New Republic,* Oct. 11, 1969.

The New York theater and those around it have promised us a lean season, and so far everyone has kept his word. Of the four new plays I have seen Off-Broadway—this year Broadway itself doesn't begin until the end of

September—the best has not been of much consequence. But there is some cheer to report. Three of the four productions were adequately directed, acted, designed, and there were elements in each that were better than that.

The increased costs of Off-Broadway production are apparent. All these plays had one setting and small casts: the giant had six actors, one had three actors, and one had two. The last was *Hello and Goodbye*, by Athol Fugard, a South African. It concerns a brother and sister, poor whites in Port Elizabeth, who meet after a fifteen-year separation. Martin Sheen, of *The Subject Was Roses* and of Joseph Papp's jungle-gym *Hamlet*, is the brother, a semi-loony young man who is sane enough to have some view of himself as a son dominated by a crippled, tyrannical father. Sheen has a bright attack, vocally and physically, that almost carries the role over its windy chasms of rhetoric. His effect is a bit larky for the pathos that presumably Fugard wanted, but he is interesting and live.

Colleen Dewhurst plays his (older) sister, who comes home after long absence to claim her share of the father's estate, not aware that he is already dead but feeling that the end is near. Dewhurst is one of my grievances against our theater, and against fate generally. She was born to be a great actress, and she has not achieved it—not yet, anyway. I'm not going to speculate about the reasons: some of them are doubtless out of a critic's province; but insofar as our theater is responsible (although she has had a few great roles), it has sinned. When she steps on stage, she still opens the old wound in me because she is so clearly one actress in a thousand. She is fine in this play (and she has not always been fine), but good as she is, she hints at something beyond, in the highest range. A world comes in with this character, there is no busyness of manufacture, it just comes in with her: vision that is clear enough to have seen the bottom, sardonic resignation, majestic animal power, the ability to generate sheer quiet. And again the hint that, if the play had been better or if the cosmos had been organized a few atoms differently, we might have seen a great performance.

William Ritman's set breaks open a poor-white shack in a way that makes the struggle for possession seem all the more degrading. Barney Simon has directed with intelligence and a sense of dynamics, but he has made the conceptual boner of letting the action spill into the aisles of this theater-in-the-round. Realist plays should stay at home, in an area of non-reality.

Fugard's previous play, *The Blood Knot*, was also a two-character work, about two South African brothers, one of whom is dark-skinned, and was a frequently effective small parable about race and about the stark condemnation of all men to live linked inseparably. It is not much less grandiosely written or better conceived than *Hello and Goodbye*, but the racial element in it makes it more arresting and resonant. Both of Fugard's plays are heavily influenced by O'Neill, and for us this is more a burden than a benefit. Just as many of Arnold Wesker's plays seem postdated Odets in America, so Fugard's new play seems something that the Provincetown Playhouse should have been doing in 1920 as a breakthrough in moral candor and the symbolic power of realistic detail. The returning daughter finds the father dead and the inheritance nonexistent, so she leaves again to face the future alone; the stay-at-home son stays at home still, deliberately forging his shackles to the past. The neo-Greek doom of families, with Pa's crutches and Ma's perfume as the equivalents of pursuing demons, with poverty as proof that we are close to the bone in human truth—no, the mode is virtually exhausted for us. Only a dramatist of huge, revitalizing intensity, which

Fugard for all his sincerity is not, could turn this play from a series of stagy "meanings" to real meaning.

The Three Sisters, by Anton Chekhov. *New Republic*, March 21, 1970.

I arrived in Los Angeles a few weeks ago feeling lucky. An engagement had taken me there just before the conclusion of the six-week visit by the British National Theatre, their only appearance in the United States, and I was in time to see *The Three Sisters*, one of the two plays they were presenting. (The other was Farquhar's *The Beaux' Stratagem*.) I left Los Angeles feeling depressed.

First, my first experience of the Ahmanson Theater in the L.A. Civic Center. I have not been in a new theater less congenial to actors and their audience since the encounter between Peter Brook's production of *King Lear* and the New York State Theater at Lincoln Center. At Lincoln Center, a lesson has been learned; plays are no longer presented in the State Theater, only ballet, opera, and musicals. The Ahmanson keeps on doing plays.

It is a huge, high auditorium with two high, deep balconies. The theater is wide, and the proscenium opening is relatively narrow, so that the stage looks like a pinhead on a broad body. This is unpleasing enough to the eye, just as the size of the place is alienating in spirit from the actors; but the worst trouble is for the ear. Words float out from that stage into a void above the orchestra, and dissolve. Sometimes they can be understood well enough, at a distance; sometimes their outlines can be guessed at before they melt; sometimes there is only our objective knowledge that the people up there are speaking and that sounds are coming from them. The whole evening is spent in an atmosphere of aural strain. (Just dandy for Chekhov, of all authors.) Lest this be thought my personal crankiness, I report that the chief topic of discussion during the intermission, among people who had been sitting around me in the orchestra, was the inaudibility of the actors.

I'm told that their voices were amplified. Insufficiently, I can assure the management. And imagine building a theater—*building* one—in which actors have to be miked. But even if they could all have been heard easily, the performance would still have seemed to be taking place up a narrow cove on the other side of an inland sea. Another triumph of civic-center theater architecture of the American 1960s.

This difficult environment probably put the visitors at some disadvantage, but they brought other disadvantages with them. The settings are by the Czech designer Josef Svoboda, whose work I first saw at this company's London theater in 1967—a production of Ostrovsky's *The Storm*. When the curtain went up there I knew I was in the presence of a "yearbook" designer—a man whose work looks impressive when reproduced in albums that summarize a theater year or era and whose real aim seems to be publication in such volumes, not service of the theater. A metallic intrusiveness was the visual tone, and the sets also had, not raked stages, but small hillsides on which the cast had to work. A member of the *Storm* company told me that a chief worry with Svoboda's sets was which buttock to tense when you stopped to say a line, so that you wouldn't tumble down the slope toward the audience.

Here, in *The Three Sisters*, Svoboda's stage is flat, but so is the feeling. The walls in the Prozorov home are made of long, thin, gray-brown rods, like frozen portières arranged in curves. He also uses these rods for the outdoor scene in Act IV. The same basic idea is in his design for a Prokofiev work in Prague, 1961, reproduced in *Stage Design Throughout the World Since 1950* (Theatre Arts Books). One effect of those rods is that they bother depth perception after a time—the actors occasionally seem to be appearing behind them, as behind vertical lines on a TV screen. But the chief defect is that they express nothing except the designer's wish to attract notice, and so they harm the production. I am not asking for Moscow Art Theatre literalness, necessarily, although literal settings usually do nothing to harm a production; if they give the actor little help, they at least give little hindrance. Svoboda's abstractions abstract nothing that is in the play and are highly unhelpful.

Especially to the director, Laurence Olivier. I saw Olivier's production of *Uncle Vanya* at the National in London in 1964—sets by Sean Kenny that at least were explicable—and excepting the performance of that basically torpid actor Michael Redgrave as Vanya, it was all sensitively done, with Olivier himself even better as Astrov than he had been with the Old Vic just after the Second World War. But this production of *The Three Sisters* is clumsy, and the clumsiness is partly attributable to Svoboda, who provides Olivier with a relatively bare and drafty stage for the Prozorov drawing room. The room looks as if the Prozorovs were just moving into, or out of, an avant-garde warehouse. The sheer maneuvering to get people physically disposed has led to some traffic jams and poor positionings, and seems to have sapped Olivier's imagination.

At any rate, the production is barren of idea and texture. I got no idea from it as to what, fundamentally, Olivier thinks the play is about or why he wanted to do it. All that happens in the vein of thematic design—and it makes me cringe to remember it—occurs at the very end. At the close of the last act we hear the band playing in the distance as the soldiers leave, Olga speaks her lines about wishing that she knew why people have to live and suffer, and, then, as the curtain descends, the distant band music suddenly changes to loud strains of the *Internationale*! Either Olivier is serious and thinks that Communism is the happy future toward which Chekhov's agony was moving, or he is being ironic. In either case, this final touch is a blatant imposition on Chekhovian delicacy—a last desperate clutch at meaning in a meaningless production.

Francis Fergusson says:

> The poetry of modern realistic drama is to be found in those inarticulate moments when the human creature is shown responding directly to his immediate situation. . . . It is because of the exactitude with which Chekhov perceives and imitates these tiny responses that he can make them echo each other, and convey, when taken together, a single action with the scope, the general significance or suggestiveness, of poetry. Chekhov, like other great dramatists, has what might be called an ear for action, comparable to the trained musician's ear for musical sound.

In this finest sense, Olivier's ear is deaf in this production.

Specifically: Maggie Smith's Masha. Smith is one of the best of English-speaking actresses, beautiful, strong, slender, and intelligent, with an admirable technique. (Except for the use of her arms. They seem to end at her elbows; the forearms dangle lifelessly. See, for example, her "cameo" in the film *Oh! What a Lovely War*.) She could be a splendid Masha, but, under Olivier, she plays it for one dominant note: anger. Certainly Masha is the angriest of the lot because the most frustrated and securely trapped, but if she is nothing *but* angry, we get something of a shrew—and a comic shrew at that. This is a Masha who is merely frustrated, in a single-strand sexual way, and whose attraction to Vershinin is reduced to a small-town, small-time escapade.

Robert Stephens is Vershinin. Another outstanding talent; but he comes on here rather like the bumptious president of the Junior Chamber of Commerce, peppy, booming his accented words like a short-wave radio occasionally tuning in. He looks immature, and he, too, overemphasizes one trait. Vershinin has sillinesses, but they must be set in a conscious context of rueful middle age or else he becomes slightly ridiculous, not humanly pathetic. This Vershinin is neither maturely melancholy nor sufficiently self-aware.

The result of these two off-balance characterizations is that their final parting—one of the most poignant moments in the modern repertoire—gets laughs from the audience, deservedly. Instead of seeing the last hope for inner life being torn from two unhappy people, we see a fussy, inept man trying to get away from a frustrated woman who is becoming just a bit of a nuisance. Olivier even lets Vershinin tug at Masha's arms around his neck—when surely the whole point of his appeal to Olga is to take her sister from him because he *cannot* tear her loose.

The Olga of Jeanne Watts is flavorless, the Irina of Louise Purnell is remote—and is the least intelligible performance in that acoustical swamp. The best performance was the Tusenbach of Ronald Pickup, touching in a tall, concave, gently firm way, although even Pickup lost the emotional center of his farewell speech. The worst performance is the Chebutykin of Paul Curran, an old-fashioned "voice" actor with nothing at all under his big noise. This company uses a translation by Moura Budberg, which sounds all right. But the best that I know is by Randall Jarrell, published by Macmillan with Jarrell's excellent and extensive notes.

Olivier in his long career has been a wonderful actor (*Oedipus*) and a disappointing actor (*Othello*), a good director (*Henry V*) and a passable director (*Richard III*). *The Three Sisters* is on the debit side of the ledger. Each of us who loves Chekhov is proprietary about him as we are about few dramatists, and each of us is quite certain that he understands the Chekhovian style. But whatever one's conviction about that style, the effect of it must be to arrive at the "single action" that Fergusson describes, using the term "action" in the Aristotelian sense. Let us say, imperfectly but concisely, that "action" is the inner motion of the play that is made manifest by the plot. No such matter seems to have troubled Olivier here—at least, not until he tied on that closing strand of the *Internationale*.

As I say, very depressing. I hope this is not the level of National Theatre productions these days. Maybe a good deal of it—I also hope—was the fault of that bloated building.

Anyway, I flew home on the new 747. *That* was exciting.

Lemon Sky, by Lanford Wilson. *New Republic*, June 13, 1970.

Christopher Walken is a talented young actor at the other end of the spectrum from, say, Zoe Caldwell. He doesn't have her technical virtuosity, and he has ambitions only towards realistic acting, even in the Shakespeare of his that I've seen. But, besides stage ease and easy charm, he has an unusual conviction of quintessence. In *Lemon Sky* he plays a late teenager (as well as the boy's older self), and we know at once that the *core* of that boy has come on stage in Walken.

Walken has an extrinsic nuisance in his life, a physical resemblance to Jon Voight, of the film *Midnight Cowboy*, another gifted actor. One distinction between them, however, is that Walken has a greater feminine quality (not to be confused with effeminacy), which I find attractive in men. And he has the strength for encompassment. There are moments in this play when everything whirls about him and, after a moment's circumspection, he seems to gather up everything that's whirling and advance with it. I hope his voice keeps developing and that every time his vowels flatten out, he means them to. With his growth, his career can grow.

Charles Durning, an actor who has only seemed passable to me previously, is here perfectly cast as Walken's father—a beer-drinking, vulgar super-male—and finds a range of humanity in the part. Bonnie Bartlett, as Walken's stepmother, supplies plain-faced, California-bungalow, suffering submission and also some credible touches of the universality that sometimes glints in the tract house. Warren Enters has directed adequately, with no suspicion of originality.

Lemon Sky, by the young playwright Lanford Wilson, is about a youth from the Midwest who leaves his divorced mother to live with his father and second wife in California, and why it doesn't work out. The dialogue is fluent vernacular, brightened by occasional inversions of cliché. ("I won't tell you my dreams if you won't tell me yours.") There are occasional perceptions—not of character but of the natural world—that verge on the poetic. But the play disappoints. It begins with an air of great portent and uses a lot of arty structural apparatus, but accomplishes little. All that happens finally is that the father accuses the son—falsely, it seems—of homosexuality, and the boy leaves. A very great deal of back-and-forth time-flow, choric comment, and comment on the play itself is expended on slight dramatic material and shallow characters. And Wilson uses, yet again, the device of telling us that a character we see is going to die soon, thus trying to win for her a degree of pathos she hasn't earned.

Wilson's play *The Gingham Dog*, presented on Broadway last year, failed through its desperate symmetries and hollow encyclopedism, but it had a trenchant portrait of a young black wife in a black-white marriage. A lot of Wilson's work seems to be based on his (white) boyhood and youth and tends to be Thornton Wilder *réchauffé*, if somewhat leaner. But it is that black girl whom I remember and who makes me care about Wilson's future.

Old Times, by Harold Pinter. *New Republic*, January 18, 1971.

Criticism of Harold Pinter has its funny side. On the one hand, there's Pinter, disclaiming scheme or theme, replying with (I think) proper tartness to those who ask him to explain his plays. On the other hand, there are the critics, explaining them, panting to supply what Pinter doesn't want. His dislike of criticism is not the usual one, a reaction to assault; quite the reverse. He is adulated, and he still doesn't want all that decoding and classifying. Yet they persist. A good example is the recently published "casebook" on *The Homecoming*, in which Pinter flatly states he has nothing to say about the play: "It exists, and that's that." Yet the book contains essays, each of which tries to fit the play into a critic's view of it as ethology or Freud or parodic Restoration comedy or something else.

The critics are quite right, of course: anyone who is moved by an artwork has an aesthetic right to try to understand why. And Pinter is also quite right; he has no obligation to explain or to accept explanations. And, possibly, *I'm* quite right, too!—to chuckle at all the above as I proceed to "interpret" his new play.

It's relatively easy to "decipher" a plot and theme in *Old Times*, which I mean to do and then move on from it. It has only three characters. An English couple in their forties are visited in their country home by a former girlfriend of the wife's whom she hasn't seen in twenty years. As single girls, they shared an apartment in London. It's easy to demonstrate that the two used to have a lesbian relationship in atmosphere if not in fact; that the husband knew them at the time, although he and they now pretend he didn't; that there's a threat that the lesbian relation will be resumed; and that the husband breaks down and cries for pity at the end. I put all this more clearly than the play does. Pinter uses overlaid "exposures" as in photography. Details do not quite jibe. Time is constantly past *and* present, as in cubist painting that shows us simultaneous views which would be impossible simultaneously in life. But my précis is supportable.

Construed from this story, the theme can be seen as the power of the female—to create a realm in which the male is trapped, a kind of golden moist web woven by women laterally through time, within which men can strut for a bit but are finally subordinated. In short, the world as the realm of Astarte-Lilith-Erda, with men allowed to delude themselves about mastery. It's not a new Pinter theme. At the end of *The Homecoming*, the one woman is seated with two of the play's toughest men kneeling next to her, begging for affection. At the end of *Old Times*, the one man has wept, then kneeled with his head on his wife's lap, while the other woman waits prone on a bed.

I don't contend that this theme was carefully selected by Pinter. He himself has said that the play began for him with a flash of "two people talking about someone else," and his statement fits what we know of his methods: that he's largely an intuitive, "automatic" writer, whose real work of design begins only as the words begin on paper. What lies behind this process is the aesthetic history of the twentieth century.

Since art began, every artist has known that he had in him something unsayable which he was trying to express within the conventions of his art and that he was, to some degree, failing to express it fully because of those conventions, which still were his means of expressing what he *did* manage to express. The better the artist was, the more keenly he felt the failure. Shakespeare, I'm sure, felt that he had failed.

In this century, artists of all kinds have begun to try various means to circumvent that failure, to circumvent the conventions of their art and to say the unsayable without the mediation of traditional forms. This is essentially the impulse behind, say, John Cage's music, Artaud's theater, and various kinds of abstract and action painting. Pinter's playwriting itself can be seen as classic surrealism, dealing with well-defined objects arranged in such a way that the point is not in their detail—the fine details are in a way a deliberate deception—but in the trajectory outlined by the way they are deployed, in the space they enclose, in the surprise and shock and laughter that the succession of these details arouses in us.

In this view the *audience* writes the play (as the audience writes Cage's music) within boundaries described by the author and in response to data and stimuli that he supplies. The pauses and silences specified in Pinter's scripts are not only musical similes, they are opportunities to "catch up"; the play rests for a moment while you draw abreast of it in simultaneous creation. Of course this process of audience collaboration is not exclusive to surrealists. It's part of all aesthetic experience, but it's a much greater part when the work's primary purpose is not mimesis or representation but to open a direct conduit between the deepest region of the author's psyche and ours.

How, then, do value judgments pertain? Once an author establishes that he is able to make these connections with us, are all his works equally good? How do I know that I like *The Caretaker* more than *The Birthday Party*, *The Homecoming* more than either, *Old Times* somewhat less than *The Homecoming*? Principally by the gravity of the material encompassed in our psyches, by the breadth of the encompassment. *Old Times* touches mysteries, but the compass seems narrower than in *The Homecoming*. The previous play seemed to entail more about more men and women, a larger aspect of the male-female cosmos, than the new work. *Old Times*, enticing as it is, *enjoyable* as it is, is less resonant.

Pinter is often compared with Beckett, his presumptive master, so a further hierarchical statement may be useful. Pinter deals with aspects of mortality. Beckett, quintessentially, deals with mortality in the purview of immortality. E. M. Cioran has pointed out that Beckett is not a nihilist but a mystic, to whom physical existence is an interruption of a greater and perfect existence. Nothing like this view is to be found—yet—in Pinter, whose "unsayable" still resides in London.

But, like Beckett, he is highly comic. Part of his comedy lies in non sequitur (a surrealist hallmark), which is often launched with furious, hilarious eloquence. I laughed quite a lot at the New York production of *Old Times*, more than I did at the London production I saw last summer, principally because Robert Shaw is a much richer actor than the man who played the part in London. (Mary Ure, the wife, and Rosemary Harris, the friend, are also excellent in the New York production, under Peter Hall's chamber-music direction.) The husband has most of the funny stuff because he is the one who is thrashing about desperately: he is the butt. Shaw appreciates this in theatrical and human terms.

All this talk of instinctive writing, of surrealism, doesn't deny the theme I cited earlier. It means only that the theme became clear to Pinter, out of his own depths, *as* he wrote rather than before he wrote. Nor does it imply that Pinter merely slaps things down on paper, any more than Magritte or Ernst or Tanguy merely slapped paint on canvas. After the impulse, the exquisite modeling.

Take the very first sight, the very first line, of *Old Times*. When the curtain rises, the husband and wife are seated in light, the other woman is standing in shadow at back, looking away. She is waiting to "enter." The visible and predictable sequence is immediately taking; before the play is a minute old, we know that relativity of time is part of the drama.

The first line is just one word. The wife says: "Dark." Then, as per the printed script, comes the stage direction: *Pause.* (!) One word, "Dark," then a pause. The other woman is *in* the dark. Is that what's meant? What kind of dark? A half dozen questions flash through our minds. The pause is to allow them—and to allow the picture—to sink in. Then the husband says, "Fat or thin?," the wife replies, "Fuller than me. I think," and we realize that they're talking about the other woman and that "dark" means dark-haired. The process is much like an open chord in music being clarified by the addition of tones.

How well it all *works.* No wonder actors love Pinter.

Writing about *The Caretaker* almost eight years ago, I admired Pinter but hoped he would be a different writer at forty and fifty and seventy. He's now forty-one and has moved from the "menace" plays to *The Homecoming*, the lyrical short plays *Landscape* and *Silence*, and this new sex-and-time teaser. His power to grow is one of the most cheering aspects of contemporary writing. He is a chief reason why the theater of the word—the *new* theater of the word that understands the unsaid—is alive.

Slag, by David Hare. *New Republic*, March 13, 1971.

David Hare, an English playwright, is twenty-three years old. Hare's play *Slag,* now on one of the four stages of the Public Theater in New York, shows him to be a prodigy. *Slag* is unfocused and sometimes boring, but it is attractively articulate and theatrically at home.

It has only three characters, three young women who are the entire staff of a run-down girls' school, running further down. The best aspect of the play is that Hare has taken a conventional comedy about a public-school staff and converted it *internally* into a macabre fantasy without much altering of externals, rather in the manner of Ivy Compton-Burnett. Some of the materials are: a kind of mod *Princess Ida*, a female sanctum with males excluded and the results thereof; satire on cultural glibness; and, the seeming *sine qua non* of British playwrights these days, a microcosm of the fate of the Empire. None of these efforts wholly succeeds, largely because Hare never clarifies his viewpoint—he just has fun; but if *Slag* doesn't always hold interest, it always commands respect. One thing the play is bursting with is promise.

Roger Hendricks Simon has staged it with vigor, humor, and a good ear. As the one virgin in the trio of characters, Roberta Maxwell gives a fine, cranky comic performance.

Follies, by Stephen Sondheim. *New Republic*, May 8, 1971.

What's all this prattle about the lack of community, of shared ethos, in the American theater? In art and experimental theaters, perhaps. In a Broadway musical like *Follies* the sense of community is as solid as it ever could have been in ancient Athens. The night I was there, the audience was *in* the show. (Almost literally. During the tumultuous applause after one number, several cheering men rose to their feet and seemed to yearn to go up there.)

What does the community consist of? In this case, pleasant nostalgia. Regret, and defiance born of regret; the lost chance and the well-we-didn't-do-so-badly-after-all feeling. Early in the show a character says, "I don't trust any music under thirty." The audience, mostly over thirty, chuckled. Later one character asks another whether he would like to be young again, and the reply is, "No, thank you, once was enough." More chuckling. I can't see why *Follies* won't run forever. ... Which is not to recommend it.

The setting is an old theater about to be torn down, a place that housed a string of hit revues between the wars. The old producer—based, of course, on Ziegfeld—gives a farewell party on stage to which he invites the girls who used to be in his shows, some of them now antique. While they meet and reminisce, the ghosts of their former selves glide among them, invisible to them, commenting silently to us.

Now that's a workable premise for a show. But *Follies* fails for me in three ways. (1) A story had to be invented, to utilize the premise. The plot and dialogue by James Goldman, the tuppenny poet of *The Lion in Winter*, are inane. (2) None of the performers is really good, and only a few of them, like Mary McCarty and Gene Nelson, are acceptable. Alexis Smith, much acclaimed, is an attractive, well-coached amateur—a less flamboyant Lauren Bacall. (3) The one element that could redeem all the above is missing: a good score. Stephen Sondheim's lyrics are occasionally clever, but his melodic invention, as he showed in *Company*, is lame. He knows the patterns of the pop music of the past and he provides numbers that whack along in the *shapes* of former hits, pounding with rhythms and repetitions until the audience is beaten into a frenzy. But the spontaneous pleasure that one gets from hearing a good new tune is completely missing.

As in *Company*, the best achievement is the scene design by Boris Aronson. He is a first-class scenic dramatist, working this time with a blend of romanticism and constructivism and greatly aided by Tharon Musser's lighting. The costumes by Florence Klotz are good, particularly the variations she worked on black and white for the ghost performers.

The climax is a fantasy called "Loveland," a sort of 1920 extravaganza in which the "present" characters appear. This mockery of old musical numbers, which has recurred on Broadway since the Second World War (as, for instance, in *Mame*), is facile and usually irritating: because it assumes that the "present" show is better than the material being mocked, when, as here, the intrinsic quality is the same in both time strata.

The big-time theater seems to be running out of the ability to nourish itself on society, so it's feeding on itself, chewing its left leg or right arm. To change metaphors, *No, No, Nanette* (which I haven't seen) is evidently a bit of baby-blanket to which the audience can cling. *Follies* is even more revealing because it *invents* its nostalgia. Imagine an album of old-time hits that never existed before 1971! Consider what the need for them means.

Well, it's a felt need, all right; and *Follies* answers it. It's aimed squarely at the audience that can afford to come to it. A perfect union, that show and its audience, replenishing one another with mutual, wry, self-satisfied admission of regrets. The Old Guard never dies, it just keeps on surrendering.

The Master Builder, by Henrik Ibsen. *New Republic*, November 6, 1971.

Michael Meyer, author of the new huge Ibsen biography and translator of several of the plays, has done a translation of *The Master Builder*, now produced by the Roundabout Theater. It deserves better. The Roundabout is an Off-Broadway group, starting its sixth year, dedicated (mostly) to revivals of classics. This was my first visit, and all I can testify to is their earnestness.

Gene Feist's direction consisted mostly of tennis-court moves. ("You take this side, he'll be over there; now exchange with him.") These simple ideas of movement paralleled his simplistic thematic concept. Paul Sparer, who has given adequate performances elsewhere, is shrunken by the demands of Solness to various postures, vocal and physical. Jill O'Hara, the Hilde, has a brassy voice with about a four-note range and none of the fresh and very dangerous spirit required.

Still, the production was not bad enough to prevent "simultaneous translation." This is an internal device for those who know and like a play, which permits them to see what every moment *ought* to be, to use the immediate performance as a mental scaffolding, if it's at least honest and serious. (Which this is.) So, translating away furiously in my head, I had a fair time at the Roundabout production of this profound autobiographical play, which searches out autobiographies in each of us.

Ibsen was himself the architect-hero, and Emilie Bardach, the girl he met in 1889, was the Hilde whom he captured on paper in 1892—the girl who rejuvenates and ages, vitalizes and figuratively kills, this mature man. It's one of the most "private" of Ibsen's plays and one of the most frightening. And it's so infrequently played that, though I wish the Roundabout had done more of the work for me, I'm grateful for a performance just good enough to let me dream of my own production while this one went on.

Narrow Road to the Deep North, by Edward Bond. *New Republic*, February 5, 1972.

Edward Bond is a greatly gifted Englishman, thirty-six years old, whose other plays that I know, *Saved* and *The Pope's Wedding*, are quintessentially religious works, concerned with the redemption of the lowest and therefore Christian. *Narrow Road to the Deep North* (at the Vivian Beaumont Theater) is different: a political parable as trite as the worst of Brecht but without the theatrical dynamics that Brecht, even at his worst, rarely loses. Bond's play has, structurally, a certain literary neatness, but it's a pedestrian narrative, not a drama at all. (And he *wants* it to be a drama.) In religion Bond doesn't preach; in politics he does.

The setting is Japan in the "17th or 18th or 19th centuries." This is hell for a director who wants to avoid preciosity, yet can't really root his work in an authentic foreign style. (Something that bedevils productions of Brecht's Chinese plays.) The story is a pat contrast between "pagan" savagery and a military-missionary Western civilization that turns out to be at least equally savage. Dan Sullivan, the director, didn't solve the insoluble matter of style or redeem the play's hollowness or use that unfortunate stage with much grace; but he did devise some telling effects, and he got passable performances from Robert

Symonds, Andy Robinson, and Cleavdon Little, who needs only a developed voice to be a valuable actor. One doesn't look for justice in the arts, but when I saw the drubbing that Sullivan got in reviews and when I thought of the Beaumont productions that have been praised or tolerated by the same reviewers . . .

The Beggar's Opera, by John Gay. *New Republic*, April 29, 1972.

The Chelsea Theater Center, founded in 1965, is one of the most discerningly adventurous groups in the New York area. Instances: last season they did a bill of one-act plays by Peter Handke; this season they did the American premiere of Genet's gargantuan *The Screens*. Their productions are often, literally, pathetic: that is, one feels pathos for the limitations imposed on them by insufficient money and facilities. Their casting is very obviously low-budget, most of the time. They play upstairs in the Brooklyn Academy of Music in a rotten long rectangular room with the playing space along one of the long sides. But they have brains and ambition.

Now they are doing a revival of *The Beggar's Opera*, by John Gay, first performed in 1728 and often revived, best-known today as the source of the Brecht-Weill *Threepenny Opera*. Gay's work is one of the earliest to be centered in the unpretty, unfashionable world, to calibrate its actions by the ethics of the outlaw and the outcast. Its world is the society of London pickpockets, whores, fences, and highwaymen. Gay used it for mirror-image political satire, no longer important, but the play lives because if you put another society out front, the mirror reflects it just as truly. Its mirth is that of people who have seen through hypocrisy, who have nothing to lose but their lives, which might just as well be lost in fun as in exploitation by others. Their difference from, say, the beasts in *The Godfather* is that these people are laughing about their lives while they can. The *Godfather* people themselves are sober hypocrites, merchandising a bloody morality.

Gay took a lot of familiar tunes, many of them from the Italian operas that were then the London rage, and wrote his own lyrics to them; so his audience had an additional sense of burlesque that we miss. But we get the lovely tunes just the same, and all of the scintillating verses. It's the music that lifts this CTC production far above any of theirs that I've seen. The score has been "newly realized" by Ryan Edwards, which I guess means newly orchestrated—very well, too; and the six players are well directed by Roland Gagnon, himself at the keyboard. All the voices are at least adequate, some better than that.

Musical plays, when the music is good and well-done, make weakish groups look better: because the music itself lends an underpinning of spirit, and the "inflections" and pacing are relatively foreordained. But when these actors are acting, they are on their own, which is often not enough. Gordon Connell and Jeanne Arnold, as Mr. and Mrs. Peachum, Reid Shelton as Lockit, have good rusty crusty flavor; but Kathleen Widdoes is possibly the first neurotic Polly Peachum, Marilyn Sokol is a Lucy Lockit who has just stepped off the BMT [Brooklyn-Manhattan Transit], and Stephen D. Newman, a vocally acceptable Macheath, is not a credible lady-killer.

Gene Lesser directed, avid for gusto and bawdiness, so there is much grabbing of crotches and bosoms, even a little urinating. John Gay is not Marivaux, and elegance is not what's wanted; but, typographically speaking,

Lesser's work consists entirely of italics and exclamation marks. His work seems especially crude alongside the nicely turned music of Messrs. Edwards and Gagnon.

Medea, by Euripides. *New Republic*, June 24, 1972.

For sheer visceral excitement, the high point of the year was a stretch of ten minutes or so in the middle of a forty-minute production of *Medea* at La Mama Theater Club. Everything I had heard about this production prejudiced me against it. It was in Euripides' Greek, with some choruses in Seneca's Latin; only a small audience was allowed, and they went through a ritual of admission. It sounded like stale Off-Off Broadwayfaring.

The first moments confirmed prejudice. We were ushered into the ground-floor theater of La Mama, where I thought we were to see the play. Then, after about fifty people had arrived, we were conducted downstairs, past actors in costume holding candles and reciting lines in Greek or Latin, along a cinder-block corridor to the basement. Here we were seated on facing benches against the long sides of the rectangular room, with members of the chorus interspersed among us. At each of the narrow ends of the rectangle were some steps and a simple doorway. The ceiling was covered with billowing burlap. I was ready to leave.

Very soon I was rooted. The director, Andrei Serban, was moving to a simple, strong idea: that the core of *Medea* is primal stuff, that comprehension of each utterance—when the play is known and the motions are elemental—is no more necessary here than in great opera. In both arts, cognitive language may even be an impediment to full release. All that we need, in gigantic drama, is the impassioned sound of words whose general meaning we know. Details of verbiage only weigh us down.

One need not take this approach as a fiat for all classic productions in order to see how it worked in this instance. During the minutes when Jason and Medea faced each other at opposite ends of that small room, storming full-throatedly at each other in a completely foreign language, I felt the blood of this ancient drama quicken as I have rarely felt it in productions of large plays.

Serban prepared for these moments with intelligent patterns of movement; with Elizabeth Swados's music-and-sounds, to create a barbaric aural atmosphere; with careful dynamics in the chorus; and, chiefly, by his success with his two principals, Priscilla Smith and Jamil Zakkai. Smith looks more like Smith College than Colchis, but she and Zakkai transcended themselves. Their bodies were completely invested in what they were doing, their voices were two full, round columns battering at one another.

All the cast, even the children, were caught in Serban's intensity, and created a seamless fabric of conviction. I keep thinking even now of the children's dangling legs as, after being slaughtered, they were handed down through a gap in that burlap ceiling to their horror-struck father below.

Serban is a Romanian, a student and associate of Peter Brook, and is now director-in-residence at La Mama. Productions there don't "run": they appear, disappear, and often reappear. *Medea* has since gone touring in Europe and may be back. Serban will presumably be back and must be watched. The stuntishness in him is much less than his main thrust: quintessential guts and revelation.

And They Put Handcuffs on Flowers, by Fernando Arrabal. *New Republic*, June 24, 1972.

Of all the well-known playwrights of the Absurd, Fernando Arrabal is to me the slightest—a hack of the avant-garde. His latest production in New York, *And They Put Handcuffs on the Flowers*, is a religious-symbolic work about the fate of political prisoners, presumably Franco's, who have long been immured and are generally forgotten. (The play is being produced at the Mercer Arts Center.) The script strains for fearless impact but ends in sensationalism (such touches, for instance, as the eating of excrement or the fellation of Jesus). After the arty apparatus and tedious candor, all that remains is blatant pathos. If that seems a callous comment, Arrabal invites it because he pretends to the much more complex and profound level of Genet's writings about prisoners.

But Arrabal himself has directed this production, and he directs better than he writes. His staging sometimes has the slamming effect that he fumbles in his ideas and dialogue. The scenes in the cell, on one side of the stage, have a fierce compacted physicality and are well performed by George Shannon, Peter Maloney, and Ron Faber. Some of the images, like a body dragged across the stage on a big open white sheet, are vivid. If this production had run forty minutes, instead of an hour and forty minutes, the play would have seemed better than it does: Arrabal's literary thinness would not have been so evident and his visual images could have been more highly selective.

A word about the Mercer Arts Center itself, the latest Off-Broadway complex, joining the (figurative) society of La Mama and the Public Theater. MAC, which is in a recently renovated building on Mercer Street, contains four theaters, a cabaret theater, a multi-media workshop, studios, a café-restaurant, a bar, and a boutique! Besides the Arrabal, MAC at present houses a dramatization of Ken Kesey's *One Flew Over the Cuckoo's Nest* and the improvisational revue *The Proposition*, among others.

Of these Off-Broadway centers, only La Mama has so far developed anything like an aesthetic character, even in the most general sense. The Public apparently wants to be like a good department store, with something for everybody. In content, the Mercer is so far much the same; in looks, quite different. The décor of the Mercer is clearly youth-oriented, with a strong suggestion of the Drug Stores in Paris and Munich and elsewhere. Socially, at least, it's interesting. People who prattle knowingly that young people today are concerned only with films ought to see the Mercer on a weekend.

Enemies, by Maxim Gorky. *New Republic*, December 16, 1972.

Upstairs at Lincoln Center, in the Beaumont, they are presenting Gorky's *Enemies*. This was a depressing experience for me. I first saw this play (same translation) last year in London, presented by the Royal Shakespeare Company under David Jones. I knew it was about worker-boss conflict in 1905, and I went with apprehension, expecting hammer-and-nail propaganda, but doing my duty to Gorky. It was surprisingly good. The workers in the play are all noble, as expected, but the upper-class characters are treated with some insight, some interest in their complexity. (Gorky had Chekhov as model for the upper-class people but only his own life as source for the workers!) The play doesn't have the organic quality of *The Lower Depths*, and its offstage suicide as a finish—again from Chekhov (and Ibsen)—had become a dramaturgic platitude by the time Gorky used it; but *Enemies* is an interesting station on the travels of Russian drama from Chekhov and Turgenev toward the Soviet future. And the RSC production was one of the best I have seen of a Russian play. John Wood, especially, as Yakov, the brother of the factory owner on whose estate it all happens, was unforgettably brilliant.

The Beaumont production gave me the Gorky I had dreaded in London: sticks, poses, clichéd Russianism, ideological blatancy. The best performance is by Philip Bosco as the factory manager who is killed in Act I, and even he could have used some tempering in this difficult part. (He comes in furious and stays furious most of the time.) Frances Sternhagen, an actress of instant credibility who seems to live wherever she lights, is good as the lady of the house. But the rest! Joseph Wiseman, the Yakov, is simply ludicrous: a gigantic stoned spider, in love with his own creepy affectations, devoid of truth or humanity. Barbara Cook, as Bosco's wife-widow, paddles chubbily around the huge stage, almost swimming from point to point. Nancy Marchand is dried-up and brittle in a part that requires richness. Josef Sommer is cheaply monochrome as the prosecutor, a role that Alan Howard made a small-scale Robespierre. And Stefan Schnabel, a general, Will Lee, an orderly, and Tom Lacy, a captain, give performances that I hope they want to forget as much as I do.

Ellis Rabb directed, in a way that is partly reminiscent of the *Twelfth Night* he did here last year. Many directors at the Beaumont have felt the need, in that unfortunately designed theater, to build out the stage, to thrust it at the audience. Here, as in *Twelfth Night*, Rabb has reversed the crescent, so to speak: has eliminated the forestage and is playing well back on that immense drill-hall stage, presumably so that he can use the turntable. He does use it well, especially in the very last moment when the room moves to show us the suicided Yakov on the lawn. (Except that it's not affecting because we don't give a damn about this Yakov.) But such a deployment forces on Rabb an approach that turns his direction into a species of haulage, getting people in from far frontiers to the playing space, getting them out again, getting them across immense reaches in the midst of intimate, soul-baring conversations.

He has thus imposed a terrible discrepancy between the physical movement of the play and its tonalities: looking for big pictures, he has warped any patterns that might have substantiated the theme. Apparently he now has an acreage complex. This forces him to such further artificiality as the moment at the end of Act II when two workers, left alone to guard the estate, are conversing quietly together. *Together*. Rabb arbitrarily forces them apart, one to each side of the enormous stage, for the sake of a picture. They are pulled apart so strenuously that one can almost hear a fabric being ripped.

The translation, by Kitty Hunter-Blair and Jeremy Brooks, has been published by Viking Press, with a preface by Brooks. In it, speaking of the RSC production, he says that David Jones understood that Gorky "put up for trial" the society of his day, not individuals; so the first week of rehearsals was spent in watching and discussing Russian films of the period and the second week in reading and discussing relevant literature—memoirs, letters, etc. Then the stage work began. This foundation of common knowledge was in fact the prime *omission* from the Beaumont production. What we saw were a lot of jobbed-in actors jobbing along, some better, most worse.

That was what depressed me, the characteristic performance of this resident theater as against the British. I know that Lincoln Center has money troubles, that the city of New York has unique cultural troubles; I know (and have reported) that most London theater is terrible and that some RSC productions are far from first-class. But why can't there *ever* be a production at Lincoln Center that compares with the best of, say, the RSC? This production depressed me because it seemed to underscore all the European commonplaces about America: one big gauche, provincial performance, thin in cultural texture.

Outcry, by Tennessee Williams. *New Republic*, March 24, 1973.

When realist playwrights die, they become symbolists. Among contemporaries, Edward Albee is only one who proves this historical principle. Now Tennessee Williams, a much more romantic realist than Albee (and a much more gifted one), moves from his familiar terrain of seamy rhapsody to the gauzy blue blue sky. His last play, *Small Craft Warnings*, was a sterile reworking of his lyricism of the lonely; his new play, *Outcry*, changes style but has much smaller craft.

Two actors, a brother and sister, are stranded in a "state theater of a state unknown." Their company has abandoned them as insane. There is no one else backstage. Ostensibly an audience—ourselves—has gathered in front, though this is not definite. Brother and sister are forced to perform for us; they do something called *The Two-Character Play*, moving in and out of it so that there is no clear border between the play-within-a-play and their private realities. Doubt gathers about their sanity. They may not even be in a theater; the whole setting, Jo Mielziner's airy sketch of a theater, may be part of their fantasy. They may really be the children of the two parents described in the "play," the man of whom has just shot his wife and killed himself.

On paper this suggests, inevitably, Pirandello, and sounds intriguing. In proof *Outcry* is an excruciating two-hour bore because Williams has only vague ideas about why he is bothering to write it. There is no affective design, no tension, no *point*, not even any stimulating ambiguity. We are given only a series of data, arbitrarily streaked—like a larded roast—with stripes of passion and torment. None of this anguish or heat ever has the slightest power on us because no ground is laid with us for sympathy or expectation. Williams simply provides a sequence of arbitrary moments, enclosed in a fancy: symbolism that asks for effect just because it *is* symbolism, rather reminiscent of little-theater pieces of the 1920s.

The most grievous disappointment is in the writing and in the roles as theatrical entities. Up to now, as we watched Williams' sad descent, we have usually had the consolation that he still had a gift for good theater language; but the dialogue in this play is on the level of "You have the face of an angel." The roles, both of them, are just bundles of spurts and relaxations, unrelated to facts as we can see them or fantasies as we can follow them. I suppose that Williams has earned the right to have everything he writes produced—the idea of an unproduced Williams play still seems somehow discourteous—but he is trying this right severely.

The producer is trying it, too. One of the two roles, the brother, is well cast. Michael York is a good actor (he was the best one in the film of *Cabaret*) with a striking theater face and a useful voice, but I wish I hadn't seen him in this play. It's like hearing a pianist, after a moving recital, expend the same emotion on empty exercises. The other role—50 percent of the cast—is given to Cara Duff-MacCormick, who is incompetent in every possible regard. Peter Glenville, the drayhorse director, plodded true to form; but in this case he did have a fearful burden to carry.

The Orphan, by David Rabe. *New Republic*, May 26, 1973.

Several months ago I was questioning the professional nay-saying of some highbrow film critics (in the *New Republic* of Sept. 16, 1972). Now I'd like to look at a reverse phenomenon—professional yea-saying by theater critics, some of whom are also nay-saying film critics. It's curious that among those who criticize both film and theater, judgment is usually much more rigorous with film. Perhaps, consciously or not, they feel that the theater needs bedside sympathy and encouragement.

Whatever the reason, most theater critics, for all publications, can be seen as a band of Sunshine Boys (and Girls) who do a lot of Positive Thinking about American playwrights and have been doing it very noticeably in the last decade or so. The result is almost always a painful graph. A new playwright of small talent is hailed by them as a big talent, gets an inflated reputation, and then, with future work, gets deflated. The decline is never the playwright's "fault" or pretense; he never *was* as good as he was said to be by others. But he is put in the false position of having disappointed the very critics who overpraised him to begin with, of having "fallen off," they say, when it was they who put him up where he should never have been.

That process—very sad for the writer—is beginning to happen yet once more in the case of David Rabe. His first two plays, produced in 1971 and 1972, got much praise and many awards. Now it's 1973. His latest play, *The Orphan*, was recently produced at the Anspacher in the Public Theater, and the critical consensus was that this writer of exceptional gifts had slipped somewhat and had written a play that didn't "work" (the current most popular critical cant word). To me, the play was merely infested with the disease that had been evident in the two earlier ones.

The Basic Training of Pavlo Hummel was one more good-hearted sentimental undergraduate play about the horrors of war—this time Vietnam—showing a simple-minded Joe being savaged by vast cruel powers, using stale expressionist fantasy and even staler rhetoric to prove its humanitarianism and high-mindedness. Then came *Sticks and Bones*, which was at least a mixed bag. A blind Vietnam veteran returns to his home and is such a moral nuisance that his family induces him to commit suicide. The family stuff, done in sharp pop-art style (the parents were called Ozzie and Harriet), had good smiling bitterness; but the soldier's purple speeches and the device of his phantom Vietnamese girlfriend were straight out of Playwriting 435 (Permission of Instructor Required). The pop elements gave me some little hope for Rabe, which the new play drastically deferred. In *The Orphan* he opted completely for the purple prose, without let-up or remorse, the kind of rhetoric that brings a tear to the eye of a third-rate playwriting instructor. The disease hasn't just recently struck Rabe, it is now simply unopposed.

Rabe took the Oresteia myth and, to make sure we got its modern application, interwove elements of My Lai and the Manson murders. These modern instances were so undigested in the script that they only intervened between us and the central myth. But what made the play ludicrous (the only word) was the language. Eugene O'Neill had trouble enough updating the Greek story in *Mourning Becomes Electra*. Rabe, trying to confront and embrace its grandeur, was like a child at an organ: his feet couldn't even reach the pedals and his tiny fists could only beat out windy squalls.

Just one sample of the language. Clytemnestra Two—for some metaphysical reason too deep for me there were two Clytemnestras—said early in the play: "When there is a thing of silver in flight, I am dirt." When you hear a good actress like Rae Allen speak lines like that, all you can feel is compassion for the very hard profession of acting, not critical impulse. And for the gifted director Jeff Bleckner, the same compassion. What patterns of movement and of speech could legitimately be evoked from this script? All Bleckner could do was to invent stuff to do *to* it.

So I won't review the production and am not really reviewing the play either. For me, it simply justified and underscored the fear I had about Rabe from his earlier work. His one apparent avenue to effective writing led through anti-grandness; his critical reception in general led him to think—or anyway didn't discourage him from thinking—that he is equipped for the grand. Now those who myopically encouraged him can no longer blink at the bankruptcy; after the praise, now come the tsk-tsks. I don't mean that once having praised him they were obliged to go on praising him forever; I mean that *The Orphan* is not much different from or worse than the work they praised; and now they have to know it.

Diatribes against the state of theater criticism are usually romantic. When was there ever a generally high level of criticism—in any country? Even in those (other) countries that have produced bodies of great national drama? Why then should there have been, despite some life-saving exceptions, good theater critics in the United States, of all places? No, my point is not that the level has sunk but that its peculiar latter-day flatulence about playwriting—and not only in the *New York Times*—has produced a euphoria where none has an aesthetic right to exist. Time after time a new writer is overpraised—and in some cases, *any* praise is overpraise. Time after time he is built up for a letdown. (And time after time the discriminating public is irritated by the praise. The latest outbursts of anger I have heard were from people who, on the basis of enthusiastic reviews in newspapers and magazines, went to see *The Hot l Baltimore*.)

Here are some instances of overpraised authors, other than Rabe, in the last decade or so, with the plays that first got big attention: Barbara Garson (*MacBird!*); Arthur Kopit (*Oh Dad, Poor Dad, Mamma's Hung You in the Closet and I'm Feelin' So Sad*); Israel Horovitz (*The Indian Wants the Bronx*); Paul Zindel (*The Effect of Gamma Rays on Man-in-the-Moon Marigolds*); John Guare (*The House of Blue Leaves*); Jean-Claude van Itallie (*America Hurrah*); Ronald Ribman (*The Journey of the Fifth Horse*); Ron Cowen (*Summertree*); Terrence McNally (*And Things That Go Bump in the Night*); and Jason Miller (*That Championship Season*). The last has just been given the Pulitzer Prize, thus putting Miller in the august company of such recent laureates as Zindel, Charles Gordone, Howard Sackler, Frank D. Gilroy, Tad Mosel, and Ketti Frings. What a list!

Each of these people either has demonstrated already that he or she was originally overpraised, or has demonstrated nothing at all, or—in my strong view—will demonstrate decline from mistaken heights. One prominent critic of film says, from time to time, that he will stake his critical reputation on a strong view he is then expressing. I would have thought that a critic stakes his reputation every time he opens his mouth. Opening my mouth now, I predict that none of the above will write anything that is even up to the level of what he has been acclaimed for. And those who acclaimed him, if they are still around and writing criticism, will go "tsk-tsk" again and will tell us mournfully that the new play doesn't "work."

It's no pleasure at all to be negative on this subject, no pleasure—for someone long committed to the theater—to make negative bets. Nor am I cementing a bias, though like any other human being, I have predispositions for or against a work relevant to my past experience with the author. (Just to stick my own neck out, I'll mention two new playwrights of whom I expect good work: Robert Montgomery, author of *Subject to Fits*, and John Ford Noonan, author of *Older People*; and, of course, the continuing talent of Sam Shepard.) But if the people listed earlier were novelists, their cognate work would evoke an editor's "Do let us see your next" or, if published, critical acknowledgment of passable competence. In the theater, where there have been so few mountains through the centuries, the critical alpinists scale molehills. No season is allowed to go by without *some* show of enthusiasm, some discovery. Either this is because of fear of monotony in reviews, or fear that the critic's editor will say, "Well, if it's *all* junk, why are we bothering?", or to pump—at the slightest excuse—some life into the theater so that it will be *there* when the really good works come along. This last casuistry is the closest to a valid reason, but even so it leads to a dreadful inflation of critical language and to public distrust.

So we're constantly being told that there is a body of playwriting talent in the American theater, that new names are added and old ones drop but that the body is constant. This is supposed to be some sort of consolation for the slightness, the ineptness, the triteness, the imitativeness, the strain, the adolescent sensibility, the lack of *necessity* in the work of the writers listed earlier, and of a number of others that could be named. It's the current American cultural curse, in many arts, to talk about talent instead of works. The public is supposed to go to the theater—and I mean the intelligent public—to see the manifestation of talent, rather than a satisfactory work. This is part of the solipsism of theater people; the more serious they are, the more fervently they believe that the audience *owes* them its presence. But the public gets tired of air pudding, and a body of talents that is a manufactory of air pudding—seemingness without substance—as opposed to reasonably satisfactory realized works.

I propose no iron legislation: despite millions of requests, I don't think my opinions should be made national theater law. Still, if *a priori* is conjectural, *a posteriori* is concrete. Just look at all the "important" new writers we've had in the last dozen years, and look at what's come of them. Most of them are candidates for that article—it appears occasionally in the Sunday drama section of the *New York Times*—in which the playwright now approaching forty comments bitterly on his trouble in getting produced or getting a run despite the fact that a decade ago he got all those praises and prizes. I would be happy (believe it or not) to be dead wrong about Rabe and every playwright I have mentioned adversely, but on the evidence I think that, in the long range, they and the public and the theater are being victimized by critical flabbiness.

The Widowing of Mrs. Holroyd, by D. H. Lawrence. *New Republic*, December 15, 1973.

D. H. Lawrence, as many of us have forgotten, wrote eight plays. One of them, *The Widowing of Mrs. Holroyd* (1914), is getting its American premiere at the Long Wharf Theatre in New Haven. Arvin Brown, the head of this resident theater and the director of this play, has seemed to specialize in British imports, some of which (like David Storey's plays) have been produced well. His decision to do Lawrence was highly sensible, but it is produced poorly.

The relation of this play to *Sons and Lovers*, published the year before, is obvious. Mrs. Holroyd is a miner's wife, thirty-seven, with two young children and a brute of a drinking, philandering husband who blames his broilings on her coldness. Another man, an electrician in the mine, loves her and wants to take her away. After a fling in which Holroyd insultingly brings home two girls, Mrs. Holroyd agrees to leave with the electrician at weekend. The next day Holroyd is killed in the mine. The play ends with two Mrs. Holroyds, the widow and the dead man's old mother, washing the body on the kitchen table, preparing it for burial. The future of the widow with the electrician is uncertain because of her guilt feelings.

The texture of the play is thin, and the dramatic line veers from the intimate and sexual to the folk-tragic in a factitiously significant way. But *The Widowing of Mrs. Holroyd* has fascinating aspects. First, though the play is unsatisfactory, it's the sort of unsatisfactory play that only a genius could write. The dialogue has real Laurentian graininess and pith. (Bernard Shaw raved about it.) Second, it shows that, as Lawrence was Britain's first significant working-class novelist, so he was also the first significant working-class dramatist. (At least, after the Wakefield Master, who wrote *The Second Shepherds' Play*, ca. 1475.) Third, the play comes from the same sources as *Sons and Lovers*, particularly the relations between Lawrence's father and mother; and it's extraordinary to see a play written by a man about his mother's sexual drama, whether he was building on knowledge or on fantasy. This Oedipal note is underscored—deliberately, I assume—by the make-up of Frank Converse, who plays the electrician. With full moustache but no beard, he strongly suggests the photographs of the young Lawrence. Converse gives an appealing, reticent, sustained performance. And there's a good performance of the older Mrs. Holroyd by Geraldine Fitzgerald, who sounds more Irish than Nottinghamshire but who cuts the hard rock of proletarian mourning and acceptance of her son's death.

Joyce Ebert is Mrs. Holroyd and is unredeemedly bad from start to finish. She is a stoutly corseted young matron whom I have seen in other leading roles at this theater and who, to put it mildly, ought never to try roles that require sex appeal. Her work in general seems based on a study not of life but of acting. In Ebert's voice you hear her theatergoing memories, not Mrs. Holroyd's experience; you see her memory of theatrical gesture even in the little flourish with which this supposedly proletarian woman puts a pair of stockings in a basket. Credibility, that minimum requirement of acting, is not Ebert's strong suit.

Rex Robbins, as her husband, merely shouts from beginning to end. The casting and the conduct of these two key roles were, of course, the responsibility of Arvin Brown, who otherwise directed competently and got an exceptionally good set and equally good lighting (as usual at the Long Wharf) from David Jenkins and Ronald Wallace, respectively. But I kept wishing for the chance to "meet" this play through the acting of, say, Wendy Hiller and Trevor Howard, who played the analogous roles in the film of *Sons and Lovers*.

What the Wine-Sellers Buy, by Ron Milner. *New Republic*, March 9, 1974.

On the morning after Ron Milner's new play opened at Lincoln Center, the *New York Times* carried five reviews of it, one by the *Times* critic, four in a big ad placed by Joseph Papp, the producer. Milner is a black writer. *What the Wine-Sellers Buy* is about black life in Detroit. Four black writers—Ossie Davis, Addison Gayle, Toni Cade Bambara, and Hoyt Fuller—had been invited by Papp to see previews of the play and to write extensive comments on it, with the promise of uncensored publication: a maneuver evidently intended to counteract expected unsympathetic response from the *Times'* white critic, Clive Barnes. As it turned out, Papp needn't have worried: the *Times* review was daintily equivocal. All five of the reviews, black and white, with one only partial exception, were extreme examples of the critical *merde* about black theater that flies through the air these days.

The play builds oases of naturalism in the middle of abstraction; so does Santo Loquasto's setting. We see two homes, with an alley between them, playing space in front of them, a shop behind, and a big backdrop that can light up with a neon collage. Loquasto has done a lot with his space but, for some reason, has given almost half his stage to House Number Two, which is used for only two scenes in a long evening. Wasteful. Those two scenes could have been played in "suggested" places, as other scenes are, and House Number One, the hero's home, where most of the action takes place, could have been much less cramped.

But that disproportion is not the worst of the evening. Milner's play trudges slowly, distendedly, and foreseeably through a dramatically trite and dramaturgically ramshackle account of black urban life, emphasizing—in sometimes lyrical black English—the desperate moral choices that face his characters. A high-school boy, Steve, comes under the influence of a rich glittering pimp, Rico (black despite his name), who, more for plot reasons than for credibility, keeps a "cover" room in the seedy house where Steve and his widowed mother live. Rico, who has a foster-fatherly feeling for Steve, unknowingly paraphrases Trotsky (the world consists of those who do and those who are done to) and urges the boy to become his partner. For a start, Rico urges Steve to "hustle" his high-school girlfriend. The boy resists but then needs money for (brace yourself) his suddenly sick mother. At first his girl is outraged when Steve suggests hustling, but later she agrees.

All this is set in a by-now very familiar street-scene context, with a chorus of blacks ranging from derelicts to dancing youths. And all this is permeated with social verity—presumably incomplete but so is any social verity. And all of it is directed by Michael Schultz in what can be called the '70s black version of 1930s Elmer Rice style, with references to filmic concepts of intercutting more patent than they were then. The performances extend from the wickedly, musically scintillating (Dick A. Williams as the pimp) to the solid (Sonny Jim Gaines, as a middle-aged suitor of Steve's mother) to the self-flagellated (Glynn Turman and Loretta Greene as Steve and his girl). Through the play I kept thinking that, though such material has been used frequently by Ed Bullins and Phillip Hayes Dean and Melvin Van Peebles and many others, still there was the compensation of the vitality of black actors. They made the *moment* alive even though one was aware that black writers had already plumbed the material, had already absorbed these traditional theatrical procedures.

Then this absorption of traditional American theater became, alas, even truer. Every impulse in Milner's play forces the hero to a downward path, toward prostitution of his girl, even to tricking her into it. She has gone to a bedroom with her first customer, and Steve is exulting. Then, for absolutely no reason on earth, or in Milner's cosmos, the girl suddenly runs back in and says she can't go through with it, she and he can find another way out of their troubles; and Steve, who has been dragooning her into hustling for an hour and has been happy about his success, equally suddenly agrees. The two clasp hands and face the moral sunrise together.

This cheesy, phony, incredible Happy Ending, a last two minutes that vomit falsehood all over the previous three hours' truth, only confirms the idea that black theater is absorbing white theater history. Up to now black theater has ingested sentimental domestic drama (*A Raisin in the Sun*) and idealistic melodrama (*The River Niger*), plays that, with all their faults, had convictions and the courage of them. Now Milner's ending is exactly the kind of upbeat, unfounded, shameless and shameful ending that was a specialty of Broadway in its busiest days. One thing that black playwrights have had up to now pretty consistently is honesty; now Milner shows that they can be just as corrupt as whites.

And, what is at least equally sickening, only one of Papp's four black critics even referred to this last-minute insulting cop-out. Hoyt Fuller said: "Mr. Milner might have served the play better by making Steve's final transformation less abrupt. While it is true that the audience is pulling for a happy ending, the too rapid change in attitude does a kind of violence to a well-drawn character." But Fuller talks about this transformation as if it were in the cards, as if it only needed to be managed better. On the script's evidence, this is absolutely false; at the end Steve is not remotely thinking of going straight. So, since Fuller really has no objection to the arbitrary fairy-tale conclusion in itself, he ends up no better than the three other blacks who voiced no reservations at all or the *Times* man who said the finish was "satisfyingly moral."

Black opposition to white criticism of black theater has had one main argument up to now: black plays, no matter how crude or trite, have clearly served the important purpose of black self-certification, and that purpose could not be shared by whites. As I've noted previously, I disagree that white critics should keep hands off, but I recognize the psychosocial truth behind that one argument. Now black critics themselves have spat on that argument by ignoring psychosocial falsehood—not to mention artistic falsehood. And they are joined by a white critic. Black and white, they are *all* finks.

Short Eyes, by Miguel Piñero. *New Republic*, April 20, 1974.

There's some temptation to hate yourself at a play like *Short Eyes*. Here is a drama cut right out of some urgent social troubles of our time, performed by people (for the most part) who know firsthand what they are talking about. And yet, within the framework of an art, it's defective—even a trifle boring. Occasionally you feel a twinge of conscience for not capitulating to it. But no. At the last, no: if it was worth doing in the theater, then the theater is worth something; and theatrically *Short Eyes* is flawed.

It's set in a dayroom of a House of Detention, presumably in New York. Most of the characters are prisoners awaiting trial on drug and burglary charges. Most are black or Puerto Rican. Most of the performers and the author, Miguel Piñero, are ex-convicts. (The bio notes in the program are a sharp change from the usual stuff.) These actors got together as a group called The Family, a theater workshop in the Bedford Hills Correctional Facility in Westchester County, working under a director named Marvin Felix Camillo. Some of the original members dropped away, these men kept together after release, and under Camillo kept working at the Theater of the Riverside Church in New York, where Piñero was playwright-in-residence. Earlier this year they produced *Short Eyes*, which was seen by Joseph Papp and was transferred to one of the theaters (the Anspacher) in the Public Theater building

The term "short eyes" is prison slang for a child molester, a kind of criminal despised by other criminals. This group of prisoners has its racial antagonisms—black against "Rican," both against the one white man—but they all unite in dislike of the white newcomer, Davis, when they learn he is a "short eyes." With the connivance of a white guard who also loathes him, they murder Davis and get it accepted as suicide. They are told later that Davis was a victim of mistaken identity, but there is a double switch: one of the prisoners, an older Rican, knows that the mistaken identity is itself a mistake—because Davis confided in him at length about his psychosexual history. He *was* guilty. But the Rican—possibly because he promised Davis confidence, possibly out of deference to Davis's widow so she can at least believe her husband died innocent—keeps mum.

The writing of the play is schizoid. The banter, teasing, homosexual play and fights are pungent, vital. They give the impression of extemporizations that have been taped and preserved, according to a scenario, rather than of dialogue written and memorized. In clumsy contrast are such passages as Davis's long confessional narrative and the examination of the prisoners by an officer, which were written on a rusty typewriter. The interest of the performance (and it does work up some interest) comes entirely from the work of the group, as group, under Camillo: a free-flowing, colorful essay in the self-histrionism of the characters, who are perhaps not so terribly distant from the performers—the creation of a kind of jungle of nativity into which Davis comes like a stranger.

That atmosphere, compressed by David Mitchell's grim prison walls, is the best thing about the evening.

But because the evening wears on and makes efforts at art that become strained, the attention wanders. One critic said that attention wanders at *Short Eyes* because the audience is busy testing out the characters' emotions in themselves. Odd how infrequently that sort of wandering occurs at *Oedipus Rex*. My attention wandered because I had faced these emotions, in these renderings, so often before—on television, in the press, on film, and in other plays. The hard, admittedly cold truth is that people who get into trouble and suffer, like people who fall in love, tend to think that because it affected them so drastically, it will automatically interest others. Once the facts are familiar—and Piñero's facts are by now very familiar—only the telling can be interesting. And Piñero hasn't much skill in telling.

There is a strong irony in his play, but I'm not convinced that he's aware of it. These prisoners very badly need some sort of superiority. The "short eyes" gives it to them, in a surge that floods across their racial and personal differences. But the inhumanity they then practice toward their "inferior" is simply an extension of the very inhumanity, the social cruelty, that put them here in the first place. So, fundamentally, they are their own persecutors. Because this underlying truth is left muzzy, because Piñero relies so naïvely on facts that have by now lost their shock value, the viewer soon conquers his impatience with himself at not being overwhelmed by the play.

In Praise of Love, by Terence Rattigan. *New Republic*, January 4-11, 1975.

English play, English star, American production. Terence Rattigan has been turning out neatly turned-out comedies and dramas since the 1930s and is still writing 1930s plays. He finds his little idea, for comedy or poignance, and he stitches his little script about it with considerable craft and no unnecessary nuisance. When the play starts at 8:00, you know that everything will be in order by 10:30, with time out for a smoke, and at least your intelligence will not have been insulted. (Remember *Separate Tables*, *The Browning Version*, *The Winslow Boy*, etc.)

In Praise of Love was produced in London as half of a Rattigan double bill (with Donald Sinden!). Presumably it was expanded to full length for Rex Harrison, whom it fits with Savile Row finish. Harrison is now the perfect Rattigan actor. What a comedown. He once was, or could have been, the perfect Shaw or Congreve or Sheridan or even Shakespeare actor. But at least this role is not a disaster like his attempt at lovableness in *Dr. Dolittle* or at physical farce in *A Flea in Her Ear*. Here Harrison is content to do a (very) minor version of Henry Higgins—a lofty, densely egocentric charmer. But how well he does it. You can see him eating up all the other actors on stage, even his co-star Julie Harris, simply by not looking at them much and justifying it with his one-man show. He times so perfectly (as when he realizes belatedly that the chess set with which he is playing is a new, expensive gift), he inflects so delightfully (who else could still make us laugh at the line "Are you mad?"), and he fulfills the requirements of stage stardom so completely. That is, he says in effect, not "I hope I please you, ladies and gentlemen," but "How lucky you all are to be seeing me." And makes it stick.

The play? It's about a wife who has a terminal disease and how she and her husband keep their knowledge of it from each other. He is a famous literary critic. (Writing for which London weekly, I wonder, in that *luxe* Jo Mielziner house?) She is Estonian born, a former Resistance heroine thirty years later. (The part was conceived for Ingrid Bergman.) None of that really matters. T. Rattigan, Gentlemen's Tailor, has made a decent suit for a good customer.

God's Favorite, by Neil Simon. *New Republic*, February 22, 1975.

Neil Simon, Broadway's one comic writer (its one serious writer is Edward Albee), presents a new play; almost simultaneously he announces that he is moving from New York to Hollywood and is less interested in the theater than he was.

His new play proves it. *God's Favorite* is one more reworking of the story of Job. (Remember Archibald MacLeish's *J.B.*? Perhaps, like me, you'd rather not.) This time the locale is a present-day Long Island suburb, and the protagonist Joe Benjamin is a wealthy Jew. Comic black servants. Comic, faintly swishy messenger of God who complains about his low take-home pay. A running gag before the play is two minutes old. (Joe's daughter comes down in the middle of the night to investigate trouble and we get a litany from her father of "Close your bathrobe.") About the play itself—its comedy as well as its purported religious affirmation—I'll only say that if I were God I'd be sufficiently insulted to shift the plagues from the protagonist to the playwright.

As Joe, Vincent Gardenia is encouraged to regress into his stock of *shtick* instead of growing in a way he has sometimes shown. The rest of the cast shall be nameless. But I name the director, Michael Bennett. This show has the look of a script that Mike Nichols rejected, so they got a director to imitate him if possible. Don't, as they used to say, take any wooden Nichols.

There is no better instance of perfect community in our theater than that between a Broadway audience and a play that they have been told in advance is a hit—particularly if it's a comedy by Simon. Well, why shouldn't these amiable people have a playwright who tickles them? I, equally amiable, ask only that he tickle me, too. He did it for me through much of *The Odd Couple* and *The Sunshine Boys*. When he fails to amuse and, worse, when he implies that there is Something Deep under his skit, or skits—both of which are the case here—his failure becomes a kind of offense.

A couple of months ago the Sunday critic of the *New York Times* told us that, this season, Broadway was coming up roses. Well, as far as scripts are concerned, including the script of *God's Favorite*, we've had only the manure on the garden up to now. Some good performances from British and American actors, but no new plays of consequence from anywhere.

Broadway, if it needs saying, is feeble. It seems to be getting feebler, since now even Simon is leaving (though Albee insists on staying). No, it won't die, so you can go on calling it the fabulous invalid if that cheers you. But if Broadway is feeble, the *theater*—meaning everything in this country that actors do in front of audiences—is kicking, irritating, troublesome: therefore alive and interesting.

The Mound Builders, by Lanford Wilson. *New Republic*, March 1, 1975.

Lanford Wilson's new play, *The Mound Builders*, Off-Broadway at the Circle Repertory Company, is better than his last one, *The Hot l Baltimore*. I thought that play (now the basis of a television series) an imitation of Tennessee Williams, hollow and syrup-covered. *The Mound Builders* has its faults, faults a-plenty, but at least they are Wilson's. So are its virtues, the chief of which is its authentic base—in Wilson's well-known feeling for the Midwest.

Two archaeology professors, one middle-aged and one young, are on a summer dig in Illinois, with their families. The story is told in flashback by the older man, accompanied by many color slides. What is attempted is a parallel/contrast between the vanished society for which they are digging and the complexities of their own lives, of modern life generally. The characters include the older man's unfaithful wife and his drinking-drugging novelist sister (apparently modeled on Carson McCullers), the younger man's pregnant wife, and the young countryman who owns much of the lake shore on which they are digging and hopes to profit by it.

It's a facile schema, the contrasts between past and present, between the university types and the young countryman, but for a time Wilson breathes some life into it. We really get the feeling that we are in mid-America (as for instance with the young wife's story of her spelling-bee championship), and there are flashes of real wit (as when someone asks the novelist whether she has a deck of tarot cards, and she replies, "No, I just look that way"). And there are some moments of genuine feeling—for instance, in the young countryman's doomed fumbling for the young wife. But finally Wilson lacks the intellectual depth to make the schema fruitful or the art to keep it from the mere filling-out of a pattern, step by overlong step. The "tragic" end is far from tragedy because I couldn't believe that the young countryman, otherwise close to all the others, would be the only one not to know either that the young wife is pregnant or that the big highway is being switched—so he will not make the money he hoped for. This plotty finagling stands out glaringly in a play on the theme of authenticity.

John Lee Beatty's setting makes imaginative use of a limited space, and, in a spotty cast, John Strasberg (son of Lee Strasberg) gives the countryman credible sensitivity and menace. Wilson himself still seems to me an ambitious undergraduate pouring out promising scripts for his professor of playwriting, but at least there are more promises here than there were last time.

The Misanthrope, by Molière. *New Republic*, April 12, 1975.

The Misanthrope, the Molière production of the (British) National Theatre now at the St. James in New York, was heralded by much trumpeting but comes pretty close to disaster. The adaptation by Tony Harrison, set in the Paris of 1966, is a mistake. The modern diction and the forced rhymes ("for" with "Goncourt") might be tolerated; but the details of the story and the values of the characters simply don't transplant.

When Oronte in 1666 insists on reading his new poem to Alceste, he is an egocentric member of his society. When Oronte in 1966, in dinner jacket, in a slick drawing room, does the same thing, he seems an eccentric buffoon, near insanity. The Alceste of 1666, who hates the hypocrisy and fawning he sees all around him, represents a reaction against the vices of courtly protocol; he means something to us by analogy with his context. But when Alceste is transposed to 1966 he loses his context and can't affect us; he just seems terribly naïve. Antigone in old Thebes is a heroine who inspires us today; Antigone in modern Greece would seem something of a nut.

The acting doesn't help. Alec McCowen is an actor of some technical snap but little innate power or color. His Alceste, instead of being a grave soul-sickened man, is an irascible egotist, a kind of schoolteacher who can't stand being crossed and who makes his points by screaming. We can't understand why Célimène should ever have cared for him.

Célimène is Diana Rigg, familiar from films and television, a very competent and vigorous actress with wit and appeal, who plays the role, complete with thin cigar, like a Noël Coward hostess. Célimène is one of the most interesting women in Molière, a twenty-year-old widow who loves this odd older man but who is just really discovering her sexuality and its power, and who finally opts for the exploration of that power instead of solitariness with the man she still loves. But Rigg isn't discovering much; at the very beginning she looks as if she had had six men for dinner and the night was young. The whole text and subtext of Molière is lost between her competence and McCowen's incompetence. (Also, she has a touch of what the English call a "common" accent: "A fine compliment *thot* is.")

Robert Eddison is pleasing as the friendly Philinte, but the director, John Dexter, keeps him standing about all night like a guard at Buckingham Palace. In general Dexter has worked with obtrusive symmetries and posed compositions that might have been passable in period costume but make the modern setting all the more uneasy. And that shiny set, with slanted stage and inexplicable swirls of drapery from the ceiling, made me uneasy in itself.

A Fable, by Jean-Claude van Itallie. *New Republic*, November 8, 1975.

After I saw *A Fable*, the latest production by Joseph Chaikin at the Westbeth Theater Center, I took down his book *The Presence of the Actor* (Atheneum, 1972) and read on the first page:

> The joy in theater comes through discovery and the capacity to discover. What limits the discoveries a person can make is the idea or image he may come to have of himself. The image can come about through his investment in his own reputation, through an involvement with approval or disapproval, or through feelings of nostalgia stemming from his desire to repeat his first discoveries. In any case, when his image becomes fixed, it limits him from going on to further discoveries.

All I can add to this prescient criticism of *A Fable* are some specifics about why I think it is a sad footnote to recent theater history. Chaikin was the founder of the Open Theater in 1963, a group that synthesized productions out of ensemble efforts of writer and actors and director, sometimes with the writer simply formalizing on paper the matters that had been worked out in rehearsal, in improvisation and inner inquiry, by the group. In 1966 the Open Theater presented two interesting works, *America Hurrah*, by Jean-Claude van Itallie, and *Viet Rock*, by Megan Terry. In 1968 they reached their height with *The Serpent* by van Itallie. With this production and subsequent ones they have often toured the U.S. and Europe. But in later productions they have seemed to be groping backward toward those first fine careful raptures. For internal reasons the Open Theater has nominally disbanded, but virtually everyone in this new production had been in the group, including the writer van Itallie and the composer Richard Peaslee.

A Fable (nothing to do with Faulkner's novel of that name) is another "collaborative work." Peaslee's music, some of it for the actors, some of it for three instrumentalists alone, could hardly be more grudging and skimpy. The six actors, wearing informal street clothes, begin by singing a chorus about the village of People-Who-Fish-in-the-Lake. Then they sit around for a while, mending a net, creating simple-hearted folk atmosphere. Then a young woman sets out from the village on a symbolic journey. She passes through a palace courtyard full of *Marat/Sade* deformed and demented people. (All other roles are played by the other five actors.) She sees the king, who asks her to find and kill the beast in his kingdom (which turns out to be himself). She passes through a country fair. She meets an ugly hermit in the woods and stays with him for a time, playing music. She returns at last to find her village leveled.

If I say that I don't get the point of this fairy tale, I must make clear that van Itallie's dialogue is absolutely *laden* with points—homiletic, false-naïve, gaseous, all reeking of smug and spurious purity. Last year I saw an "independent" production of his play *The King of the United States*, which was an imaginative victory by the director Allan Albert over an insipid political fantasy-satire full of high-school insights. This year van Itallie becomes the Khalil Gibran of the avant-garde.

Last year Chaikin did an "independent" production of *The Sea Gull* that, except for the passable performance of Leueen McGrath as Arkadina, was a clumsy barbarism, revealing how far Chaikin was from a command of representational acting. In the years immediately preceding, the last years of the Open Theater, he had demonstrated that (in his own terms) his image had become fixed, limiting him from further discoveries. Like so many explorers in the arts, he had made a breakthrough and had then sat down.

Through the 1960s Chaikin was a figure of some seminal force, in America and abroad, particularly appealing to young people who were looking for new ways of being truthful in the theater. Diluted from Grotowski though much of his work was, Chaikin showed some poetic imagination of his own—for a while. Lately he has been drawing heavily on credit that is running low. In my review of *A Chorus Line* (in the *New Republic* of June 21, 1975) I suggested that the idea of a musical derived from the synthesis of its cast's experiences, even some of the show's devices, owed a debt to Joseph Chaikin. Increasingly Chaikin owes debts to himself. *The Mutation Show* a few years ago fed desperately on the vocal-kinetic work of his earlier shows, thinned out now because the miming and vocalizing had much less rich subjects to work on and thus seemed centered on celebrating the methods themselves. This is even more the case with *A Fable*: familiar Open Theater tactics are here applied to hollow stuff and now appear not only stale but merely self-gratifying.

Trelawny of the "Wells", by Arthur Wing Pinero. *New Republic*, November 8, 1975.

Joseph Papp, the theatrical Gatling gun that mostly fires blanks, has opened his new season with a dud. At the Vivian Beaumont in Lincoln Center, where he promised us a season of classics, he opens with Pinero's *Trelawny of the "Wells"*. Apparently Papp uses the word "classic" (as film people often do) synonymously with "old." He did a production of this play downtown at the Public Theater in November of 1970, and I noted at the time that, buried in this trumpery antique, there is a core of cultural history: a turning point from romantic to realistic theater. But an awful lot of baggage has to be hauled getting to and away from that core.

The present director, A. J. Antoon, has shifted the setting to the U.S., as he did with his good production of *Much Ado about Nothing* three years ago. I'm less upset about this shift than others have been. The Pinero doesn't travel as well as Shakespeare because it is more realistic in detail; nonetheless, New York of the late nineteenth century was still greatly under the levy of British class ideas (see James and Wharton), and the stratification necessary to this story is therefore almost as valid in New York as in the original London.

But the casting is generally deplorable, and although Antoon has moved the play nicely around the stage, the performance has no central style. Walter Abel, as the crusty old "aristocrat," is making up for a largely pallid career by overcoloring now. The most agreeable members of the 'Wells' company, the theater gypsies who are contrasted with Abel's ménage, are John Lithgow as the leading man, Michael Tucker as the aspiring playwright, and Meryl Streep as a successful alumna. Mary Beth Hurt has the title role; she has some dignity and appeal as the matured Trelawny, but she isn't credible as the earlier successful actress of purple romance.

The settings and lighting by David Mitchell and Ian Calderon are beautiful and make the best use I have so far seen of the deep Beaumont stage. At the start of each act we are looking at a Victorian theater stage, with some old flats and an old drop; these then rise into the flies as a setting glides forward from behind them onto the thrust stage of that old theater: so the idea of a play about the theater is neatly reified. But, as they say of bad musicals, you can't whistle the scenery. The handsome looks of this production don't compensate for the inadequate performance of a play that would be tolerable only if superbly performed.

Ice Age, by Tankred Dorst. *New Republic*, December 20, 1975.

I read Knut Hamsun's *On Overgrown Paths* in 1969, and it has haunted me ever since. I was reviewing a new translation of his early novel *Victoria* (in the *New Republic* of February 1, 1969) and was freshly convinced of his genius, a genius that was coming back into light after the cloud thrown over his career by his support of the Norwegian Nazi party and his praise of Hitler. Rereading some others of his books, I came across his last work, then new to me: *On Overgrown Paths* (P. S. Eriksson, 1967), a kind of journal interspersed with memoirs, written during the years 1945 to 1948 when Hamsun was interned on suspicion of treason, first in a hospital, then in a home for the aged, then in an

Oslo psychiatric clinic. It's a short book, done in a style that can be called close-mouthed, wry, patient, solitary.

He was eighty-six when he was arrested. Apparently the Norwegian government was trying to find him mentally incompetent in order to excuse his political behavior so that they wouldn't have to punish him, but he stubbornly and very competently insisted that he had known what he was doing. Their Nobel Prize author—he and Sigrid Undset are the only two that Norway has had—would not let them off the hook. He passed all the psychiatric tests and, in a sense, forced them to find him guilty, which they did in 1948. He was heavily fined, though the fines were later reduced; if he had been younger or obscure, he might have been shot. He died in 1952, aged ninety-three.

The obvious parallel is with Ezra Pound, but Hamsun is personally much more appealing; he has none of Pound's nastiness and viciousness. Hamsun's book—in a taciturn, unbending manner—compels. If one knows some of his best work, his memoir is disturbing in at least two ways. How could a writer of such powerful human insight have subscribed to a ruthlessly anti-humanist politics? When does one stop honoring honor and courage? Leni Riefenstahl's Nazi documentary *Triumph of the Will* is frightening because she had filmic genius, employed for odious propaganda, that makes us viscerally respond. But here, alone and unpopular, past propaganda, is this stubborn old man refusing to bend, and you find yourself finding him—it's the only word—admirable. His book is shaking because it shakes the bounds of human encompassment.

Evidently the book has haunted the German playwright Tankred Dorst. Now fifty, Dorst is the author of a number of plays and opera libretti performed throughout Germany. (He has been in the U.S. twice: as a prisoner of war and as a writer-in-residence at Oberlin.) His play *Ice Age* is based on the Hamsun memoirs; it has been done in several German cities, including Berlin, has been filmed for German television and produced in Australia, and is to be produced in Britain. Now the Chelsea Theater Center, in the Brooklyn Academy of Music, presents the play in Peter Sanders' translation.

It's as easy to understand why so many people have wanted to produce *Ice Age* as it is to understand why Dorst wanted to write it. The subject is tantalizing. But tantalizing subjects don't always make satisfactory plays. In this case, at least, one can legitimately use a worn rationale: *Ice Age* is the kind of unsatisfactory play one is glad to have seen. The dramatic trouble is central: the central figure is a portrait, not a protagonist. The Old Man, which is all he is called, observes, comments, responds, but he initiates nothing and does not change. The core of his persona is to initiate nothing and not to change. There can be drama in stasis, as Beckett has shown, but Dorst doesn't venture that far. He sees the Old Man's stasis as a handicap, not an opportunity, and he tries to compensate by adding material that is meant to make the play function in relatively conventional terms.

Most of this added material is strained. He sets the play in one place, an old-folks home, and he surrounds the Old Man with contrasting old people, blithering about complicated trivia. To dramatize the moral complexities and the effect of the Old Man's character, Dorst invents a young ex-partisan named Oswald, son of a rich collaborator, who has wanted for a long time to kill the Old Man, who tries to shatter him with symbolic charades, and who is himself shattered by the old man's fixity. If the character of Oswald had been written well, and had been played well in this production, it might have crystallized some of the feelings that Hamsun's book gives the reader. Instead it's all merely arty.

And Dorst does some funny fiddling with the Old Man's wife. She was, as he says, much younger, but he omits the fact that Hamsun's wife (who had previously been married to a German) was believed to have intensified his pro-German, anti-American, and anti-British feelings. She was herself in prison at this time and served three years. Dorst converts her into a bland, baffled woman with a flabby son, who brings the Old Man muddled news of his farm and wants only to do everything he wishes.

There are a few good scenes, particularly one in which the Old Man encounters an old-timer named Kristian from his part of the country. They smoke a pipe together and count up which of their acquaintances are dead, chuckling because they are still alive. This encounter, drawn from a somewhat different scene in the book, strengthens the essence of the Old Man, his rootedness in his soil and community, his consecration of the life that gave him life. And there is an earlier scene in which the Old Man takes a word-association test given by a psychiatrist. After he answers a particularly inane question, he adds quietly: "I've written thirty novels."

But the strength of the play, which is also its weakness, is that it works not in dialogues or clashes but in the *being* of the Old Man. He becomes vivid as a man who loves simplicity, his language, his people, his farm, his mind; who hates slovenliness and lack of self-discipline—and can therefore find plenty to mock in democratic society. He says that he wanted to see Norway take her place in a Germanic union. (And Dorst might have added, from Hamsun's strong statement to the court: "I could call to mind that every single great and proud name in Norwegian culture had first journeyed through Teutonic Germany in order to win the acclaim of the world at large. It was not wrong of me to remember that.") The Old Man rests his support of Hitler and the Quisling party (as in the book) on his ignorance of the Nazi tortures and his desire to save Norwegian lives from being wasted in futile resistance, particularly in aid of the Britain he disliked.

If it could be proved that Hamsun really knew of the Nazi crimes in Norway and elsewhere, then his book and this play would take on very different colors. But he was an old man when the war started, living an isolated rural life, reading only a doctored press. That is explanation, not excuse, but it helps to explain how he was able to remain steadfast to an ideal abstracted from its barbarous application. (When in fact Hamsun later learned of the horrors, he refused to comment on them, as if acknowledgment of the horrors would have been a way out for him, a way to regret his past. It's almost as if, by rejecting acknowledgment of the horrors, he was punishing himself for his mistakes, making himself live with them without admitting them.)

Dorst has an excellent ally in Roberts Blossom, who plays the Old Man. (He was Gatsby's father in the recent film.) Blossom grounds his fine performance in a perfectly realized center: hard, lonely, self-imprisoned within himself. Arne Zaslove, the director, has done his best work with Blossom. The rest of the cast is indifferent when not hurtful, except for Roger DeKoven's juicy Kristian. If there were such a thing as a modernistic ice cube, the inside of it would look like Wolfgang Roth's setting. The Chelsea Theater Center has often produced interesting plays, not often as moderately well as this one. With all its shortcomings, this production at least brings us Dorst's and Blossom's disdainful, doomed old lion.

Rich and Famous, by John Guare. *New Republic*, March 13, 1976.

In the current crop of overpraised young American playwrights John Guare is one of the few with readily discernible talent. It was discernible even in his disappointing *House of Blue Leaves*, which eventually won everything but the Nobel Prize and the Congressional Medal of Honor. His early short plays like *Muzeeka* had imaginative release and exuberant humor, but nothing of his that I have seen, including his screenplay for the Milos Forman film *Taking Off*, came close to satisfying.

So it continues with his latest play, *Rich and Famous*, just produced by Joseph Papp (Newman Theater). It consists of the fantasies of a young playwright on the night of the first preview of his first produced play, after writing 843 previous scripts. (Part of the fantasy, I guess, is that, though this is the first preview and there's talk of a major cast change before the opening, the newspapers review it, disastrously.) He goes through a series of scenes with a drag queen, a childhood sweetheart, a smooth Jewish Broadway composer, his Bronx-Irish father and mother, and the haunting image of a boyhood pal who makes it as a picture star just as this play flops. William Atherton, of *The Day of the Locust* and *Hindenburg* films, plays the writer. All the other parts are played by Ron Leibman, of such films as *Where's Poppa?* and *The Hot Rock*, and Anita Gillette, best known from television.

A great deal of Guare's dialogue is sharp and resourceful. He wrote several songs, music and lyrics, that are pleasant and clever. Some of the set-pieces, especially those for Leibman, are show-stoppers, patently manufactured but nonetheless effective. But I'm left again with the feeling that what Guare needs is a sympathetic collaborator. After he has shot all his fireworks, and he has some, almost every one of his scenes is residually trite and static. The scene with the former sweetheart is full of familiar, grubbily overtugged heartstrings. The scene with the uncomprehending parents is *that* scene again, this time Irish instead of Jewish. Even the scene with the *doppelgänger* film star at the end concludes with a flashy gag, with only a strained relevance to the play.

The script, then, has no dramatic conclusion or thematic issue. Guare is the writing equivalent of a talented actor who needs a good director and flounders without one. The actual director here, Mel Shapiro, does some good work. Shapiro is hell on Shakespeare, traditional (*Richard III*) or mod (*Two Gentlemen of Verona*), but he breathes and expands in fantastic work, as here and with John Ford Noonan's *Older People*. As for the actors, Atherton is very agreeable but seems pallid next to Leibman, who has all the showy stuff and charges into it loaded with more nightclub comic business than you could shake a stick at. Anita Gillette herself lacks the cartoon range for this kind of quick-change work.

Boy Meets Girl, by Bella and Sam Spewack, & *Secret Service*, by William Gillette. *New Republic*, May 8, 1976.

The Phoenix Theater, like its mythological namesake, keeps trying to rise from its ashes, but the ashes keep catching up with it and by now it's quite a pile. The Phoenix was started in 1953 and was, I believe, the only institutional theater in New York at the time, doing seasons of revivals and new plays, including new musicals. It waxed and waned and kept on waxing and waning, but whether doing one or the other, it displayed no fire, no ambitions toward anything like unified style, not even the dubious goal of aesthetic propaganda. It was—like the Circle in the Square and the Beaumont today—simply a group that did seasons of plays, for subscribers if it could get them, with no permanent ensemble and with many different directors. However, in its various forms and alliances through the years, in New York and on tour, the Phoenix has maintained one thing: an aroma of weak high-mindedness. Basically the Phoenix has always seemed to me the perfect matinée theater for club-ladies.

No theater can exist that long without some achievements. The Phoenix has presented me with some nice memories, most of them from their first home in the former Yiddish Art Theater down in Irving Howe country. There I saw Fritz Weaver's striking small-part début in Sidney Lumet's malformed production of Shaw's *The Doctor's Dilemma*; Tyrone Guthrie's lovely productions of *The Pirates of Penzance* and Pirandello's *Six Characters in Search of an Author*; and Irene Worth in Schiller's *Mary Stuart*. But most of the Phoenix work that I saw was dullish do-gooding or worse.

Then it joined forces with that lackluster repertory company, the A.P.A. (Association of Producing Artists), under that lackluster director Ellis Rabb (whose current production of *The Royal Family* continues his pedestrian career). After five years the Phoenix divorced itself from the A.P.A. and started its own repertory company under T. Edward Hambleton, one of the founders in 1953, who is still running the Phoenix. (The repertory was only seasonal, not continuing, and hardly any of the actors continued as "company"; but that's par for the American course.) The productions that I saw—of Molière, Congreve, Dürrenmatt, Pirandello—were miserable, and I gave myself a brief vacation from the Phoenix. Now I've seen their two latest productions—revivals of American plays—which are only marginally better (at the Playhouse Theatre.)

Boy Meets Girl, by Bella and Sam Spewack (1935), is a typical Broadway farce of the between-wars era. It's about Hollywood, but it could have been about shoestring Broadway producers or a nightclub girl in a college dorm or horse players, as other l930s hit farces were. As playwriting they are all just juggling to keep you distracted from the very fact of the juggling. The authors always seem to be performing in front of a caliph who will have them beheaded if they bore, so they sweat and strain with ever-wider frightened grins. The plays themselves always make me think of balcony stairs. I see the authors sitting in the back of the theater on the balcony stairs at rehearsals in Boston or Philadelphia, portable typewriters on laps, frantically rewriting.

Kaufman and Hart's *Once in a Lifetime*, one of the best of the breed, is also about Hollywood and is much better than *Boy Meets Girl* because it's built on something interesting: the arrival of sound. *Boy Meets Girl* (which was filmed in 1938 with James Cagney, Pat O'Brien, and Ronald Reagan) has to make its own way, so to speak, with no better material than the stock stuff of Hollywood extravagance and zaniness. The plot is pumped and whumped and is never well enough manufactured to be really funny, only frantic. (The one funny line falls flat here. The curtain goes up on a movie producer dictating to his secretary; he begins: "My dear Signor Pirandello . . .")

The historically important aspect of this play, of all Broadway comedy of the period, is not the writing but the fact that out of it was developed a unique style of directing and acting, one of the few clearly individuated American theater styles. The ace director in that style was the man who first did *Boy Meets Girl*, George Abbott; such fast-talking actors as Lee Tracy and Allan Joslyn were leading performers. It was all sharp, bright, brassy, with a tempo imposed from without, not generated by the script. Unlike British and French farce styles, its intent was fundamentally to keep life out, to create a small, fast, perfect mechanism—which it frequently did. It had about as much relation to "motivated" acting as trapeze work has to ballet. (Reportedly Abbott once told an actor at a rehearsal to cross from right to left on a certain line. "But what's my motivation?" asked the actor, "Your motivation," said Abbott, "is that I'll kick your ass out of this theater if you don't.")

I certainly don't mourn the virtual end of that style, but when a play of that era is revived, who today is going to direct and play it? Certainly not John Lithgow, who directed here and who keeps things rushing but who has small sense of comic phrase and point, and who simply doesn't know when members of his cast are dismally unfunny. Of the company Lenny Baker (the boy in the film *Next Stop, Greenwich Village*) is a mild surprise as a bespectacled wild screenwriter, but the rest are mostly wretched, particularly Mary Beth Hurt, who is back again with the Betty Boop voice and cuteness that she used in Congreve and Pinero and also uses later in Gillette.

The matter of style, a different one, is also the root of the other failure, William Gillette's Civil War melodrama *Secret Service*, which he wrote in 1895 and played for decades. (Richard Dix, resplendent in Confederate uniform, filmed it in 1931.) Melodrama was a staple of the nineteenth-century American theater, but its style, as distinct from subject, was not greatly different from European models, in writing or in acting. Stylistically, *Boy Meets Girl* is much more peculiarly American than *Secret Service*.

But if a forty-year-old style is remote from this company, an eighty-year-old style is more than twice as remote. So, under their addled director Daniel Freudenberger, they make the worst possible choice: they kid the play—and they make it even worse by not kidding it consistently. The play is done more or less straight until the villain arrives and cavorts as in a summer-camp romp: then *both* approaches are used alternately. At its best the show almost touches the sweep and gesture of melodrama, particularly with Meryl Streep, the heroine, who has some historical imagination and has good looks that are timeless—she looks good in any period. John Lithgow (who directed *Boy Meets Girl*) starts dashingly enough as the hero, but he throws it all out the window later in cartoon, even though the program notes that Gillette's distinction was naturalism in a florid era. Freudenberger evidently induced these betrayals out of ignorance or lack of confidence, even though he put in, before each scene, authentic period songs, sung authentically. Without inflating *Secret Service*, there's a small daring in the script that the director never faces: the villain is a true Confederate patriot, in a play set in Richmond; the hero is a Northern spy. Gillette was clearly relying on actors' qualities and at least some truthful character discrimination to guide audience sympathies, not on Freudenberger horseplay.

It's deplorable—not because *Secret Service* is worth much more than the paper it's written on but just *because* it's not much of a play and is not worth reviving unless one makes an honest effort to re-create the theater of which it was a part. Theater people are always eager to mock the popular theater of the past—e.g., the Royal Shakespeare Company's revival of Boucicault's *London Assurance*—as if our own popular theater were Olympian.

James Tilton designed both plays, the farce adequately, the melodrama drearily. The same body of actors performs in both plays and demonstrates more of the handicaps of repertory than of the blessings. Both productions are part of the Phoenix's season of American plays, apparently chosen for the Bicentennial. The Phoenix celebrates that event just as it has done most of its work in the past twenty-three years—with well-meaning fumble.

The Runner Stumbles, by Milan Stitt. *New Republic*, June 12, 1976.

Here is still another instance of our theater's frenzy to push a writer merely because he is serious and is not completely devoid of ability. Milan Stitt's play *The Runner Stumbles* had a "showcase" presentation at the Manhattan Theater Club, then a production at the Hartman in Stamford, and now has been brought to Broadway, at the Little Theatre. All those votes of confidence have been given to a work that—if one could imagine it as a novel—would get a "let us see your next" letter from a good publisher.

The play deals with love between a priest and a nun in raw north Michigan at the turn of the century (suggested by an actual murder case). The love is unconsummated. After a stormy scene the nun is found dead, and the priest is accused. His innocence is established at the end, but it could easily have been done at the beginning.

It's all accoutered in fussy dramaturgy—flashing back and forward from the trial to the events discussed—which cannot conceal the fact that we know from the beginning that the nun and priest will eventually reveal their mutual love and that the play has nothing else to reveal. Stitt makes much heavy weather about clarifying views of God and service en route, but it's only padding on a thin story. Once again a tender of seriousness in a playwright, genuine though the tender is, has been accepted as genuine seriousness.

Stephen Joyce, one of our better actors who is not yet fully appreciated, is forceful and flawless as the priest. The director, Austin Pendleton, has laid out the play well, but has permitted rough edges in some performances.

A Texas Trilogy, by Preston Jones. *New Republic*, October 23, 1976.

Preston Jones, a Texan now forty years old, has for a number of years been an actor at the Dallas Theater Center. During 1973-74 he wrote three full-length plays about a West Texas town. During the last two years, word of those plays has spread, as they were produced first in Dallas and then in other resident theaters around the country. Last spring the three plays were produced in repertory at the Kennedy Center in Washington, D.C.; now those Kennedy productions have been brought to New York (at the Broadhurst Theatre), and now the fact that they have disappointed many in New York has been ascribed to their advance publicity.

There's no reason at this too-late date to dwell on U.S. publicity inflation. In the theater, as I've noted before, that inflation is often caused by critics pumping away in the hope, indirectly, of sustaining their jobs. But how could an American trilogy, after numerous prior productions, be done at the Kennedy Center and then be headed for New York without stirring up hoopla? To blame that hoopla for a letdown is a new high in disingenuousness.

Anyway, an effort of such scope deserves scrutiny. Here are (necessarily) brief descriptions of the three plays. All are set in Bradleyville, Texas, during the twenty years after 1953. The order in which one sees them is irrelevant to the author, but by coincidence I saw them in order of declining interest. *Lu Ann Hampton Laverty Oberlander* takes place in three acts that are ten years apart. We see Lu Ann as a squirmy high school girl meeting the boy she will marry; as a bar-haunting divorcée with a small daughter; as a weary widow with a teenaged daughter. *The Oldest Living Graduate* is about an aged rich rancher, confined to a wheelchair, who was a colonel in the First World War and is the most ancient alumnus of a Galveston military academy. His fiftyish son wants to use a ceremony in honor of that last fact to promote a business deal, for which he needs some property of the old man's. The colonel holds on to it for sentimental reasons; then has a stroke at a lodge meeting, and gives it to his son. *The Last Meeting of the Knights of the White Magnolia* is about that same night, during which a small group of seedy white supremacists meet in a fusty hall in the colonel's hotel to induct a new member and keep the lodge alive. It's only a series of rube vaudeville skits building up to the colonel's stroke, which happened offstage in the previous play.

The productions don't give the plays enough help. Ben Edwards' settings look cheap and drab, as settings even of cheap, drab places. (Yes, producing these three plays was expensive, but I'm talking about results, not problems.) The cast is spotty. As the tripartite Lu Ann, Diane Ladd seems more concerned with sinking her teeth into three showy parts than in the woman herself. She gives us résumés of every performance we have seen of a bouncy teenager, a tight-dressed beautician, and a straggly-haired housewife. She is helped principally by the fact that she is doing all three in one evening: if she were doing only one, the mechanics and vacancies would be clearer.

Fred Gwynne, the old colonel, has some force and color but also some self-indulgence. Certainly the *character* is a ham. (For myself, I'd like to see all old people in wheelchairs banned from stage and film: they're always either lovable or hateful bores.) But Gwynne embroiders the part with elaborate double gesture and mugging. Patricia Roe works sharply as his tart daughter-in-law; Lee Richardson works with his usual honesty as her husband; James Staley and Baxter Harris are authentic as swain and second husband of Lu Ann. The rest—of comment on the acting—is silence.

Alan Schneider directed the plays and, at its best, his work is unobtrusive. But there are many moments that obtrude. In *The Oldest Living Graduate*, for instance. Character A sits on a sofa center while B stands at the end of it; A gets up and walks behind the sofa while B comes around and sits on it—

again and again. In *Knights of the White Magnolia*, for another instance, Henderson Forsythe has a long silent minute wandering around the stage at the end, as he closes the meeting room, which in tempo and detail is agonizingly trite.

Of course, a "regional" playwright like Jones can be relied on for "regional" dialogue. People talk about "Worlds War One," the phrase "by God" is inserted everywhere ("this by God town"), the colonel's word for "stupid" is "bumble-dicking," high-school Lu Ann calls nice things "neat-o," and so on. Moreover, Jones conveys that these people, as in other well-knit communities, love conversation and deal with their lives in language.

But in Jones's character portrayals something spurious creeps in. The author quite clearly knows these people, but he has allowed his experience and observation to be crammed into clichés of stage and film. Lu Ann is a conglomerate out of William Inge and others; Colonel Kinkaid is in the line of latter-day Lionel Barrymore nasties; the Knights are a troupe of rube comics out of old local-yokel plays and films. (See Griffith's *Way Down East*.) Of course these clichés originally had some basis in life: all fictional stereotypes have. But without sufficient power of revitalization in their use, all we're conscious of is that they've been used before. The past weight of past plays and films has crushed Jones's honest intent into patent theatrical manufacture. It's something that has happened before to writers of serious purpose and insufficient talent.

That insufficiency is further apparent in his structures. These are linear, realistic plays: if Jones had written three such plays *well*, it would have been wonderfully refreshing in an age that thinks innovation equals value. But his idea of exposition is to have A ask B some leading questions so that we can get information, or to have B tell A things that A already knows for the same purpose. And all three of his plays are so thin that he has to pad blatantly (the checker game and Josh Mostel's scene in Act I of *Lu Ann*; the scene with the handyman in Act I of *The Oldest Living Graduate*). Structurally worse than these matters is the fact that Jones feels the need for late ironic disclosure in two of the plays. Near the end of *Graduate* we learn that the son has all along owned the property he's been begging his father for, legally awarded him because the old man is mentally incompetent. We're supposed to believe, and can't, that the son has gone through all this begging just because he wants his father to *give* him something; and a drama of dynastic contest is thereby subverted to a weak Oedipal ploy. At the rueful end of *Knights of the White Magnolia* a leading Knight says he has known all along that the lodge is finished; so the whole evening, in which these buffoons have been trying to get a young man to join them and keep them going, becomes retrospectively even more tedious than it has been.

The themes of the three plays are discernible but affectively dull. In *Lu Ann*, the best of the three, the heroine is at the end in more or less the position her mother was in at the start, and what has been outlined for us is the frustration of petty ambitions and banal desires. A possibly important subject, if intensely treated; at Jones's level it produces only glib pathos. In *The Oldest Living Graduate* we get a murky image of the past's false grandeur being ground under the money millstones of the present, a kind of parallel movement to *Knights of the White Magnolia*, in which racism—a component of that grandeur—is shown to be fading away.

The dim effect of these themes, and the tinniness of character portrayal and structure, are rooted in fundamental indecision: how does Jones feel toward his characters? Why has he written about them? Is he being satiric? Is he being sympathetic? Is his purpose, in a sense, historical? Is he deliberately *all* these things? It's impossible to say; and this basic obscurity of intent is what makes his work lurch from point to point, occasionally somewhat moving in a facile way, until it ends in general muddle.

The entire enterprise is at last only a managerial phenomenon: the fact that three new plays by one author were presented in repertory on Broadway. I confess a special disappointment. I had hoped that the Jones trilogy would be a proof of national theatrical vitality, of theatrical decentralization at a high level of quality. But these plays have the opposite effect: they underscore the word "provincial."

Sly Fox, by Larry Gelbart. *New Republic*, January 15, 1977.

O rare Ben Jonson. And getting rarer. When theater people think of his *Volpone* these days, they usually think of a show that could be derived from it, rather than the play itself. Even fifty years ago the Theatre Guild sidestepped Jonson to produce an English translation of Stefan Zweig's German version of *Volpone.* José Ferrer revamped the play in 1947. In 1964, Bert Lahr starred in a musical adaption called *Foxy* (which, curse the luck, I missed), and now comes *Sly Fox* (at the Broadhurst Theatre), a play "based on *Volpone*" written by Larry Gelbart, co-author of *A Funny Thing Happened on the Way to the Forum* and scripter of the TV series "M*A*S*H."

Gelbart has transposed the play to San Francisco in the late nineteenth century and has otherwise altered it drastically, but it's still about a rich miser and his clever servant who fool three would-be inheritors into thinking that the rich man's death is near—and who keep milking the greedy ones for gifts. Some of Gelbart's dialogue is good trapeze work, some of it is only moderately clever. (A naval officer says he has medals "too numerous not to mention.") George C. Scott is vigorously zany as Foxwell J. Sly; and he also doubles as a pistol-packin' judge out of Mark Twain. Hector Elizondo is nimble—and Irish!—as his servant. Of the three avaricious ones, two are very good comics: Jack Gilford and Bob Dishy. (My only real laughs came when Dishy choked between avarice and marital jealousy as he offered his luscious young wife to the supposedly dying Scott, and could hardly get the words out.) Arthur Penn directed the show with more release and relish than I expected from a man whose recent films have been increasingly knotted with psychological convolution.

But most of the time I just watched the patterns being made, pretty decently, and didn't laugh. Partly this is because Jonson's comic morality play has been thinned into farce. It just isn't a farce plot, it's the scaffolding for a savage indictment. More, farce has to be believable in its own landscape in order to be funny, and I just couldn't believe that these were the shenanigans of nineteenth-century San Franciscans. The whole thing smells of wrench and discomfort.

But it did give me an appetite to see Scott in *Volpone*. Or in a real farce, Feydeau or Pinero or any other. He can easily swerve his fierce power into farce channels to make himself a more intensely loping, ravaging Groucho.

Anna Christie, by Eugene O'Neill. *New Republic*, May 7, 1977.

Why won't Liv Ullmann go home? What a strain it is for those like myself who love her to hear her struggling through English. I almost said "see her struggling" because it's quite clear that her unease with language affects her physically. Anyone who has watched *Scenes From a Marriage* on PBS (the subtitled series) must have noted the difference between her English introductions, strangulated, even simpering (and themselves subtitled!), and the controlled, beautifully true acting in Swedish. If she wants to continue a career that began splendidly, she has to resist the con men who want to put her in their pockets. She played Nora unforgettably at the Beaumont, but she had often done *A Doll's House* in Norwegian. If she has done *Anna Christie* before, it doesn't show.

Of course a trouble with her departure, for us, would be that if she confines herself to the Norwegian theater, we won't see her. And a trouble for her with Swedish films now would be that Bergman isn't there. She recently made a film in Germany with him in English, and I have my fingers crossed for both of them. One solution would be Bergman's return to Sweden. But anyway, until she proves otherwise, I wish she would get out of the English language. I don't think there's anything else to say about her performance of Anna.

The production is drearily (not grimly) designed by Ben Edwards, whose lighting fadeouts at the end of acts always leave a last stellar glow on Ullmann. José Quintero, renowned for his direction of O'Neill, doesn't increase that renown here. One instance of his clumsiness: at the end of Act II he has old Chris, Anna's father, sit on the forestage just a few seconds before the curtain descends. Then Chris has to get up and scamper out of the way as the lights dim.

Chris is played by Robert Donley, who gives the best performance: with grizzle and gruffness and a pitiable weakness in himself that he keeps blaming on "dat ole davil sea." Mary McCarty's acting as Marthy, the old scow, is factitious. John Lithgow, the Mat Burke, who is supposed to be all solid bull muscle, a stoker, is lightweight and fluttery. Rescued from the sea in Act II, he enters in overalls and torn undershirt looking like an overgrown Tom Sawyer plucked from a raft. The least that Jane Greenwood, the costume designer, could have done was to put him in a clinging jersey that would have made him seem substantial. But that wouldn't have helped his high-pitched voice; and couldn't Quintero have done something about Lithgow's flaccid hands?

Still, in one view, I was glad to see the play, which I've seen before only in two film versions: silent with Blanche Sweet (1923), and Garbo's first talkie (1930). Its dramaturgy, full of clumsy manipulations, directly contradicts its tonality: the construction is that of the James O'Neill period, here used for the New Realism. But there are some illuminations in it, particularly about O'Neill's subsequent work.

Primarily *Anna Christie* is an example of early twentieth-century American naïveté about realism. The great European dramatists of the nineteenth century had, in general, borne down veristically on the bourgeois life around them. For O'Neill, one of the first American dramatists to respond to that veristic impulse, truth in art was pretty much limited to squalor—just as he had felt that in order to see life he himself had to become a sailor, booze it up, and brothelize. He had treated middle-class life in such plays as *The First Man*, but, in his early days, his best strength was with sailors and stokers and hardscrabble farmers, probably because he believed that their lives were *"realer."* *Anna Christie,* for all its attempt to appear at home in seaminess, is really a bit wide-eyed and adolescent in its awe of the underside. (Compare early Hauptmann and Heijermans.)

Thematically, *Anna Christie* forecasts some aspects of O'Neill's belated maturity. Like *A Touch of the Poet* and *Long Day's Journey into Night* and the lesser *Moon for the Misbegotten*, it is fundamentally about immigrants in America and the psycho-cultural shock of transplantation. And as in *Journey* and *Moon* and *The Iceman Cometh*, the view of women's morality is black-and-white: there are Good Women and Bad Women, easily distinguished. As in the last plays about his family, the hero is Irish Catholic, living by a double standard. Anna says to Mat, who has bragged of his prowess with whores: "You been doing the same thing all your life, picking up a new girl in every port. How're you any better than I was?" His reply: "Is it no shame you have at all?"

That leads to the ending of the play. When it was first produced in 1921, O'Neill was hit by some critics for what they considered an arbitrary happy ending. Mat should not have returned when he found out about Anna's past, they implied, Anna should have slipped back into a brothel. O'Neill said it would have been "obvious and easy" to make the ending tragic, and, though this may have sounded like fancy footwork at the time, I think he was right. First, there would have been no drama, only an unwinding, if the play had consisted simply of revelation to one character of something we've known from the start, with consequent collapse. More important is the fact that the ending states one of O'Neill's favorite themes: redemption. In this case, it's woman's redemption by man. Mat forgives Anna only after she swears on a cross that she really loves him and that she has changed because of her love for him. This conclusion—the roustabout whoring sailor forgiving the whore because she really loves him—has an irony far removed from a conventional happy ending. O'Neill had a clear sense of this irony and (in this play anyway) a limited faith in redemption. He wrote to George Jean Nathan: "The happy ending is merely the comma at the end of a gaudy introductory clause, with the body of the sentence still unwritten. (In fact, I once thought of calling the play *Comma.*)" When you consider what their future is going to be like—Mat off at sea most of the time, Anna alone—the play's seeming final period looks very much like a comma. That irony is the most interesting aspect left in *Anna Christie*.

Otherwise Engaged, by Simon Gray. *New Republic*, June 26, 1977.

If Noël Coward had been born in 1936, like Simon Gray, he might have written Gray comedy. The locus has changed from frivolous London high society to the bookish London middle class, the dramaturgy has shifted from careful plot to seeming meander in order to reflect the New Aimlessness, the dialogue now includes the frank as well as the brittle, but the basic principle is much the same. A writer who can spin light dialogue, like a silkworm, simply spins along until he has enough for an evening, then stops. Despite the latter-day layer of intellectual-social reference and some last-minute emotional tug, the aim is to make two hours pass pleasantly if possible.

Somewhere in the second of the two acts of *Otherwise Engaged* I felt that Gray remembered he needed a conclusion, so he began to slip in some cautions about the hero's emotional aloofness. Until then Gray had simply got laughs out of the sheerly theatrical device (not psychological study) of a hero who does and says little while a string of characters in various frenzies come and pour out their troubles or passions to him. *Butley*, Gray's previous play, was somewhat better because at least Butley was a bastard from word one; his characterization wasn't an obvious afterthought.

The hero is named Simon Hench. (It's as if Edward Albee had named a hero Edward Calvert.) Trying to spend a day alone listening to records, he is interrupted by, in turn and usually more than once, a troublesome tenant from his top floor, his older brother, a literary friend, friend's present girl, another girl's presumable father, and his own wife. The play is like a thread reeling along that, as it comes near its end, is knotted to another thread so that the reeling can go on. No growth, just replacements—a series of "two" scenes between Simon and one person after another. We get the feeling that he's like a quiet ping-pong champ taking on all challengers. (There are as many as three people on stage only when someone happens to enter before the present visitor leaves.)

Tom Courtenay, known from such English films as *The Loneliness of the Long Distance Runner* and *Billy Liar*, makes his U.S. stage début as Simon—and doesn't kid about it: he's on stage the whole evening. Courtenay has calmness and nice timing. Of the others, all American or Canadian, the best is Lynn Milgrim as a sexy intellectual bitch with just the right sexy intellectual insolence.

Harold Pinter's direction itself is shocking. His ear is excellent, but his eye is weak, as he showed earlier this season in his direction of *The Innocents*. He's like a fine radio director with no sense of space or movement. For instance, the two brothers stand face to face for minutes in Simon's living room, talking. I wanted to shout at them to sit down.

But there are some laughs. And at least Gray operates with ease: he doesn't paw at you, *à la* Tom Stoppard, like an unbearable bright child.

Antony and Cleopatra, by William Shakespeare, & *All for Love*, by John Dryden. *New Republic*, September 24, 1977.

It couldn't have been planned, still the effect was wry. The main theater for the Edinburgh Festival is the (refurbished) Assembly Hall in the Divinity School of the university. In the courtyard of the school is a heroic statue of John Knox. Two of the productions in the theater this year were versions of the Antony and Cleopatra story, Shakespeare's and Dryden's. And there, as we trudged up the steps twice to watch passion undo the fevered pair, was the stern figure of Knox, author of the trumpet blast against "the Monstrous Regiment of Women."

This was the 31st Edinburgh Festival but my first visit. It's a huge twenty-day international enterprise: plays, concerts, recitals, dance programs, and exhibitions, (Rex Harrison was scheduled to do a one-man show drawn from Bernard Shaw's theater criticism!) These are only the main events. Much more numerous are the dozens of so-called Fringe events—remember *Beyond the Fringe*?—productions by small groups and university theaters from all over the world. I had the chance to see only two main shows and two exhibits of work by the German photographic genius August Sander (1876-1964).

Shakespeare's *Antony and Cleopatra*, done in heightened Elizabethan dress, was a slightly mitigated disaster. First, the playing space in the Assembly

Hall is too cramped for spectacular plays. But, after we concede that pictorially we were seeing digest versions of the Antony and Cleopatra plays, the direction by Toby Robertson was bumpy. For instance, if ever a stage direction was implicit in Shakespeare, it's that the two lovers should make their first entrance together, close to each other. In my mind's eye I always see them borne in on litters, reclining side by side. Even in these narrow Edinburgh quarters, it was possible to do something other than have Cleopatra come in alone, turn back to the entrance, and *call:* "If it be love indeed, tell me how much"; then have Antony appear in the entrance and call back: "There's beggary in the love that can be reckoned."

Dorothy Tutin, known on Broadway and in films (e.g., *The Importance of Being Earnest*), is a leading British actress of some ability, but her Cleopatra kept reminding me of a bosomy schoolmistress doing the part in front of her class and thereby hinting at things in her private life to titillate her girls. Of fiery majesty, none. Any Cleopatra who cannot whip the bringer of bad news with frightening fury is wasting her and our time.

Alec McCowen, last seen on Broadway in Molière's *The Misanthrope*, himself was ludicrously miscast as Antony: a spindly, screeching Cockney clerk, bewigged and costumed for a party. The one taking performance was by Derek Jacobi, who was so good as Andrei in Laurence Olivier's film of Chekhov's *Three Sisters*. Jacobi played Octavius Caesar and immediately registered distinction.

I had never seen Dryden's *All for Love*. Possibly because expectation was low—Dryden after Shakespeare, for heaven's sake—I had a pretty good time. It would have been better if the director, Frank Hauser, had done a bit of cutting toward the end, particularly in Dryden's extended arrangements to finish with the picture of the dead pair seated next to each other on thrones, but the play has life and some music and was staged, in heightened Restoration dress, as deftly as possible in that space.

John Turner, an experienced actor whom I can't remember seeing before, explicated Antony quite competently. His wife, Barbara Jefford, who was Molly in Joseph Strick's wretched *Ulysses* film, was a bit matronly for the serpent of old Nile—I sometimes thought I heard her girdle stretch—but it was workmanlike work.

What's most interesting about the play, however, is why Dryden wrote it. About this, one must guess. Dryden adored Shakespeare; in fact the title-page of his play (1677) says: "Written in Imitation of Shakespeare's Style." But that, taken alone, is a declaration of insanity: no mentally competent, let alone talented, poet could possibly set out to imitate Shakespeare on a Shakespearean subject without something additional in mind. True, Dryden said in his preface, "By imitating him I have excelled myself," and many artists of many kinds have improved themselves by taking the right masters. (This was Dryden's first tragedy in blank verse after years of writing in rhyme.) But that doesn't quite explain why he invited comparison by choosing the very same subject that a god-poet had chosen.

I infer two reasons. First, the shape. This, as many have noted, is very much a neoclassical play. Dryden pokes at the French in his preface, but Racine cannot have been far from his mind in structural terms (though the language itself imitates Shakespeare, as he says). To this end, Dryden concentrates on Antony and makes the play much more *his* tragedy, in classic mode, rather than a double affair. Dryden even neatens history by bringing Octavia, Antony's wife, to Egypt for a confrontation with her husband and his mistress—a dramatic license exceeded only by Schiller when he had Elizabeth and Mary meet in *Mary Stuart*.

Second, as he says in his preface, Dryden wanted to retell the story with strong moral emphasis: morality was a leading critical concept of the neoclassicists. It's always seemed odd to me that Dr. Johnson, who thought Dryden a great poet, should have held that this play's "one fault" was that Dryden had "recommended . . . conduct which through all ages, the good have censured as vicious, and the bad despised as foolish." That judgment would have puzzled, possibly grieved, Dryden.

So my guess—clarified by this production—is that Dryden "took on" a poet past adjectives, not to compete with him artistically but to make a critical statement and to make it more vividly by using the same subject that the giant had used. The result is far from a dry text. I can't quite see why one should ever do the Dryden play *instead* of Shakespeare; but done in repertory with it, as here, the production proved that the play is playable and that it illuminates some perspectives of change in art and society.

The Dybbuk, by S. Ansky. *New Republic*, January 14, 1978.

The border between life and death is the territory of S. Ansky's famous Yiddish play *The Dybbuk*—in fact, its first title was *Between Two Worlds*. Ansky wrote the play after a three-year study of Jewish lore in the *shtetlekh* of the Ukraine during the second decade of the twentieth century. It was first produced in 1920, shortly after the death of Ansky (a pseudonym for Shloyme Zanvl Rappoport), by the celebrated Vilna Troupe of Lithuania.

Today *The Dybbuk* seems part of the consistent flow of Eastern European Jewish life. But, according to Nahma Sandrow, the latest historian of the Yiddish theater, it was otherwise. In *Vagabond Stars* (Harper & Row, 1977), her recently published and invaluable book, Sandrow says of the play:

> Only a few years before, it would have been impossible, among Jews struggling to free themselves from orthodoxy. Now, on the other hand, as even political ideologies were dimming as an alternative faith, and as life seemed so miserable and dangerous that faith would have been a great comfort, a degree of escapism and nostalgia contributed to the magic of *The Dybbuk*.

In short, the play didn't grow spontaneously out of the assurances of the times; it was a deliberate regenerative effort whose success was heightened by a hunger of the times.

Joseph Chaikin has directed a production at the Newman (in the Public Theater) intended to bring the play closer to *our* times. Chaikin, known internationally for his work with the now-disbanded Open Theater, has used a new translation by Mira Rafalowicz, shaped with Rafalowicz into a new version. The impulses toward the new version, highly condensed and somewhat altered, seem to be those that Jerzy Grotowski followed in his version of Calderón's *The Constant Prince*: to concentrate on modern approaches to acting and directing;

and, through this use of modernity, to strike through to the cultural and mythic roots of the work—to use the new as a way of reaching the old. On both scores this production seems to me only partially successful.

A *dybbuk* is a spirit that haunts the living. The story tells of a poor and devout scholar, Chanon, in love with and loved by a girl named Leah, whose father affiances her to a rich youth. Chanon dies in the anguish of his loss. His spirit is then invited by the unhappy Leah to her wedding, invades her body, and forestalls the wedding. After a painful exorcism, the *dybbuk* of Chanon leaves the body of Leah. She dies, and the lovers are reunited in death.

This may sound like mystical romance—I saw it played as such by the Bucharest Yiddish State Theater on a New York visit—but there are materials in it of much greater depth than *Lucia di Lammermoor* or *Peter Ibbetson*. Chanon is a student of the Kabbalah, a mystic system held to be as old as the Torah itself: it runs alongside the holy books that are open to all but is accessible only to the elect. Chanon is therefore somewhat at odds with the Hassidic Jews among whom he is studying, who warn him against unorthodoxy and the dangers to which he is exposing his soul. He persists: and the weakness brought on by this persistence makes him vulnerable to fatal shock.

Kabbalist teaching places sacred importance on the sexual act, holding that the union of male and female principles, through male and female bodies, is an approach to divinity. The Kabbalist here loses his body before he is able to united with his beloved's body: so his spirit joins her body in a union that is symbolically sexual as well as metaphysical. The dead lover takes her body to prevent a live lover from having her. The mystical and sexual aspects, even Freudian aspects, of such a story are only some of its richnesses. This play, like some of Samuel Beckett's, is a view of values as seen by a soul that is halfway across the life/death border even at the beginning.

Chaikin and Rafalowicz have seen these qualities in *The Dybbuk*, but Chaikin has realized them only tepidly in the production. Bruce Myers is excellent as the exalted Chanon. Jamil Zakkai is strong as Leah's father, and Richard Bauer has some of the necessary force as the exorcising rabbi. But Sonia Zomina plays a grandmother right out of the Bucharest theater tradition, in contrast to the others, and in the key role of Leah, Marcia Jean Kurtz is weak. As a presence, physical and vocal, Kurtz simply doesn't provide what she should provide: the locus of the drama.

The setting, a few vaguely constructivist pieces by Woods Mackintosh, is too open and airy: it allows the enclosed feeling of the play, the *shtetl*-synagogue feeling, to be dissipated. The lighting by Beverly Emmons is either unimaginative or downright harmful. Most of the time the lighting evokes no "colors" at all, no "sculpture"; and why is there a harsh white light on the dead Chanon when he reappears? No, I'm not asking for hokey ghost lighting; still, why that harsh white?

And why does Chaikin have the dead man sitting in his old chair when he comes back to disrupt the wedding? It's comical. Do the dead get tired? In the center is the bride writhing with his *dybbuk* inside her; and there he sits cozily downstage right, close to the audience, in that bright white light, speaking in unison with her. Chaikin's staging, in general, is facile. The opening pageant of Hassids in prayer, bowing and reading; the chorus of women with their Tyrone Guthrie movements in unison: all this is easy and trite picture-making. Some of the staging is even clumsy, like Leah's last backward crawl to join her lover behind her.

Chaikin's production of *The Sea Gull* a few years ago was a calamity. *The Dybbuk* is better, but it's merely mediocre. It does little to alter my opinion of his artistic stature, which is far below the beatification accorded him by his acolytes.

Fefu and Her Friends, by María Irene Fornés. New Republic, February 25, 1978.

In terms of sheer activity, the New York theater is tremendous. If you mean more than Broadway. At the moment (first week in February), there are only twenty-eight shows on Broadway, with only three openings for the month. But the total of Off-Broadway and Off-Off Broadway productions is 118, with much more to come in the month. I don't need to say that I don't see all of them, but maybe I ought to note that I see a great many more than I report on and thus have a fair sense of the pulse and the body. What follows is a review of a bruited production in the busy world away from the not-so-Great White Way.

The author of *Fefu and Her Friends*, María Irene Fornés, is herself one of the stalwarts of Away-from-Broadway theater. A Cuban émigré, she has been writing since 1961 and has won admirers for such plays as *Tango Palace, Dr. Kheal*, and the book of the musical *Promenade*. Almost as much as for her writing, she is admired as a moral force in the non-Broadway theater, organizing, supporting, and working at every kind of job to help. (I once saw—and liked—part of a film she never finished, made with a dancer.) My admiration for her is strong in all ways except the most relevant one, her writing. To me it has the defects of self-reliant sincerity—nothing much more comes to me from the stage than that the author utterly believes what she is saying. The tone of the language tends to the flat—the purplish passages in this new play are egregious and troubling—the characterizations and the themes are all collusively tacit: that is, they ask for a coterie audience that will grant in advance the depth and humor of the work. This is not pretense by Fornés: it is just insufficiency.

Fefu was first produced in May 1977 at an Off-Off Broadway theater, where I saw it; has now been moved in slightly altered form to an Off-Broadway theater, where I have seen it again; and has been published in the Winter 1978 issue of *Performing Arts Journal*, where I have read it. It has been highly praised by many, including Susan Sontag. After three visits, it remains a work of no consequence for me.

It's a house-party play set in New England, 1935. Fornés must know that the house-party play is a '30s cliché (J. B. Priestley's *Dangerous Corner*, etc.); but I think she thinks that she has moved *through* the cliché by using only female characters and by having no plot. The only coherent of the action is the fact that an older woman, Fefu, has invited some younger women to her home to plan an appeal for funds for some educational project. The point, really, is supposed to be the characters of these women, their relationships, and the natural community of women. All these matters are too ill-developed to be rewarding.

Two further elements hurt. First, symbolism—the first instance I can remember in Fornés's writing where she has drawn on the overtly poetic, and it's painfully bad. Early in the play Fefu fires a shotgun out of a French window at her husband, who is never seen. It's a family game; the gun is—probably—always loaded with blanks. One of the guests is a hysterical paralytic (played by Margaret Harrington, the only interesting performance) who hasn't walked since a similar incident some time ago, whom we see walk mysteriously in one scene, and who is symbolically shot at the end when Fefu kills a rabbit outside. In all this material, Fornés's reliance on her simplicity, which anyway I have thought misjudged, gives place to nervous grabs at portentous ambiguity.

The other element is a device involving the audience. The opening and closing sections of the play are watched conventionally from our seats. In the middle of the play the audience is divided into four groups, each with a shepherd, and each group is taken to four rooms in Fefu's house. Each group sees a scene in each room—it's the same scene in each room done four times for each of the four groups that visit. Then the four groups, each having witnessed each of the four scenes, go back to their seats to become again the audience *en bloc*.

I doubt very much that Fornés thought of this four-part walk-around as a gimmick. Probably it signified for her an exploration of simultaneity (since all four scenes are done simultaneously four times for the four groups), a union of play and audience through kinetics, some adoption by the theater of cinematic flexibility and montage. But since the small content in these scenes would in no way be damaged by traditional serial construction, since this insistence on reminding us that people actually have related/unrelated conversations simultaneously in different rooms of the same house is banal, we are left with the *feeling* of gimmick, intended or not—the feeling that mechanical aggrandizement has been impasted on a play with the specific gravity of a novel by Lois Gould or a film by Paul Mazursky.

Fornés directed—harmlessly, I would say, except that most of her casting is poor. She has been so anxious to have her people "unactorish" that they are figuratively invisible, except for Harrington and (differently) for Rebecca Schull, the Fefu, who confuses smugness with maturity.

***A Prayer for My Daughter*, by Thomas Babe. *New Republic*, February 25, 1978.**

Joseph Papp's productions continue apace at his various auditoria in the Public Theater, and if pace were all, be would be the Reinhardt of our day. Instead, he is the R. H. Macy of the theater—lots of stuff, attractively advertised, lavishly poured forth, with something for almost everyone but not much for the most demanding.

Among the plays I've seen so far this season at Papp theaters is *The Mandrake*, an adaptation of Machiavelli's *Mandragola* by Wallace Shawn, directed by Wilford Leach and done with all the elegance and skill of a boozy, bawdy faculty romp at a third-rate college. There is no intermission in this two-hour show, and after an hour I prayed for a blackout that would at least give me a chance to leave. My prayer was answered. (I waited long enough to get a glimpse of the girl who is heralded throughout the first hour as wonderfully beautiful. No comment.)

I also saw (one act of) *Landscape of the Body*, one of John Guare's Saroyanesque gushings—gushings that have been pampered so long, one can doubt that Guare now has enough discipline to organize his modest talent into a realized play. *Landscape* made some fanciful symbolic use of a beautiful young woman and a detective pursuing her.

This is the season for symbolic detectives. Only a few weeks before the opening at the Anspacher of Thomas Babe's *A Prayer for My Daughter*, I saw another writer's play directed by Babe at the busy Playwrights' Horizons on far West 42nd Street—*Two Small Bodies*, by Neal Bell. It was a two-character play about a detective and a woman suspected of murder (based on Alice Crimmins), and it was supposed to float up into some an stratosphere of guilt-and-purification. All it did for me was to make me glad of the return of Catherine Burns (remember the film *Last Summer*?), whose vitality triumphed over Babe's geometric direction.

Now comes Babe's own play, *Prayer*, which too is about detectives and suspected criminals and mystic evocations therefrom. July Fourth in a police station. (*En garde*, symbol hounds!) Two detectives, one fat and one thin. (That, see, is contrast.) They have arrested two homosexuals on suspicion of murder, one a middle-aged guru-type, the other a young, druggy, wistful gay-whore type. (Savior and Magdalene, perhaps, up to date and *à la mode*.)

Of the four performances, three are imitations of film and TV stock-in-trade, with Jeffrey De Munn most offensive as a fake Al Pacino detective. Only Laurence Luckinbill as the guru acts moderately respectably, and perhaps that's because his character is so muddy that there was no stereotype for him or his director to refer to. That director was Robert Allen Ackerman, who is interested primarily in electricity but whose voltage is very low.

As for the script, aside from the labored dialogue, if a play can be considered apart from the words through which it lives, aside from the creaky construction to leave certain duos alone on stage together at various times, the play is governed by an undergraduate impulse to inflate. Instead of, for instance, writing a play about two detectives and two homosexuals that, by bearing down intensely on who they are and how they interact, *revealed* large themes, Babe, with the swagger of the writer who has big ambition but small insight, uses the four men simply as armatures onto which he plasters lashings of Meaning. I won't detail the plot: I'll simply record that the fat detective's daughter is threatening suicide over the phone, that the young gay strips naked in the second act and hugs the fat man, who embraces him as his "daughter," that the youth seizes the fat man's pistol tucked in the back of his belt and shoots the detective in the rump, and that the fat man sits there with a bullet in his ass while the news comes in on the phone of his daughter's death and while spacious-but-terse pronouncements about good and evil are pronounced.

I've seen two previous Babe plays at one or another of Papp's theaters: *Kid Champion*, which struggled turgidly to turn a rock star into a symbol of Our Rotten Age; and *Rebel Women*, a Civil War drama in which a Southern belle matched wits (among other things) with General Sherman in order to save her husband, a drama with somewhat less credibility than *Tosca*.

The Public Theater is unquestionably a nursery for young playwrights, but many of them are so cosseted that they remain infants.

A History of the American Film, by Christopher Durang. *New Republic*, April 22, 1978.

A History of the American Film is the wrong title. It ought to be called *A History of American Film Skits.* From the very opening (at the ANTA [American National Theatre and Academy]), with its burlesque of Lillian Gish rocking the cradle in *Intolerance*, right through every predictable stereotype of character and situation, right through Cagney and Bogart and *Casablanca* and *Citizen Kane* to the present day, this is an expensively produced rehash of jokes seen earlier and often better. Comden and Green were doing it in *Billion Dollar Baby* in 1945 (and they surely weren't the first), and it's been going on pretty steadily since then, particularly on television. Sid Caesar, Red Skelton, Lucille Ball, and Carol Burnett are only the first names that come to mind. Christopher Durang, the author of this highly-heralded show, and his composer Mel Marvin, have nothing to add—except a tenuous fantastic story to try to link the skits together.

To be clear: it's not satire on Hollywood life, like *Once in a Lifetime*. It's burlesque of things that Hollywood has implanted in the world's store of images: Busby Berkeley numbers, patriotic numbers, religious numbers, and so on. Satire is the first infirmity of youthful minds. Irreverence is one of the most precious gifts that new writers can give us, but imitative irreverence is pretty depressing.

April Shawhan does well enough as the heroine who goes from braids to bra-less and Bryan Clark is sharp in a variety of character roles, but Gary Bayer lacks force in a variety of heroes. Swoosie Kurtz herself is turning from the promising actress she was only a few years ago into a one-woman wisecrack business. I'm afraid we're watching another Elaine Stritch in the making. The director, David Chambers, threw a lot of bustle into the enterprise, but then there wasn't much else to throw in. The program credits the "sound design" to Lou Shapiro. I assume that Shapiro is hard of hearing and has pitched the amplification of every smallest line to help those similarly afflicted.

Ballroom, by Michael Bennett. *New Republic*, January 27, 1979.

Ballroom (at the Majestic Theatre) is the new musical by Michael Bennett, who devised *A Chorus Line*. Two fundamental faults keep it from the entertainment value of the previous show. *A Chorus Line*, it seemed to me, derived from Off-Off-Broadway "matrix" techniques, and was possibly suggested specifically by Joseph Chaikin's *Mutation Show*, with the performers' lives providing the material of the show, with the line of performers holding up large photographs of themselves before their faces. *A Chorus Line* wanted to tug heartstrings, all right, but at least it had some seeming self-reflexive materiality. *Ballroom* derives from a sentimental TV drama by Jerome Kass in the *Marty* vein: homely folks or old folks or both need love, too. It makes a beeline for the heart, so it doesn't get there.

The second basic fault is the setting of the story, a Roseland-type ballroom for older folks in the Bronx. Apparently Bennett chose this subject because, as in *A Chorus Line*, the natural activity in the place is dancing. (Again Robin Wagner supplies a mirrored setting in an attempt at the Chinese-boxes effect—a dancing show about a dancing place.) But in the first show the *characters* were dancers; here they are only people, dancing. So most of the dancing is only ballroom dancing, hyped up a bit. Much of the time we watch Dorothy Loudon, the lonely middle-aged heroine, dancing with Vincent Gardenia, the lonely middle-aged hero, on their way to romance. I can see the likes of Loudon's dancing on any dance floor. I can see better than Gardenia anywhere. Who wants to watch *them* dance for much of two hours?

The music, by Billy Goldenberg, isn't bad. The book, by various visible and invisible hands, is. As I listened, I kept seeing typescript pages in different colors, for rewrites and inserts.

If Bennett wants to go on doing dance-musicals about dance-places, why doesn't he stick to professional dance-places?

The Bacchae, by Euripides. *Saturday Review*, November 1980.

Greek tragedy lies on our theater today like an outsized mantle, so rich and big that it's a mite embarrassing. As literature, the plays beggar praise; and a continual flow of new translations simultaneously brings us closer to the originals (as we are told) and brings them closer to our imaginative embrace (as we can see). But on stage, if they are to accomplish the very same ends, they present problems of accommodation. Our theater, faced with these titanic works, has to devise strategies to encompass them.

Shakespeare's tragedies try the outer edge of our brains and spirits, and in that trial they exalt our humanity. Greek tragedies seem to *reside* on those outer edges; they exist in the territory that a *Hamlet* or *King Lear* must travel to. This is not to pronounce that the Greek plays are greater than Shakespeare's—which isn't an opinion one tosses off *en passant*. But Shakespeare's tragedies live within conventions of society and theater much nearer to our own. With the Greek plays, if they are to bless us as they can, we must mediate, not through reduction but through awareness that the community of which these plays are emblems no longer exists, and that compensations must be found by a theater that is not truly emblematic of any comparable whole community.

Michael Cacoyannis, the Greek-born and British-trained director, is well aware of this need for strategies, and he fills that need. I'm not speaking here of his films of the tragedies but of his stage productions that I've seen: *The Trojan Women* (1963) and *Iphigenia in Aulis* (1967), both at New York's downtown Circle in the Square, and now a third Euripides work, *The Bacchae*, at the uptown Circle in the Square. The Cacoyannis strategy is simple. He begins with the fact that virtually nothing is known about the way these plays were first done or about the music and dance that were integral to them. Then, out of study and commitment, he *invents* an Athenian theater that is internally consistent, that is just stylized enough to seem ancient and strange but not so far off that the plays seem like unwrapped sarcophagi—a theater exalted in tonality yet close enough so that our actors can operate in it and we can comprehend.

Other strategies work differently, in some ways more effectively. Since Cacoyannis's earlier direction, the best Greek productions I've seen were *Medea*, *Electra*, and *The Trojan Women*, done at La Mama by Andrei Serban with music by Elizabeth Swados. Over several years I saw each play eight times and would go again tonight if I could. The Serban strategy was, essentially, not to perform the plays but to perform the myths on which the plays were based and which were very old when the plays were written. The cast spoke no English, mostly

Greek with some Latin, so that we concentrated on massive sculptural ideas, visual and emotional, not on character or nuance.

The Cacoyannis strategy doesn't come near the immensity of Serban, but he gives us much greater refinement of detail. And it's helpful in *The Bacchae*, this terrible tragedy of a city's denial of a god and that god's revenge. Because the city of Thebes refuses to recognize the divinity of Dionysus (or Bacchus), the god entices the women of Thebes—led by Agave, the king's mother—into revels on a nearby mountain. When the king, Pentheus, tries to imprison Dionysus as a fraudulent intruder, the god tricks Pentheus into dressing as a woman so that he can spy on the women's revels. The women discover the spy and, in their ecstasy, rend him to pieces. Agave, still ecstatic, comes back to Thebes bearing the head of her own son, which she thinks is a lion's head. At last the Bacchic frenzy leaves her, and she realizes what has happened. Relentless, Dionysus proclaims that his punishment of her and her son is just.

Now, since Dionysus/Bacchus is the god of wine and love and joy, it would be easy to treat the play as a pat Freudian analogy—the body's revenge for the denial of the body. Certainly that truth is included, along with other truths, but Cacoyannis sees *The Bacchae* as a classic drama of those truths to which Freud is a latter-day testimony.

As the first step toward bringing the play close while keeping it large, he has made a new translation, condensed but not synoptic. Sometimes it slips into the uneasy colloquial ("all dolled up"), but generally the language cuts in large-scale sweeps with a modern edge. The setting by John Conklin is a simple black floor, for a stage surrounded by the audience, with entrances at the usual Circle apertures and with silver trapdoors in the center for the appearance of the god and the chorus of women—who are Bacchae (his devotees) from Asia. The lighting by Pat Collins underscores the Cacoyannis approach: it suggests grandeur yet it often lays in shadow and highlight to concentrate attention and almost to suggest cinematic focus.

The cast is mostly excellent. To get the worst over at once, that superb actress Irene Papas is disappointing as Agave. True, she has the most difficult part: one long scene at the end, in which she enters dionysically rapt holding her son's head, then has a dialogue with her anguished father (the admirable Philip Bosco), then comes slowly to her senses, and, after all that, must plumb and convey horror. This is one scene that needed more graduated lighting, more support with sound and music. Perhaps it was the lack of them that forced Papas to strain, to use the upper third of her voice so much. Still, knowing this wonderful woman's gifts, I can't believe that her performance won't come under firmer control.

For the rest, nothing but praise.

Cacoyannis has continued his strategy by casting the Asian Bacchae mostly with black women. (The one white woman is not only egregious but the weakest of the group.) Their movement and speech fit sinuously their devotion to their god. And two young men, both new to New York, are extraordinary. John Noah Hertzler, as Pentheus, has resonance and poise. Pentheus is not a character in the modern sense: he is a statement, an attitude, until prurient curiosity undoes him. Hertzler seems to sense this, seems to bring with him a ground for his anger at Dionysus and works that anger through differing shades, so that we get a believable, blinkered young monarch.

Christopher Rich, the Dionysus, makes a stunning début. Rich, one might say, is Cacoyannis's best strategy to connect us to the play, and he does it—has to do it—from Moment One. It opens "cold": Dionysus steps out, tells us that he is a god, that he is being mistreated, and that he is angry, and we must believe it all at once or you might as well scrap the rest of the play. To do it either in remote rhetoric or apologetic vernacular would kill it. Rich does neither; he is immediately vivid, golden, graceful, clear, commanding. He fixes in his body and in his reading the divine made visible and credible. It's all the more powerful because Rich suggests the mysterious androgyne, the lithe and sensuous feminine (not effeminate) combined with male force. No American actor other than Christopher Walken has that combination or shows such possibilities for a fine classical-modern career. Our theater being what it is, let us all cross our fingers for Rich.

But not before applauding Cacoyannis. His major moment—the Agave scene—is incompletely realized; but his discovery of Rich, his use of Hertzler and the others, his sense of how to "place" a Greek play for modern viewers, all put us in his debt.

Coming Attractions, by Ted Tally. *Saturday Review*, March 1981.

Coming Attractions, by Ted Tally, has been called by critics a funny satire. This is not quite true. It's funny, all right, but Tally takes some standard satirizable aspects of American life—TV, celebrity-selling, beauty contests, etc.—and shows that they are now far beyond satire.

When the play begins, four bound and gagged hostages are sitting on stage, and Lonnie, a young fellow with a gun, is shouting his demands to cops out front. (What he wants is celebrity. Among his demands: a personal appearance on "60 Minutes.") A man with a tape recorder, apparently a reporter, tells the cops he's going in to talk to the kid. Lonnie is happy; he thinks he's going to get publicity on the networks. "Networks!" says the man. "For four lousy hostages?" The networks are off covering someone who's holding fifty hostages. But the man can help Lonnie. He's not a reporter, he's a talent agent named Manny, and he knows how they can both cash in—TV, books, movies.

Manny devises a persona for Lonnie, with a skeleton costume, and sends him out to shoot people who answer their doorbells. ("Trick or treat?" Blam.) Lonnie becomes the fabulous Halloween Killer, shoots twenty-eight people, is captured, and goes through legal maneuvers that assure him plenty of time before he comes to trial. Meanwhile, he does television shows and, disguised as Miss Wyoming, he crashes the Atlantic City beauty pageant to kill Miss America on camera. ("I'm talking network," says Manny, who planned it. "I'm talking prime time.") But a fatal flaw cracks Lonnie: he falls in love—with Miss America.

It does him in. After zooming through the show-biz stratosphere, after showering show-biz benefits on everyone he meets—each witness, each cop writes a bestseller—Lonnie ends in the electric chair. On prime time TV, of course. He dies "live." (Just before airtime, the warden asks the television director some Actors' Studio questions about his "role.") And this funny show ends with Lonnie frying.

The pitch of the story, as you can see, is insane, but it is only dailiness goosed a little higher. *Coming Attractions* isn't a chuckly old-fashioned nudge like

Kaufman & Hart's *Once in a Lifetime*; it isn't a grab for titters like Christopher Durang's recent spoof of chic New-Yorkniks, *Beyond Therapy*. These could be called satire, which, in H. W. Fowler's definition, aims at amendment. Tally is describing a condition that *is*—exaggerated to underline a blackly comic reality—without the slightest hope of amendment.

His method is touched-up mimesis. Before you go to the theater, you turn on the TV news and see, in this order, a murder in Northern Ireland, a sexy blonde selling you new cars, and deaths by arson in Jersey City. Then you go to *Coming Attractions* and hear Tally's newscaster say: "We interrupt 'Celebrity Funeral' to bring you a news update." Which is the satire?

Tally's ultimate triumph is his initial perception. He sees that most of the usual American subjects for cartooning have now been made corny by life, not cartoonists; and he uses that fact as his launching pad.

From the start of his career, Tally has shown a sense of the *Zeitgeist*. His first play, *Terra Nova*, written in 1976 while he was a student at the Yale School of Drama and performed since then in many theaters in several countries, is about Scott of the Antarctic. When I heard the subject, before I saw the play, I thought: "The 'Vietnam time' is over. A young man has written a play about courage." Authentically, with no thought of fashion-mongering, Tally had responded to social atmospherics. *Coming Attractions* proceeds from the same core of aptness, confronting some acceptances that have become central in our culture.

The show is not all Tally. A number of songs, music by Jack Feldman, lyrics by Bruce Sussman and Feldman, fit their moments neatly. The theater is the Off-Broadway Playwrights' Horizons, and the setting by Andrew Jackness makes more than the most of the tiny stage. Rotating panels on both sides, sliding panels in the back give the illusion of space spilling in. André Ernotte directed—with assistance on the musical numbers from Theodore Pappas—and Ernotte surprised me. I've seen several of his productions, also his Belgian film *High Street*, and thought them strained or sluggish. *Coming Attractions* never strains to be vivid, is never dull. Ernotte's staging is fluent and deft, and his casting was perfect.

Griffin Dunne as Lonnie and Larry Block as Manny do very well. One part each. But the sparklers are the other five people who play a lot of parts with the specially enjoyable freehand dash of sharp skit performers. Christine Baranski as Miss America, June Gable as a TV reporter, Jonathan Hadary as a pop star, Dan Strickler as a prosecutor, Allan Wasserman as a smiling Arab terrorist in a guest spot on a variety show—and all of them do much more—are cruelly right. *Coming Attractions* is about repulsions, not attractions, and they aren't coming, they are here. Tally is a Jeremiah disguised, wittily, as a wit.

Key Exchange, by Kevin Wade. *Saturday Review*, September 1981.

If Lanford Wilson in his plays pretends to grasp more than he can, a newcomer named Kevin Wade grasps more than he pretends to. *Key Exchange* (at the W.P.A. Theater, Off-Off Broadway) is, and is something more than, a bright little comedy about three young New Yorkers, two men and a woman, who bike on weekends in Central Park. The dialogue is in that partly secret language that every young generation invents to keep older people out—or at least to make elders look foolish if they use it. Wade flourishes it with wit and point.

Brooke Adams, familiar from *Days of Heaven* and other films, is a photographer having an affair with Ben Masters, a novelist. In the park they meet Mark Blum, an ad copywriter, biking alone on the day after his wedding. In a neat mosaic of weekend meetings on the bike path, we follow the seesaw Adams-Masters liaison and Blum's reports on his marital troubles. All three of them are concentrated on their bodies. We see them only in biking shorts, massaging or exercising or resting to ride again. When they don't talk about biking, they talk mostly about sex, sportively or quite seriously.

Adams is hungry for commitment (something Blum already has encountered in marriage), a term that gives Masters the shakes. Her standards were set by her father's devotion to her dying mother, described in touching detail, standards of love *in the past*. But Masters says: "I want to have my cake and have my cupcake, too." He wants Adams and himself to have other dates. Finally he gets her to accept his code so that they can continue; paradoxically, it splits them, though they still care for each other. Blum meanwhile suffers through his wife's sudden desertion of him for another man, then her sudden return... for how long?

The exchange of keys is a move by two people toward commitment, and the risk of commitment is a recurrent theme these days in plays and films by young people. (Wendy Wasserstein's play *Isn't It Romantic*, Albert Brooks's film *Modern Romance*.) Commitment means the future, and it's the profound lack of confidence in the future that seeps through Wade's chitchat. Lightly but implicatively he sketches the tip of a chilling iceberg, and his winning cast plays his comedy with that knowledge. I'd bet that the intelligent director, Barnet Kellman, started with the depths and worked upward to the surface brightness. Kellman's closing touch translates Antonioni into American. Adams and Masters part. He's facing front; she wheels her bike out toward the back, then pauses to wave goodbye backward over her shoulder. She doesn't look at him, and she doesn't see that he doesn't see the gesture. It's a tiny mod epiphany.

Crimes of the Heart, by Beth Henley. *Saturday Review*, January 1982.

The Pulitzer Prize for drama is looking up—a little, anyway. Since 1957, when it was given to America's greatest play, O'Neill's *Long Day's Journey into Night*, the only time the Pulitzer award hasn't made me cringe at least slightly was when it went to Sam Shepard's *Buried Child* two years ago. This year it has gone to a first play by Beth Henley called *Crimes of the Heart*, produced Off-Broadway in 1980 and now moved to Broadway, in which a limited but authentic dramatist's voice can be heard.

The success of the play is, to some extent, a victory over this production. Henley is a Mississippian who writes about small-town life in her home state, and this has been taken as an almost arbitrary injunction to treat her play like one more slice off a standard Southern loaf. In point of fact, Henley is a quietly tenacious pursuer of horror, a writer shaken into pitch-black comedy by the buried terrors in the superficially smooth, tabby-cat lives she has seen. The trouble with the tone of this production directed by Melvin Bernhardt is that, for too long a time, it leads you to expect one more hyper-detailed, gabby decline into hominy-grits entropy. The play has figuratively to fight its way through the opening half hour or so of this production before it lets the author establish what she is getting at—that, under this molasses meandering, there is madness, stark madness; and that the only factor that keeps these characters out of asylums (insofar as they *are* kept out) is their mad humor about themselves, which translates almost chillingly into our looking at them as comic.

The play concerns three sisters. (Forget Chekhov—there's no connection.) They are played by: Lizbeth MacKay as the sister who lives in the house whose kitchen we see; Mia Dillon as the sister who has just returned from her home with her husband nearby; and Mary Beth Hurt as the sister who has just returned from Los Angeles. As the play opens, MacKay comes into the (mammoth) kitchen, puts a birthday candle in a cookie, and silently sings "Happy Birthday"; and my teeth clenched in readiness for another drawling ode to Loneliness. But in contrast to this opening tonality, here are some of the matters that come to light. MacKay is much more upset about the death of an old horse than by her grandfather's stroke and coma. Dillon has shot her husband because she doesn't like his looks and, while he lay bleeding, offered him lemonade; as part of his criminal prosecution of her, he sends her lawyer some photographs of her taken *in flagrante* with a fifteen-year-old black boy; she says the pictures will ruin her but manages to forget about them completely for twenty minutes or so. And Hurt, who comes on in a mini-skirt as the standard Hollywood returnee who has been lying to her family about her career, discloses that she has been hospitalized for psychosis. In short, what begins as more wistfulness under the wisteria eventually becomes a compound of giggle and decay on the edge of an abyss.

I take Henley as serious, not as a parodist—a lightweight daughter of Faulkner rather than a diluted Tennessee Williams. This opinion is strengthened by a reading of her subsequent play, *The Miss Firecracker Contest*, which has already been produced in Dallas and in Jackson, Mississippi, and which continues to probe the grotesquely comic vein of horror in a small town in her state. And still another play of hers, *The Wake of Jamey Foster*, will have been produced in Hartford, Connecticut, by the time this review appears. She is twenty-nine.

To praise Dillon, MacKay, and Hurt would be like praising a jeweler for fixing a watch: if he can't do that, what *can* he do? For competent actors, these roles are easy—which is to compliment the author, not knock the performers. Bernhardt's approach, to let the horror seep in slowly, is better suited to conventional suspense than to a play that needs an index of its import from the start. It isn't blatant weirdness that's wanted, but something akin to what Eric Thompson did with Ayckbourn's *Absurd Person Singular* or Charles Marowitz (in London) with Orton's *Loot*, where we were subtly but swiftly informed that the play was stranger than it seemed to be.

Crimes of the Heart has faults. Too much of the action occurs offstage and is reported. Frequently Henley uses an irritating device: Character B repeats the last words of what Character A has just said. ("She shot him in the stomach." "In the stomach?") But she has struck a rich, if not inexhaustible, dramatic lode: the tension between the fierce lurking lunacy underlying the small-town life she knows so well and the sunny surface that tries to accommodate it. *Crimes* moves to no real resolution, but this is part of its power. It presents a condition that, in minuscule, implies much about the state of the world, as well as the state of

Mississippi, and about human chaos; it says, "Resolution is not my business. Ludicrously horrifying honesty is."

The Dining Room, by A. R. Gurney. *Saturday Review*, May 1982.

A. R. Gurney has written the Gentile counterpart of James Lapine's *Table Settings*, which was done at the same New York theater (Playwrights' Horizons) two years ago. Lapine's play was about an urban Jewish family and centered on their dining table—a quite conventional family play, the script of which had been figuratively cut into snippets and shuffled so that the unconventional time sequences could seem to lend it depth. Gurney has done virtually the same thing with a conventional chronicle play about a New England Wasp home. To the dining room come the different generations of a family, friends, lovers, prospective new owners of the house; but instead of a chronological parade, we see their appearances overlap and interchange, see them older before younger, see a character from a succeeding scene enter unseen by other actors in the current scene so that there's "comment." All this hocus-pocus, in itself almost a convention by now, has been applied to banal characters, complications, and dialogue. If you taped a month of a soap opera, then jumbled the tapes, you'd get—with a slightly lower order of writing—much the same result.

All the cast do well enough, but not doing well in these familiar roles would be—or ought to be—cause for withdrawal of their Actors' Equity cards. Likewise for the director, David Trainer. My sole astonishment is at Gurney's energy in being able to address this mass of platitudes, spurred only by the technical trickery of the time mix.

A Soldier's Play, by Charles Fuller, & *Colored People's Time*, by Leslie Lee. *Saturday Review*, June 1982.

This year's Pulitzer Prize in drama went to Charles Fuller for *A Soldier's Play*, but in my view it really went to the Negro Ensemble Company, which produced it. Fuller's play is another mediocrity—a very attenuated work, indeed. A black soldier is murdered on a Louisiana army base in 1944, and the investigation is conducted by a black captain. After much mechanical dragging-about and some pleasant musical interludes, it's finally revealed that the murder was committed because of racism among blacks—the dislike of some blacks for the failure of other blacks to "rise" by basically white standards. Thus this intra-black enmity is a not-so-oblique result of subservience to white racism. A pungent point—dated, I hope—and worth, in the context given here, a good half-hour "historical" play. Instead, we get two hours of "Come in, sit down, tell me where you were on Thursday night" prolongations.

What chiefly holds the play together, insofar as it *is* held, is Adolph Caesar's raspingly fierce performance as a tough professional-army sergeant. But all in the cast are good and do their enriching best. Which is why I think the Negro Ensemble Company is the real winner of the prize. Its plays are usually mediocre, never better, occasionally worse; but the actors are generally excellent and seem to improve the plays. If they could find scripts as good as they themselves are, the NEC would be one of the outstanding theaters in the English-speaking world.

The company proves it again in a subsequent production, another mediocre play: *Colored People's Time*, by Leslie Lee. The title is a phrase often abbreviated to "C.P.T." among black people; it means that they live by private clocks, not necessarily matched to white chronometry. Lee's play consists of thirteen scenes intended to give a capsule history of black people in America as seen from the inside; it begins with runaway slaves in 1859 and ends with the victory in the Montgomery, Alabama, bus boycott of 1956. Not one whit of enlightenment, in any historical or dramaturgic sense, comes from the script, but a good deal of humanity, understanding, suffering, and pride comes from the nine versatile actors. Outstanding among them, each in several roles, are the NEC stalwart L. Scott Caldwell, the appealing Debbi Morgan, and the reliable Charles H. Patterson. The scenery by Felix E. Cochren and the lighting by Shirley Prendergast are, as is too often the case with NEC productions, so unremarkable that they must be remarked on.

Colored People's Time was directed by Horacena J. Taylor, whose work I've previously admired in *Nevis Mountain Dew* and *Old Phantoms* and who seems to me the Negro Ensemble Company's premier director. Under her hand the tiny stage of the Off-Broadway Cherry Lane Theater is never stifled, and each of the seedling scenes flowers as far as it can.

La Cage aux Folles, by Harvey Fierstein. *Saturday Review*, November-December 1983.

Nothing in our theater is quite like the experience of attending a Broadway smash hit. The audience seems to ascend from enjoyment to quivering excitement, and if the show is a musical, which the biggest hits usually are, it keeps ascending into the mystically communal. Apparently this is the closest that an American audience can come to what Athenians felt at the Theater of Dionysus in the fourth century B.C.: union through exaltation by the events on the stage.

At *La Cage aux Folles*, the near-frenzy that tingled through the huge auditorium during the show, the rapture with which the audience responded to every purportedly comic or emotional line, to every musical number, even to the costumes and scenery, gave me a great deal more pleasure than the show itself. Dionysus might well have thought the occasion unworthy, but he couldn't have quarreled much with the effect. The ecstasy went even further. When we all came out of the Palace Theatre after the show, a small crowd had gathered to watch us. It wasn't opening night; there were no celebrities and flashbulbs. People just wanted to gaze enviously at the elect group that had been admitted to the temple, that had been privileged to witness the most desirable rite that Broadway currently offers.

Well, what *is* this wonder of the age, which had huge box-office lines before it reached New York, which seemed divinely ordained as a smasheroo even before it opened out of town? It turns out to be a paradox: an up-to-the-minute subject in comfy, old-fashioned garb. That subject is gay rights, the right to gay life. The structure of the show, its song and dance and the architecture of its book, would have delighted your grandparents.

Those who saw the popular French film on which the show is based will be less surprised at the paradox, because the film itself was a conventional farce with an unconventional twist. A young Frenchman is bringing his fiancée and her stuffy parents home to dinner with his father, who owns a nightclub in St. Tropez. Father lives with his club's star, who, in farces of the past, would have been, say, a stripper. The complications would have come from disguising the stripper as a *Hausfrau* to fool the prospective in-laws. Here "she" is a transvestite, a drag queen called Zaza. (The show's title means "cage of queens.") So the problem is to pass "her" off as a him, a pal. A couple of decades ago, the club owner had a heterosexual fling, hence the son; since then, he and Zaza have been father and "mother" to the boy, and now Zaza's devoted, "maternal" self must be shunted aside. Feelings are hurt; troubles, as troubles will, ensue.

That's the nub of the musical's story, too, and it's so thin, conflict is so long delayed, that a stopgap dramatic moment has to be whipped up to bring down the Act I curtain, a conflict so flimsy that it's resolved six minutes into Act II.

Stock though the show's texture is, much of it is competent Broadway trade goods, professionally turned out. The songs by Jerry Herman are not up to his *Mame* level, thus are automatically below his *Hello, Dolly!* level, but he's a veteran Main Street tailor of standard patterns. He knows how to fashion the expected *shapes* of musical numbers, and if his melodic invention is not what it has been—possibly excepting "With You on My Arm"—Herman, helped by Jim Tyler's adroit orchestrations, delivers a score that is tolerable without being memorable.

Arthur Laurents, who directed, has done such work before, though he is better known as a playwright (*The Time of the Cuckoo, Home of the Brave*) and as author of books for musicals (*West Side Story, Hallelujah, Baby!*). Here Laurents has shopped up a batch of trite delayed turns and poignant exits, mellow moments and carpentered climaxes, as if from a mail-order catalogue for directors. Despite his dismal staging, however, he gets a passable performance from Gene Barry (yes, Bat Masterson of TV) as the "husband" of the middle-aged homosexual pair; Barry comes across as the ace used-car salesman of all time. Laurents gets an even better performance from George Hearn as Zaza, the "wife." Hearn deals smoothly with the external feminine aspects—gesture, movement, and management of clothes, including spiked heels—and, more important, he has enough insight into Zaza's drag character to give his acting a sometimes touching verity.

John Weiner, as Barry's affianced son, is a walking declaration of industrial hardship—current hardship in the theatrical industry. So few musicals are produced these days that there's only a small corps of available juveniles from which to select. Hence, I suppose, Weiner. On the other hand, the older generation is also cornily represented by Jay Garner as the stuffy future father-in-law.

The chorus line of a dozen show "girls" (show persons?), the dancers in the St. Tropez nightclub, consists of ten transvestites and two women. The twelve are identically costumed; still, it's easy to spot the women. Near the end of the show, the twelve disclose their genders through street clothes, and the audience cheers as if they all deserved Medals of Honor for social bravery. I thought they deserved praise for surviving Scott Salmon's choreography. This is Salmon's Broadway début after choreographing "over 100 network television shows." About ninety-nine of them spilled over onto the Palace stage.

One of our best costume designers, Theoni V. Aldredge, splashes in with appropriate *art nouveau* parody. Aldredge has discernment among vulgarities. For *Dreamgirls* (a much better show), she supplied an endearing garishness; here she kids the dance-line costume vulgarity with an edge that underscores the camp of the queens' dancing. David Mitchell's scenery is notable because it does nimbly what musical-show scenery has been doing at least since *Mame* in 1966: much of the time, it changes before our eyes. Not only does one setting flow into another, but the proscenium opening narrows or widens as needed. This is more than extravagant display: it's an acknowledgement of the audience's conditioning through the flexibility and shot variation of film and TV.

Yet, after all the pro and the less-pro comment, we are left with one fundamental item of dismay, the debasement that is probably the reason for this show's tidal-wave success: the book. It was adapted from the film (itself adapted from a Paris hit play) by Harvey Fierstein. He is the author of, and played the lead in, *Torch Song Trilogy*, the truest and most enlightening American play about homosexuality that I know. *Torch Song* began in the tiniest of Off-Off-Broadway premises, then moved to Off-Broadway, then to Broadway, where it rightly won this year's Tony Award for best play. Presumably success brought Fierstein a chance at the Big Time, to write the book of this musical, and much of the press is rhapsodic about how, after a long, hard struggle, he has made good. To me, he has made goo.

Torch Song Trilogy dramatized the difference of the homosexual from the heterosexual, the rights and benefits of that difference. Because he told some truths, Fierstein was given the chance to betray those truths, and he grabbed the chance. Admittedly the script of the French film was undistinguished, but Fierstein went to work to make it less distinguished. His book, abetted by Herman's lyrics, tells us over and over that basically we're all alike, that the homosexual has triumphed by finding the courage to proclaim what he is, and that he is just one more human being, interchangeable with anyone else on the block, except for the way he makes love.

This isn't equality; this is mush. This is to say that blacks are no different from whites, Jews from Gentiles, women from men, when the real value of these groups is in their differences. The test of any sane society is in its ability to welcome those differences, to grow by them, not to push them all into a cross-cultural Waring blender.

If the book of *La Cage aux Folles* had been by Laurents, whose *West Side Story* cosmeticized urban racial strife and whose *Hallelujah, Baby!* reduced American black history to fortune-cookie homilies, the effect would be no less disgusting, but the surprise would be less. Fierstein turned his back on a brave and talented achievement to boil up some golden molasses. His book for his musical makes the plush audience feel, at least for two-and-a-half hours, that the difficulties and pain and acuteness and sensibilities of homosexual life are the same as those of any other life, that we all just haven't understood one another up to now, that *La Cage* brings that understanding, and that our self-congratulation—which is what the closing ovation amounts to—seals a compact of social unity forever. No wonder it's a hit.

Still, the fact that it's a hit is, contradictorily, the most redeeming thing about it. The utterly extrinsic power of the Broadway hit, as such, almost compensates for the show's social pabulum. Success, not social honesty, is what the show is for, what Broadway is for. Broadway is the only American theater locus that can provide gargantuan success in a world where success is prime. That's why, despite sags, Broadway will survive: it makes the smasheroo possible.

Einstein on the Beach, by Robert Wilson. *Saturday Review*, March-April 1985.

Beginning with its title, *Einstein on the Beach* seems to possess substantial meaning, but it ends by having virtually none. Like almost all the Robert Wilson pieces I have seen, it centers on the imaginative spending of much money. He needs so much money and has such a limited audience—though a zealous and articulate one—that his work must be funded. (That's why he does most of his work abroad, where funding is easier and expenses lower.) But his spending is not Ziegfeld extravagance, it's his aesthetic reason for being.

Wilson productions have scripts (by himself and others) but not stories, utterances but not conventional dialogue. Often the speeches consist of words, or even sounds, arranged for contrapuntal litany, even when unaccompanied by music. The scenes range from two people sitting before the curtain to dancers moving through open space to immense complex settings full of actors and singers and dancers. But, as with Wilson's *The Life and Times of Joseph Stalin*, among others, the title is not much more than a springboard for his fantasy.

This production, we're told, has something to do with the fact that the world opened by Einstein has left us stranded (Nevil Shute's phrase) on the beach. An early (beautiful) scene shows a small boy standing on a very high structure watching the slow approach of a giant locomotive. (Everything approaches slowly.) Possibly this is to suggest the young Einstein's fascination with machinery. In the last scene a bus rolls in slowly, and the driver delivers a long, irrelevant monologue. I don't know what this suggests about Einstein. In between we have seen disconnected sequences, almost all of them individually lovely: moving Plexiglas cubes, a duet on the observation platform of a train, a trial, a lighted bed floating up from the floor to the flies against a black background, a cross-section of a three-story house. None of them connects organically with the title. All of them are the fruit of Wilson's particular powers: to design scenic pieces and movement and, with Beverly Emmons, lighting to shape theater space and kinetics in ways that expand our experience.

In this view Wilson can be construed as the latest in an ancient theatrical line, the manufacturers of public spectacle intended to ravish audiences by showing them what they could not see elsewhere—a line that begins with the mock naval battles in flooded Roman amphitheaters and continues right up through *Ice Capades*. This is not to trivialize a contemporary artist of exceptional sensibility, simply to show that his roots go back much farther than one would think. Wilson is called avant-garde, but there is something of the traditionalist in him as well.

The element in the show most supportive of the title is a violinist in the pit orchestra, perched higher than his colleagues, bewigged and moustached like Einstein. He implies that we are all now dancing to Einstein's famous fiddle, even though this is not what we see on stage. This brings us to Philip Glass's score for this "opera," as it's called. That score has the effect of being too simple to describe. Often it consists of scales run continuously up and down, with key changes, sometimes actually sung to the syllables do, re, mi, etc. The music isn't melodic or dramatic in any usual sense; it's mesmeric, as it helps to entrap us in the four-and-a-half hours that this gorgeous work of non-meaning takes to roll before us.

The common tag for Wilson is that he is something new, a "theater painter." It is an old profession; *he* is new, bringing to his work (much since *Einstein*) modern perceptions. Wilson carries forward this spectacle theater for an audience impatient with the cracker-jack prizes of plot and the consolations of explicit meaning, who want their vision enlarged.

Strange Interlude, by Eugene O'Neill. *Saturday Review*, June 1985.

Eugene O'Neill is unique among American dramatists because, after arduous apprenticeship, he wrote tragedies of world stature. He is unique among great dramatists because his apprenticeship lasted most of his life. Only three of his later plays, written after he was fifty, inarguably attained the quality that he had been struggling toward for twenty-six years.

One of the earlier plays, the gargantuan *Strange Interlude*, was recently revived in London and, with most of the same cast, was brought to New York. Performed with fair deftness—if that word can apply to a nine-act work almost five hours long—this production at least gave us the chance to see how fundamentally heroic O'Neill's life had been. Nothing really mattered to him except the committed struggle of the artist with the unseen and unknowable. He never wanted to wrestle anyone but angels.

To see this play now is to have both an advantage and a disadvantage as against its first audiences in 1928. Now we know the masterworks that followed—*The Iceman Cometh, Long Day's Journey into Night, A Touch of the Poet*—so we can see *Strange Interlude* as part of an ultimately triumphant pilgrimage; but we can also be impatient because we know there's better O'Neill to see, as if we were listening to Wagner's *Rienzi* instead of *Tristan*.

The basic theme of this play is the mission of the Eternal Feminine, the Earth Mother—not woman as divine, but the divine as woman—and how men, believing they serve their own wills, in fact serve her will, thus serving the beauty and survival of the human race. (O'Neill often claimed August Strindberg as his master, but this is much more of a Shavian theme.) Through nine acts and some twenty-five years, O'Neill chronicles how Nina Leeds, a New Englander who has lost her young love in World War I, contracts a marriage; aborts a pregnancy; contrives pregnancy by another man; raises her son and sees him married; buries her husband; dismisses her lover; and, at the last, unites with an asexual novelist who has long been an acolyte at her shrine. Thus she fulfills her functions as wife, mother, love goddess, and unreachable goal.

But a chronicle it is, alas. The whole work, stodgily characterized and sometimes distressingly written, would be merely grandiose except that, despite its blatant defects, one can sense the agonizing reach toward myth. O'Neill wanted to plumb the sources of sexuality and mortality, to disclose the powers that lie outside human control. As it eventuated, he succeeded in this quest when he stopped concocting plots and puppets, when he plunged into his own and his family's past, the truth and troubles of his Irish-American background. But it's the very grandioseness of *Strange Interlude* that provides the small interest it retains. As a neat little package of a play, it would have no interest at all.

Aside from its length, the play's most famous element is its use of soliloquy in the presence of other people. Of course the aside is an ancient convention in the theater, but O'Neill revived it as an instrument of modernity, an attempt to incorporate in drama the texture of the contemporary novel. On stage these asides might be handled in various ways—for instance, change of voice or of lighting. The most striking aspect of the recent production was that *nothing* special was done about these spoken thoughts; the actors simply delivered them as part of their dialogue. This led, quite deliberately, to some blurring of the borders between the inner and outer worlds of the characters, but this blurring gave those otherwise wooden characters their richest ambiguities.

This treatment of the asides was only one of the good choices made by the director, Keith Hack. The second was to take the dominant tone of the performance from the surprising ironic humor in this glum work. Hack couldn't treat *Strange Interlude* as a comedy of manners, but it's probable that only a British director and British actors, easy in such comedy, could, or perhaps would have wanted to, treat the play in anything like that style. It helped.

Chiefly contributing was the performance of Nina by that exemplary actress, Glenda Jackson. She attacked the immense role like an adventure, meeting its challenges—its burdens—with virtuosity. As often as the role permitted, she was moving, even in such a baroque passage as, "The present is an interlude . . . strange interlude in which we call on past and future to bear witness we are living!" And always the tawny Jackson voice coursed through the long play tirelessly and entrancingly.

I can't call this production an artistic success; the play itself prevented it. But it was as painless a way as possible to get firsthand theatrical experience of an evolution—the evolution of a man determined to be a genius, who later succeeded.

Chicago, by John Kander, Fred Ebb, and Bob Fosse. *Slant Magazine*, November 26, 1996.

Chicago begins with a man stepping before the curtain to tell us that we are about to see a story of "murder, greed, corruption, violence, exploitation, adultery, and treachery," all those things "dear to our hearts." This makes us nervous. When a big Broadway show proclaims its daring, we can brace ourselves for pretty mild stuff. So it proves. As a subversive act in which we are supposedly complicit, *Chicago* is quaint.

The origin was otherwise. This musical is based on a play of the same name that was written in the early 1920s by Maurine Watkins, a Chicago reporter who had gone to Yale for George Pierce Baker's celebrated playwriting course. As part of her course work, Watkins wrote the first draft of this play, which lambasted and lampooned corruptions in the Chicago that she knew. It was produced in 1926, and took its place in the post-World War I theater's surge of cynicism. Within a few years, Broadway also saw such plays as *Broadway*, *The Front Page*, *Burlesque*, and *The Racket*, works intended to rip the rosy trappings off several pieties in America's new, bitterly enlightened age.

This cynical *frisson* attended the two film versions of *Chicago*, in 1927 and 1942 (titled *Roxie Hart*), and was apparently on hand as late as 1975, when John Kander, Fred Ebb, and Bob Fosse made a musical of the play, directed by Fosse. We're now told that the musical was ahead of its time back there in 1975 (though it ran 898 performances and had been a successful play fifty years earlier), and that today, at last, its moral challenge is acceptable. Today, in fact, *Chicago* is about as challenging as a Victorian peep show. Could it really have been otherwise twenty-one years ago? Some have said that the effect of the O. J. Simpson trial and other recent moral circuses have helped this musical's revival. Well, America has always liked to think of itself as a time-ravaged innocent. (Even Edith Wharton looked back to long-lost innocence.) It was always a dubious chastity. This citing of O. J. is only the latest fantasy on the subject, summoned to explain the new success of a show that was never a failure. But, luckily for those who will flock to this latest Broadway hit, Kander and Ebb and the present producers still take its moral daring seriously, which enables them to give it some life.

In Al Capone's Chicago, Roxie Hart, a married night-club chorine, shoots her lover and engages a smooth lawyer, Billy Flynn, to get her off. He sets out to do this by making her a newspaper-headline sensation. This steals the spotlight from a fellow prisoner, Velma Kelly—a vaudevillian with two murders to her credit, whom Flynn has also been publicizing before trial. The pursuit of justice soon becomes the pursuit of post-trial vaudeville contracts. Complications follow, of course, involving Roxie's nerd husband, Amos, and her sudden claim to be pregnant.

The book of the musical, by Ebb and (the late) Fosse, flexed the play to bring in a total of six other attractive murderesses, dancers all, with seven males to partner them. (What are the males doing in a female prison? The gods of musical theater scoff at such questions.) In the current production—I didn't see the 1975 version—the show is viewed as a show: old-fashioned vaudeville (presumably done to save production costs). The band is onstage center on a raked platform, with conductor, just the way big bands like those of Xavier Cugat and Lawrence Welk used to appear, with the performers coming out of a runway in the middle, or around the edges, of the stand. From time to time, as at the start, someone addresses the audience, which reminds us that everyone up there knows it's just a performance. This is all to the good: it spares us any pressure to take this "shocking" story seriously.

Kander's music is rhythmically apt but melodically flaccid; Ebb's lyrics don't always escape the banal. We know what the songs are supposed to be doing, but they rarely soar past serviceability. Two pleasant exceptions are "Razzle Dazzle," in which Billy Flynn and the company expound their philosophy of deceit, and "Class," in which Velma and the butch prison matron lament the decline of good manners. The arrangements by Ralph Burns and Peter Howard add a welcome lift to the score, especially with a tuba.

Ann Reinking, who worked with Fosse, has choreographed *Chicago* "in the style of Bob Fosse," says the program. The result is mostly carnival kooch dancing *in excelsis*, tempered with nifty acrobatics, with all the women in slinky, transparent black. Because the bandstand takes up most of the stage, all the dancing and almost all the action must take place in what used to be called "One"—the first plane of space parallel to the footlights—except for the sporadic use of tall ladders that swing out from the wings. Reinking uses every inch of space ravenously.

She causes some discomfort, though, by playing Roxie herself. She played that role in the latter part of the 1970s run. Now, whatever her actual age is, the passage of time shifts our attention. Instead of focusing on her performance, we keep marveling at how well she has kept her body in shape and that she is as precise and limber as anyone on stage. The face and the line of the neck have been less fortunate. It's hard to believe that this Roxie is Velma's coeval, more or less, and that she could be pregnant. Even those who don't know the facts of Reinking's career and are more chivalrous than myself may have some difficulty here.

Bebe Neuwirth, as Velma, is little help to Reinking in this regard. Neuwirth is tart, cool, sexy—and, alas, clearly younger than her co-star. Besides, she has something that Reinking, for all her show-biz finish, lacks: a winning arrogance. Neuwirth doesn't work to win us over. She owns this stage, she seems to say, and we're lucky to be there, to have the chance to appreciate her. It's the kind of serfdom that only an exceptionally talented performer can dare to offer. Neuwirth dares; and we accept.

As Billy Flynn, James Naughton sings surprisingly well and is almost sufficiently overweening. Joel Grey, who made his first success in an earlier Kander-Ebb musical, *Cabaret* (1966), is Roxie's husband and plays him for pathos: not exactly a one-note performance, more of a half-note. Mary Sunshine, a newspaper sob-sister, is played by D. Sabella, whose odd billing is eventually explained—in yet another act of "daring" (the "D." stands for "David").

The Resistible Rise of Arturo Ui, by Bertolt Brecht. *Theater*, Fall 2003.

Bertolt Brecht's *The Resistible Rise of Arturo Ui* was presented in October 2002 by the National Actors' Theater (NAT) in New York, and the result was less a production than the scene of a traffic accident. Colliding there were the NAT's flimsy schema, the ambition of Al Pacino to play Arturo, and the sway of Simon McBurney, the director. All through the performance I felt that I was surveying wreckage.

The first victim was the National Actors' Theater. What is it? Not what its title says it is. It is not national—it is located in New York—and it is no more an actors' theater than any other production. The enterprise was launched in 1991 by Tony Randall, who had large but gauzy ambitions, questionable judgment, and a lot of money that he had earned in television. (It was supplemented by donors.) The NAT under Randall has presented a number of great plays with widely varying artistic results, but it has never resolved into a company with perceptible long-range purpose. Continuity and growth and a sense of ensemble have been blatantly absent. I have seen fewer of their productions than has Michael Feingold (of the *Village Voice*), and he writes, "I have been going to the NAT for a decade now, and I still don't know what it is." This Brecht instance looked as if Pacino's ambition had crashed into whatever was left of Randall's nebulous aims and had left the *raison d'être* of the NAT even more shaky. Whether it will survive this collision and what its future productions will be are questions that do not bate the breath.

The Brecht play was done in an auditorium at Pace University, not only with Pacino in the lead but with a number of well-known film actors in the cast, including Randall. The venue and the cast announced that some high-salaried people were proving their anti-commercial humility. The nub of the venture was, of course, Pacino's long-nurtured ambition to play Ui. He had done it in his pre-film days in Boston, and in 1974, after his first film successes (including *The Godfather*), he had rehearsed it in a workshop at the Public Theater. "We will evaluate it," Joseph Papp had said while the workshop was in progress, "and then groom it for the Vivian Beaumont," the Lincoln Center theater that he then managed. Evaluation must have been negative; the production never opened.

Thus early, however, Pacino was a bifurcated figure. Besides his first films, I saw him Off-Broadway in *The Indian Wants the Bronx* and *The Local Stigmatic*, on Broadway in *Does a Tiger Wear a Necktie?*, and at the Beaumont in *Camino Real*, and had recognized that this long-waisted, short-legged actor was, at his best, a high-voltage dynamo. I followed his screen career with recurring admiration, but I knew—it was no secret—that he had concomitant theater plans. Among them were Arturo Ui, Richard III, and Herod in Wilde's *Salomé*, all of which he had already performed. (The third of these monsters he has recently done again in a public reading.) Now that he has brought about this large production of the Brecht play, perhaps his Arturo ambition is satisfied.

His yearning for Arturo has always seemed peculiar from the sheerly theatrical point of view. Perhaps it meant little to Pacino that the play has never ranked high in the Brecht canon. (Martin Esslin, an apostle of Brecht, called it an ambitious project that failed.) More pertinently to Pacino, the title role is not the dominant one. Brecht, writing in 1941, wanted to demonstrate analogically how a gang of thugs had taken over Germany, and he peopled his play with broad cartoons of the important figures in the Hitler chronicle. His symbolic setting is Chicago, where gangsters are cornering the cauliflower market and seizing widespread power, and the play's structure makes Arturo a tool rather than a protagonist. The notes in the Willett-Manheim edition of the play, articulating Brecht's intentions, state that "Ui is presented as a passive plaything in the hands of strong men." Quite apart from the accuracy, even in analogue, of this view of Hitler, the role is a strange ambition for a big-name actor. In any case, it was a disappointment for the audience that expected a true Pacino performance and got instead an amorphous person dragging about in a leather overcoat and checkered pants, piping his lines in a high voice.

Toward the end of the first half of the production, Arturo tried to improve his persona by taking lessons in deportment from an old actor (played by Randall). This attempt to revamp the flaccid with the classic did not help. All through the second half of the play Arturo was once again limp. Pacino moved around the often dimly lighted stage with a remoteness that added to its dimness. In any case Pacino faced an uphill fight all the way. The gangster charade for the Hitler story is so thin that its very transparency vitiates it. We wonder at the juvenility of Brecht's analogue rather than being stung by it.

The dominant figure in the production was the third factor in the collision, Simon McBurney. This English director, best known for his work with the Complicité of London, began with the choice that faces every director of a revival: commitment or salvage. Does the director believe in the play's continuing vitality, which he will serve with his imagination? Or does he fear that the play is dusty and needs all the shaking up he can give it? A still-memorable instance of the first approach was Peter Brook's *A Midsummer Night's Dream* in 1971, which, despite flutterings, conveyed Brook's love of the play. McBurney's *Arturo Ui* was of the second kind. It conveyed fear—fear that the play was torpid, obvious, and dated and that it was the director's obligation to conceal these faults. In consequence McBurney desperately poured ingenuity into and all over the play.

Brecht had asked that it "be performed in the grand style with obvious harkbacks to the Elizabethan theater, i.e., with curtains and different levels." (He had written it in blank verse with some mock-Shakespearean moments.) McBurney supplied the different levels, three of them, mostly suggested by lights, and he also supplied steps leading down into the audience that were never used. But in not quite Elizabethan style, he festooned the play with rear projections, clips of mobs, fights, and landscapes. In Act II he included clips of Hitler and crowds and subtitles about Nazi history, thus explaining—in effect, maiming—the allegory that was being played in front of them. With Paul Anderson's lighting, McBurney created an ambience of murk in which the actors, all of them grotesquely made up, frequently struck poses like *tableaux vivants*. Their voices were amplified (thus muddying George Tabori's adaptation of the text) in an attempt to increase presence. These maneuvers, along with many more, served McBurney's secret purpose: to distract us from the play itself. Sweating to hold the audience's interest, McBurney imperially squashed any trace of the NAT's thin classical identity and of Pacino's usual zing.

The cruelest aspect of this collision is that McBurney was right to take the salvage road. The play is, on its own, inert. I remember some tremors in the 1963 Broadway production—directed by Tony Richardson with reference to the Berliner Ensemble production—that were chiefly due to Christopher Plummer's stoat-like Arturo. But Pacino, and not just because he is not Plummer, could not provide tremors because the play is by now dead on arrival, and McBurney's artificial respiration failed. As Martin Esslin says, the play was never much. Now it is a burdensome corpse.

This is hard to regret. Outweighing any aesthetic lapses in the play is its historical grossness. It is an offense to history. The Nazi rule of Germany was not imposed by a bunch of gangsters. It was installed by the German people. Of course there were dissidents—up to 1933 a great many—but, as noted, the very clips of ecstatic crowds that McBurney used were a contradiction of Brecht's thesis. The image of a docile people being taken over by thugs is utterly fraudulent.

A further highly relevant matter: Brecht never mentions, symbolically or otherwise, the Nazi exploitation of centuries-old German anti-Semitism. He wrote the play in Finland before leaving for the United States, intending to present to this country a view of Germany in an American mode—"the gangster play." This gangsters-versus-honest-citizens approach permitted him to omit aspects that would not help his purpose, a purpose that concerned him and other exiled German intellectuals during the Hitler years. They wanted to distinguish between the Nazis and the best of Germany. (Thomas Mann, in California, wrote to Brecht in 1941—the year of *Arturo Ui*—assuring him that he had recently given a lecture in which he warned "against equating what is German with what is Nazi.") Any hint of the Jewish fate in *Arturo Ui* might have clouded Brecht's intent. Odd as it may now seem, the Brecht who was so critical of Germany before Hitler wanted, during the Nazi era, to protect Germany's good name. This play, sanitized of anti-Semitism, can be seen as part of that effort. As the world knows, Germany was the source of much that is marvelous in the humanities and the sciences, but as the world also knows, Germany was not the guileless victim of Nazi gangsters.

Well, let's look on the relatively bright side. The smashup in the NAT production may have a healthy purging effect. Through the collision of Randall's muzzy motives and Pacino's peculiar insistence and McBurney's worried fussing, perhaps *Arturo Ui* will at last be laid to the rest it has long deserved.

THEATER FEATURES

"The Trail of the Splendid Gypsy: On Edmund Kean." *Horizon*, **March 1962.**

In Shakespeare's *Twelfth Night* one of the minor characters remarks, "If this were played upon a stage now, I could condemn it as an improbable fiction." The line might serve as an epigraph to the phenomenon of the actor Edmund Kean, a prodigious Englishman whose private life was as theatrical as his public career. Kean could be said to have originated the type of the tortured, flamboyant actor, becoming in the eyes of his generation and those that followed it an epitome of romanticism. He first appeared on the American stage in 1820, and he came back to it again in 1961, as the central figure in a lavish musical named after him. In the intervening century his life has served as the material for a number of dramatists, even though some of them—like Alexandre Dumas and Jean-Paul Sartre—felt it necessary to alter details for the sake of credibility. Art, after all, insists on certain restraints that do not hamper reality.

Edmund Kean was the illegitimate son of a London actress-cum-harlot named Ann Carey, granddaughter of that Henry Carey who, some claim, was the author of "God Save the King." Kean's birth date is often given as November 4, 1787, but as Giles Playfair points out in his excellent biography, a more likely date is March 17, 1790. Charlotte Tidswell, the remarkable woman who helped to rear the boy, remembered that she was summoned to the mother's childbed on a St. Patrick's Day; and a playbill of the year 1801 refers to Kean as "The Celebrated Theatrical Child . . . not eleven years old." His father, also named Edmund Kean, was a surveyor's apprentice who committed suicide in 1792. His uncle, Moses Kean, who died in the same year, had been a ventriloquist-entertainer and the lover of Miss Tidswell.

Aunt Tid, as Kean grew to call her, was a sensible woman and a competent supporting actress who spent forty years on the London stage. She took care of Edmund for long periods when he was a child. She provided the framework of morality from which he often wandered and the basic view of his art from which he never swerved: a passion for emotional truth. The facts about his childhood are relatively few. He was not only taught acting by Aunt Tid, he was trained as a pantomime Harlequin, a tumbler, a singer and dancer, and a bareback rider. It was an age that adored theatrical prodigies, and the boy made a number of appearances. Among them was a trip to Wales, where he gave a private performance of Hamlet for Lord Nelson and Lady Hamilton.

Kean's adult career began when he was about fifteen years old where all acting careers began in those days, in the provinces. There were three first-class theaters in London: Drury Lane, Covent Garden, and the Haymarket. To appear at any other London playhouse was to get yourself blacklisted by the major theaters; and to get an engagement at one of the major theaters an actor had to prove himself in out-of-town theaters. Kean spent nine years in the provinces.

To some extent his physique must have worked against an earlier rise to fame. The public was used to "Roman" stars of noble presence, and Kean was short. (His autopsy report gave his height as 5 feet 6¾ inches.) His voice, although there are reams of testimony about its varying powers, was not a round, unblemished column of golden sound; it sometimes tended to hoarseness. His face, too, was more striking than conventionally handsome: lean, vulpine, with scowling brows and glittering dark eyes. In addition, the style of acting he was developing must have worried some managers. It often moved audiences, but it was new and highly personal—not without poetry but much more "natural" (what we should call "realistic") than the current fashion. London was not eager for him.

The story of his nine years in the provinces is one of grinding work, poverty, disappointment, and humiliation. Explicitly the story proves his persistence, and implicitly it reveals the reasons for his growing alcoholism and other excesses. Today we can only marvel that the fire (and that is the operative word in Kean's life) was not extinguished by heartbreak and simple hunger. One episode will illustrate. In 1811 he was left stranded in Ireland by a tight-fisted manager. He had by then married an actress named Mary Chambers, nine years his senior, and had two sons, Howard and an infant, Charles. They landed in Whitehaven, England, in July with a bundle of clothes and books, a dog, and not one penny. They decided to make their way to London, where Aunt Tid could at least shelter them until Kean could find a decent engagement. It took them five months to reach London.

They traveled, he and his wife and two small children, from village to town to village, in carts and wagons when they were given rides; eating as they could, not eating when they couldn't; sleeping in the worst beds of filthy inns when they could afford that luxury. (Even when they couldn't afford it, Kean drank.) When they arrived in a place where there seemed the slightest possibility of scratching up a few shillings, Kean would engage a hall, write out a few playbills, and get the town crier to announce the show. He and Mary would perform scenes from various plays; he, *solus*, would do songs, dances, and imitations. Thus they made their progress to London, where they arrived in December.

In the provincial theaters he played all kinds of parts—often danced and tumbled—hoping always for the London engagement that would establish his fortunes and give the opportunity to his quality. At last the chance came, but not before some further turns of the knife. Despondent of ever reaching the three best London theaters, in October, 1813, he accepted an engagement for the following January at the Olympic, a minor London house. On November 16th, six weeks later, he received the long-desired offer from Drury Lane. Six days later, on November 22nd, his cherished son Howard died. Wrung with grief, Kean had to trot back and forth like a hopeful dog from Drury Lane to the Olympic, begging the Olympic to release him and Drury to be patient. The tangle was finally cleared; his Drury Lane début was set for January 26, 1814, as Shylock.

Theaters operated differently in those days. Their closest modern parallels are opera houses. Every sizable theater had a more or less permanent company and a standard repertory, and would engage a visiting actor for Shylock much as an opera house might engage a Rigoletto today. He would arrive a day or two ahead of time with his own costumes, go through a minimal rehearsal to establish outlines of movement, which varied little from theater to theater, and then would appear. A "directed" production, in our sense of the word, was virtually unknown; audiences went to see individual performances.

History is lucky as far as Kean's London début is concerned. On that bleak winter night William Hazlitt, jewel among critics, was present. There were, he said later, about a hundred in the pit, for Drury's business had fallen off. (Kean's engagement was one of several desperate attempts to find an attractive new star.) Hazlitt wrote in the *Morning Chronicle* of January 27, 1814: "Mr. Kean (of whom report had spoken highly) last night made his appearance at Drury Lane Theatre in the character of Shylock. For voice, eye, action, and expression, no actor has come out for many years at all equal to him. The applause, from the first scene to the last, was general, loud, and uninterrupted. Indeed, the very first scene in which he comes on with Bassanio and Antonio, showed the master in his art, and at once decided the opinion of his audience." Kean knew it. He ran home to his lodgings after the performance and exclaimed: "Mary, you shall ride in your carriage, and Charley shall go to Eton!"

In many an actor's life the interest of the story would dwindle here. A struggle for recognition—but afterward just a straight, climbing line of success. The success certainly came. Through the years he essayed the great parts, one after another: Richard III, Hamlet, Othello, Lear, Coriolanus, and some lesser but rewarding roles like Sir Giles Overreach in Massinger's *A New Way to Pay Old Debts*. He was received better in some than in others, but he became the darling of Drury, of London, of Britain. (There is still today a Kean Street off Drury Lane.) By 1816 a London newspaper said that Englishmen had stopped talking about the weather when they met in the street; instead they asked each other what they thought of Kean's Giles Overreach.

But the marks of his struggle, his chancy boyhood and youth, had not been erased. He drank, he gambled, he roistered. His marriage, which had never been good, grew worse now that poverty did not chain the pair together. Perhaps worst of all was his realization that not even reaching the pinnacle of his profession would bring him social acceptance. In the theater he was imperial; in a ballroom, to which he might have been invited as an amusing curiosity, he was, as the law once put it, a rogue and vagabond. This was an abnormally sensitive man of whom it was said that he could see a sneer across Salisbury Plain. To live in a stratified society and be treated as a lackey by his intellectual and spiritual inferiors was a very hot and real hell for Kean.

He did not lack for praise. Byron, who was much involved in the affairs of Drury Lane, was overwhelmed by him. After he saw Kean for the first time Byron wrote in his journal: "By Jove he is a soul! Life—nature—truth without exaggeration or diminution." Kean's sister-in-law wrote to a friend: "Lord Biron [*sic*] is enchanted with Edmund and is like a little dog behind the scenes, following him everywhere." Byron presented gifts to Kean—a Turkish sword and a snuffbox—and addressed a poem to him which began:

> Thou art the sun's bright child!
> The genius that irradiates thy mind
> Caught all its purity and light from heaven.

Coleridge provided the most frequently quoted line on the subject: "To see Kean act is like reading Shakespeare by flashes of lightning." Shelley intended Kean to play the Count in *The Cenci*. Keats, who said, "One of my ambitions is to make as great a revolution in modern dramatic writing as Kean has done in acting," wrote his one finished play, *Otho the Great*, for him. (The actor, with good theatrical sense, however, never played in either Shelley's or Keats's literary drama.)

But Kean did not lack for trouble, either. His hurricane temper, occasional drunkenness, and illness brought him into conflict with managers. His personal life seethed until it erupted in a suit by one Alderman Cox against Kean for "criminal conversation" with Mrs. Cox. Kean and Mrs. Cox had, in fact, been lovers for some years. That she was a rather permissive lady and that her husband had probably known this, were considered irrelevant. After a newspaper orgy of scandalous articles and cartoons, the alderman was awarded £800 in damages.

Professional and personal troubles combined on the night in January, 1825, when Kean returned to the stage after the alderman's victory. The house was packed and hostile; the audience kept up a storm of booting and abuse, punctuated with orange peels, so that although he played out the entire role of Richard III, not one word was heard. He continued to fight back night after night, insisting on playing and delivering curtain speeches, but he made little headway against the hostility and decided to give the ostentatious moral outrage time to subside while he toured America.

He had made one previous American tour in 1820, when he had been only the second London star to visit this country. His predecessor was George Frederick Cooke, who died in New York and was buried in St. Paul's Churchyard, where a monument to him was erected by Kean. New York, Boston, Philadelphia, and Baltimore had welcomed Kean, but on his return trip to Boston he incensed an audience by refusing to play because there were too few people in the house. The action was inexcusable, and there was no reason now for Kean to expect anything but the rude reception he unmistakably got when he went back to Boston a third time. Yet other American cities, as far south as Charleston, hailed him and restored his finances and confidence. On this tour he also acted in Montreal and Quebec, and in Canada was made an Indian chief, perhaps the first visiting European celebrity to receive this honor. He was much struck by the ceremony. Later he had a portrait painted in his chief's costume, and used often to put on headdress and buckskin when the firewater was in him.

After more than a year's absence he returned to England to find that the public had forgiven him. The *Times* of January 9, 1827, reported: "When the curtain rose, a general cry of 'Kean! Kean!' resounded from every part of the densely crowded house." But his health, ravaged by drink, work, and temperament, was declining. He had frequently to cancel engagements, he could not learn new plays, and sometimes he even "went up" in old parts. Still he blazed, fitfully but forcefully, up and down Britain and on his one professional visit to Paris. He wrote his estranged wife a pitiful appeal for reunion, which she ignored. He was, however, reconciled with his son Charles and to Charles's choice of acting as a career.

Indeed, his last appearance was with his son. On March 25, 1833, he was announced for Othello at Covent Garden with Charles as Iago. He got as far as the scene in which he cried, "Othello's occupation's gone." (Even collapse knew its cue in Kean's life.) Then he became ill, and then unconscious. He was put to bed in a nearby tavern and a few days later was moved to his house in Richmond. He died there in May, aged forty-three. In another room of the house lay his battered old harridan of a mother, to whom he had recently given shelter. She died twelve days later.

The force of his art became a standard by which other performers were measured. Writing of the tragedian William Charles Macready, Leigh Hunt said, "It is to be recollected that Mr. Kean first gave the living stage that example of a natural style of acting, on which Mr. Macready has founded his new rank in the theatrical world." To the theater Kean brought a burning, intense style in contrast to the large Handelian classical manner of the school of John Philip Kemble. Beyond this he had an extraordinary effect for an actor: he was a stimulus to the finest artistic minds of his time. He was for them the embodiment in the theater of romanticism—that movement in which art tried to attain universals through the closely examined adventures of the individual soul. To contemporary poets and visionaries Kean's acting was, in Hazlitt's phrase, "an anarchy of the passions," a revolution for which they hungered and which he demonstrably abetted.

As late as 1898 Kean's reputation was still potent enough to serve as a dramaturgic instrument. In Pinero's *Trelawny of the "Wells"*, aristocratic Sir William Gower objects to his grandson's engagement to an actress. To him, actors are mere gypsies. Then Sir William learns that the girl's mother played with Kean, whom he himself had seen years before; and in the line that changes his attitude and the temper of the play, Sir William says: "Kean! . . . Ah, he was a *splendid* gypsy!"

In the musical play *Kean*, Peter Stone, the librettist, and Alfred Drake, the star, presented a Kean whose antecedents were recognizable but whose direct descent was from a different source. Stone and Drake, if they were not completely consistent with historical facts, certainly kept faith with the "stage" Kean, as he has been represented for a hundred and twenty-five years in the work that was the basis of their show: a play by Alexandre Dumas *père*, lately revised by Jean-Paul Sartre.

Drake's production, like Dumas's play, told the story of Kean, the "King of London," in the early nineteenth century, a reigning actor dear to the crowd not only because of his talent but because he has made his way up from their midst. He is in love with a countess, the wife of the Danish ambassador, and is himself pursued by Miss Danby, a stage-struck young heiress. The Prince of Wales, a friend of Kean's, asks him to give up the Countess to avoid an international incident. Kean suspects that the reason for the request is that the Prince wants to woo her. On stage with Miss Danby, he sees the Prince and the Countess together in the royal box, breaks out of his part (Othello), and insults the Prince. In a final scene, where the Count visits Kean's house, Miss Danby comes out of a bedroom at the last moment to draw suspicion away from the Countess, who is hiding in another room. Kean is forgiven by the Prince, is reconciled to Miss Danby, and all ends with a Gallic shrug that accepts the pleasantly inevitable.

Thus the musical comedy, and thus in essence the play by Alexandre Dumas, first presented in 1836. The history of that play has nearly as many twists as the plot itself. The first twist is that Dumas didn't write it himself—not completely, at any rate. Edmund Kean played in Paris for the first and last time in 1828, and shortly thereafter two busy French playsmiths devoted a total of five days to writing a play about him. Their names were Frédéric de Courcy and Marie Emmanuel Guillaume Marguerite Théaulon de Lambert—the latter gentleman mercifully called Théaulon for short. The play languished unproduced, perhaps because its subject was still alive. Three years after Kean's death the manuscript was brought to Dumas, who was rapidly becoming the most popular dramatist in France. On April 30, 1836, a Dumas play, *Don Juan de Maraña*, was produced in Paris and failed. It was doubtless inconceivable to that fat literary fountain that the theatrical year could proceed without another play of his, so he took over the Théaulon-de Courcy work—probably at the suggestion of Frédérick Lemaître, the great actor, who wanted to play Kean—and altered it to suit Lemaître and himself. Théaulon and de Courcy disappeared from the title page of the play.

Jean-Paul Sartre, a later "collaborator" of Dumas's, asks: "What's Alexandre Dumas's part in this story? I suppose we'll never know. What's sure is that he signed the play and was paid for it." However, in his memoirs Dumas refers to "Kean's terrible glance in *Othello*," so it seems likely that he saw Kean act, was moved by him, and had more than grist-to-the-mill interest in him as a subject. *Kean, ou désordre et génie* was produced at the Théâtre des Variétés on August 31, 1836, just four months after the previous Dumas play, and was a great success for author and actor. Lemaître felt so proprietary about the work that when another actor presumed to play it some years later, he plastered Paris with signed posters stating: "I am the only real Kean."

The play was subsequently translated into German, Italian, Spanish, Portuguese, and Danish, and continued to be played in French; Lucien Guitry performed it in the 1890s. In Germany it was a particular favorite, and the late Albert Bassermann was among those well known for portrayals of Kean. When the lurid Ermete Novelli toured America in 1907, the play, in Italian, was a staple in his repertoire.

It was performed in English in New York in the mid-nineteenth century, but its most successful English adaptation was made for his own use by Charles Coghlan, the British-American actor-manager, and first presented in New York in December, 1897. For an unaccountable reason he called the adaptation *The Royal Box* and, even less accountably, changed the names of all the characters. Kean himself became James Clarence, and the reviewers were kept busy exercising their parentheses. "In this scene we see James Clarence (that is, Kean) ..." Coghlan had success with *The Royal Box* and two years later was on tour with it when he died in Galveston, Texas. In full fustian fig, the Coghlan version was revived in New York as late as 1928 by the road star Walker Whiteside, and even in those speakeasy days, it managed to run thirty-nine performances.

Dumas's play has twice been filmed. The first, silent version was made by Russian émigrés in Paris in 1922, was directed by Alexander Volkov, and starred Ivan Mozhukhin. The second version was made in Italy after World War II with Vittorio Gassman. The former film is by far the better known. When William Whitebait, the eminent film critic of the London *New Statesman*, retired recently, he wrote a valedictory article in which he remembered, among the highlights of his youth, that "the audience at the Studio des Ursulines so bravoed Mozhukhin in *Kean* that the film had to be stopped and the passage replayed."

As Lemaître induced Dumas to revise the Théaulon-de Courcy script, so in 1953 another actor persuaded Jean-Paul Sartre to revise Dumas. The eloquent Pierre Brasseur had played the role of Lemaître in Carné's film *Les Enfants du Paradis*, and this led him to consider reviving one of that actor's roles. The old play needed refurbishing, and Sartre agreed to do it, partially out of admiration for Brasseur, possibly partly as pure theatrical *jeu d'esprit*. One could attribute all kinds of "existential" characteristics to Kean as a Sartrean character: a man outside society seeking to engage with it; a man hovering between realities, aware that the adulation he receives is paid to the less real of his selves; a man tormented by internal conflict into a keener awareness of the anguish of existence. It would not be difficult to make a Sartrean case for *Charley's Aunt*. Sartre himself claims little more than that he "scraped off a bit of rust and mildew." In so doing he provided Brasseur with an excellent vehicle.

The author of the recent *Kean*, Peter Stone, was not the first one to consider the musical use of Dumas's play. On April 18, 1850, Giuseppe Verdi wrote to the manager of the Teatro la Fenice in Venice: "Tell Piave [the librettist], in order to spare time, that if he hasn't been able to find the Spanish drama I indicated, I suggest *Kean*, one of Dumas's best dramas. So many fine things can be done with this play without losing time. I could begin work in a month." The Spanish drama referred to was Gutiérrez's *El Trovador*. Piave may not have found it; but another librettist, Cammarano, did. It became *Il Trovatore*, and the subject of Kean never, alas, rose with Verdi again.

The Broadway musical version, adapted by Stone from Sartre and hung with songs by Robert Wright and George Forrest, satisfied what might be called a Kean tradition. Actors were responsible for initiating the first two adaptations, and the new one came about at the instigation of Alfred Drake, who drew up the first scenario for this production.

From Dumas to Stone the play has never claimed to be biography; it diverges in several respects from the facts. The play's hero is not married, presumably because Dumas thought his audience would have less sympathy for the torments-in-love of a married man. Kean was not in life an intimate of the Prince Regent; his only recorded contact with the Prince was the gift of a royal purse of one hundred guineas, as a mark of favor, shortly after his Drury debut. The Prince put his box at the disposal of the king of Prussia and the emperor of Russia so that they might see Kean play Othello, but there is no proof that he and Kean ever met. The play's hero is a conscious self-dramatizer, a French mixture of Schnitzler's Anatol, Mozart's Don Giovanni, and Leoncavallo's Canio, with a *soupçon* of Byron. The real Kean, although his actions often superficially resembled those of the fictional one, was the protagonist of a tragedy, not a romantic melodrama. He juggled his assignations, boozed with his cronies, and insulted his audiences as the fictional Kean does, but unlike in the play, there was never a hint in all this of light-heartedness, of true gaiety. It is the frenzy of a man none the less sentenced for being self-sentenced. Among his papers was found an introspective poem with the lines "Whipt in his childhood, in manhood trained, / In all the vices which the fallen strained."

The jigging London urchin and the starveling provincial player—even the illustrious international star—could never in remotest fantasy have imagined that some of his life would he acted after him "in states unborn and accents yet unknown." But this theatrical genius has indeed found popular immortality in a colorful melodrama. Kean's sense of humor was limited and bitter; still, he might have enjoyed this irony.

"An Invitation to Some Comic Authors." *New York Times*, **January 16, 1966.**

Well, what about comedy? The Broadway theater tells us that serious plays are so risky that it has to avoid them. The assumption we are encouraged to make is that, on the other hand, Broadway compensates for this with the quality of its comedies. But is this the case?

Barefoot in the Park and *Luv*—helped greatly by Mike Nichols' pastry-chef touch—are flakily light much of the time. *Cactus Flower* lives up to its name by finding a little bloom in the midst of a lot of dryness and thistles—a few good Abe Burrows gags, his don't-look-back, hurry-up direction, Barry Nelson's dependable professional performance. *The Odd Couple* itself starts with a situation based on a genuinely comic perception, which is then exploited not for further perceptions or developments but for gags. The technique is that of revue-sketch writing, spun out to three acts.

And these are among the best comedies on hand. . . .

My point is not to belabor established shows but to question the assumption about Broadway: that, since it must specialize in comedies (it says), comedy is where it shines. (There is a similar assumption about musicals—equally debatable at the moment.) Most of the comedies and farces we get are so repetitive they appear federally decreed to conform. As the second-act curtain approaches, we know the lovers must quarrel. When a situation is lengthily predicted to go in a certain direction, we know in advance that it will go in another. A bland question always brings a tart answer. And when an author gives particular signs of floundering, we brace ourselves for the one sure-fire, guaranteed laugh-getter: he will have a character use the phrase "son of a bitch." (Sadly, I acknowledge that it never completely fails.)

In a society that, we are told, is incapable of tragedy, in a theater that, we are told, could not afford tragedy even if it existed, where are the comedies, then? The ones that relate to our lives, that is—not to last year's hits.

It is arguably idle to call for high tragedy in America. But if this country is prospering in any art at present, it is in the comic novel, with such writers as Joseph Heller, Bruce Jay Friedman, Elliott Baker, and John Barth. We all know that good novelists are sometimes not good dramatists; still, many have succeeded, and, at the least, they have historically been interested in trying. Why aren't these contemporary men writing for the theater? Why doesn't Mordecai Richler send us something from Canada? Jules Feiffer, where are you? J. P. Donleavy, you who wrote the excellent *Ginger Man* and then hobbled it in dramatization, isn't it time to swing as freely in comic drama as in comic fiction?

These writers are all gauchos of the sacred cow, and shouldn't we assume that they would like nothing better than roping and tying another one—perhaps on the stage? One even dares to ask the same question of Terry Southern, who seems in some danger of becoming the house black-humorist to Hollywood.

These are some of the writers—only some—whose talents show excellent promise of being adaptable to the stage, whose presence would give substance to the implication that this is a prime theatrical time for comedy. It would be willfully naïve to assume that, even if these men wrote good plays (a bet certainly worth making), every Broadway management would necessarily embrace them. But there are some interested producers, it seems, and there will probably be others, as the generations change and as the influence of a changing audience is felt more and more.

Besides, although Broadway bulks first, it is not the whole theater, not even in New York. Whatever the disappointments in Off-Broadway's development (many, many), an appetite for fresh comedy continues there. This season has seen two one-act comedies by Douglas Turner Ward, *Happy Ending* and *Day of Absence*, which, though distended, were both trenchant and pertinently funny. *Veronica*, which I was unable to see, was reliably reported to be a good comedy. And *The Mad Show*, a modest and modestly produced revue at the New Theater, is a constantly amusing display of blithe knife-work. I do not contend that all comedy must be black or satirical in order to pertain today. *A Funny Thing Happened on the Way to the Forum*, which justified its title, was sheer farce—with music. Few among us are too stern to enjoy romantic comedy, when it is not insipid. (*Barefoot in the Park*, flimsy as it may be, is a case in point.)

During the last eight years, I was much concerned with films, and independent filmmakers frequently told me how they itched to tell the truth about race problems or world peace or drug addiction or other matters about which the big studios fudged. All fine and necessary, I thought, but why didn't one of them itch to tell some truth about falling in love and wooing and marrying—which the studios also fudge? With, for example, such actresses on hand as the Harris ladies—Rosemary and Barbara—what male would not be interested in a little vicarious romance? What female would not respond to such protagonists in plays that dealt honestly with aspects of her own feminine experience?

There is an ironical parenthesis here. Some of our comic writers make a sharp division between their personal lives and their views of the world. They marry, pay their insurance premiums, and play with their kids—while they write satires about the corrosion of society. One reality does not necessarily disprove another, however. Ever since *As You Like It*, good comic dramatists have also been analyzing the reasons for their happiness when and where they were happy. But, whatever the kind, let this comedy come; only let it be genuine.

For in its rush to prove that there is no room for the serious, Broadway has fostered a flood of imitation comedies—often derivative of George S. Kaufman. This usually means an attempted fusillade of wisecracks coming from the confrontation of the cynical with the naïve or stupid. Kaufman's plays—mostly collaborations—were an apt expression of the between-wars era when the middle class began to enjoy mild joshing about itself, so long as the gibes were directed at its inept members by superior ones. Now the audience has altered, and comic plays themselves have altered insufficiently.

What Kaufman did was not easy, or lots of others would have done it, too. Many are still trying. But the time is out of joint—out of those old joints, anyway. (The current revival of *You Can't Take It With You*, at the Lyceum Theatre, is a pleasant exercise in nostalgia and will not, I hope, prove a stimulus to further imitation by dramatists.) A new wave of comic playwrights—serious and relevant comic playwrights—has every reason to appear; and could, I think, prove that it is wanted simply by appearing.

"Sartre's Theater and Ours." *New York Times*, **February 13, 1966.**

Many of the outstanding plays of the French theater come from part-time playwrights. Men of letters-in-general also write plays—such authors, past and present, as Camus, Mauriac, Claudel, Gide, Cocteau, Montherlant, and, pre-eminently, Sartre. There are, of course, plenty of French dramatists who write little other than plays; but in France, as in other European countries, the drama is often part of any imaginative writer's interest. This fact derives from a cultural attitude toward the theater quite different from ours in the United States. Wallace Fowlie says the following, in an essay on Sartre: "Traditionally in France, the theater is looked upon as a domain that the leader of a new movement is anxious to capture and utilize." It is an astonishing idea to Americans. Quite apart from difficulties of production in our theater, no such tradition has ever existed in this country.

Imagine a leader of the New Left—or a John Bircher, for that matter—anxious to "capture" the theater. No, alas, it cannot be imagined. We get some plays responsive to current conditions, like recent ones by the black writers James Baldwin and LeRoi Jones. We get some adventures in form, like "happenings." But there is no sense in America that a new intellectual or artistic movement must "utilize" our theater.

To Jean-Paul Sartre, in another tradition, the theater has been an inevitable adjunct (along with the novel) to his philosophic and political work. During the German occupation of Paris, for example, he produced *The Flies*, a moral and political allegory that uses the classic Orestes story. During fifteen years after the war he wrote eight more plays as vehicles for differing aspects of his developing ideas. Those that are best known in the U.S. are *No Exit*, *The Victors*, *The Respectful Prostitute*, and *Dirty Hands* (which in 1948 was produced here in a poor version called *Red Gloves*).

The Condemned of Altona, recently given its American premiere by the Lincoln Center Repertory Company, is Sartre's latest play, written in 1959. He wanted to make a full statement on matters that were then troubling him, and it is culturally significant that he chose to make it in the theater. The occasion was France's Algerian war. Sartre had been in the French army during the Second World War, had been a prisoner, had escaped and worked for the Resistance. He had, we know, some pronounced ideas on the subject of Nazism and Nazi methods. Now his own country and the Algerians were engaged in practices that—political justice aside—proved yet again that no nation or race has a monopoly on animal cruelty or evil. This can hardly have been a surprise to him, but the instance moved him so greatly that he wrote this play.

The insistent iron of Sartre's mind is indicated by the fact that he set the play in postwar Germany. Only fifteen years before he had seen France ravaged and drained by the Germans. Now he had chosen to use Germans as exemplars of his belief that countries are not moral entities, that good and evil are accessible to all, that after all these centuries all men are still trying to learn how to choose. His collective protagonist is a rich German family of shipbuilders. The father had dealt with the Nazis when they were in power, on the theory that governments come and go but money and industrial empire remain. The older son has imprisoned himself for thirteen years in an upstairs room of the huge family home, self-condemned to an effort to understand how he, who had at first resisted Nazi brutality, had himself become a torturer and murderer on the Russian front.

With the younger son's wife as catalyst, the play moves to the theme that there is no real atonement for evil, that the world cannot change by phantoms of remorse or perfection but only by the reality of responsibility. It is the lack of responsibility (which, in a phrase he made famous elsewhere, Sartre calls "bad faith") that is the universal source of evil.

In art, Sartre is not the pioneer that he has been in philosophy, criticism, and politics. He is not remotely a member of the French avant-garde—although he certainly appreciates it, as witness his book on Genet. For his own work, he seems to have decided early in life what a play should be. He prefers conventional forms and has a taste for melodrama. (In fact, he has found time to rewrite an unabashed old melodrama, *Kean*, by Alexandre Dumas.) He likes highly theatrical images and—in the old-fashioned sense—"strong" situations. This is not to say that Sartre's plays are in any way sloughed off or patronized. Neither are they merely propaganda or thesis plays. Whatever their quality in the end, he clearly means them to have a vital theatrical existence.

Yet *The Condemned of Altona*, although it has a provocative dramatic base and confronts large issues with a large soul, is not an entirely successful work. It lacks the carefully wrought structure of *No Exit*, the consistent, cumulative suspense of *Dirty Hands*. Sometimes it seems to lose control of its symbols, and it skirts the absurd (with a small "a"). It flutters between large-scale drama and small-scale domestic quarrels. But since this imperfect play certainly merits production, it needs the very best theatrical treatment it can get.

At Lincoln Center, it gets from Herbert Blau, the director, considerable intellectual understanding and considerably less theatrical art. The ideas in the play are made clear, and they frequently have force, but, in stage terms, this production is pedestrian. It seems almost as if Blau were saying: "Here is what it is about. And in this scene the actors stand here to say it or move here, or sit there." There is small sense that the point of the production is its theatrical life rather than its content of ideas; and without the former, if a play is any good at all, the latter is weakened.

Fortunately for all of us, Blau imported George Coulouris to play the patriarch, but as in Lincoln Center's production of *Danton's Death* (by Georg Büchner), he has again committed errors of miscasting that Stanislavsky himself could not have overcome. As the older son, Tom Rosqui gives—in the abstract—a good, sardonic performance; but he is so wrong in person and personality for the essentially romantic part that he works against the cohesion of the drama as a whole. Carolyn Coates, the sister-in-law, is, in some ways, a taking actress, but she lacks the fire needed to propel this play to its climax.

The problems of establishing a competent American repertory company today are enormous. But we, as audience, must face what we are given. Blau chose this cast, and if their shortcomings have limited them, the burden is self-imposed. Yet, because Blau understands *The Condemned of Altona* intellectually, because the play has considerable intrinsic interest and is not, for him, as far out of reach as was *Danton's Death*, this is on balance the most rewarding production of the Lincoln Center company so far. One wishes that it were not so necessary to give such negative praise to what is meant to be New York's civic theater.

It is easy to cite the commercial defects that keep the American theater in general from being the arm of cultural life that the theater is in France. At Lincoln Center, however, the defects are in art. One had hoped that this company would be a galvanizing force for a surge of theatrical creativity in New York. One still hopes so. But, as of now, one may doubt that, if we were lucky enough to have the voice of a Sartre among us, the Lincoln Center company would have convinced him that their theater was a place in which he had to speak.

"Brecht—In Theory and Fact." *New York Times*, **April 10, 1966.**

During *The Caucasian Chalk Circle*, by Bertolt Brecht, which I saw twice and enjoyed twice at the Vivian Beaumont, I was additionally amused by some seeming contradictions. The play was written by a man whose theater theories have proved weak; it derives from a political philosophy with which I disagree; and it teaches a moral point that is simple—possibly too simple. Yet I believe it is a fine play.

The contradictions are connected, I think. First, the theory. Central to Brecht's view of the theater is the Alienation Effect, which is probably the most over-exploded idea in modern drama. Leaving out books and longer essays, I should like to have a box of (pre-Castro) Havana cigars for every Sunday article—like this one!—which, after a Brecht production, explained that the Alienation Effect may read well but does not work on stage. The explosion of the theory seems to me both irrefutable and irrelevant.

Brecht, of course, did not mean "alienation" in the usual sense. He meant to induce a certain perspective in audience members. When they witnessed an action, he did not want conventional, close empathy from them; he wanted them to perceive the history that had led up to the action. To take an example from *The Caucasian Chalk Circle*, the rescue of the baby by the kitchen maid is not meant to wring us in conventional fashion. The combination of the mimed action and the narrator's "chilly" song, says Brecht, "makes evident the terror of a period in which motherly instincts can become a suicidal weakness."

Well, it doesn't. Even if the music were better than the Lincoln Center production's weak score, this abstract historical point would not be made. What does happen is the emphasis of our customary double consciousness. Every theatergoer has this consciousness latently. He knows that he is watching pretense at the same time that (if all goes well) he believes it. Brecht, in this rescue scene, wants us to be more than usually aware of the play as play and ourselves as audience. It is essential that we be convinced by the stage action or there can be no double consciousness; it is also essential to him that we see the actors as actors.

But the result is not as he hoped, a perception of historical cause. It is, first, a refreshment of the faculty of theatrical participation; and, second, a vision—through that faculty—of the differing levels of consciousness in life itself. So the failure of Brecht's theory, as he intended it, is finally irrelevant because it succeeds in other modes. Besides, whether a success or a failure, that theory is only one of the fruits of Brecht's fundamental philosophy—the worldview that, in additional ways, gives his best plays their power and pertinence.

Brecht was a Communist and an atheist. From these beliefs comes his work's fierce opposition to bourgeois morality and to the generally accepted tenets of humanism. For him, the belief that man is alone and without gods does not (as it does for some existentialists) automatically elevate man to almost divine status. He does not see man as replacing God.

Why, then, are his best plays of interest to those who are not Communists and who may not be atheists, either? There are at least two reasons, I think. First, it is obviously not necessary to be a Communist to know that Marxism has altered our view of society. The materialist view of history and behavior cannot now be ignored any more than it need be solely venerated. Brecht is far and away the best dramatist of this view who has so far written. What we can accept in that view has never been truer in art than it in in his work.

Second, in general artistic terms, it seems increasingly possible that we are moving to the end of a long age of subjective art—art that reproduces the individual and whose chief purpose is "identification." In his essay "Beyond Bourgeois Theater," Sartre writes: "Why do men live surrounded by their own images? . . . Why must we also have our portraits in our room, why must we see representations of ourselves in the theater, why must we walk in the midst of statues that represent us, why must we go to the movies and always see ourselves again? . . . I think that people live in the midst of their own images because they do not succeed in being real objects for themselves."

Perhaps a greater degree of self-knowledge (of becoming "real") is helping to terminate the age of "self" explorations in art. Painting and sculpture, for example, are no longer largely concerned with miming the human form and environment or even the imagination and fantasy. The humanist tradition of art is being severely questioned by many kinds of artists. To be sure, human life is not likely to cease being the most interesting subject to human beings; but art, which had more and more intensely plunged into subjective experience in the last two centuries, may be coming to the end of that particular cycle. (To return to it, no doubt, at some future date.)

Brecht, from his own sources and impulses, anticipated this. Whatever his theoretical formulations, his artistic instincts and insights were those of a genius who had outdistanced his time. Although it was for doctrinaire social and political reasons, he, too, was trying to make an art that superseded a reveling in emotion, that was more than a reproduction of domestic familiarity. He wanted to pierce, not merely through the front doors of our apartments and houses, but right through to the quintessences of our lives.

Although his plays have surface resemblances to traditional drama, essentially his work proclaims his belief that the old drama is dead: the drama whose point often was to reassure us, to tell us how wonderful and safe we are, by italicizing us on stage. What we need (he says) is a drama that will show us how deluded we are: how capricious life is; how only the recognition of certain universals—of unpleasant disorder and unpleasant order—can save us from destroying ourselves.

As for *The Caucasian Chalk Circle* itself, it is one of Brecht's least overtly propagandistic plays, but his Marxist views underlie it. Out of this foundation, this is a play that teaches an ultra-simple lesson. But so does *The Taming of the Shrew*, and, similarly to *The Shrew*, Brecht uses the didactic road on which the play travels as a chance for theatrical display. He reworked an ancient Chinese legend for his story, which is set in the Caucasus—after a modern prologue—in 1200 A.D. Two women contend for a child: the mother who abandoned it and the maid who adopted it. A judge puts the child in a chalk circle and asks each woman to take an arm and pull the child out. He awards custody to the one who cannot bear to hurt the child. Moral: Anything belongs rightfully to him who will do best by it.

Simple enough. (Debatable, too; but so is the lesson of *The Taming of the Shrew*.) The point is that, in reaching this lesson, we have followed the maid and the baby through war, narrow escapes, and farcical misadventures. It is entertaining, but not merely so; Brecht wants us to see a parallel between these arbitrary stage effects and the accidents of life. Yet he also shows a difference. The maid's life is at the mercy of Brecht, a knowing man; but (he implies) our lives are at the mercy of blind or inimical forces. To dramatize this, he neatly unties all knots at the end in ways that would be unlikely in reality.

Thus, to resolve the contradictions with which I began, Brecht's Alienation theory, failing in its stated intent, hits another mark. His Marxism gives the melodramatic horseplay here an inescapable hard edge. His almost stoical use of character, instead of psychological and emotional delving, gives the play's texture a cool modernity. And his teaching of a simple lesson gives him the chance, in *The Caucasian Chalk Circle*, to tell a charming story.

"An Alternative Theater: Off-Off Broadway." *New York Times*, May 1, 1966.

It might be argued that the best thing to say here about the Off-Off Broadway theater is nothing. A certain obscurity, even cliquishness, befits a minority theater, and it is not necessarily unhealthy. Lack of popular acceptance is probably good for its character, and this is not the same thing as lack of popularity with its own audience. Partisans have already objected that several productions from Off-Off Broadway were recently elevated to Off-Broadway: Lanford Wilson's plays at Theater East, two bills at the Martinique, three programs at the Cherry Lane. (With no political analogy intended, the relationship among Off-Off Broadway, Off-Broadway, and Broadway is something like that among Beijing, Moscow, and New York. Each one thinks the one ahead of it has gone "soft.") Let's just say that the Off-Off Broadway theater exists; is producing a great deal of work, some of which is interesting; and has some chance of improvement in its own terms. It cannot be as completely ignored as some of its devotees would like.

The rising cost of work in Off-Broadway theaters has, in the last seven or eight years, spurred the production of plays and other theatrical events in Greenwich Village cafés, in churches and other venues in the Village, and in acting-school workshops. Naturally, this movement has greatly increased the creation of material specifically for use in these places. Here are some productions of such material, of varying length, that I have recently seen on Off-Off Broadway: a murder drama in which games are played with time in a manner reminiscent of Alain Resnais's films; a "camp" musical about the Egyptian queen Nefertiti; a documentary about the tax-evasion trial of Judith Malina and Julian Beck of the Living Theater; a slapstick comedy set in a firehouse; a fantasia about an aging nympho and a young narcissist at Coney Island; and, to confirm the oddity of mixtures, revivals of a Strindberg mother-hating play (*The Pelican*) and one of Maeterlinck's most velveteen pseudo-poetic dramas (*The Death of Tintagiles*).

Easily the most important aspect of Off-Off Broadway is its spirit. Its intent, like that of "underground" film, is to be open, permissive, free, and venturesome. Off-Off Broadway wants to be the theater that does what cannot or will not be done elsewhere. As such, it is welcome. As such, on the basis of what I have seen, it is also somewhat disappointing. Criticism of individual plays apart (for one thing, most of them were put on for limited runs and have already left), here are some general observations. The actors are usually either students of obviously differing ages or those who may be called professionally amateur. It is generally poor acting, sometimes painfully so. Kevin O'Connor, in the six short plays done at the Martinique, is an exception—outstandingly the best actor I have seen in Off-Off Broadway works.

Design and lighting are necessarily sketchy, and are at their best when intended to be amusing. The most interesting production element is the directing. Outside of Tom O'Horgan, again at the Martinique, these directors do not seem to have much insight into acting. But in shaping the physical profile of plays, they often show ingenuity and a kind of engaging abandon—slapping in techniques and effects like painters gone drunk on color. These directors also have a good sense of biological adaptation: they utilize the particular places in which their plays have to live. Actors' entrances at La Mama are often made through the audience because the dressing room is at the rear of the café—so the directors put that fact to some use. The fire chief in the firehouse play, at Judson Memorial Church, makes his entrances down a pole because there is a permanent balcony over the stage; Tintagiles died over behind a door near the bar because that was the only other usable door in the Caffé Cino.

The production styles range from the flat documentary effect of the Beck-Malina docu-drama to the extreme slapstick of the firehouse play—which is so intense in its use of custard pies and dousing in a tank that it takes on a tinge of ballet. (Both of these productions, incidentally, were the work of the Open Theater, a group that produces plays in several Off-Off Broadway houses.) Nothing in any of this staging is new; the novelty is in seeing the use of a wide and uninhibited range of techniques.

The playwriting has an equally wide range of style and quality, including tenuous "little-magazine" meanderings, "in" jokes for the regulars, and material of substance in such writers as Sam Shepard and Lanford Wilson. Perhaps Leo Rutman may also be included with this Off-Off Broadway group: his interesting, if overlong, *They Got Jack* was produced at the posh Off-Broadway Establishment Theater, but only on three Monday nights—so it may qualify here. Indeed, a good test *not* to apply to these writers is whether they can go on to Off-Broadway or Broadway itself. Some of them do so, of course, and all concerned may turn out to be the better for it, including the theater. But Off-Off Broadway does not think of itself as a series of farm teams feeding the major leagues, any more than "underground" film exists as a training ground for Hollywood. It exists to be itself.

That, as I say, is the chief disappointment for me of Off-Off Broadway so far: "itself" is only sporadically vital. There is more feeling of coterie than compulsion, more of an obligation to keep a bohemian atmosphere alive than of much urgency about what is actually being done in it. Still, that is probably both Off-Off Broadway's defect *and* its value: a mode of operation is being maintained without a great deal of striking content as of yet; but unless such a mode is maintained, better unconventional material may find no place to flourish.

For the uncommitted visitor, Off-Off Broadway can be called "chance" theater, then. First, there is the matter of mere detail: bills and performance times can vary from announcement to announcement—to be found in Village newspapers. (Most performances are given between Thursday and Monday evenings.) More important, to visit these theaters is to run a fair risk of boredom. The worst of this is that the boringness is quickly apparent and that, in a café theater, it is difficult to leave (without becoming part of the show!). Then again, I have not been more bored at any of these theaters than I have been on Broadway several times this season.

And, at least, in the Off-Off Broadway theater, one can always feel some peripheral sense of contribution. I do not suggest grim self-sacrifice on the altar of tedium. I have enjoyed some Off-Off Broadway plays. But if the evening turns out badly, at least one has helped to maintain a theater movement that has some promise of promise. A metropolis as large as New York's, a culture as complex, can afford alternative theaters. Off-Off Broadway is not yet of any strong cultural importance that I can see; but there is no reason why, possibly by virtue of its very looseness and omnivorousness, it cannot develop a healthy kind of artistic anti-tradition.

"Bored But Very Vital: Chekhov's Theater." *New York Times*, **May 15, 1966.**

Boredom and apathy are highly interesting subjects. As ingredients of drama, they begin to be important in the elegant comedies of the Restoration and early eighteenth century, but there they have a particular function: they are attributes of people who have never had to work for a living and who rarely think of useful occupation otherwise. Indeed, high comedy in any period is virtually impossible without a social caste that has a great deal of time on its hands.

Through the nineteenth century, boredom and apathy take on other colors, as the middle class rises and as the humanity of the working class becomes more and more insistent. Boredom is still generally a function of characters of wealth and/or position, but it is no longer restricted to comedy. And in comedy it often takes on a new, bitter note. In Alfred de Musset's *Fantasio*, for example, the bored hero says the following:

> If there were a hell, how soon I'd blow my brains out to go and see it all! What a wretched thing is man! ... There are times when I yearn to sit on a parapet, look at the river flowing by, and start counting one, two, three, four, five, six, seven, and so on until I die.

These lines, written in 1834, might almost come from Samuel Beckett.

Now, in these days of Beckett, of Pinter and Ionesco, of Antonioni's films, boredom and apathy are by no means exclusive to characters of wealth and position. They are usually symptoms of disappointment, in characters of widely varied status who are intellectually and spiritually unsatisfied.

The turning point in the history of apathy in drama occurs in the works of Anton Chekhov. All his major plays deal, in one way or another, with the theme of transition: from a dying society to a happier life to come on earth. His characters' listlessness and apathy are part of the curse of anachronism—in people born too late to live the life for which they were conditioned, too early to live the life they can envision. In his first full-length play, *Ivanov*, Chekhov drafted an early, if incomplete, version of this condition, and a chief trouble with the current New York revival at the Shubert Theatre is that the condition is outlined but not colored. John Gielgud, as Ivanov, states the matter clearly enough without convincing us of it emotionally.

Ivanov, though hardly one of Chekhov's most deeply developed characters, is not merely a congenital floater. He is a man who was once vital and engaged but is now resigned. He advises a younger man as follows:

> Don't try to fight the world single-handed . . . keep away from rationalized farming, schools to educate the peasants, revolutionary speech-making, and all the rest of it. That's where I made such a stupid mistake. Those things sap your vitality, they wear you out.

He also counsels the younger man to marry someone perfectly ordinary, even if she is dull and commonplace. Ivanov went against his society by marrying a Jewess, and as both his love and his rebelliousness cooled, he found himself in an anomalous position that only made his life more wearing.

Thus Ivanov's condition is not upper-class languor, it is the middle-aged fate of all those who are political romantics in their youth. Although injustice has existed for some centuries, they expect that, just because *they* take up the cudgels, injustice will quickly disappear. When this does not quite happen, they take it as proof of the foolhardiness of their beliefs and actions; and they settle down to a later life of facile disbelief and disparagement. It is the temper of this background that is missing from Gielgud's portrayal, and the lack of it makes his performance much less affecting than it could be.

Ivanov's life-view, though, is only a partial statement of what we get in Chekhov's later plays—in, for instance, the Prozorovs in *The Three Sisters*. In the character of Ivanov there is severance from the present without any hope, however tenuous, for an imagined future. But there is an even greater difference: in dramaturgy. In *Ivanov* apathy is the very subject of the drama. It causes the action and the conclusion. In the later plays, apathy is only the medium in which the drama occurs, the great shadowy forest through which the characters move, encounter, and part.

To wit: it is soul-sickness itself that estranges Ivanov from his wife and keeps him—after her death—from marrying Sasha. In *Uncle Vanya*, all the characters live in a decaying society and, it's true, are plainly conditioned by it; but Dr. Astrov is a man full of plans and hopes. He declines to marry Sonya only for the straightforward reason that he does not love her, and he has no affair with Ilyena, the married woman whom he loves, only because she flees him. This is possibly the prime reason why the later plays, like *Vanya*, are more interesting than *Ivanov*. For Chekhov came in them to use social malaise simply as environment, and compressed the drama into channels that run fiercely but quietly through it.

This truth—of the passion broiling under the muted surface—exposes the vulgar mistake that Chekhov's plays are nerveless odes to negativism. In fact, no view of life displeased Chekhov more. His own medical and artistic careers are proof enough. Gorky records that a plump and well-dressed lady once began to prattle to Chekhov in what she thought was Chekhovian language: "'Life is so boring, Anton Pavlovich ... And I have no desires ... my soul is in pain ... it is like a disease.' 'It is a disease,' said Anton Pavlovich with conviction. 'In Latin it is called *morbus imitatis*.'"

There is a touch of imitation—or at least of self-indulgence—in Ivanov, though not in Chekhov's subsequent major characters. Their apathy is the hushed agony of those caught between perception of the present and perception of the distance to the future, yet who somehow mean to live. Through all his plays, then, the use of apathy runs as a decisive current in the history of drama. But particularly in such later works as *The Sea Gull*, *Uncle Vanya*, *The Three Sisters*, and *The Cherry Orchard*, Chekhov, more than any playwright before him, understands that condition as a barometer of social climate, an insight into moral health—of a country, finally, as well as its citizens.

"A Life in the Theater: Harley Granville-Barker." *Horizon*, **Autumn 1975.**

In 1970 the Royal Shakespeare Company came to New York with Peter Brook's production of *A Midsummer Night's Dream*, which was hailed as revolutionary. In some ways that was true, but what was generally unknown was that Brook's production was in a revolutionary tradition, a tradition begun before World War I by the English director Harley Granville-Barker. "Barker's productions at the Savoy from 1912 to 1914," Robert Speaight has written in *Shakespeare on the Stage*, "looked ahead in a pretty straight line to Peter Brook's *A Midsummer Night's Dream* at Stratford more than fifty years later." For it was Barker who pioneered in stripping Shakespearean production of nineteenth-century scenic and musical baggage.

My point is not to diminish Brook, who has inherited from the past as all alert artists must, but to identify and explore that inheritance. Granville-Barker is one of the most extraordinary and extraordinarily versatile figures in the history of the English-speaking theater, an artist whose influence, long after his death, remains strong on both sides of the Atlantic even when his name is unknown. (The very spelling of that name is a bit of a muddle. After his second marriage Barker hyphenated his middle and last names, so some indexes list him as Granville-Barker, Harley. His biographer, C. B. Purdom, calls him Barker, and I'll follow suit.)

Early in his life Barker reportedly said that he planned to spend ten years as an actor, ten as a director, and the rest of his life as a writer. He did hold more or less to that schedule, though the decades overlapped somewhat. Presumably he meant that in his later years he would concentrate on playwriting, which he had begun early, and he did indeed write some plays and translate many in those years; but what he did not foresee was that he would spend his last twenty-five years out of the working theater—as a scholar, principally concerned with the essays by which he is new best known, his *Prefaces to Shakespeare*.

All four of those careers had their true distinctions. His acting made a strong impression on many critics. Max Beerbohm wrote of one Barker performance in 1904 that it had "just that mastery of climax and anti-climax which makes an artistic whole." Of his directing, John Gielgud, who worked with Barker in 1940 on one of his rare returns to the theater, said: "I never saw actors watch a director with such utter admiration and obedience. It was like Toscanini coming to a rehearsal." Of his playwriting, J. B. Priestley said in 1967 that Barker "is undoubtedly one of the most original, intelligent, and sensitive English dramatists of this century." And of his *Prefaces*, Arthur M. Eastman says in *A Short History of Shakespearean Criticism* (1968) that Barker, as no one else in that history, "helps us to a sense of the stage actuality of a Shakespearean play."

It is possible—possibly easy—to fault Barker in each of his four professions, but the fact that he achieved genuine eminence in all four of them stamps him a genius. What makes him relevant today, not just a rueful-fascinating historical figure, is the way he affected the theater in which some of us work and which all of us attend. What makes him biographically interesting are the elements of tragedy in his life, tragedy that is endemic to the theater.

Barker was born in London in 1877, the son of a rather nebulous real-estate agent who was descended from clergymen. His mother, much more influential him, was the granddaughter of an Italian physician who had immigrated to England. (Bernard Shaw, who met Barker at the turn of the century, said that the younger man "had a strong strain of Italian blood in him and looked as if he had stepped out of a picture by Benozzo Gozzoli.") Mrs. Barker was the chief breadwinner of the family by means of a then popular entertainment, the poetry recital. She toured Britain and America. Her son could not have had much formal education—the first anomaly in a career marked by intellectual rigor— because he spent much of his childhood traveling with her and at times recited items on the program. He made his first appearance as actor in a provincial English theater in 1891, and the following year, aged fifteen, made his London début as a "3rd Young Man." Evidently he showed some quality, although he was no immediate sensation, because he kept finding work and kept progressing.

About this time Barker began writing plays. His first, a collaboration called *The Weather-hen*, was produced in London with some success in 1899. Barker was twenty-two. That year he read a minor role in a copyrighting performance of Shaw's new play *Caesar and Cleopatra*. In those days the copyright law was such that at least one public performance of a play had to be given in order for the author to hold his rights. (Sometimes he would merely get some friends, actors or otherwise, to come to a hall one morning, tack a hastily scrawled performance notice on the board outside, and have his friends read the script aloud on stage.) The importance of this particular performance was, first, that Barker was selected for it, and, second, that it brought him together with the forty-three-year-old Shaw and thus helped initiate a great era in the English theater.

The meeting of Barker and Shaw helped change the latter from a published but rarely performed dramatist into a famous theater artist in Britain and, soon, the world. Barker did this partly by his acting of important Shaw roles. Shaw said he was "humanly speaking, perfect" as Marchbanks in *Candida*, which he played in 1900, and subsequently Barker played in the first productions of *Man and Superman* (John Tanner), *John Bull's Other Island* (Father Keegan), *Major Barbara* (Adolphus Cusins), and *The Doctor's Dilemma* (Louis Dubedat). He influenced Shaw because, quite inferably, the author had him in mind when writing those roles and because his performances contributed substantially to the productions that ensured Shaw's theatrical place. That might have been monument enough, to have been inspiration and executant for a great dramatist, but it was a lesser part of Barker's career, even of his contribution to Shaw's career.

Barker had begun directing in 1900, and by 1904, at the age of twenty-seven, he had done five productions, including a bill of short plays, two of them by Maeterlinck, and a full-length play of his own, *The Marrying of Ann Leete*. Then came two significant events. He married Lillah McCarthy. a stunning, exceptionally gifted actress with whom he had once toured; and he joined forces with a manager named J. E. Vedrenne to run the Royal Court Theatre (nowadays known as the home of the English Stage Company, producers of John Osborne and other prominent playwrights of the last twenty years).

The Barker-Vedrenne partnership was no ordinary managerial move. It was, as it turned out, the major effort of Barker's life toward the goal that mattered most in his life: the establishment of a permanent theater of high quality. He and the critic William Archer had already written a book-length study called *Scheme and Estimates for a National Theatre* that set forth, in ostensibly practical terms, the means to realize a vision. The means was not forthcoming, so Barker sought another avenue. He and Vedrenne decided to do a series of matinees of plays of merit. They began in October 1904, with some backing from friends, including Shaw, and by the following February they took over the theater completely.

The Barker-Vedrenne management of the Royal Court lasted until June 1907, when money difficulties intervened, but during that relatively brief time it changed the shape and intent, even the frustrations, of the English theater. From that time on, the level of playwriting, of general artistic tenor, was affected by the Royal Court venture: achievement and disappointment in the theater were measured against the Barker-Vedrenne record.

In the course of those three years the Barker-Vedrenne management gave 988 performances. Shaw loomed largest in the list with 701 performances of eleven of his plays. They also produced plays by Euripides (in Gilbert Murray's new translations), Ibsen, Galsworthy, Hauptmann, Schnitzler, Yeats, Masefield, and Barker himself. He directed many of the plays and acted in many, sometimes in those he also directed. Seasons of serious new plays are not unfamiliar these days (partly because of Barker's effect, in the United States as in Britain), but in those days such seasons were virtually unknown. The previous century had been one pre-eminently of acting, usually star-centered rather than ensemble work, and of generally abysmal playwriting, usually tailor-made for stars. The intellectual and aesthetic changes that were already roaring through the other arts and that had already blown away much of the fustiness in continental playwriting had left the English-language theater almost untouched. This director-actor-playwright, twenty-seven when he joined with Vedrenne, changed all that in just three years. He did not move our theater en bloc to Parnassus, but from then on it could at least know what it was missing. Further, perhaps foremost, it established Shaw in the position from which he has not yet been budged: as the greatest dramatist after Shakespeare in our language.

It also established Barker. At thirty he was now a figure of first consequence. The end of the Royal Court days marked the end of the ten years as actor that he had "scheduled" for himself; he acted very little thereafter. Now he concentrated on directing, which profited enormously from his acting talent and experience, and on writing plays. His first play of lasting worth, *The Voysey Inheritance*, had been produced at the Royal Court in 1905, directed by himself with himself in the leading role. The plot concerns a respected old solicitor who, just before he dies, informs his son and partner that the firm is operating fraudulently. The son must decide whether to expose matters and bring about ruin or keep up the fraud until he can set things right.

In 1907 came *Waste*, again directed by Barker with himself in the leading role, a play about a brilliant young politician who has a casual affair that wrecks his career and prevents him from doing the great good he might have done his country. In 1909 came *The Madras House*, directed by Barker but without him in the cast. *The Madras House*, too, deals with inheritance of a sort— the passing of a successful fashion house from father to son—but thematically it deals with changes in men's view of women and with women's changing view of themselves.

All three of these plays contain elements of, in Max Beerbohm's phrase, "breadth and brilliancy." All three of them show, again in Beerbohm's phrase, how "deeply influenced he was and is" by Shaw. Still, of all the dramatists influenced by Shaw, Barker is easily the best, and if his "original contributions to our dramatic literature" are not quite the "treasures" that Shaw called them in his obituary article, they are still far too good for oblivion.

Paradoxically, his plays, his works in permanently available form, have had less effect on the theater than his work in ephemeral form: his directing. His production of new plays at the Royal Court and elsewhere had demonstrated his diamond-bright intelligence, his hatred of stagy cliché, his great sensitivity to character nuance, his extraordinary ear. Now he began to apply these attributes to Shakespeare. To some his work seemed raw and disturbing, but his intent was to unite the best of what he took to be the Elizabethan manner with the best of the modern. He believed in suppleness of verse-speaking (music but not music for its own sake) and the speed of speech and action that are implicit in the very structure of the Elizabethan stage: he believed in simple design and costume and lighting chaste and strong, rather than lots of stage freight and upholstery.

With the aid of a rich peer, Barker was able to make one more attempt at establishing the beginnings of a theater close to his ideal, at the Savoy. He was highly dissatisfied with the job-lot life of the commercial theater, so much so that he had even talked about immigrating to Germany and becoming a naturalized citizen there. Several visits to that country had strongly impressed him with German regard for the institution of the theater and willingness to subsidize it (which is still true). But at least he was able to start work at the Savoy.

His productions of Shakespeare there began with *The Winter's Tale* in September 1912. Critics said it was not Shakespeare, it was post-impressionism. Amid the uproar, writes C. B. Purdom, "there were those who recognized new factors . . . freedom from subservience to the actor-manager, freedom from elaborate staging, faithfulness to the text, and the conviction that Shakespeare was not a dead classic but a dramatist for the twentieth-century theatre."

Two months later Barker produced *Twelfth Night* at the Savoy. Other work intervened, and he did his last Shakespeare production, *A Midsummer Night's Dream*, at the Savoy in February, 1914. In his entire career he directed only four Shakespeare plays—there had been a production of *Two Gentlemen of Verona* ten years earlier—but they have touched the theaters thinking about Shakespeare ever since.

His ten years as playwright were overlapped by his ten as director. And those years in turn were overlapped, were ended at last in a way that wrenched him out of his whole style of life.

In the winter of 1915 Barker brought three productions to New York: Shaw's *Androcles and the Lion*, Anatole France's *The Man Who Married a Dumb Wife*, and Shakespeare's *Midsummer Night's Dream*. Press and public were startled but engaged, as they were by the two productions of Greek plays that Barker did in American college stadiums in the summer of 1915. Then a change, sudden and profound, came in Barker's private life.

In a sense not at all cynical, this change might be said to reflect a desire, perhaps unconscious, to emulate Shaw even further. Barker's playwriting, as noted, was indebted to Shaw. He joined the socialist Fabian Society, in which Shaw was prominent, and he resigned from the executive board of that society when Shaw did (although Shaw remained a socialist all his life while Barker filtered away). The very example of professional versatility, though Barker's was much lesser, was set by Shaw. Now a different sort of example may possibly have affected Barker: Shaw's marriage to an adoring rich woman.

Barker's own marriage to Lillah McCarthy had seemingly been good. They had worked together at the Royal Court and the Savoy, and she was with him in America playing leading roles for him. But in New York Barker met Helen Huntington, the wife of an American multimillionaire, and they fell in love. His affection for her was genuine: there is no more reason to doubt that in his case than in Shaw's. (More reason to believe it in Barker's case, perhaps, because, unlike Charlotte Shaw, Mrs. Huntington was not rich in her own right. Her husband had endowed her generously when they parted.) But given the importance of Shaw in Barker's life, it is hard to believe that some idea of living *à la* Shaw did not occur to Barker.

The effect on Lillah was cruel, devastating. She left America with Barker in June 1915, believing that his relationship with Helen was over. But he was back in New York in September without her, and in January of 1916 Lillah got a letter from him asking for a divorce. "She went at once to Shaw," says Purdom, "who said that he, too, had heard from Barker by the same post." Years later Lillah described that evening in a passage from her memoirs that was omitted from the published book (all references to Barker were deleted, at his insistence):

I went all frozen on a cold January night. . . . Shaw greeted me very tenderly and made me sit by the fire. I was shivering. Shaw sat very still. . . . How long we sat there I do not know, but presently I found myself walking with dragging steps with Shaw beside me . . . up and down Adelphi Terrace. . . . He let me cry. Presently I heard a voice in which all the gentleness and tenderness of the world was speaking. It said: "Look up, dear, look up to the heavens. There is more in life than this. There is much more."

If that sounds unlike the usual image of Shaw, it fits the image of a protective parent, which is how he saw himself in relation to the young genius and his gifted, beautiful wife. After Barker returned to England, Shaw saw him as often as he could, despite his sympathy for Lillah. But the friendship could not continue. Barker's new wife detested both Shaw and the theater itself. She felt that the workaday theater was an unworthy place for a man of Barker's intellect and writing abilities, and she disliked Shaw, possibly because he was a link with and reminder of Lillah, but more surely because he was happy in the theater, appreciated Barker's gigantic theatrical gifts, and wanted him to keep on using them.

Unquestionably Shaw was grievously hurt by the breach, though he sometimes spoke lightly of it. He wasn't even informed of the second marriage, which took place in July 1918. A month later Shaw wrote to Barker: "It would be convenient occasionally to know something about you. I surmise that you are married: but it is only a surmise. . . . I have refrained, with an exaggerated delicacy, from asking you questions for a year or so. Now I do ask them bluntly." The reply is not known, although they met later that year.

Unquestionably Shaw had looked on Barker as a son-in-art. (At one time there was even a rumor in London that Barker was his natural son.) In his biography of Shaw, the Irish critic-playwright St. John Ervine says that a few years after the second marriage, he was driving in the country with Shaw and they passed the road that led up to Barker's palatial new home. "I said to G.B.S.: 'Harley Granville-Barker lives up that road.' He looked at it in the odd way he had when he was moved, and, almost as if he were indifferent, said, 'Oh, Harley!' But when G.B.S. was as terse as that he was under deep emotion."

Thus, if Barker had made his second marriage because he was consciously or unconsciously modeling himself on Shaw, the result was to split him from his model. It was a Shavian irony.

His marriage was also to split him from the theater. After 1918 until his death in 1946, save for a few excursions, most of them quite brief, he did nothing in the theater. He wrote about the theater, principally a book called *The Exemplary Theatre* in which he restated his aims for the theater he had not been able to make and argued for a closer relationship between the university and the theater. He lectured from time to time. He translated, some French plays on his own, some Spanish ones with his wife. He finished his fourteen illuminating *Prefaces to Shakespeare*, each one an essay on a particular play, the one on *Hamlet* so long that it is a complete book in itself.

And he wrote two more plays, of debatable quality but of high vicarious interest. *The Secret Life* (1923) is about a retired English politician who is persuaded to run again for Parliament and a probable cabinet post, but who quits the campaign to visit the woman he loves, who is dying—in America! *His Majesty* (1928) is about an exiled king who makes an effort to regain his crown but is sent again into exile. It is hardly intrusive to see these plays as devices of psychological projection.

Of Barker's brief returns to the theater, the chief one was the ten days he spent, at John Gielgud's invitation, attending rehearsals of the latter's *King Lear* production in 1940. Gielgud devotes a chapter to this experience in his autobiography *Stage Directions* and says: "[Barker] had only ten days to work with us on *King Lear*, but they are the fullest in experience that I have ever had in all my years on the stage." To read Barker's preface to *King Lear* is to read intellectual exegesis at its most practical, a theater mind intent on exploring the text with performance as its imperative. To read the nine pages of notes that Gielgud made of Barker's specific suggestions for voice and movement—Gielgud gives them as an appendix—is to glimpse the theatrical gifts that underlay the essayist's gifts. To read both is to perceive the breadth of the man and the extent of the loss in his virtual retirement from a directing career at the age of thirty-eight.

In 1930, twelve years after their marriage, the Barkers moved to Paris. It was to be their place of residence, except for their exile during the Second World War, for the rest of their lives. Barker hyphenated his name to please his new wife, and they established themselves in a grand duplex apartment that had a staff of eleven. During the war they lived in New York, where Barker did some work for the British Information Service. He lectured at Yale, Harvard, and Princeton, and his book *The Use of the Drama* grew out of a series of lectures he gave at Princeton.

Before he came to America he had already become a legend, remote from almost all his former theater associates, especially his former closest friends, the Shaws. In 1943 Shaw sent a postcard, one of his favorite literary forms, to Barker in New York: "Charlotte died last Sunday, the 12th of September, at half-past two in the morning. She had not forgotten you.... You will not, I know, mind my writing this to you. She was eighty-six. I am eighty-seven." Three years later Shaw wrote his obituary article about his former friend, twenty-one years younger.

Why did Barker leave? Why, before he had begun to reach the height of his one gift that can inarguably be called great, did he forsake the theater? He sometimes answered that question. He wrote to Gielgud in 1937 that he had pinned his faith to the establishing of a permanent national theater and "finding it... no go, I got out." He had said in 1915, rather wryly, "Since we cannot do away with the theater, let us make it as good as we can." He had tried, in epoch-making fashion; but frustrated by the war and increasingly wearied by frustration, he finally allowed himself to be led away.

There are reasons beyond his theater idealism, of course, that help explain his susceptibility to persuasion. "When Barker was young," says Purdom, "it was the thing to be a writer, while to be an actor was to belong to a despised profession. He never grew out of this state of mind." He always preferred the company of other kinds of artists, of politicians and intellectuals, to that of people only in the theater. There was certainly an appetite for misconstrued gentility in Barker that made him vulnerable to Helen's immense loathing of the workaday theater. But fundamentally it was his inability to realize his visions that made him willing to give up.

In 1916 he even wrote a one-act play called *Farewell to the Theatre* about a famous actress who gives up her career because she cannot have it at the level she wants. That and his two subsequent full-length plays are his apologia in disguise. The history of the theater contains other successful people who felt themselves cursed with theatrical talent, gifts they could exercise only in a place they disliked. William Charles Macready, the English actor, was an international star for three decades until he retired in 1851; the last two words of his voluminous diaries, after the entry noting his retirement, are *"Thank God!"* (Italics his.)

The tragedy of the English theater was that it could not give the right home to an artist of Barker's vision. The tragedy of Barker is that he looked for the excuse to leave: that a residual Victorian ache for propriety aggravated his artistic frustration and sapped his will to fight further. And the tragedy is compounded because it is quite clear that in the library of his Paris apartment he was "directing" on paper, putting into his Shakespearean and other essays the force and wisdom that might have gone into the establishment of a history-making theater.

The oddity is that he nevertheless did make history; that, despite his disproportioned career, he has had a huge influence, seen and unseen: on those who knew from whom they were learning, and on those who learned from him whether they knew it or not. In 1967 the English critic Ivor Brown said, "Barker established the status and proved the value of the [director] in this country." In one way the statement is exaggerated; Barker was not the first. In another it is too modest: he also affected the United States directly, by his productions and writings, but continuingly by the cultural osmosis that brings important artistic influences from England to America and vice versa. Whenever we see a director concerned with unity of concept, a company concerned with authenticity of style and the idea of a permanent ensemble, we can know that they are in some degree the progeny of Barker. Whenever we see a university supporting a professional theater and professional training, we can know that the program is to some integral extent the result of Barker's *The Exemplary Theatre*. As for Shakespearean scholarship, few competent Shakespeareans would deny the vitality that Barker pumped into that body.

In his early play *Waste*, the young politician-hero, Trebell, objects to high-flown talk about the influence of God on man's search for knowledge and says that he wants to converse in prose. His opponent in discussion says, "What is the prose for God?" Trebell replies, "That's what we irreligious people are giving our lives to discover." The theater proved too prosaic for Barker to discover his god in it, but before and after he left it, he did work that still helps those stubborn enough to hope.

"Theater As You Like It: A Round of Applause for Repertory." *Horizon*, **Autumn 1976.**

Hardly a month goes by without one more definitive article on the fate of the American theater, and almost every one prescribes the repertory system as the solution to all problems—or at least as the requisite first step toward solution. Well, the idea of repertory certainly is important to our theater today, so it is important to have a clear understanding of it. Let me begin my own comments by examining the word itself.

It doesn't mean what it looks like. "Repertory" doesn't mean "repetition." A repertory theater does indeed repeat plays, but the word comes from the past participle of the Latin verb *reperire*, to find. The *Oxford English Dictionary* gives three meanings for "repertory"; abridged, they are (1) an index; (2) a storehouse; (3) repertoire. If we look then under the most pertinent meaning, "repertoire," we find: "A stock of dramatic or musical pieces that a company or player is accustomed or prepared to perform."

This definition is a small miracle of compression. It not only gives the quintessence of the idea, sometimes misrepresented even by presumed repertory supporters, but it also includes the term with which repertory used to be interchangeable and with which it is now often confused—stock. Today a stock company may or may not have a permanent ensemble; it performs plays successively, for one or two or however many weeks, then discards them. Throughout most of the nineteenth century a stock company was a repertory company: a stock of people, in a relatively permanent ensemble, who had a stock of plays to choose from and perform. The only element left out of the OED definition is alternation: a repertory company varies its bills, giving a play one or two or three performances, then bringing it back after having performed other plays.

This system, which may today strike some readers as a fancy, idealistic plan, was for centuries the only form of theater practice. That is the prime historical point. The idea of repertory is not a professorial or critical theory; less than a century ago it was universal and commonplace in Great Britain and America (as it still is in Europe). The reasons it was abandoned cannot be ignored, but what we are discussing is a return, not a novelty.

During the first thousand years or so of the Christian era, the formal theater was under the Church's interdiction, but traveling players kept working underground. As Jacques Burdick writes, "Forced together by circumstance, mimes, actors, acrobats, rope dancers, and musicians joined forces to survive." After the Church began to use formal theater for its own purposes around 1000 A.D. and began to draw on professionals to assist, actors moved out of the underground to prosper in the new sunlight. By the middle of the sixteenth century they were familiar on the Continent and in England.

Actors traveled. Audiences didn't. Many people might never go ten miles from home in their entire lives; they had neither money nor transport nor, often, permission. Since there simply weren't enough people in any one place to make up many audiences, actors had to be vagabonds or starve. Even if they wanted to stay a week in one place, actors had to have seven plays in repertoire, a stock of goods to offer like any other traveling tradesmen, so that the available audience who came on Monday would come again on Tuesday and for the rest of the week. Traveling with just one play would have been stupid, and staying in one place would have been unthinkable.

But the latter idea became possible as the Renaissance wore on, as towns and cities grew larger. Since there were now more people with more money and more leisure time living in larger compact areas, some troupes could stop traveling, or at least vary their traveling with extended engagements in one place. But just because companies now were, or could be, fixed in one place, this did not mean that they would alter the "stock of wares" idea of their traveling days. In Great Britain—therefore in America, too, as the colonies built theaters and developed a profession throughout the eighteenth century—audiences were conditioned to the scheduling of Play A on Monday evening, Play B on Tuesday, C on Wednesday, with perhaps A returning on Thursday.

Cities, though growing, were still not large enough in the eighteenth century to support extensive runs of one play at a time. If a new production was a success, it took time for news of it to travel among the maximum potential theater audience; the spacing out of performances of that production allowed that time. Besides, the bulk of any theater's repertoire was standard works, not new plays. If Smith made a hit as Othello, it was Smith whom people were coming to see, not a new play, and it was better business to tease the audience by spacing *Othello* out among other standard plays, rather than to present fifteen or twenty performances of it in a row.

"In the early period [of the nineteenth century]," states Edward Mammen in *The Old Stock Company School of Acting*, ". . . the stock theater was the only form of professional theater organization. . . . A system in which a single group of actors presented many plays during a season was obviously well adapted to the comparatively small and isolated communities of these years." But change was coming. Beginning in 1810 with George Frederick Cooke, English stars began to tour the United States. Often traveling alone, they would simply take over the leading roles in a local theater's productions of standard plays. Lesser actors, both British and American, also tried to set themselves up as touring stars because such tours quickly became cachets of eminence. Increasingly, local managers had trouble drawing audiences to productions done solely by the resident company, without some glamorous visitor.

To compound this intrinsically theatrical problem came the invention and extension of the railroad. In 1849 there were fewer than six thousand miles of track in the United States. In 1860 there were more than thirty thousand miles of track, much of it west of the Mississippi. In 1869 the golden spike was driven in Utah, and transcontinental trains came into service.

This immense technological development had a huge impact on the theater. Stars could, of course, now travel farther, more easily, and more quickly; and now they could take some of their own supporting players with them, to make sure that important supporting rules were played as they wished in a local theater. This led, in short order, to what was then called the "combination" company: the *complete* acting company with star(s), along with all costumes and scenery—what we would today call a road company. These combination companies, for reasons of economy, usually traveled with one play, so a successful company amounted to a long run of one play done in numerous places.

The railroad also had another effect, less marked by theater historians: now the audience could travel, too. People from small towns went much more frequently to cities where they saw grander theater productions, which they could then compare with local fare. The "small and isolated communities" that Mammen mentioned became larger and less isolated, and the public became too demanding for what must have often been the shoddiness of local theaters.

Because of these cumulating factors, the decline of the stock company was rapid in the latter half of the century. In 1860 there were more than fifty stock companies around the country, and in 1871 there were still some fifty. But by 1878 there were only twenty; by 1880 seven or eight. Seven years later there were four, three of them, paradoxically, in New York.

The stock companies were pushed out by the combination company, which still is essentially our predominant theater practice—one play produced to run as long as possible, in one place or on tour, with a group of actors assembled only for that play, with a physical production built only for that play. For a local manager, the chance to book an entire show, complete with scenery, was a financial boon. Previously he had to pay a corps of actors every week and provide his own scenery; now he could book "packages" when he needed them and when they were available, with almost no overhead in other weeks. And those packages came festooned with personalities and with proven reputations.

Thus we got the long-run system. An enormous amount has been written, with truth, about the defects and ill effects of that system, but most writers scant the improvements that it brought about. The first improvement was in the direction of plays. During the centuries of stock, plays were not rehearsed as they are today. Most plays were standard items, and each theater had a venerable prompt-book for each play—also more or less standard—containing the entrances, exits, principal movements, and "business" for the cast. When a new play was produced, the movements and effects were usually worked out in collaboration between the cast, the stage manager, the prompter (if he was old and trusted), the author (if he was present and respected), and the manager of the house. No one person was expected to have the overall artistic vision and control of the present-day director.

It was around the middle of the nineteenth century that the director came into being. As more and more reliance was placed on the success of one play in one production, more and more care was spent on its preparation. Under such artistic mentors as Dion Boucicault in Britain and America, and Augustin Daly in New York, the theater gained a person who had something of the relation to a production that a conductor has to a symphonic performance.

That increased reliance on one play at a time led to an increased investment—of money, time, and taste—in scenery and costumes. (Previously most stock theaters had used a stock of scenery, and actors had usually provided their own costumes.) Once again art and economics went hand in hand. When more money was invested in scenery and costumes for a play, more performances of that play had to be given to repay the cost; the "run" system made those added performances possible.

But the most radical effect of the change from repertory to the long-run system was on the playwright. First and most obvious, he could make more money. Prior to about 1850, a new play might be given by a stock theater for as long as a week; then, if it was successful, it would be placed in the repertory to alternate with other plays. In general a new play would get, in the course of a season, a maximum of some forty non-consecutive performances.

The playwright's success thus became vital to the theater's success. Previously, a new play that failed was simply withdrawn; the theater continued—with its standard repertoire and perhaps another new play or two. But with the end of repertory, audience interest shifted from player to play. The search for successful new plays became the theater's prime interest, and it is still our theater's dominant drive.

By 1900, allowing for very few exceptions, we can say that the stock/repertory theater, with a relatively permanent company, had disappeared. The carefully directed and specifically designed one-show-at-a-time theater had taken its place, and a manager did a new production only when he had a new script of promise. It was a revolution in theater practice.

With this revolution came a change in attitudes toward repertory. As we have seen, for many centuries repertory had been virtually the only form of theater operation. Then the theater altered its way of making a living; and repertory, after it had been supplanted by the long run, became revered, yearned for, apostrophized, and etherealized. It was as if the theater had practiced repertory for all those centuries out of high-mindedness (not for cold cash reasons), had somehow slipped from grace, and now depended on a return to that earlier, untainted, idealistic system for salvation.

Mournful statements began to appear about the loss of the stock company, particularly as a school for acting. But Mammen, who did as reliable a study of acting as is possible through research alone, shows that in the early nineteenth century the beginner at the Boston Museum theater had to learn entirely on his own; in the middle of the century, as runs lengthened, there was some balance between careful instruction and variety of roles; toward the end of the century, as the long-run system took over, chances for variety disappeared but "the apprentice stood a far better chance of adequate instruction." Yet, despite these facts, the idea of repertory as school and as professional fulfillment became more and more hallowed.

In 1904 William Archer, the English critic and dramatist, and Harley Granville-Barker, the English genius who was an actor, director, dramatist, and critic, collaborated on a book called *Scheme and Estimates for a National Theatre*. The authors' assumption, based on the past of the English-speaking theater and the continuing practice of the national and municipal theaters on the Continent (which, through benefit of subsidy, have not changed to this day), was that their proposed theater would have to be a permanent repertory company. Archer and Granville-Barker conceded some points skimped on by other enemies of the long-run system before and since: "Beyond all doubt, the supersession of the old stock company by the long-run system has done a very real service to the stage. It has encouraged a finish, both in playwriting and acting, which the older conditions never allowed. It has broken a tradition of slovenliness." But then they went on to stress the shortcomings of the new system, especially the typecasting, in which actors are cast repeatedly in the roles that they closely resemble and develop only narrow specialties: "Under the old system talent and skill were expected to work impossibilities; under the new system little is left for them to do." Repertory was "the only practical system" for the national theater they envisioned, with a permanent company, and with the plays alternated and (remember the word *reperire*) retained.

That British national theater had to wait a long time for its birth, but in the Edwardian decade several attempts were made in England to establish repertory. Between the two world wars the repertory movement continued to struggle and managed to stay alive, pre-eminently at the Old Vic in London and the Memorial Theatre at Stratford-on-Avon. After World War II the Old Vic finally became the National and the Stratford company, eventually rechristened the Royal Shakespeare, opened a London base. Both companies, with fluctuations, have done admired work. There is no question as to whether repertory can pay its way in Britain; it can't. Both of these companies are kept going by government subsidy far beyond anything the United States has ever given to the theater. Still, they have had considerable public support and have, additionally, become tourist attractions. By and large these companies are true repertories, in which many actors remain for many seasons.

In the United States the outstanding attempt at repertory between the wars was made by Eva Le Gallienne, who was also involved in the first attempt after World War II. Le Gallienne's Civic Repertory Theater ran on Fourteenth Street in New York from 1926 to 1933, and the American Repertory Theater, where she was one of three directors, ran on Columbus Circle in New York only from November 1946, to February 1947. In the intervening years, costs had greatly increased, other attractions for desirable actors had opened up, and the public had lost the habit of repertory.

The money situation for American repertory has improved in recent years because of more chances for subsidy. In 1957 the Ford Foundation began its Program in Humanities and the Arts, which has been especially helpful to repertory theaters. Other foundations have also helped substantially. In 1965 the federal government began the National Endowment for the Arts, one aspect of which has been theater assistance. (I have to note that the projection of the National Endowment for theater aid in 1975 was $6.5 million, while West Germany's annual support of theaters stands at about $35 million.) Still, partly in response to recently available financial aid, there are now about fifty resident theaters throughout the United States. Some of them call themselves repertory companies, and a few of them come close to the definition. Their work shows at least a clear recognition of the repertory ideal and, however incomplete or abortively implemented, tries to move toward that ideal.

Why? Why has repertory *become* an ideal? Why has the standard commercial practice of the last century become the utopia of our time?

Early in the twentieth century the long-run system began to show its defects. Its virtues were as described, but it soon became apparent that, under the new system, the theater had been converted from modes of continuity into hundreds of separate little enterprises, each one born to die however long the death was postponed. Actors, now usually typecast, were not only deprived of variety but of the chance for refreshment and improvement of a role that alternation provided. If development of theater artists had never been as consistent under the old system as was now nostalgically imagined, it had become practically nil in the long-run system. Since the object of production was now to see how long a play could run before it was permanently discarded, most of the plays chosen were those that the largest number of people would rush to see as soon as possible.

As these defects became clearer, some noted theater people began to argue for a return to repertory to revive and expand its advantages. Some of them, like Archer and Granville-Barker, realized that those advantages had rarely been properly exploited; they resolved to make amends. But since repertory was no longer the mainstream, those who favored it immediately became exceptions, somewhat rarefied. The support of repertory quickly took on the color and trappings of a Cause among many theater people.

Theater people, since enthusiasm on the subject, until relatively recently, was generally restricted to professionals outside the theater—critics, professors, and the like. In the nineteenth century, repertory had, so to speak, been commanded by the audience. Now the audience was either unconcerned or satisfied with the new order. Then, during the last decade or so, came further changes. First, among actors. American actors had *talked* about repertory for sixty years as the ideal form, as a home, as a place to develop and sustain; but in my experience and observation they had done this talking only when they were out of work. When they had jobs, in commercial shows or films or in radio or television series, they only sighed about it ruefully or mentioned it not at all. But as more resident theaters were established, more and more actors, particularly young ones, began to develop a deeper revulsion toward commercial conditions. I don't maintain that actors no longer want fame and big money and that no golden offers would lure them away from the Ashtabula Rep. I do maintain that more actors, particularly young ones out of university drama schools who may also have served internships at theaters abroad, have been less willing to throw themselves on the meat markets of Broadway and Hollywood and are trying to find rational ways to invest their theatrical lives elsewhere.

The attitude of playwrights, too, has changed. Around 1950 the best English-language playwrights became repelled by Broadway and the West End and started writing for Off-Broadway and its London equivalent. This took them out of inhuman money pressures but not necessarily out of the long-run system. In England, which has the two best English-language reps, a further move toward rep was especially logical, because many of the most desirable actors and directors were connected with those companies. Harold Pinter gave his plays *The Homecoming* and *Old Times* to the Royal Shakespeare Company to be performed in a repertory schedule. Many other playwrights have done the equivalent.

For the playwright this brought less money, at least for the first production; and the first production is often the most lucrative. It also meant making do with the actors in the company most of the time, instead of selecting from the whole corps of working actors. Although there were exceptions to this, where actors were jobbed in for specific new plays (as they are for some revivals), fundamentally the playwright was still moving toward repertory. What led him there, I believe, was not only the absolutely incredible financial conditions and consequent strictures of Broadway, but a growing feeling that what was good for the theater was good for the playwright and that repertory was good for the theater. To help such a theater it was necessary to find actors and an audience for whom to write. As many playwrights learned, the question, Whom am I writing for? is not easy to answer. Repertory theaters, organic, related to a community, may be part of the solution.

Other kinds of theater artists, designers, and directors, who had also benefited at first from the change to long runs, began to see virtues in repertory. All of them knew that every theatrical profession had benefited in some way from the long-run system but that this system had outlived, by seventy years or so, its usefulness to anything but the straight business theater. These professionals wanted to take what they had gained from System Two back into a bettered System One.

And that may not even have been the most significant development for repertory. The American audience now seems to be changing. The repertory theaters around the country, of which there are a few, and those close to repertory in method, of which there are many more, are reporting high attendance rates. None of these theaters is rid of the need for subsidy: on the contrary, subsidy is increasingly necessary as costs zoom ahead of ticket prices. But audience response around the country is growing. People don't go to touring shows or local affairs in ritual fashion as they once did. They are sick of road-company dregs and jerrybuilt local productions. They subscribe, in great numbers, to the professional resident theater.

Certainly a great deal of that subscription is only a new kind of social ritual. But such support, always present in any public art and not to be snooted at, helps keep those theaters alive. And one important group for whom they are being kept alive—possibly the most important in a long view—is the best part of that audience: those who go out of hunger, not rote. That best audience exists. I have seen a bit of it myself and I have heard a lot about it from directors and managers of theaters around the country. Spattered with television sludge, jostled by the sweaty hysteria of "serious" magazines, choked by the many weeds in the garden of film, they seek refuge in something that a theater—a good theater—can give them; and they realize that one of the most rewarding ways in which a theater can operate, can serve them, is repertory.

Is repertory the best form? For directors, what they may possibly lose in rehearsal time in a repertory schedule they gain in chances for ensemble exploration and cumulative power, in less need for the break-in period of the one-shot production. Scene and costume and lighting designers usually have to work less lavishly in repertory but can work more ingeniously, more consistently in their general intent, with ample chance for variety. The playwright makes less money with a repertory production, but he has what serious writers want so desperately these days, a habitat.

But it is the actor who gains the most, with a theater and artistic family, with accrual of roles, and the chance to improve in them—if he can withstand, or wants to withstand, or at least can visit temporarily, the other fields that will beckon. Even though, or possibly because, the actor gains most from repertory, he is the theater professional least likely to remain in it. Of course he is the only one who needs physically to remain. The playwright's work can be done subsequently in other places in other ways while he remains with the theater. The designers can remain while their work is used subsequently elsewhere. Even a director can take a leave of absence to do a guest job elsewhere. A member of the acting company doesn't have these options without interrupting his work in his own theater. On the other hand he gets more from it.

Is that all? Is that enough? Most of these advantages would come from a "series" season, a company that did one play for, say, a month, then another for a month, and so on. The audience would still see the work of an established company, would still have the chance to see the same actors in different roles throughout the season. But is there one inarguably unique asset of repertory theater?

Yes. *Reperire*. We have a heritage of great world drama. We rarely see much of it. We can never see all of it and can never have a sizable portion of it available to us in any theater's repertoire. Still, a corps of repertory theaters could produce and keep on tap a growing number of great plays so that American audiences, as they came along through the years, could have the chance to see some of those titanic works at least once in their lives, even if in some cases it meant going to other cities. Reading those major plays is always possible, always wonderful, but it cannot be sufficient. A good theater should prove that.

This is not to say that a repertory's only function is to keep the classics alive; but it is to say that such work cannot properly be done in any other theater form. By doing repertory, an American theater can make many other things possible for other American artists, including playwrights.

So it may be that the hour of repertory is returning. Not by using the term as an arty shield against criticism of incompetence. Not by using it as an aggrandizing label on any theater that happens not to be a long-run establishment. But by using the method truly, better than before, both to keep the past available to the present and to give the present a better place to speak to the present.

I have to note, finally, that I don't *believe* all the above will happen. Belief, in these matters, is for rhapsodists. But it seems reasonably reasonable to hope. The ingredients are there. They can be fused by talent and by will.

"Why We Need Broadway: Some Notes." *Performing Arts Journal*, **May-September 1985.**

The numerical decline of productions is not my subject, nor the drive to save some buildings from demolition. I'm concerned with Broadway as social phenomenon, civic flourish, sensory experience.

I look at two stubs for a Broadway show that my wife and I saw last night. The tickets were priced at $35 apiece. I'm struck with a comparison. When we married in 1943, the rent for our furnished apartment was $62 a month. Even after allowing for increases and inflations, I'm left with a grotesque disproportion between the cost of occupying an apartment for a month in 1943 and occupying two knee-cramped chairs for two hours in 1985.

Compensation is meant to come, of course, from what we saw and heard during those two hours. Disregard the fact, for this argument, that the compensation rarely comes; what is always true, whatever the quality of the show, is the price.

And the matter of price is why I never get the fullness of Broadway theatergoing. As a member of the press, I receive free seats. Most press people simply couldn't go as often as we must if we had to pay; our journals couldn't afford it. But free tickets put me in a relation to the show that is quite different from others in the audience—a difference that doesn't apply Off-Broadway or at films precisely because those other tickets are cheaper. No matter what the price stamped on my Broadway ticket, I don't pay it. I never ask myself whether the show is worth the money, however one defines worth.

In a quite real way, this is regrettable. A central part of the Broadway experience is the spending of money—the conviction that you have or have not got your money's worth. To get your money's worth—a criterion that cannot be equally pressing in other theaters—is one of the seductions with which Broadway tantalizes.

To charge Broadway prices in a regional theater would not provide the same thrill, even for a good show. It would be like charging Lutèce prices for a good local restaurant. Broadway prices for touring shows are the closest that one can come to the Broadway thrill away from Manhattan.

The matter of price connects with the paramount reason that Broadway is needed. The ticket price does for the audience what Broadway does for theater people themselves. It is the only locus in the American theater where American success is possible. Without Broadway, work in the theater would offer top levels of fortune only at about the level of a bank branch manager. Why should Americans who choose theater work have no chance at success comparable to success in other fields? Academics and lithographers and medical missionaries can have other motives for choosing their professions, but the theater is work in a success mode. Why should the choice of theater as a profession arbitrarily deprive one of a whirl at the great U.S. roulette wheel? It would be democratically unfair for Broadway not to exist.

Every year Broadway gives some theater people success. Every year Broadway gives some theatergoers their money's worth. On both sides, a gratification that is unique.

Not so many decades ago, Broadway was in effect the only American theater, if we concede that the rest of the country saw little but Broadway plays either before or after their New York residence. All theater people, including the most serious, aspired to Broadway, if only because there wasn't much else to aspire to. In the years since 1950 or so, that has ceased to be true, as other theaters grew. Some of our best theater people work elsewhere. Broadway, which used to be ecumenical, which included the most serious and the most trivial, now concentrates largely on material that is irrelevant to serious audiences. The obvious reason is rising expense, not decline in audience quality. The cultivation of the average American is demonstrably higher than it was when the Broadway range was wider. Broadway has priced itself out of seriousness, out of limited appeal, even though those limitations are broader than they would have been forty years ago. Most of what happens on Broadway hopes to reach the biggest audience, not the best, and must hope so.

This has led to the elevation of the pseudo-serious play. It has always been prominent on Broadway, even when it had genuine competition. Elmer Rice and Robert E. Sherwood and Maxwell Anderson and Philip Barry were always on hand to win their prizes and acclaim, but they were accompanied a good deal of the time by O'Neill and Williams and the best of Europe. Not now, not to anything like the same degree. Now the pseudo serious rules the Broadway roost, virtually unchallenged.

I think this is probably all to the good. I think the separation of the pseudo-serious from the truly serious, by the firm hand of the financier, is probably a benefit. Let there be a place where *The Real Thing* and *Children of a Lesser God* and *'night, Mother* can be considered top quality and can run and run. Plenty of other theaters now exist, in New York and around the country, to accommodate truly good work. Let there be a locus for the cheesecloth serious that really doesn't want a strong light behind it. Let there be a pantheon for the mediocre. It helps to clarify judgment. Production on Broadway doesn't arbitrarily mean mediocrity—*Glengarry Glen Ross* is a splendid exception—but

Broadway success is a pretty strong hint. And that's a help for the serious theatergoer who is not eager to waste time, money, or dignity.

These notes, I emphasize, are not meant satirically. I have lived in three cities: New York for most of my life, Rome for a year, London for half a year. Rome, despite its beauty, is, as many Romans will tell you, a dull place to live, and one reason is that it has no theater center. It has numerous theaters, more now than when I lived there, but no center. For a New Yorker, a city is not a true metropolis without a theater center like Broadway or the West End, a center that is a glittering spinoff from a two-thousand-year history, an entertainment zone that is in itself set apart as a showplace. New Yorkers *feel* the presence of Broadway whether or not they go there, whether they care for the theater or not. There's an old joke about a man who goes into a luncheonette and asks for coffee without cream. The counterman says, "We don't have any cream. You'll have to take it without milk." The New Yorker who wants his coffee black wants it without cream.

Compare American theater and American television. In television we have one public network that, however soggy and spotty, attempts programs of high quality; and we have three major networks and many minor ones that sell goods with intermittent chunks of programs designed to sell those goods. In the theater world, it's just the reverse. We have one commercial channel, Broadway, and numerous other channels that, however soggily and spottily, try to concentrate on work of high quality.

I don't want commercial TV to disappear. I think it presumptuous of those lofty-minded people who keep trying to upgrade it. (I'm excepting programs harmful to children.) People who want *Dallas* and *Hill Street Blues* have as much right to watch them as others have not to watch them.

Similarly, people who want to see *A Chorus Line* twenty times—they exist—have as much right to their addiction as I have to be well satisfied with one viewing.

No serious critic can review TV steadily. I've known some who tried and were battered down by the shows fairly quickly. No serious critic ought to be asked to review all Broadway material. In the television world, serious criticism, if there is any, has no discernible effect. In the Broadway world, serious criticism ought to be just as irrelevant.

After I was fired by the *New York Times*—I was their theater critic for eight months in 1966—I wrote an article called "Drama on the *Times*" (*New American Review*, no. 1) in which I said:

> The job [of theater critic on the *Times*] should not be construed as a contest between art and commerce. Patent commerce should be allowed to be as commercial as it likes, unmolested. The newspaper can satisfy its journalistic obligations by running a notice of the opening written by a reporter.... Art critics do not review billboards; music critics do not review dance bands.... The present imperative for the critic to review every Broadway show seems to me a debasement of his function... and an invasion of a businessman's business rights. A man who manufactures popcorn has the right to sell it, without interference, to anyone who wants to buy it. But the man who manufactures popcorn

theater productions has to suffer the intrusion of a powerful dissuader who doesn't like popcorn.

The practice continues, and continues to be harsh on both the popcorn purveyor and the critic.

I went on to explain that I wasn't inveighing against light comedies and musicals as such. Quality is the question there as elsewhere. Who is not lifted by a really good light comedy? *Barefoot in the Park*, directed by Mike Nichols, had no ambition but to be good pastry, and it succeeded. As for musicals, they are the most serious reason for the continuance of Broadway.

New musicals get produced elsewhere; occasionally they move to Broadway. (The most ironic success in Broadway history is *A Chorus Line*, which began as an anti-Broadway action in a workshop Off-Broadway.) But for a century the best talents in the making of musicals, whatever they were at the moment, have resided and flourished on Broadway. In one of the most relevant of clichés, the Broadway musical is America's unique contribution to the theater of the Western world.

More, the good Broadway musical is, in theater terms, America's greatest contribution to memory, to nostalgia, even to a sort of collective unconscious. I wouldn't want the score of *Oklahoma!* not to exist in my memory. *Pal Joey*, *Guys and Dolls*, *My Fair Lady*, and *West Side Story* don't rank in recall with Olivier's Oedipus or the three Grotowski productions I saw, but they are equally ineradicable.

Broadway, for self-evident reasons, has been the mecca for musical talent. My chief worry about Broadway now is not whether it is a help or hindrance to serious playwriting but whether it will continue to summon those musical talents. I hope that the shift in cultural energy, from Broadway to film and radio and TV and now MTV, will not weaken the continuance of the Broadway musical, as grand and splashy as the Off-Broadway musical is said to be intimate.

In his book *The Public and Performance*, Michael Hays begins with an essay on "Theater Space as Cultural Paradigm," and he begins that essay as follows:

> Until recently, the social value and function of the buildings, the architectural forms that enclose the theater event, have remained largely unexplored territory. Critical investigation has instead focused attention on the smaller space of the stage. . . . This larger theatrical space exists, however, and is first signaled by the willingness of actors and audience to converge in a specific place at a specific time. It is, in fact, the choice of locations that first announces the conceptual as well as the spatial structure of the theater event. . . . And it is also this theater space that first allows us to propose a connection between the ordering principles of the theater event and those of society at large.

Hays is concerned with the fixing of the large proscenium, with the size of staircases and foyers and promenades, in nineteenth-century French and German theaters as exponents of *haut bourgeois* sway and appetite. He says nothing about theater *districts*. But his method of inquiry can be applied to the growth and expansion of Broadway in the Times Square area around the turn of the century. The sweep of the Paris Opéra interior, designed to reflect the grandeur of the swelling French middle class, had its mirror image fifty years later in the congestion of Broadway, the cramping of new theaters between office buildings and hotels, the cramping of the lobbies, of the rows of seats. New York theater building was patently constricted by real estate and construction costs, but those very constrictions were part of the being of New York life, part of the buzz and intensity of Manhattan, the impulse to compress as much as possible into that slender island. One can infer that the Tired Businessman of the 1920s, who was supposedly the archetypal Broadway patron, found a facsimile of his own pressures and bustle in the pressures and bustle of Broadway. Possibly the very compactness, the space-saving of Broadway seemed to reflect his own principles of business drive.

The congregating of theaters was a tacit comment on American expediency. Why scatter theaters around a city when their very proximity made such conveniences as restaurants and parking more accessible, made it easier to go from one theater to another if the first one was sold out, and when it set up a reciprocal buzz of energy? Without that congregation, there would be no theatergoing *crowd*. That crowd told the New Yorker he was on Broadway and told the visitor he was in New York.

Physically diminished though Broadway is, the idea of the crowd still operates, a crowd that heads toward the same general area, then breaks off into separate pockets. That crowd is as close to a sense of community as the New York theater comes at present. Dingier than it used to be, going to Broadway is still a unique experience because of Broadway excitement. The loss of that excitement, which of course has nothing to do with what goes on in the theaters themselves, would be a national cultural loss. It's difficult to imagine a future America in whose theaters that Broadway hum does not sound as at least the signal of one end of territory.

Ghelderode said, in the *Ostend Interviews*, "if it is bad, the theater gives rise to pleasure, if it is good, to joy." Since the Renaissance, history shows no theater that has always been good, always—in Ghelderode's terms, joyful. Such an idea is inhuman. Let there be, always, a "bad" theater that gives pleasure. Let our only quarrel with it be when it doesn't give pleasure. Let there be a physical center for such a theater. The existence of that "bad" theater helps to keep the molecular structure of the whole theater intact.

"George Bernard Shaw: Twentieth-Century Victorian." *Performing Arts Journal*, May 1986.

> Surely, George Bernard Shaw possessed more energy, physical and mental, than any other man who ever lived. I am not surprised to learn that he suffered from migraine: How else could Nature persuade him to take a rest?

Thus W. H. Auden began his review of the second volume of Shaw's collected letters (*The New Yorker*, November 25, 1972). Similar comments figure in virtually every review of the first two volumes of letters; they recur in the reviews of Volume 3, published in 1985 by Viking (989 pp.), once again under the superlative editorship of Dan H. Laurence. This third volume, which is to be followed by a fourth and final volume, covers the years 1911-1925 and contains 578 letters and postcards. Samuel Hynes, reviewing this volume (in the *New Republic* of July 15 & 22, 1985), uses data from Laurence and a calculator to fix some statistics. Says Hynes:

> ... the three volumes of letters published to date, containing just over 1,900 letters in all, amount to less than .08 percent of Shaw's total output. If the complete letters were to be published, they would fill 390 volumes. To write a quarter of a million letters, Shaw had to average nine a day, 365 days a year, over an extraordinarily long life, while at the same time writing plays, prefaces, novels, tracts, music and art criticism, and a vast amount of casual journalism.

To which I would add that Hynes omits Shaw's theater criticism—in my view the best in the English language. Hynes could not have known of a volume called *Agitations* published (by Ungar) later in 1985, containing more than 155 of Shaw's letters to the press, unreprinted elsewhere, edited by Laurence and James Flambeau. To all of which I would also add that, besides his writing, Shaw frequently spoke and debated at meetings for social and political causes, that for several years he was a municipal officeholder, that he was an early and active member of the Fabian Society, that he was a co-founder of the Labour Party, the *New Statesman*, and the Royal Academy of Dramatic Art.

These facts are both less and more impressive when Shaw, born 1856, is seen as a product of Victorian conditioning. Put the facts above against most contemporary lives and they seem Himalayan; compare them with some of Shaw's contemporaries and you see that, in rough data at least, he is a man comparable to other men and women of his time. Some examples. Henry Mayhew (1812-87) wrote theater ballads and burlesques and farces and co-founded *Punch* before he went on to write his immense landmark sociological studies, *London Labour and the London Poor* and *The Criminal Prisons of London*, as well as his quite different *German Life and Manners*. George Henry Lewes (1817-78) wrote, translated, and adapted innumerable plays, acted a bit, became a distinguished theater critic, co-edited *The Leader*, co-founded and edited *The Fortnightly Review*, wrote a four-volume *Biographical History of Philosophy*, a study of Comte, a two-volume biography of Goethe, and a five-volume work called *Problems of Life and Mind*. Tom Taylor (1817-80) was professor of English for two years at the University of London, was called to the bar, was secretary to the Board of Health for twelve years, translated *Ballads and Songs of Brittany*, became editor of *Punch* and art critic of the *Times*, and wrote or adapted over a hundred plays. Seen in this context, Shaw's prodigality is less anomalous, more like Mozart seen against the Mannheim School or Shakespeare against the Elizabethans.

Contradictorily, the facts of Shaw's achievements become even more impressive when posed against the careers of most of his contemporaries. In them, their energy seems concentric, whirling in a closed circle around their lives and era. With Shaw—and this may be a partial definition of genius—the energy seems to whirl forward, to burst continually into a succession of futures, not through prophecy as such but through intense perceptions treated candidly that lead from his day into areas not widely perceived in his day yet familiar to us. His energy, then, by giving him extraordinarily clear perception of his own times also, as we can see, gives him avenues to movements, ideas, revelations to come.

Here I offer some instances of that forward thrust, those "modern" insights. I reviewed the first two volumes of Shaw letters in relatively traditional fashion (see my book *Persons of the Drama*), demonstrating the breathtaking range, the implicit and explicit development of the ideas of his plays, and much, much more (including sheer garrulousness) that are again present in the third volume. I concluded, and believe even more firmly, that essentially what Dan Laurence is doing is hewing out a great new posthumous Shaw work to add to the canon. But with Volume 3 I thought I might vary response by selecting some of the major instances of Shaw's mind bursting forward and relate them to the body of his work and thought.

The first instance comes early in the book. In March 1911, he wrote to Gilbert Murray, some of whose Greek translations had been produced at the Court Theater in the previous decade when Shaw was associated with it. He said he had heard that Murray had just translated *Oedipus Rex*, supplied a funny three-page parody of the play, then continued:

> Jocasta . . . says that men have often dreamt thus of their mothers . . . Let us get a little nearer home. I very seldom dream of my mother, but when I do, she is my wife as well as my mother. [In 1911 Shaw's mother was still alive. He had been married for thirteen years.] When this first occurred to me (well on in my life), what surprised me when I awoke was that the notion of incest had not entered into the dream: I had taken it as a matter of course that the maternal function included the wifely one; and so did she. What is more, the sexual relation acquired the innocence of the filial one, and the filial one all the completeness of the sexual one. This surprised me the more, because my theory, as you may have noticed in my books here and there, is that blood relationship tends to create repugnance . . . I am not very appreciative of the psychiatrists; but there may be something in their theory that repressed instincts, though subconscious, play a considerable part in our lives . . . anyhow . . . you may possibly see that there is a great poetic and psychological drama in it.

Shaw never wrote precisely that drama, but he had already dealt symbolically with the wife-cum-mother figure, Mrs. George in *Getting Married*, and later dealt symbolically with the father-daughter union, Shotover and Ellie in *Heartbreak House*. (In fact, as Arthur Ganz points out in his acute short book on Shaw, the implicit incest theme recurs in his plays, though Shaw explicitly denies it.) Even earlier, Shaw had perceived the delicate subconscious interplay of filial-sexual feelings. Reviewing *Parsifal* at Bayreuth in 1889, he comments on the scene in Act Two in which Kundry, by speaking to Parsifal of his mother, entices him into a kiss that changes his being:

> And that long kiss of Kundry's from which he learns so much is one of those pregnant simplicities which stare the world in the face for centuries and yet are never pointed out except by great men.

Wagner was the great man in this instance, but Shaw supplied the subconscious response to comprehend the "pregnant simplicity" some years before "the psychiatrists." I don't contend that Shaw was a pre-Freud Freudian; yet it seems clear that he was aware quite early of the buried territories of the mind that lay open to the future's exploration.

In August 1911 John Galsworthy, always active in humane causes, though sometimes foolishly, pressed for a moratorium on the manufacture and use of airplanes, for fear that they would eventually be used in warfare. He appealed to his friends, Shaw included, to sign a statement on the subject. Shaw replied:

> I can't sign that absurdity: I might as well revive Fielding's suggestion that armies should fight with their fists ... We know perfectly well that aerial warfare will *not* be ruled out ... no matter what pious wishes we express. It may be horrible; but horror is the whole point of war; the newspapers will be really jolly when showers of shells alternate with showers of mangled aeronauts on crowded cities ... the really interesting question is how far the new development will make an international combination against war irresistible. Nations will not stop fighting until the police makes them: the difficulty is to organize and effectively arm your European-North American police if you get it.

Shaw's awareness of Freud's *thanatos* (as well as *eros*) had long been part of his thought. The most memorable of all instances is the Devil's long and bitter speech about mankind's love of killing, in the Dream Scene of *Man and Superman*. In this reply to Galsworthy, Shaw not only briefly reiterates the Devil's view, he foresees the flat inevitability of the military use of the airplane; and before the First World War, let alone the founding of the League of Nations, he foresees the need for such a body, as well as the difficulties that still plague the United Nations today.

An Irish puppeteer named Clunn Lewis wrote to Shaw in May 1913 to ask about his interest in that kind of theater. Shaw said:

> In reply to your inquiry as to what I can find to interest me in marionettes when I am accustomed to have at my disposal for the performance of my plays actual living actors and actresses of the greatest talent and beauty, who can move and speak of their own accord without having strings pulled, and who can change the expression of their faces with every shade of emotion in the drama, I will tell you something that will perhaps surprise you; and that is, that it is just because your dolls can do none of these things that they are so interesting and instructive to all technical students of the stage ... The dramatic effect is sometimes actually greater than that produced by living performers. Nobody who has not seen marionette shows can be persuaded to believe this; but it is so ... I could name actors—among

them one no less eminent than Henry Irving—delayed for years in their career because they never learnt from a puppet-show how much must be done by suggestions and illusion, and how fatal to this is a too industrious effort to imitate and simulate every action or symptom of emotion instead of merely setting the audience to work to imagine it.

A bit circuitously but quite cogently, these remarks connect with the future.

First, they remind us at once of Kleist's "On the Marionette Theater," with its sublime lines: "Grace appears most purely in that human form which either has no consciousness or an infinite consciousness; that is, in the puppet or in the god." Idris Parry, who translated the essay, further reminds us that in Thomas Mann's *Doctor Faustus* Leverkühn reads the Kleist essay as a comment on human existence and that Hugo von Hofmannsthal thought the essay was the most perceptive piece of philosophy since Plato. I don't of course suggest that Shaw's comments rank with Kleist's essay, only that they resonate against it.

Note, too, that Shaw's very last play, *Shakes versus Shav* (1949), was a brief blank-verse bagatelle for puppets. "This," said Shaw at age ninety-three, "in all actuarial possibility is my last play..." He was right; he died the following year without attempting further work. He wrote this piece because he had been sent two puppets, of Shakespeare and himself, and had been asked to compose a piece for them. He said: "I have learned part of my craft as a conductor of rehearsals... from puppets," and he warned against technological improvements:

> I can imagine the puppets simulating living performers so perfectly that the spectators will be completely illuded. The result would be the death of puppetry; for it would lose its charm with its magic. So let reformers beware.

In July 1919 a journalist named F. V. Conolly wrote to Shaw from New York to tell him that a company of black actors had been formed there to make black films. Then Conolly asked if Shaw thought "a black company could depict Shakespeare, Shaw, or Archer [!], or would they be limited by their color to portray comedy?" Shaw answered:

> Negroes act very well, usually with much more delicacy and grace than white actors . . . The notion that there is anything funny in a man or woman being black is as childish as the notion that there is anything funny in being white, though no doubt the first white men in Africa must have elicited shouts of laughter from adults, and terrified the children into convulsions . . . As English actors have never been prevented from playing *Romeo and Juliet* by the fact that they are not Italians, and nobody's enjoyment is spoiled by the fact that the play is not written in Italian, so a performance by a black company would be just as enjoyable as a performance by a white one if the acting were equally good.

Shaw does not touch here the matter of "color-blind" casting—mixed companies, with talent alone as the criterion—but he wasn't asked about that; and what he does answer seems to reach forward from 1919.

All his life the subjects of racial differences and prejudice were in his mind. In his blank-verse play *The Admirable Bashville* (1901) a Zulu chief visits London and asks: "Are these anemic dogs the English people?" His English host's reply is an inversion of the Prince of Morocco's lines in *The Merchant of Venice*:

> Mislike us not for our complexions,
> The pallied liveries of the pall of smoke
> Belched by the mighty chimneys of our factories,
> And by the million patent kitchen ranges
> Of happy English homes.

In 1932 Shaw also wrote a long story called "The Adventures of the Black Girl in Her Search for God"—a story whose form recalls Shaw's passion for John Bunyan and Voltaire—at the end of which the Girl marries a redheaded Irish Socialist. (Obviously more than racial egalitarianism is involved here.) The following year Shaw wrote *On the Rocks*, a play that takes place entirely in the Cabinet Room at No. 10 Downing Street. One of the ministers is an Indian, Sir Jafna Pandranath, and in the course of a heated argument, a Tory minister calls him "only a silly nigger pretending to be an English gentleman." Sir Jafna responds with a long speech as beautiful and as beautifully made as a Handel aria, concluding:

> I return to India to detach it wholly from England, and leave you to perish in your ignorance, your vain conceit, and your abominable manners. Good morning, gentlemen. To hell with the lot of you.

After he leaves, the Prime Minister says, "That one word nigger will cost us India." To repeat: this was written in 1932.

The topic of Shaw and James Joyce's *Ulysses* has been much discussed, particularly in regard to Shaw's alleged prissiness. Two letters settle the matter, I think. The first is in this volume. In June 1921 Sylvia Beach wrote to Shaw, inviting him to subscribe in advance for a copy of the book. His response:

> I have read several fragments of *Ulysses* in its serial form. It is a revolting record of a disgusting phase of civilization; but it is a truthful one; and I should like to put a cordon round Dublin; round up every male person in it between the ages of fifteen and thirty; force them to read it; and ask them whether on reflection they could see anything amusing in all that foul-mouthed, foul-minded derision and obscenity . . . It is, however, some consolation to find that at last somebody has felt deeply enough about it to face the horror of writing it all down and using his literary genius to force people to face it.

Admittedly, this is a somewhat hygienic, utilitarian view of the "fragments" Shaw had read, but it's clear that his disgust was with Dublin, not with Joyce or his "literary genius." Then, unfortunately, Shaw displayed that cantankerous whimsy to which he was prone by refusing to subscribe for a copy of the book. (Joyce had predicted that he would decline, had in fact even bet on it.)

This refusal helped feed the myth that Shaw had been revolted by the book and had burned his copy. Such a story was published in *Picture Post* in May

1939. Shaw wrote the magazine on June 3rd (the letter is in Richard Ellmann's edition of Joyce's letters):

> The story is not true . . . Having passed between seven and eight thousand single days in Dublin [a reference to the single day of *Ulysses*] I missed neither the realism of the book nor its poetry. I did not burn it; and I was not disgusted. If Mr. Joyce should ever desire a testimonial as the author of a literary masterpiece from me, it shall be given with all possible emphasis and with sincere enthusiasm.

The writer of this letter, supporting the premier modernist of world literature, was eighty-three at the time.

Agitations contains a letter from Shaw to *The Academy*, 29 June 1907, in reply to a Lady Grove who, a month earlier, had heard Shaw deliver a lecture called "The New Theology," had been offended by it, and had written a letter. The passage in Shaw's talk that had apparently aroused Lady Grove was this:

> If I were God, I should try to create something higher than myself, and then something higher than that, so that, beginning with a God the higher thing in creation, I should end with a God the lowest thing in creation. This is the conception you must get into your head if you are to be free from the horrible old idea that all the cruelty in the world is the work of an omnipotent God, who if he liked could have left the cruelty out of creation, who instead of creating us . . Just think about yourselves, ladies and gentlemen. I do not want to be uncomplimentary, but can you conceive God deliberately creating you if he could have created anything better?

Replying to the outraged lady's objection to his concept of an "ignorant and inexperienced god," Shaw said:

> . . . the intellectual problem is to find a tenable conception of a force which, though it has produced cancer and epilepsy, tetanus and diphtheria, curved spine and hare lips and the impulses of poisoners and torturers as well as love and beauty and divine ecstasy, is nevertheless a force with honorable intentions. My theology supplies such a conception and Lady Grove's does not . . . The old-fashioned gentleman who felt that God would not lightly damn a man of his quality has given place to a lady who declines to be saved by a deity who is not absolutely first-class in every particular.

Or, as he wrote to Tolstoy three years later (the letter is in Volume 2 of the Laurence set):

> To me God does not yet exist; but there is a creative force constantly struggling to evolve an executive organ of godlike knowledge and power: that is, to achieve omnipotence and omniscience; and every man and woman born is a fresh attempt to achieve this object.

This belief, probably the most familiar of Shaw's beliefs, runs through too many of his works to begin citing them. The pressing truth is that, today, in a post-Hitler, post-Hiroshima, and (we must now say) post-Chernobyl era, though terminologies may differ, every man and every woman working in the world could not work, would not work, without some belief in Shaw's belief. Shaw's new theology is an especial reassurance for those of us who doubt organized religions and who also know that, whether we call ourselves agnostics or atheists, we act for reasons larger than the ones we—sometimes cynically—give ourselves.

To my knowledge, the best book about Shaw since Eric Bentley's is *Shaw's Moral Vision*. by Alfred Turco, Jr. (Cornell, 1976). In the closing section Turco writes:

> In Shaw's view, human salvation ultimately hinges on the capacity of the species to come to terms with retrograde elements of its biological and cultural heritage . . . Having begun by holding that the individual must survive in order to be saved, Shaw ends by holding that the species must be saved in order to survive. Are we essentially a race of Julians, who will destroy ourselves by fixation on the limitations of the past, or of Wotans, who will surpass ourselves by commitment to the possibilities of the future? Or will it be superseded when the Life Force demolishes both man and the cycle of eternal recurrence that has thus far constituted the history of the "unchanging human heart"?

The title of Turco's closing section is "The Tragic Optimist."

I emphasize that the Shaw quotations above, from a large and a small collection of letters, were extracted from a bustling throng of ideas, and are by no means all that could have been chosen to underscore what the world's theater knows through his plays: his continuing pertinence.

"Howard Brenton: A British Firebrand, Lost in Translation." *New York Times*, April 23, 2006.

Raging, singing, embracing, mocking what is shoddy in the world around him, the English dramatist Howard Brenton has written more than forty plays, long and short. In Britain he is grouped with such contemporaries as Edward Bond, David Hare, and Caryl Churchill. Yet, unlike them, Brenton is hardly known in the United States. Some years ago I gave Susan Sontag a copy of *Sore Throats*, the Brenton marital drama of 1979, which I had seen in London and which I thought would interest her. Next morning about 8:30, she telephoned and, almost angrily, said, "Why haven't I heard about this play?" I couldn't give her a precise answer then, and I still don't have one. The production this month of *Sore Throats* by the Theater for a New Audience will at last extend the skimpy list of Brenton productions in New York and may help to justify her irate question. Meanwhile, some hints to an answer may be found in an overview of his work.

Much of Brenton's writing has been about thoroughly British subjects; some of his dialogue is in untranslatable dialect; his politics are radical. Although examples of such matters can be found in British imports that have been performed here in the last thirty years (Broadway generally excepted), certainly

Brenton relishes the role of provocateur. In one interview he offered the opinion, since often quoted, that the theater is "not the place for measured discussion, it is the place for really savage insights." Savage insight figured in *The Romans in Britain*, which ran into censorship troubles in 1980, not because of the savagery of the Romans when they invaded in 54 B.C. nor because it interwove their tactics with those of the British in Ireland in 1980, but because of its "insight" about a homosexual rape.

This uproar was recalled last year when the National Theater in London announced that it would present Brenton's new play, *Paul*, about the apostle. Before it opened in October 2005, the theater received 200 letters of complaint, some of them arguing in advance that the play would violate the new law against religious hatred. But there was no disturbance during the run of *Paul*, no prosecution. In fact, Brenton's play presents a Paul who, unlike the other apostles and their less exalted version of events, fervently believes in the Jesus of the Gospels.

Religion has had a recurrent fascination for Brenton, possibly sparked by his father, who had become a Methodist minister after twenty-seven years as a policeman. Two relatively immediate responses: a dubious character in one of the son's plays has a "copper" father, and Brenton wrote a fiery short play about John Wesley, the founder of Methodism.

He started working in the theater after getting a degree in literature in 1965 from Cambridge (a place he loathed). He joined a fringe-theater company that included Hare, who directed several of the early Brentons and became a frequent collaborator. (The best-known result came in 1983 when they co-wrote the highly successful *Pravda: A Fleet Street Comedy*, which presented Anthony Hopkins in a role that reminded many of Rupert Murdoch.) The young fringe company toured Britain, and Brenton himself did some acting, but principally he wrote.

His view of the English theater in the late 1960s was, to put it gently, skeptical, like his view of politics. He has often called himself a Socialist, though, as with the earlier Socialist George Bernard Shaw, it is difficult to find overt Socialism in his plays. Like Shaw's, Mr. Brenton's politics are clearest in his choice of subjects and his attitude toward them. In 1969, for example, he wrote two plays. *Revenge*, his first full-length production in London, deals with a convict who is released from prison with one thought in mind: to nail the detective who sent him up. The detective and the convict are played by the same actor, a device used to underscore some moral generalities in Britain. *Christie in Love* is about an actual serial killer named John Christie, who had already been executed. The play moves fantastically through the mind and dreams of the murderer, not to justify him but to deepen the horror of being that man and knowing it.

Brenton's abstention from propaganda has not diverted him from political subjects. For instance, *The Churchill Play*, written in 1974, uses the device of a play within the play to slice away at inflated Churchill mythology. The whole work is conceived, Brenton says, "as it will be performed in the winter of 1984 by the internees of Churchill Camp somewhere in England," a sort of concentration camp for dissidents. (The date that the author selected is plainly Orwellian.) Churchill returns in the course of the play and says he wants to be prime minister again. When he is told that he can't because he is dead, he says,

"That hasn't stopped others." In *Weapons of Happiness* (1976) Brenton uses another actual figure, Josef Frank, the Czechoslovak Communist who was hanged after the Prague show trials of 1952. Here, however, Brenton rescues Frank and makes him a refugee working in a London potato-chip factory, where he comes into contact with the dewy ideas of the young English radicals around him.

It hardly needs underscoring that Brenton's range has been extraordinary. But there is more. Besides his plays, he has written a novel, poetry, and essays. In addition, for the National Theater he has done translations of Brecht's *Galileo* and Büchner's *Danton's Death*, and for the Royal Shakespeare Company he has translated both parts of Goethe's *Faust*.

In his own work the aesthetic qualities are varied, even deliberately contradictory. He has very often blended realism and fantasy, turning his plays almost physically about as if to display their subjects from different vantage points, yet the characters and the dialogue are intensely naturalistic. What is consistent in his work is a pungency, a sense of intent, a determination to propel the theater through entertainment—which he never ignores—to a plane of immediate, disturbing verity. He writes for the most part as if playwriting were a morally grave responsibility with which he has been charged.

Sore Throats, which begins previews at the Duke Theater on 42nd Street this weekend, is as realistic a play as any Brenton has written. Any fantasy in it is the characters', not his. He bears down here with acetylene heat on two people, a man of forty-five and a woman of thirty-nine, who have just been divorced and who now move through strophes of strenuous conflict and unforeseen linkages and sheer phantasm that leave them emotionally naked.

In the sort of contrast that is not unusual in Brenton's career, his next play, to be presented at the Globe Theatre in London next summer, is about the medieval lovers Abélard and Héloïse. Still, with all the richness of Brenton's career, and in one sense because of it, Susan Sontag's question remains. Perhaps a clue to his neglect here is in one of his poems. In 1979 he published "Sonnets of Love and Opposition." In No. 30 he presumes to ask Shelley, himself a radical, for "a tip" about writing. The poet gives him some stringent advice, ending, "Declare you are a public enemy / Of kingly death, false beauty, and decay." To which, in the last line, Brenton replies, "Ta, Percy. I'm on my way."

But not, unfortunately, to New York, or at least not very fully up to now. Perhaps Shelley's counsel, followed wholeheartedly, helped to delay him.

"Our Debts to the Duke: A Note on the Duke of Saxe-Meiningen." HotReview.org, August 2006.

Everyone who goes to the theater owes a debt to the Duke of Saxe-Meiningen. Though Georg II (1826-1914) ruled his tiny German duchy liberally and justly, he figures in our lives for rather different reasons. From youth he had been passionate about the arts, had studied painting and music, and when he came to the throne in 1866 one of his early actions was to found a theater company. That company, recruited by the duke himself from the best available German-speaking professionals, was dedicated to the classics and important new plays (including those by Ibsen), and it was the duke himself who set the theater's tone and fixed its ideals. In this process, he consolidated the profession of the theater director.

In Germany, outstandingly among all countries, vestiges and hints of what we might call directing had preceded the duke. There were efforts to do more with production than to follow the rubrics in prompt-books and to invest the play with whatever costumes and scenery a theater had available. But it was the duke, beginning in 1866, who first insisted that all plays be costumed and set for specific productions and who rehearsed his actors with unifying design, precision, and thematic tenor.

This phenomenon, occurring in the little town of Meiningen, was astonishing enough. (Imagine, say, Lincoln, Nebraska, becoming the vanguard of theater production in America.) But in 1874 the duke began a practice that made his company a major influence in the history of the theater. He sent his company on tour. He could not accompany it, of course; he had a duchy to run. But he had an able deputy who kept the performances well up to the duke's mark.

The Meininger, as the company came to be known, toured Europe for sixteen years, ranging from Russia to England. Their influence—basically, the duke's influence—was immense. Stanislavsky went to see them on their two Moscow visits; Henry Irving feted them in London. (They were planning an American visit in the 1890s, but the deputy died, and there was no one to lead them.) The duke maintained the company thereafter and occasionally sent them on tour, but mostly he kept them at home. Still, they had done their influential work. Through the Meininger's tours, the idea of the truly directed production was established in the theater. It is not the slightest exaggeration to say that when we attend a theater performance, traditional or heterodox, the impulse to create the unified production that we see had its origin in the vision of Georg II.

But that is not all. Our debt is larger than is usually acknowledged. Georg was also passionate about music. For many years he maintained a symphony orchestra—and for fewer years an opera company—in his tiny capital. Wagner called it the best orchestra in Europe. The principal conductor for five years was the pre-eminent Hans von Bülow; Johannes Brahms came to Meiningen to play with von Bülow's orchestra. That in itself would be noteworthy if merely a historical fact. However, eventually more immediate to us, in 1885 von Bülow engaged Richard Strauss as his assistant conductor—with a five-month contract.

Strauss, who was then twenty-one, had already proved to be one of those almost unnerving prodigies with whom the course of music is bedecked. He had already written two symphonies and a violin concerto—all of them performed—along with numerous sonatas and songs and chamber works. But he had shown no interest in the theater. Bryan Gilliam says, in his *Life of Richard Strauss*, that, besides the influence of the major musicians with whom he was associating,

> there was another aspect of Meiningen ... that would profoundly shape Strauss's career many years later: that of the theater. The Meiningen Theater of the 1880s was one of the finest in Germany, and Strauss the avid theatergoer took full advantage.... Richard's letters home [to his father] suggest a strong attachment to the stage.... His diaries and letters document his exposure to Schiller, Kleist, Shakespeare, Ibsen, [Albert] Lindner, and others. Such an intense preoccupation with the theater ... was a major factor in his move from tone poem to opera.

Strauss himself said in the memoirs that he wrote many years later:

> During this particular winter the famous Meiningen Theater Company did not go away on tour, and naturally I was there every night for the splendid performances. When I took my leave of the duke and his wife [in April 1886], Frau von Heldburg [the duke's wife and his leading actress] . . . bade me a gracious farewell with the words: "His Highness the Duke and I are very sorry to lose you so soon . . . You have been the best *claqueur* we have had in the theater for a long time.

Still vivid in Strauss's mind were the duke's "magnificent" productions of the classics, particularly distinguished by "the direction of the crowd scenes, in which every move was plotted with the greatest care, and by the stylistic verisimilitude of the staging." Strauss also gives us an example of the duke's discipline:

> One New Year's Eve [1885] the rehearsal went on until 9 o'clock, 10, at last it struck midnight, the duke stood up, everyone breathed a sigh of relief. The duke: "I wish the company a very good New Year, the rehearsal may continue!"

In fact it took six years—six very busy years in which he created the "tone poem"—before Strauss began his first opera, *Guntram*, but it seems fair to agree with Gilliam that the idea of opera composition might never have grown in Strauss's mind without the Meiningen experience. In time Bernard Shaw wrote, "Strauss produced works for the musical theater that maintained it at the level to which Wagner had raised it." So, in addition to our theatrical debt, when we are at a Strauss opera, when we tremble with *Elektra* or revel with or soar with *Der Rosenkavalier*, a little throb of gratitude is due the man I can't help thinking of as our duke.

RECORDED DRAMA

The Lady's Not for Burning, by Christopher Fry. *Saturday Review*, December 29, 1951.

The terrifying thing about records, as those who make them know, is just precisely that they are recorded. "Live" performances can be improved; but a record once released is like murder committed. One ought to be very sure and very proud of it before doing it. Generally, manufacturers of musical records realize this, and most of the performances they release at least justify their existence in permanent form.

This admirable rigor has not yet infused the field of dramatic records. Here, one often feels, the intent is taken for the deed; and the fact that a good play has been recorded clouds the point that something less than the austerity of a Beecham or Toscanini (to say nothing of their creative abilities) has governed the production. Obviously dramatic recordings can be no better than the theater with which they are contemporary. But in the theater one can make allowances for the exigencies of production; on records, where more factors can be controlled, there is little excuse for anything but the best possible.

As for the recording of Christopher Fry's *The Lady's Not for Burning* (Decca set DX 110), some who saw this play a year ago felt that they would rather be reading than seeing it—not a compliment to any play, however well-written. It was so exclusively concerned with brocaded language that its production in a theater seemed superfluous; its lack of valid theatricalism tended to make it boring. But on records—where a playwright's failure to fill theatrical requisites is less damaging, where attention can be satisfied with sounds—Fry's play is highly entertaining indeed. He has still to clear himself of the charge of substituting rhapsody for characterization and story; and an air of collegiate preciousness still tinges the work. But there is a great deal of fun and an occasional thrill to be had from his verbal pyrotechnics. Perhaps he will become the first great writer for records!

One hopes that Fry is decently grateful to his extraordinarily good cast. With the exception of Penelope Munday, who mistakes twitter for ingénue appeal, the same good actors who labored under a more or less undramatic burden on the stage succeed more fully when the focus is shifted to voice alone. John Gielgud is addicted as ever to tremolo: when a sentence or phrase ends in the consonant "n" or a vowel, it does not 'scape him lightly; but he endows his lines with bite and barb. He has always been at his best in ironic comedy. Pamela Brown is womanly and rich. In spite of a rather reedy voice, Richard Burton conveys considerable reticent charm. The others, especially Eliot Makeham's crinkly Chaplain, are equally engaging.

There is slight confusion in places because entrances and exits are not always clear, nor do we know to whom some lines are addressed. But the net effect is intelligent entertainment. It is to be hoped that many ladies (and gentlemen) are for Frying.

Hedda Gabler, by Henrik Ibsen. *Saturday Review*, April 26, 1952.

This is the first of a projected series of complete recordings of famous plays, presented by a firm (Theatre Masterworks) whose theatrical luminaries are Eva Le Gallienne and Margaret Webster. The venture is off to a commendable start, in terms of performing quality, because of Le Gallienne's portrayal of Hedda and her fluent, actable translation.

Le Gallienne has been playing Hedda for twenty-five years and there are no secrets in the part for her. One may wonder at her fondness for a character so desolate of attraction, one who lacks even the fascination of thorough villainy, but the fact remains that she creates a Hedda of texture and dimension: wiry, cruel, and frantic for unattainables. The rest of the cast, as is usual in recorded plays, is a decidedly mixed bag. The best is Andrew Cruickshank, whose Judge Brack has a refined diabolism. Carmen Mathews is adequate as Mrs. Elvsted, but her voice is so similar in quality to the star's that, at times, only Le Gallienne's greater incision of speech marks the transition from one character to the other. Curious casting, indeed. David Lewis as Tesman is more radio than real. As Løvborg, Richard Waring, an actor of some force in the theater, continues to reveal limited means in this purely aural medium; his voice is simply not an engaging instrument. The characters and scenes of each act are described by Webster.

As for the play itself, it seems to have completed an odd cycle. When first seen, it was thought unworthy because it invaded unmentionable moral areas. It overcame that objection as those areas were admitted to the province of art. But now it seems unworthy for another reason: it tells us nothing about human beings that has not since been much better expressed elsewhere; and without the virtue of pioneer revelation, the display of Hedda's egomaniacal behavior seems archaic and gratuitous. Then, too, the play's flabby motivations and naked contrivances, for a time concealed by, or forgiven for, the author's social purpose, are now hard to accept. Surely the definition of a classic is a play that continues to move us, not one that once had importance.

Bernard Shaw said of another Ibsen play: "It will be flat as ditchwater when *A Midsummer Night's Dream* will still be as fresh as paint; but it will have done more work in the world." The same might be said of *Hedda Gabler*, which, artistically speaking, has passed to its reward. However, those who for their own reasons want to hear a good performance of the title role will find it in this album.

The Importance of Being Earnest, by Oscar Wilde. *Saturday Review*, August 29, 1953.

"In matters of grave importance," says Gwendolen Fairfax, "style, not sincerity, is the vital thing." Thus, through one of his characters, Wilde laid down the basic precept not only for *The Importance of Being Earnest* but for all artificial high comedy. Meaning is much less important than manner because the characters' lives have no meaning: they have only elegance.

The principle of playing high comedy is a paradox: to seem fundamentally bored but to be continuously interesting. For the essence of these characters is that they have nothing to do; they are occupied only with varyingly desperate searches for means to pass the time. No problem is too slight—the choice of a restaurant or the best way to eat muffins—but they seize on it for debate, hoarding it because it may be hours or even days before anything else arises to provide an occasion for talk. What keeps these people from boring *us* is their eloquence. What makes them amusing is the contrast they provide with our own lives of alarm-clock risings and monthly payments on the car. Therefore if they lose one jot of the style that is their *raison d'être,* they become like melted ice cream: not quite the same thing, though the ingredients may not have changed.

All this is demonstrated by a new album in the Theatre Masterworks series (Vol. III), a production of *The Importance of Being Earnest* directed by Margaret Webster. Maurice Evans plays John Worthing here with verve and comic perception, which will be no surprise to those who have followed his career since his Dauphin in *Saint Joan* and have known all along that his forte is comedy. Stella Andrew is charming and conjures up a porcelain-figurine Cecily. But the others of the cast— good and less-good actors together—are simply lost. Lucile Watson as Lady Bracknell gives the impression throughout of hurling herself against stylistic doors that refuse to open. (Whoever has heard Edith Evans say "Mr. Worthing! Rise, sir, from this semi-recumbent posture!" will not readily settle for less, and Watson offers a good deal less.) Mildred Natwick, so often justly admired, is merely saddening as Miss Prism. Memories of her Madame Arcati in *Blithe Spirit* led one to expect more, but here she flounders as if she had (temporarily, one hopes) lost the compass points of comedy. The kindest word to apply to John Merivale as Algy and Leueen McGrath as Gwendolen is inept.

The fault, of course, is Webster's, in casting and direction. She continues to be something of a contradiction. She writes perceptively about plays, but her practice as director lacks her perception as theoretician. Style and design aside, consider the primary matter of speech in this recording. Why juxtapose the pretty English accent of Andrew and the hard Yankee "r's" of Natwick? How believe that Watson is a British aristocrat in a cast containing Evans, Robin Craven, and John Williams? Better to do the play with an all-American cast, one would think, even though there seems little point in producing this British *reductio ad absurdum* in anything but the British manner. Certainly, there is no point in playing it without figurative arched backs. This production is lamentably round-shouldered.

Romeo and Juliet, by William Shakespeare. *Saturday Review*, November 28, 1953.

It is a pleasure to be able to report to prospective theatergoers and record purchasers of 1963 that if Claire Bloom develops as she should and benefits by prudent direction, they will have the opportunity by that time to see and hear a Juliet of poetic and extraordinarily moving beauty. The Old Vic recording (RCA Victor LM 6110)—a virtually complete performance of the play—records Bloom's first essay of the part, which bears about the same relation to her future performance that Margot Fonteyn's first Swan Queen, in *Swan Lake*, bears to her present triumph. That RCA saw fit to preserve this Juliet is more a tribute to faith than good judgment.

Bloom, whose lovely dancer in Chaplin's *Limelight* is so warmly remembered, is temperamentally and vocally exactly right for Juliet. She has what Booth Tarkington once called "the bride quality"; she has a voice of range and (still largely suppressed) power; she has the ability to melt and chill your bosom. What she lacks most right now is simplicity. For example, she makes pointless pauses: "If that thy bent of love [time out for heaven knows what and now let us resume] be honorable." She is addicted to—or perhaps has been directed to employ—upward curlicues at the ends of speeches that belie meaning and destroy reality. She also lacks the Handelian line that is essential to the great Shakespearean roles, and whose absence is especially notable where clauses occur between parts of a verb ("So Romeo would, were he not Romeo called, retain...").

But Bloom has the essential magic. Not all the misdirection, all the choppiness, all the undeveloped artistic intelligence can entirely smother it. Listen to her in Act III, scene 2, where she quite misses the impetuosity of "Gallop apace" but progresses to the real anguish of "Romeo is banished!" Or listen to her potion scene, a strange mixture of emptiness and mystery. She is entirely unmoved by the thought of stifling in the vault but pierces hard with the line about dashing out her desperate brains. Experience and sound advice will make this young lady a consistently fine actress.

Next in importance to the play is Romeo, in which Alan Badel, at his best, merely skims the surface. At his worst, towards the end, he sounds, not tragic, but as lugubrious as a despondent muezzin calling the reluctant faithful to prayer. Too, he lacks proportion; he expends as much emotion on bidding the apothecary get something to eat as he does on his suicide.

The two actors' plums in this play are the Nurse and Mercutio, minor parts that can make stunning effects. In the first, Athene Seyler is excellent, a juicy old vulgarian full of loving guile. As Mercutio, Peter Finch is leaden in the Queen Mab speech and achieves the considerable feat of dying—in that scene which is an actor's boon—without evoking pathos. The venerable Lewis Casson, for his part, is properly warm-hearted as Laurence, a truly "comfortable friar." The rest of the cast is unexceptional but not unexceptionable.

It is worth noting that a number of odd things happen to the text in this recording. Two examples out of many that might be given: in Romeo's "My life is my foe's debt," where the last word rhymes with "Capulet" in the preceding line, that last word is changed to "thrall." In the Mantua scene, the perfect line "Then she is well and nothing can be ill" is rendered "Then nothing can be ill for she is well," to jibe with an alteration in Romeo's previous line. The same meaning but not the same music.

The level of performing quality in acting records is still far below that of musical records, a fact unaffected by this album; but at least here we are given glimpses of Claire Bloom's possible future.

THEATER AND FILM

"End of an Inferiority Complex: Theater vs. Film." *Theatre Arts*, **September 1962.**

Four-and-a-half years ago, when I began reviewing films regularly, my attitude towards them was that I loved them and was not ashamed of it. I had been educated for the theater and had worked in it a little; and although I had been going to films constantly since I was six, I felt about them *vis-à-vis* plays much as a dog-lover feels about dogs: he is devoted to them but does not confuse them with people. Now, many months and films and plays later, I have to face the fact that my inferiority feeling about films is outmoded; was outmoded then; that, for a New Yorker, most of the best theatrical experiences in that period came from the screen, not from the stage.

I shall not discuss which form is superior, an issue about as meaningful as the old debate on art versus science. But a comparison of this period's plays and films reveals some interesting facts about true status and forward motions. In this comparison I include both foreign and domestic films. If it is argued that most of the rewarding films of the period came from abroad, the same thing is true of plays; so honors (and dishonors) are even. I use New York as a locus because more plays and films are available here than anywhere in the country.

My attitude toward films was not unique and is still widely held. In fact, with many people trained for or fond of the theater, it is immediately assumed and infrequently questioned. Where does it come from? In my own case it arose from some sense of the theater's antiquity, immortality, force; from awe of the ideal theater that has existed at a few moments of history and is always hypothetically possible. With the exception of music, the theater seems to me the most immediately powerful and, if need be, irreducibly simple art. "Two planks and a passion" is more than a cant phrase.

On the other hand, film seemed for the most part a not quite self-sufficient offspring of the theater, often entertaining, variously seductive, sometimes magnificent, but rarely able to stand unpatronized by some such compensating thought as, "Very good—for a film." Additionally (and these points are still true) the vast majority of films from every source—Hollywood, Britain, Europe—were trivial and stereotyped. *Star* by no means implied *star actor*. The conventions of the commercial film were expected to disregard the verities of life.

The screenwriters I knew disparaged their work and longed to write plays. Screen actors who had been in the theater talked about it as the heaven from which they had fallen; screen actors who had never been in the theater either said the stage was *passé* or that they didn't dare to attempt it—two sides of the same coin of inferiority. Successful film directors said that some day they would "prove" themselves by directing successful plays. The theater was thus not only the source of several elements in films but, more importantly, its implied source of standards.

I knew, as did all these people, of films at their finest: Charlie Chaplin, Sergei Eisenstein, Vittorio De Sica, René Clair. I knew, too, that for more than a generation films had been the darling of European intellectuals, that there was a very vocal and literate group who ranked the film second to no art. To me and my friends, film buffs though we were, this smacked of Left Bank crankishness—like equating Duke Ellington with Beethoven just because one thoroughly enjoyed Ellington; cultism made sacrosanct with aesthetic verbiage. No admiration for Jean Renoir's *Grand Illusion* or Eisenstein's *Battleship Potemkin* or Chaplin's *Modern Times* could alter for us the basic distinction between an art that came from a machine and one that was live. When films were beautiful, they were the best works of a second-rank art. The hierarchy of the forms made fine art expected in one and surprising in the other.

My expectations of the theater have not changed. My view of films has altered. To maintain my former view would not only be difficult but close to mad. Since early 1958 New York has seen some good and moving plays, a few memorable ones. But consider what has happened in films. It is stark understatement to say that no force in the theater has equaled the impact or importance of two new creative forces in films: Ingmar Bergman and Michelangelo Antonioni. No new social drama surpassed Jack Clayton's *Room at the Top* or Karel Reisz's *Saturday Night and Sunday Morning*. No farce approached Billy Wilder's *Some Like It Hot*. No religious play (especially Paddy Chayefsky's *Gideon*) could touch Jules Dassin's *He Who Must Die*. Satyajit Ray's Apu trilogy demonstrated again some purities possible *only* to film. Federico Fellini's directorial virtuosity, bright and hard as a diamond, was without a theatrical equivalent. Nor did the theater match the airy comic gifts of Philippe de Broca. There was no play about the effects of war that compared with De Sica's *Two Women*.

In the theater, with Tennessee Williams at best repeating himself, with Arthur Miller absent, there is general agreement that the outstanding dramatists of the period were Samuel Beckett, Jean Genet, Eugène Ionesco, John Osborne, and Jean Anouilh. Beckett's *Waiting for Godot* is possibly the best play of the time—so pre-eminently the best play of the Absurd Theater that most of the other plays of that school seem to be taking place inside it. Genet's *The Blacks* is a fierce conduit of bile that gushes and stuns its audience. Ionesco bites, although he meanders; Osborne bites, although he whines and falsifies. Anouilh plays intelligent theatrical games with the ingenuity of a nineteenth-century French dramaturge tinged with contemporary caustic. Among Americans, Edward Albee has painted some effective pastels, Jack Richardson has earned the painful word "promising," and Jack Gelber's *The Connection* caused more stir than any American play of the period, a fact that may illuminate our poverty to future historians. Lillian Hellman's *Toys in the Attic* was a piece of ice-sculpture by a craftsman who clearly felt she had been idle too long and was desperate for material. Two Eugene O'Neill bequests, *Long Day's Journey into Night* and *A Touch of the Poet*, reminded us that there were giants in those days, clubfooted though they may have been.

It is possible, of course, though unlikely, to think that all the plays above were superior to all the films named. But the point is not primarily to rank them but to show that an inferiority complex about these films, as against these plays, is out of order. They cannot *automatically* be rated below the plays just because they are films. They are entitled to the sternest standards of criticism, to unapologetic appreciation.

A further look at plays and films of the time provides wider ground for considering the two forms at least equally fruitful. That further look is intensified because, by inevitable coincidence, some plays and films dealt with the same themes. As an epic of modern man facing certain death, does Garson Kanin's *A Gift of Time* excel Akira Kurosawa's *Ikiru*? Does Gore Vidal's *The Best Man* tell us more of the interior of political man than Ralph Thomas's *No Love for Johnnie*? Among romances about prostitutes, is Richard Mason's *The World of Suzie Wong* more enjoyable than Dassin's *Never on Sunday*? To a layperson reasonably literate in Freud, would you recommend Henry Denker's *A Far Country* over Guy Green's *The Mark*? Is Michael V. Gazzo's *A Hatful of Rain* as tenable a social melodrama as Robert Rossen's *The Hustler*? By laugh-machine standards, are there as many chuckles in Jean Kerr's *Mary, Mary* as the Bob Hope-Lucille Ball *Facts of Life*? Between two explorations of anti-black prejudice, does Lorraine Hansberry's *A Raisin in the Sun* register more vividly than Stanley Kramer's *The Defiant Ones*? As an odyssey of amoral adventuring, is Williams' *Sweet Bird of Youth* more pungent than Jean-Luc Godard's *Breathless*? My own answer to all the above is no.

Perhaps conditioned by reluctance to admit that the theater is not *ipso facto* superior, we ask whether the argument for film's equality is not due to a temporary decline in playwriting. The decline is inarguable and the reasons are many. Like all movements in art, this decline is caused, extensively, by factors outside art—social, political, economic—too complex to investigate here, which resulted in a theater increasingly money-hobbled and "hit"-directed. The interests of the theater today and the new hurdles to production (backers wives' opinions, theater-party approval) deflect serious talent from writing plays. The historical fact seems to be that when a society wants an art form, talent arises to supply the need (painting in the Renaissance, opera in nineteenth-century Italy). A case could be made that serious plays, tragic *or* comic, are not wanted by our society today. Writing talent exists, richly, variously. A year that produces first novels like those of Walker Percy, Edward Adler, and Reynolds Price can scarcely be called barren. But the writing talents of our time, whether they could succeed dramatically or not, are rarely drawn to plays because they cannot feel that the theater is penetrable by them or important to the audience they want to reach.

Nevertheless it is not merely the flatness of the current theatrical countryside that has destroyed inferiority feelings about the film. Although that flatness has helped to make the view clearer, film's merits would stand if the theater's last four-and-a-half years had been crammed with treasures. My former attitude changes because it becomes increasingly plain that different standards must be applied to film: separate but equal, equal but separate.

The old strictures about films as *against the theater* are still valid. A film is created almost as much by technicians (cameraman and cutters) as by artists (actors, writers, directors). The film is essentially not congenial to language. (All the Shakespeare films prove this.) The film does not permit sustained acting; further, skillful directors and editors can synthesize a performance where the talent is minimal. (Marilyn Monroe could not sustain a ten-minute vaudeville sketch, but Billy Wilder wrung a few hundred snippets of scenes out of her and wove them into her amusing vocalist in *Some Like It Hot*.)

But, true though these strictures are, all they do is compare films with the theater, and we must no longer use theatrical standards to judge films. It is a historical fallacy. Films must be judged by an aesthetic that is consonant with its resources, methods, and highest potentials. To refute the strictures above by *appropriate* argument: there are indeed more technicians in a film, but the notion that this means the mechanical deep-freeze of art is about as sound as saying that good writing cannot be done on the typewriter. The theater uses some technicians; the film uses more. At what precise number does art die? Obviously all that matters is the result. If our bosoms are truly wrung, it is irrelevant to dismiss the work because the sound engineer and special-effects man contributed. We should know how it happened; but how can we claim it *didn't* happen?

As for language, if film is not its best medium, still a film can be well written (Orson Welles's *Citizen Kane*, among others); and film has non-verbal languages of its own that the theater is denied. They include montage; metaphors of motion by which the audience can be transported as easily as the actors; and the art wrung from sheer physical action—from the elemental chase to the scurrying of the tiny car in Jacques Tati's *Mr. Hulot's Holiday* to Max von Sydow's ritual bath and revenge in Bergman's *The Virgin Spring*.

However, it is the matter of acting that is the heart of the theater's assumed superiority. If Miss Monroe's voice in a play could not puff past the tenth row, why is that a relevant criterion for her performances in films? Many a fine singer can "act" well in his singing but is hopelessly ham in his acting; no one thinks that nullifies his validity in his own medium. The superiority of theater acting over film acting—sustained work over "piece" work done out of sequence—rests on the false assumption that if acting is not done in the theater *per se*, it is not acting. Film underplaying is not, by definition, easier than most contemporary stage playing; it is simply more internal, not non-existent. The ability to jump into the middle of a scene, without build-up, does not demand the power of sustenance of the stage but it demands keen powers of concentration and imagination, as any stage actor can testify who has been interrupted in rehearsal, then asked to resume in mid-scene.

Most conclusively, again, the results speak for themselves. The techniques of film may aid screen actors in ways that the stage actor, coached by his director but now alone, is not aided. But the performances of the best film actors are *performances*—designed, projected work, fired by empathy and imagination and the talent of re-creation. I cite, among many, the film acting of Paul Newman, Marcello Mastroianni, Toshiro Mifune, Sophia Loren, and Jean Simmons. (A double bill of two inferior films, Mervyn LeRoy's *Home Before Dark* and Stanley Donen's *The Grass is Greener*, would show how sadly Simmons is underrated.)

Twenty-six years ago Otis Ferguson wrote in *Theatre Arts*:

> The movies have had a hard time in the court of criticism, finding themselves generally in the position of being guilty until they prove themselves innocent. . . . The prosecution can always cite ten bad pictures to the one good picture found by the defense . . . Hence pictures as art are simply not, not nearly; and there is nothing left for the defense to say except that art shall not live by its bad works alone, and that

anyone in the more established fields who squinted down the tradition and saw only the fertilizer and not the flower would be punished horribly.

This statement could almost be applied to today's theater. But never mind, the theater has always been judged by its best achievements, its potentialities. And so film stands now: most of its works ephemeral and bad, as are most works in all arts; free of the shadow of its antecedent art; with a future at least as bright as the theater's. To put it negatively, the bonds of commercialism are no longer worse in one place than the other. Positively, the attractions of film to serious writing, directing, and acting talents will increase because, here and abroad, there is a sense of social response to film, a sense that it is wanted, that it is acutely attuned to our age. With the interplay of timeliness and talent, all things—though doubtless difficult-—are possible.

An old trouper once said to me of a famous star: "He used to be an actor but now he's in the movies." I'm glad that my old friend hasn't accompanied me to films and plays during the last four-and-a-half years. The experience might have crushed him. Only theater-trained people—like him and, in a lesser way, myself—have persisted in the assumption of the theater's superiority even when we loved films. But the figurative head of the film is no longer to be patted. It stands independent and too tall.

"To Be Taken as Directed: Some Plays (Not Movies)." *New York Times*, May 22, 1966.

By now it has become unwritten law that film is a director's medium and the theater is a writer's medium; but all unwritten laws ought to be written down once in a while so that they can be examined. Some recent plays make the second part of the proposition worth examining. At least they show how much the playwright is at the mercy of his director, a mercy that is sometimes hard and sometimes helpful.

For example, Isaac Babel's play *Sunset*. It is rather slender in dramatic development, almost as much a tale as a drama; but it is a small treasury of skin-bursting, vitality-packed characters, and it is enriched for the theater by the flood of comic-dramatic emotion that sweeps it along. At the 81st Street Theater, however, the director Aldo Bruzzichelli has imposed on this juicy, passionate play a halting, gaunt, ponderous conception that, in my view, maims its spirit. The competence of the actors, who were presumably chosen by Bruzzichelli, is generally low, but even with a cast equal to the concept he has foisted on the drama, we would get, I think, only a better executed misconception.

Babel's protagonist, in this play set amidst the Jewish community of Odessa at the turn of the century, is Mendel Krick, a brawling old giant of a man, tyrannical to his family, a drinker and lecher. His egocentric devotion to his desires and his refusal to recognize anyone else's rights, or even the passage of time, are seen by the author through a spectrum composed of bitter admiration and ironic comedy. Bruzzichelli has converted this man into a taciturn neurotic—diluted Dostoevsky instead of full-blooded Babel—and even such a character is, under his direction, played only in mechanical externals by Martin Rudy. The rest of *Sunset* is distorted in kind.

Here, then, is a prime case of the schism that can exist between a play as written and a play as seen by an audience. At the 81st Street Theater, Babel's words are spoken, in a good translation by Mirra Ginsburg and Raymond Rosenthal; but in terms of intent, and also, in numerous instances, of specific stage directions, it does not seem to me that Babel's work is on view.

An example in reverse is the production of Saul Bellow's *The Last Analysis* at the Theater of the Living Arts in Philadelphia. In the original New York production the play was treated more or less as a realistic Jewish-American comedy in the vein typified by Sam Levene, who played the TV-comic hero. In Philadelphia the play has been directed by George Sherman with complete sympathy for its imaginative, fantastic, farcical-poetic qualities. Sherman gives the Bellow drama the chance to be fully what it is: an imperfect, inconclusive but extraordinarily stimulating work. (And a second hearing, as well as reading, emphasizes how well written *The Last Analysis* is.)

These matters were discernible in New York, but for the most part only through a layer of misconception imposed by the director. Further, Sherman has helped David Hurst to a performance of the spiritually beset hero that makes him a great deal more than the Catskill comic we got in Manhattan. Hurst renders him as an outsized buffoon-hero of our dilemmas—like a Picasso clown cavorting, grimacing, and being heartbreakingly foolish for us all.

Yet how many in the New York audience blamed the author of *The Last Analysis* for shortcomings that were not his? In Philadelphia the important shortcomings that exist are Bellow's, as are the achievements. Handicapped only by some weaknesses in the permanent acting company at that theater, Sherman has rendered his author whole.

Still a different kind of example is available in Baltimore at the Center Stage, which is presenting *The Chinese Wall*, by the Swiss dramatist Max Frisch. As we have come to expect from Frisch, this play consists of an obstreperously clever theatrical concept used to explicate a sophomoric moral idea. Its purpose is to warn us of atomic destruction, and its method is extravaganza: one of those plays in which characters from many periods of history are deployed hopefully to create a feeling of profundity and scope.

Douglas Seale, the director, chose to do *The Chinese Wall* either because he disagrees with this estimate of the play or because he thought it provided theatrical opportunities, or both. Whatever the reason, Seale has staged Frisch's drama with imaginative fireworks. He has chosen a circus ring as the basic metaphor, a device that makes the play theatrically viable, and has invented quantities of vivid stage business. No director could supply the thematic substance or continuous interest that this work simply does not have, nor could he make it finally satisfying; but Seale has done the best possible service to Frisch by meshing gears with the author's intent and propelling the play to some superficial life.

In the theater of our time—at least until "happenings" take over—plays do not begin without a script. Between us and the author are the performers, as boon or blockade; and in the last century or so, the controlling figure of the director has arisen (incidentally, soon after the rise of the virtuoso musical conductor). Nowadays no author comes to us except through the mind and sensibilities of a director. This does not make the theater as much a director's medium as the cinema; one has only to compare film scripts and play scripts to see this quite clearly. But it does often make the director the decisive element in theatrical performance, for good or less good.

One advantage of the theater over films—and a factor that swings the theater's balance to the writer—is that a play can survive one production to be produced again. (Hollywood remakes of earlier movies are not really a relevant analogy.) How lucky for me to have been able to see this second production of *The Last Analysis*. With all gratitude to Douglas Seale, I hope never to see *The Chinese Wall* again. As for *Sunset*, how fortunate we will all feel—even, I believe, admirers of the present production—if we can one day see it produced by a more perceptive director.

"Gabriel Blew His Horn: On Bernard Shaw and Gabriel Pascal." *Theater*, **Spring-Fall 1997.**

The anatomization of Bernard Shaw goes marvelously on. In the near half-century since his death, editors have quarried in lode after lode of his Himalayan life's work. In addition to the swelling critical literature on his plays, books continue to appear in which Shaw's own non-dramatic writings are collected under one heading or another. Some of these collections are *Shaw's Music*, in three volumes; *Shaw on the London Art Scene, 1885-1950*; *Shaw on Shakespeare*; *Shaw on Dickens*; *Shaw and the Doctors*; his writings on Ireland; his writings on religion.

Then there is the correspondence. Dan H. Laurence, prince among Shaw editors, who did the music volumes, has also done a four-volume edition of the letters—containing about 2,500 items, but he warned that "Shaw, by conservative estimate, must in his lifetime have written at least a quarter of a million letters and postcards." There is also a volume of the correspondence with Ellen Terry (the only letters published during Shaw's lifetime), a volume each of correspondence with Mrs. Patrick Campbell, Granville-Barker, Siegfried Trebitsch (Shaw's lifelong German translator), and Lord Alfred Douglas; and a volume of Shaw's letters to the press.

The line continues, and continues to amaze. In 1995, the University of Toronto Press began a series called *Selected Correspondence of Bernard Shaw*. The first two volumes were *Theatrics*, letters on theater subjects edited by Laurence, and Shaw's correspondence with H. G. Wells, edited by the general editor of the series, J. P. Smith. Now comes volume three: Shaw's correspondence with Gabriel Pascal, the producer of three Shaw films, edited by Bernard F. Dukore and titled, aptly, *Bernard Shaw and Gabriel Pascal* (1996, 224 pp.).

How many of the letters in these Toronto collections are also available in the four-volume set? Very few. There are more Toronto collections to come, of correspondence with one individual or with a group of individuals in a particular field—literature and socialism, for instance. In effect, one of the many awesome facts about Shaw is his *oeuvre*'s increase after his death.

Bernard Dukore has done much beneficent work on Shaw, notably his editing of the *Collected Screenplays* and of the four volumes of Shaw's theater criticism (the best performance criticism ever written in English). In his introduction to this new book, Dukore sketches the biography of Pascal, which is about all that can be done with his life. Almost everything that Pascal wrote or said about himself is factually questionable. He was born in Hungary "probably" in 1895. His real name was something else. He invented various romances about his origins to help him move along, entered the German film world in 1914, did something uncertifiable in World War I service, then re-entered the German film world—but Dukore has been unable to verify any of his claims. With the arrival of Hitler, Pascal moved to Hollywood.

He told a story, again dubious, of a chance meeting with Shaw on the beach at Cap d'Antibes in the summer of 1925. Spurred by this encounter, true or not, he made his way to London in 1935 and managed to get an appointment with Shaw. Dukore says he was "a likable, flamboyant, Munchausen-like, self-dramatizing impresario with enormous charm, *élan*, blarney, and chutzpah." He reminded Shaw of their (alleged) meeting, then trumpeted that he had come to make adequate films of Shaw's plays, as against the previous Shaw films, and that he meant to devote the rest of his life to the project. He also announced that his total fortune was the half-crown coin in his pocket. After a week's consideration, Shaw gave him license to film *Pygmalion*.

Their correspondence, with Dukore's helpful annotation, discloses fascinating facts, but these facts only deepen the mystery of Pascal. Until now he has often been regarded as a continental con man who bamboozled the aging Shaw into giving him the rights to some plays that wealthy studios had been pining for. But this view overlooks Pascal's accomplishments: the production of the *Pygmalion* film and the production-direction of *Major Barbara* and *Caesar and Cleopatra* (lesser though the last one is). Where did this man really come from? Where did he acquire his experience? He certainly practiced his profession well, even if with plenty of smoke-and-mirrors and a high wind of verbiage. But at the end of the book everything we learn about what he did with the filming of Shaw's plays only makes the mystery of his origins more tantalizing.

Not many will want to read all the business details in Pascal's longer letters and telegrams—arrangements, re-arrangements, projects, requests—laced as they are with heavy doses of obsequiousness to Shaw. (Sample: "You know how difficult it is to keep one's own personality, small or big, in the presence of your infinite personality.") Still, Pascal provides a vivid picture of film-world wheeling and dealing. And Shaw does indeed reveal more facets of that "infinite personality."

Through these letters we glimpse Shaw films that were never made although they were much discussed. (Among them, Herbert Marshall in *The Doctor's Dilemma*, Alfred Lunt and Lynn Fontanne in *Captain Brassbound's Conversion*.) It's painful to think of these performances hovering out there in some Maeterlinckian cosmos of the unborn. These letters also tell of oddities. Shaw had some correspondence with, of all people, Mary Pickford, who was supposed to back a Pascal film. In *Caesar and Cleopatra*, Caesar's speech to the Sphinx, which, as delivered by Claude Rains, is the loveliest moment in the film, was almost botched by the developers of the negative. Arturo Toscanini was supposed to conduct a Rossini chorus for *Major Barbara*, but Pascal's budget wouldn't allow it. in September 1940 the filming of *Major Barbara*—that salvationist-diabolist play about a munitions manufacturer—was delayed from time to time by air raids.

Think, then, of Shaw himself. He was seventy-nine when his association with Pascal began, and it continued until his death at ninety-four in 1950; yet he was meticulous in business detail (in his whole career he never employed an agent), keen in artistic device, and sparklingly aware of what was happening in theater and film. In February 1940 he wrote to Pascal: "There is a young actor named Guinness whom you ought to see."

Shaw's encounter with the film world, which had begun with a couple of poor Shaw pictures in the early 1930s but was now at its height, is especially striking when compared with the late-nineteenth-century theater circumstances in which his theater life had started. A particularly fine place to examine those early circumstances is *Henry Irving's Waterloo*, by W. D. King (University of California Press, 1993). King fixes on Shaw's review of Irving's production of a one-act play by Conan Doyle, *A Story of Waterloo*, and uses that review as catalyst for an analysis of the confrontation between the fully flowered nineteenth-century theater and the arrival of a new, progressive theater embodied by Shaw. This new Shaw-Pascal collection can be seen as somewhat symmetrical in relation to King's book: it shows the 1894 herald of a new theater at the end of his life engaging a still newer art.

I once met Claude Rains, and in the course of our chat, I mentioned Pascal. Rains, in his gorgeous voice, responded with comments unprintable here. About some of Pascal's business practices, perhaps those comments were just, but Dukore's volume makes something else crystalline. One more of Shaw's innumerable accomplishments was to perceive the potential in this Autolycus figure and to guide him to at least partial fulfillment. Pascal died only four years after Shaw, aged sixty. (His one post-Shaw Shaw film was *Androcles and the Lion*, which proved how much he needed Shaw's piloting. However, he had started arrangements for the creation of *My Fair Lady*.) His fifteen-year collaboration with Shaw enabled this "flamboyant" man to find powers in himself, of energy and vision, that surpassed even his previous self-estimate.

"Shakespearean Projections, or the Bard on Screen." *Theater*, **Winter 2002.**

"The best in this kind are but shadows," says Theseus as he watches a play in *A Midsummer Night's Dream*, but Shakespeare, visionary though he was, could not have foreseen how topical and debatable that thought would become. Shadows, black or tinted, are the material of film, and few subjects in the Shakespeare field generate more heat than the advantages and disadvantages of putting his plays in film form.

Here are two new books on this much-discussed subject, and the issues are so rife with dissension that before discussing these books, it seems fit that the reviewer state his position. In more than forty years of film criticism, I have often said that Shakespeare cannot be filmed, not if it is truly to be Shakespeare and just as truly to be film. Shakespeare is text: the words. Almost every theater production of one of the plays makes minor cuts, in consonance with contemporary audience sensibility and conditioning, but that cutting never—well, almost never—controverts the belief that what keeps Shakespeare immediate is the language. All the action derives from and leads back to the language. If it were otherwise, Charles and Mary Lamb's *Tales from Shakespeare* would suffice to keep these plays with us.

In film, whose aesthetics I have been exploring through those decades, language is generally much more compressed than in the theater. This is not nearly so rigid a rule as some believe—think of Uncle Jack's farewell in *The Magnificent Ambersons* or the professor's address to the faltering strikers in *The Organizer*—but, to put it basically, few films have been made primarily because of the language in them. Yet no other prime purpose seems valid in a production of Shakespeare in any medium, and that priority is forsaken in a Shakespeare film. An important exception will follow below, but as a matter of artistic aptness, long stretches of language, particularly in diction of the past, are usually uncomfortable in film. With tolerable reduction, we can say that Shakespeare is language and film is not.

No critic can possibly approach any topic, let alone this fraught one, with a completely open mind. (How can a critic's mind be completely open if the critic really cares for the art?) Thus, with one figurative eyebrow raised, this critic approaches these books.

Note first that there is a relevant chronology in Shakespeare films, ordained by the history of film itself. Shakespeare plays were being filmed long before speech was possible. Very soon after Thomas Edison and the Skladanowsky brothers and the Lumière brothers presented the film medium to the world—without sound—the production maw of the screen began to gulp down Shakespeare. Odd as it may seem now, there were hundreds of silent Shakespeare films. Many of them greatly condensed the plots or consisted only of selected scenes, but the species proliferated. (In 1968 Robert Hamilton Ball published an account of them, *Shakespeare on Silent Film*, and subtitled it, with neat quotation, *A Strange Eventful History*.)

The fact that all these films were forced to be silent resulted, willy-nilly, in a divorce. Action was separated from text. Bits of the text were frequently inserted as intertitles, but they often seemed mere obeisance. These pictures were only Shakespeare stories. Admittedly, some of those silents served a poignant purpose. In the 1970s I saw the scenes of *Hamlet* that Johnston Forbes-Robertson had filmed in 1913. It was hardly the performance that in 1897 Bernard Shaw had called "a true classical Hamlet" with "continuous charm, interest, and variety," but still I was glad of the chance to see Forbes-Robertson in motion. There are many similar opportunities.

The arrival of action before language meant that when sound came along, the text was an addition to the Shakespeare film, not its first cause. (The earliest "talkie" was *The Taming of the Shrew*, made in 1929, starring Mary Pickford and Douglas Fairbanks and sporting the notorious credit "By William Shakespeare with additional dialogue by Sam Taylor.") Anyone who thinks that the original priority has not affected concepts of latter-day Shakespeare film need only look at the implications in these two books.

The Cambridge Companion to Shakespeare on Film (2000, 366 pp.), edited by Russell Jackson of the Shakespeare Institute at the University of Birmingham (England), contains eighteen essays on various aspects of the subject by members of faculties in Europe and America. Jackson provides an introduction and the opening essay. In his introduction he says, "It is probably as much of a mistake to ask whether 'film' can do justice to 'Shakespeare' as to reproach 'Shakespeare' with being inappropriate material for 'film.'" He frees himself of that "mistake" very quickly in his essay "From Play-script to Screenplay," where he says, "Akira Kurosawa's 1957 *Macbeth* adaptation, *Kumonso-djo* (commonly known in English as *Throne of Blood*), includes none of the original play's words but can be said to adopt (and indeed enhance) the play's fusion of psychology, superstition, and politics." Kurosawa was most certainly a genius, and *Throne of Blood* is one of his major works, but to believe that a film version of *Macbeth* transmuted into another culture—without Shakespeare's language, even in translation—can "enhance" this play is to make one's view of Shakespearean adaptation all too clear.

Jackson quotes Graham Greene's comment, made during Greene's film-critic days, that he was "less than ever convinced that there is an aesthetic justification for filming Shakespeare at all," that "the effect of even the best scenes is to distract, much in the same way as the old [Beerbohm] Tree productions distracted." If W. H. Auden's recently published *Notes on Shakespeare* had been available to Jackson, he might have quoted, "Most movies of Shakespeare make you want to say, it's very nice, but why must people say anything? You want to *see* everything." Greene and Auden are both contending that the text is unavoidably scanted in a Shakespeare film and that this loss is crucial. Jackson disagrees: "The modification of the text of the theatrical original . . . is not so much an unavoidable and regrettable consequence of filming, as an opportunity the director forgoes at his or her peril. . . . The *mise en scène* of a film is a vital element of the cinematic experience . . . and in Shakespearean films it retains this importance, rather than becoming a reprehensible competitor with the spoken word." Both Greene and Auden might have sadly agreed.

As do, cheerily rather than sadly, almost all the contributors to this *Companion*. They analyze films cinematically, and in essence there is little disagreement or dissent about the subordination of the text. It is, for them, secondary to the action and the action's presentation. From this complex collection I concentrate on a few excerpts that deal with this (absolutely central) theme. In the second essay, "Video and Its Paradoxes," Michele Willems notes: "The status of the spoken word thus appears as the main variable in the transcoding of a play for the cinema or for television. . . . Each director has his own way of solving the tension between the Shakespearean text and cinematographic visuals, which Roger Manvell referred to as 'oil and water.'" (In 1972 Manvell published a book called *Shakespeare and the Film*.) "Oil and water" is not quite an apt figure. Oil doesn't win out over water, but almost invariably, visuals win out over text.

In "The Tragedies of Love on Film," Patricia Tatspaugh says of Renato Castellani's adaptation of *Romeo and Juliet*, "His screenplay, which retains approximately 36 percent (approximately 1,081 lines) of Shakespeare's script, significantly alters the original." This is not hard to believe. A retention of only 36 percent of the lines (1,081 is to Tatspaugh an approximate figure) would significantly alter *Charley's Aunt*, let alone *Romeo and Juliet*. She concedes that "Castellani's textual alterations and embellishments lessen the effectiveness of the big scenes," but she states this clinically, without judgment one way or the other. In discussing Orson Welles's *Othello*, Tatspaugh first says, "Welles relies on visual effects to amplify the heavily cut text and to contribute to the presentation of the principal characters. Then she notes, "The sharp and moving visual images, which appeal primarily to the eye, undermine the tragic intent." Agreeing that visual images tend to appeal "primarily" to the eye (rather than the ear?), we can still question the worth of an *Othello* film that undermines "the tragic intent" of the play.

Harry Keyishian, in "Shakespeare and Movie Genre," wants to "illustrate the relationship of Shakespeare movies to movie genres" by commenting on three films of *Hamlet*. Look at one instance. He sees Laurence Olivier's version as a *film noir* and cites what he considers affinities between this film and the *noir* genre. He strives so hard to make these points that he never mentions that Olivier tore the text to tatters, discarding about half of the play; omitted Rosencrantz and Guildenstern completely; and opened the picture with the specious and patronizing voice-over, "This is the tragedy of a man who could not make up his mind." (At least J. Lawrence Guntner mentions most of these matters when he discusses this film in another essay.) For my part, rather than considering Keyishian's views critically daring, I was glad to see this picture consigned to *film noir*.

Most of the essays, however, make interesting points on aspects other than the text, and two of them are especially illuminating. In "The Comedies on Film," Michael Hattaway says, "It is difficult to find cinematic equivalents for Elizabethan theatrical codes of place and space.... Film, in contrast to theater, does not deploy frames but uses masks." He thus posits a major difference between the concepts of space in theater and film. Any scene of a play takes place in a selected fragment of the world. Any scene of a film takes place in the whole world. When a theater actor leaves the stage, he steps into the wings. When a film actor moves off camera, even if it is an indoor scene, he steps into the rest of the world. "The [film's] problem is to manipulate and shoot unstylized reality in such a way that the result has style." I take this to mean that in the adaptation of a play, any play, film has always to deal with this inherent spatial difference between the two arts.

Samuel Crowl's essay "Flamboyant Realist: Kenneth Branagh" is especially welcome because it deals with the man who has done the most to temper my own views on the subject of filming Shakespeare. When I first saw Branagh's *Henry V*, I felt that I was entering a territory that I had thought could not exist. Here was a film that, if we allow for little more abridgment than a stage production might indulge, concentrated on the text. Almost incredibly, it clearly treasured the text as the picture's reason for being.

What was even more exciting, Branagh himself spoke with a miraculous blend of vocal styles, a blend of theater and film. He maintained the verse as verse, with lift and rhythm, yet he never floated away from the contemporary viewing audience. He was neither a theatrical elocutionist nor a vernacular Shakespearean trying to prove that he was a regular guy. As director, he kept the whole cast in harmony with his approach. To cap the triumph, the cinematic elements were splendid. (Who can forget Derek Jacobi as the Chorus striking a match in the dark to begin the film? Or Branagh and Emma Thompson profile to profile in the wooing scene?) Not all of Branagh's subsequent Shakespeare films have maintained the high level of his *Henry V* but in all of them his own performances have exulted in vitalizing the texts, and all of them have shown cinematic ingenuity.

Crowl says that Branagh is "the first director of Shakespeare films to mix Olivier's attention to the spoken text with Welles's fascination with camera angle and editing and [Franco] Zeffirelli's visual and musical romanticism." If we assume that Crowl means Olivier's speaking of the text that he decided to retain, the opinion rings solidly, especially the comment on Zeffirelli (best known as an opera director). Of this book's contributors Crowl is one of the few to emphasize the matter of music, specifying Patrick Doyle's score for *Henry V*: "Doyle's score, at the close of Agincourt, swells from a single voice singing a *Non Nobis* to a huge choir supported by a full orchestra." More: I would add that Doyle's score at the start of Agincourt, swelling reticently under Branagh's rendering of the St. Crispin's Day speech, is like a surfboard carrying its rider up and over the crest of a gigantic wave.

In her 2000 book *Framing Shakespeare on Film* (Ohio University Press, 275 pp.), Kathy M. Howlett deals with eleven films, eight Shakespeare and three derivatives: Kurosawa's *Ran*, which is abstracted from *King Lear*; Gus Van Sant's *My Own Private Idaho*, which has a tenuous relation to the Falstaff-Prince Hal story; and *A Midwinter's Tale*, Kenneth Branagh's lark about a tatty *Hamlet* production. This selection may seem odd, in light of her title, but she advises us at the outset that her book

> is an effort to expound those rare visions that have captured the imaginations of American film audiences by demonstrating that Shakespeare is still centrally in these films, despite their deviation from the text or radical reformulation of character and situation. The successful Shakespeare film can transform Shakespeare's text while remaining rooted in Shakespearean conceptions.

This is, at least, forthright. Howlett, who teaches English and cinema studies at Northeastern University, clearly believes that there is some magical quintessence called Shakespeare that remains after one deviates from the text and reformulates character and situation. Of what, we can wonder, is that quintessence composed? The stories?

The frame in her title means something different to Howlett than to Michael Hattaway. Howlett: "When I speak of cinematic framing I do not simply refer to the rectangular screen that permits the audience a view of the action but to how the arrangement of objects within the cinematic frame interprets the Shakespearean story according to a dynamic of space existing between the camera and the objects it surveys." In contrast to Hattaway's subtle point, this is only a reworking of the familiar truth that by the composition of the frame, the director emphasizes or diminishes the elements within it, and it is of course as true of *kung fu* films as of Shakespeare.

Howlett devotes a chapter to each of her choices, except for a chapter that handles two together. Here is a fair instance of her approach (and prose style):

> Franco Zeffirelli's *Hamlet* (1990) illustrates discursive practices within a single frame. For while the audience attends to what might be called the "topic frame" of the film—Shakespeare's *Hamlet*—the film also exhibits other recognizable influences that introduce variation in the organizational principles of Shakespeare's play. By introducing a new frame encoded with familiar patterns from a popular American film genre, the Western, Zeffirelli involves the viewer in a frame-making cognitive activity that challenges the viewer to new insights about the nature of Hamlet's conflict. However, many film and Shakespeare critics

do not find these changes meaningful. . . . What [these critics] do not see is that this director taps into aspects of Shakespeare's *Hamlet* that resonate within the context of American mythology and film.

As one of those myopic critics, I offer reservations here. Even if we allow that the ultra-European Zeffirelli might have conceived *Hamlet* in Western mode, Howlett's tracings of the Western motifs in this film seem strained. They consist largely of ticking off the shots in which we see Hamlet against the sky or in large spaces or on horseback, an approach that could convert Pabst's *Don Quixote* into a Western.

Here is the closing sentence of Howlett's book, in a chapter about the Branagh *A Midwinter's Tale*, a film that is for me only a moderately amusing caprice: "Ultimately, what *works* in this film is its ability to draw the audience from the textual center to a level beyond that of style, plot, character, or theme, where one may discover an immanence of meanings." Or, it is imperative to add, one may not. Her peroration is yet another statement of the idea in Jackson's introduction: "The modification of the text of the theatrical original" is an opportunity that the [film] director forgoes at his or her peril. It is on this rock that the Shakespeare-film enthusiasts build their church.

Some conclusions and some conniptions. No argument by any of the writers in these two books overtly questions that Shakespeare is pristinely Shakespeare's text. What these critics do advance, in various forms and from various angles, is the belief that the alteration or gross reduction or rearrangement of the text is justified by the enrichment that film and video can provide. As a veteran film lover and critic, I am unconvinced. Most of the contributors to these books—and there are several other such books—so blithely assume that drastic film alterations of Shakespeare are helpful that they evoke a mixture of irritation and fear. If these are the teachers of Shakespeare today, what of Shakespeare tomorrow?

A recognition, almost an admission, is essential. The plain, insistent fact is that a new art form has evolved since the arrival of the sound film. What is needed, and what is scantily treated in these books, is clear perception of this new form, clarity about the fact that Shakespearean film is not Shakespeare on film but a separate art, a melding of Shakespeare with film for which no adequate name has yet been devised. A few exceptions exist, chiefly the best of Branagh. In his *Henry V* and *Much Ado about Nothing* and *Hamlet*, he put Shakespeare on film, with cinematic flourish yet without converting the plays into film scripts. His best work does not belong to this new art. In that new art, Shakespeare is only a collaborator, like a screenplay writer, instead of being the object of the enterprise. Setting Branagh aside, we can be reconciled to the new form, can even rejoice in it, if it is seen candidly for what it is.

The obvious analogy with this new form is Shakespearean opera. Almost two hundred operas have Shakespeare librettos. (An often overlooked fact: Wagner's second opera, *Das Liebesverbot*, was based on *Measure for Measure*.) At least three of these operas are glorious masterworks: Verdi's *Macbeth*, *Otello*, and *Falstaff*. Verdi responded swiftly to the arrival of Shakespeare in Italian translation. The first production of Shakespeare in Italy was in 1842; Verdi finished *Macbeth* in 1847. But there is a vast difference between the general view of Shakespearean opera and that of Shakespearean film. Great as Verdi's three works are, no one would think of going to them in order to study Shakespeare, not just because the language is Italian but because the music is why the work exists. What one relishes in those operas is the effect that the plays had on Verdi's musical creativity.

If the analogy with opera were followed, then what would be studied in a Shakespeare film is the effect the play had on the director's creativity. This point is certainly made in the two books discussed here but—a crucial omission—without stipulating that these films are not those plays. They are other works. These films are a twentieth-century invention (the Shakefilm?), some of which are well worth study in themselves and as themselves. (As are some of the performances: e.g., Celia Johnson as the countess in *All's Well That Ends Well*, John Gielgud as Clarence in Olivier's *Richard III*.) But the assumption that merely because a film of a play is available, it is therefore an acceptable substitute for the text, even an improvement—that assumption is fearsome. The film-for-text substitution happens; it will surely happen more and more frequently for teachers and students who are more and more visually oriented. If only the field were seen as the study not of Shakespeare but of the new form. Think of Verdi ...

BOOK REVIEWS

A History of American Acting, by Garff B. Wilson. *New York Times*, July 24, 1966.

The history of any art is the history of the world in which it was made. Or ought to be. Garff B. Wilson's *A History of American Acting* (Indiana University Press, 310 pp.) at least recognizes the obligation.

Wilson's book is an unusual attempt to chronicle a nation's acting, as distinct from the history of its theater as a whole. To write about performances that one has never seen is at once a height of presumption and of devotion. One can never really know what one is talking about; yet an effort to set the past in some sort of understandable order is not only helpful but—if one cares about the art at all—just plain interesting.

With the help of contemporary reviews, comments, and reminiscences, one can hope to recapture the flavor of individual actors and performances. (There are also phonograph records of some nineteenth-century actors, though the author does not mention them.) But it is the flow of influences, interactions, inheritances that such a historian must plump for, and Wilson, a professor of dramatic art at Berkeley, knows it. He even interrupts his narrative four times for "Notes on the Setting"—the changing of relevant historical-social backdrops.

Yet these crucial matters are only described, not illuminated. We are told of the various schools, such as the heroic, the classic, the emotionalist, and so on. And we are given some background information. But the two are not meaningfully related. What in American life evoked these schools? How did the schools co-exist (as they often did)? And why, in drastically altered times, did some of them survive? For example, Robert Mantell (unmentioned by the author), who acted well into the twentieth century, was surely a descendant of the heroic school of Edwin Forrest, thriving in a very different age. Why was he still popular? A Method actor's criticism of Wilson might be that he merely "indicates" but does not fulfill.

His book is also rather flatly written. "It is certain that Forrest's physical and vocal make-up had real influence on his style of acting and on the way he interpreted roles." Aside from the home-mechanics prose, is there an actor of whom that remark could not be made?

There are other reservations. Wilson's comments on modern actors are sometimes curious. He believes that Judith Anderson, Helen Hayes, and Katharine Cornell can all claim kinship with the classic school—presumably because all have played roles of "high seriousness." (He cites Hayes's Harriet Beecher Stowe and Cornell's Elizabeth Barrett.) He sometimes apportions space oddly: Clara Fisher, a popular personality performer, gets two pages; Margaret Anglin, a great artist, gets six lines.

Still, if Wilson's book does not completely fill a need, it is at least a useful stopgap. Merely by arranging this material in a continuous narrative, he has thrown some matters into highlight and has collected some curiosities. The most striking matter is that modern stars—the biggest—are shackled, compared with those of the nineteenth century. I do not mean the fact that the old-timers had luxurious private railroad cars and no income taxes. I mean that this is now the era of the playwright, not the actor, and no modern American star can function long without new plays.

A hundred years ago the star would not have been similarly bound. He could, if he liked, spend his life selecting roles from a large established repertory. The special advantage of this circumstance was that he could outfit himself with a career tailored completely to his talents and even expressing his artistic principles. Today such a performer chooses, too, of course, but within a much narrower range, and he may have a long, successful career without actually fulfilling himself.

This book refreshes a conviction that most performances, as ensembles, must have been ghastly. There was no director in our sense, only a stage manager with a prompt-book. Actors frequently supplied their own costumes. Rehearsals—if the star was visiting a local company—were less than minimal. What the audience got was brilliance from one or two performers. This was the basic aesthetic rationale of that theater, and it is not completely untenable—as the Metropolitan Opera used to prove regularly.

Then there is the matter of the drama criticism of the day, which fitted its theater. We tend to dismiss that criticism because of its pillowy style and its sentimental judgments of plays; but its power was in its response to acting. William Winter, who was the drama critic of the *New York Tribune* from 1865 to 1909, is ludicrous today in his distaste for Ibsen and his praise of various hack playwrights, but his comments on actors are often miraculously individualizing and vivid.

And then there is a matter that is glaringly obvious once it is pointed out. In the great century of immigration, the American stage must have been a conglomeration of accents. A number of leading actors were born and trained in England, a surprising number were Irish. At least two were Continental and learned English to appear in the United States. (A teacher of mine had once played with the Polish-born Helena Modjeska and used to do an imitation of her charming accent as Juliet.)

Some curiosities recounted by Wilson:

Charlotte Cushman, the first native-born American tragedienne of stature, occasionally played male roles and once was the Romeo to her sister's Juliet.

In Rochester, New York, which had a large German-born population, Booth was once advertised as "Herr Edwin Booth," and a riot broke out in the theater when he began to speak in English.

When David Belasco discovered the young Mrs. Leslie Carter, he decided to train her. He recruited an entire company to support her, and for two years rehearsed her in forty plays—which were performed for him alone.

Anyone concerned with the development of American acting theory will find the matter more sensitively traced in several chapters of Christine Edwards' recent book *The Stanislavsky Heritage*. Yet Wilson's book, by reason of its scope, shows nineteenth-century American acting, like American literature, forming itself on English models; and, again like literature, finding a native voice (in large part) through comedy. Such comedians as Joseph Jefferson and William Warren were not the artistic equivalents of Mark Twain and Bret Harte, but their work in American comic roles embodied comparable impulses toward a statement of familiar life.

Life—vitality—is the key word. Through all the furbelows and fustian, the fake Shakespearean poetic dramas, sheer abundance and abundant vitality glow. Nonetheless, nostalgia must be guarded. Heaven be thanked that we have been spared most of those shoddy shows and patchwork productions. But how wonderful it would have been to see great actors in a day when the theater existed for them.

Melodrama Unveiled: American Theater and Culture, 1800-1850, by David Grimsted. *New Republic*, September 28, 1968.

Most histories of the American theater are poor stuff. The majority are just serviceable pedantry; the rest are usually either "glamorous" or intellectually thin or both. Very exceptionally a history is factually valuable and is also a work of grace and insight—the great example is George C. D. Odell's fifteen-volume *Annals of the New York Stage*. But most of them are pretty discouraging to a reader who has enjoyed such critical art histories as, say, Lewis Mumford's *Sticks and Stones* or Alfred Kazin's *On Native Grounds* or Wilfrid Mellers' *Music in a New Found Land*.

Things theatrical are looking up. The literature is a long way from richness, but at least there is row some realization that it has been poor. The last few years have produced, for example, Garff B. Wilson's *A History of American Acting* and Jane DeHart Mathews' *The Federal Theatre, 1935-1939*, neither of which is first-rate but both of which in any case understand their obligations. Now David Grimsted has published the best book on its subject that I know and one of the few American theatrical histories that can be recommended to the general reader: *Melodrama Unveiled: American Theater and Culture, 1800-1850* (University of Chicago Press, 285 pp.).

The title, *Melodrama Unveiled*, is literally apt but too constricting. Grimsted's real subject is in his subtitle, *American Theater and Culture, 1800-1850*. Certainly he shows us how melodrama *was* unveiled, but he also shows us why; and that history is much more interesting than the genre itself. At any rate, the book is considerably larger than a study of melodrama, which the main title implies. Grimsted writes intelligently and well about the theater as a socio-cultural function, as the result of give-and-take between itself and the world around it. His book is a product of thought, not merely of plodding research, yet it is documented thoroughly. (But why so few illustrations—and only in the endpapers?)

At the end of the eighteenth century, the American theater was influenced by some legacies of the Enlightenment and some impulse to fulfill Columbia's destiny as the home of the New Man. Shakespeare was the staple of most theaters, along with other classics, and a good deal of the drama criticism of the time urged the theater onward and upward. Ambitious American plays were written and produced (as well as less ambitious native plays and entertainments). There were even several proposals for publicly subsidized theaters. However short-lived, there was the sense of a historical moment.

The quality of production in the early nineteenth century must often have been ragged; how could it have been otherwise? Grimsted writes: "Within a week a theatrical company might offer as the evening's feature play a melodrama, a Shakespearean tragedy, an opera, an eighteenth-century comedy, and a fairy-tale play." These were only the feature offerings; there was almost always a comic afterpiece. And all of these works were performed by the same company, more or less, including the opera. (The tragedienne Charlotte Cushman made her début in Mozart's *Marriage of Figaro*.) Still, whatever the quality, theaters flourished all over the country. By the middle 1820s New York was recognized as America's theater center, but by the middle 1850s there were fifty-eight American communities with permanent theaters. These in addition to numerous traveling troupes and touring stars.

As the population grew, as the frontier became a fact for many and a metaphysical presence for all, and as cultural independence from Europe became a passion, the theater changed and responded. The classics—of British drama particularly—were certainly not abandoned, but a new, popular drama began to appear and increase. This form, too, had a European origin: the play that ushered melodrama into the United States was French—Caignez's *The Voice of Nature* (1803). But melodrama was quickly naturalized; it became the vehicle of the age's ethos, truth, and hypocrisy. Grimsted says, apropos of an archetypal play called *Rosina Meadows*:

> Its conventions were false, its language stilted and commonplace, its characters stereotypes, and its morality and theology gross oversimplifications. Yet its appeal was great, and understandable. It took the lives of common people seriously and paid much respect to their superior purity and wisdom.... And its moral parable struggled to reconcile social fears and life's awesomeness with the period's confidence in absolute moral standards, man's upward progress, and a benevolent providence that insured the triumph of the pure.

Before chuckling complacently at the past, look at tonight's TV Western. Even if it's "adult"—that is, has a varnish of cynicism and sexual liberality—it conforms essentially to Grimsted's description.

The Astor Place Riot in 1840 was a turning point in American theater history. It was the outgrowth of rivalry between two stars, the American Edwin Forrest and the English William Charles Macready. The latter was playing in New York, and Forrest's supporters agitated against him on straight chauvinistic lines. ("Down with the codfish aristocracy!" "Huzza for Native Talent!") On the night of May 10th, a large mob gathered outside Macready's theater. They became unruly, and the military were called to aid the police. Shots were fired; twenty-two people were killed or died of wounds, and thirty more were injured. I have always thought of this riot as a drastic expression in vulgarized form of the idea that (among other critics) Walt Whitman presented in the *Brooklyn Eagle*: the idea that American art was in bondage to Europe, that even Shakespeare represented "the mighty aesthetic scepter of the past," that an American drama "*must* rise." Now Grimsted makes a further illuminating point:

> The riot marked an end to the conglomerate appeal of the drama.... One theater was no longer large enough to appeal to all classes.... The country had grown, and grown apart. The theater after midcentury followed this development. It expanded and divided—into legitimate drama, foreign-language drama, farce, vaudeville, circus, burlesque, minstrelsy, opera, symphony—each with its separate theater and separate audience. One roof, housing a vast miscellany of entertainment each evening, could no longer cover a people growing intellectually and financially more disparate.

Given its own clear track, melodrama roared ahead; and Grimsted explains why that genre became predominant, why we did not get the great national drama that Whitman and others wanted.

Part of the reason was that serious writing was still associated with historical subjects. "But nineteenth-century audiences understandably craved a drama reflective of their own situations and standards." Part of it was the serious playwright's addiction to blank verse. Not that the language of melodrama was realistic, but at least its prose was an elevation of the familiar. ("Melodrama," says Eric Bentley, "is the Naturalism of the dream life.") Also, the popular plays made use of specific localities—numerous theaters around the country had their own playwrights—and they had a strong sense of social apposition in their heroes' vocations. Noblemen were out, the honest farmer was in. Very soon he was joined by the urban workingman, or "mechanic," as he was then called. (There is still a pipe tobacco sold in rural America called Mechanic's Delight.)

In his last two chapters Grimsted examines the structure and "vision" of melodrama, and here one can have only sympathy for him. There is absolutely no literary or dramatic interest in these plays today; they are only cultural-historical phenomena. Nineteenth-century melodrama is practically indistinguishable from its parodies—on paper, at least. Actors of the time must have developed some special skills in it because they were playing "straight." (You can see some of it in such early films as Griffith's *Way Down East*, and you can at least sniff the genre in some Donizetti and Verdi operas.) Unlike some current cultural commentators, Grimsted does not try to exaggerate the worth of popular material simply because it was popular. He explains why melodrama came about and what it represented. He assumes, quite rightly, that it is important to us because it was human, American, and precedent of many elements in our own culture. But he says he has read 250 of these plays. I've read perhaps twenty-five in my life, and I bleed for him.

The brute fact is that, in contrast to every significant European theater of the period, the nineteenth-century American theater left *not one play* of vital consequence to us, of more than museum interest. Yet it was unquestionably a theater that was vital to its audience. The paradox in that condition is both a strength of the theater and one of its miseries.

***More Theatres*, by Max Beerbohm. *New Republic*, November 8, 1969.**

Rupert Hart-Davis, the English publisher and editor, has refused to abide by Max Beerbohm's judgment on his own drama criticism. We are the gainers. Beerbohm selected about one-third of his critiques in the *Saturday*

Review for his now-famous collection *Around Theatres* (1924). Hart-Davis has collected the other pieces, hitherto not reprinted, in two volumes. *More Theatres, 1898-1903* has just been published in the U.S. (Taplinger, 624 pp.). *Last Theatres* is to follow next year.

Beerbohm remains the greatest English-speaking drama critic who didn't really care about the theater. (The breed has proliferated.) In sheerly theatrical terms, he had little vision and less concern, but he also had exquisitely idiosyncratic tastes and the social sensibility of an invisible, aristocratic imp—all these expressed in that purling, soothing-impertinent style.

Still his limitations, as limitations will do, gave him certain advantages. For instance, he perceived the importance of *The Importance of Being Earnest* when the best of English-speaking critics, Bernard Shaw, did not. And there are passages in this new collection that might have been written this year:

> When a man dramatizes one of his own novels, his natural vanity prevents him from sacrificing the many things that have to be sacrificed if the play is to be a good one. Also, his natural vanity prevents him from believing that any audience can include any creature so degraded as not to have read his book. His play, therefore, is as likely to omit many essential things as it is to include many that are quite superfluous. The result is dreadful.

This seems to me a fair comment on Elliott Baker's dramatization of his own very good novel *The Penny Wars*, which recently opened and closed in the same week.

Bernard Shaw: A Reassessment, by Colin Wilson. *New Republic*, November 22, 1969.

Colin Wilson says that he has been a Shaw disciple since childhood. He thinks he knows him "as well as Keats knew Shakespeare or Dr. Johnson the Bible." Thus his book, *Bernard Shaw: A Reassessment* (Hutchinson, 306 pp.), which has given him more trouble than anything he has ever written (he is thirty-eight and has produced twenty books, including an autobiography), is about Wilson as well as Shaw. The intensity of his replies to the critics of Shaw, and the sensitivity of his antennae to negative signals about Shaw's current reputation, suggest that he feels he is now suffering something of Shaw's own fate. Shaw was doomed to be misunderstood, we are told, because he spoke against the prevailing literary culture, and spoke truth.

Wilson asserts that the prevailing culture, both before World War I and after, was largely one of romantic nihilism. Shaw on the other hand was a "vitalist." He wanted to do something for the world rather than sit and complain about it; but for his pains Yeats compared him to a sewing machine, Eliot said he couldn't read him, Pound called him a ninth-rate coward, and even H. G. Wells—who was briefly a fellow Fabian and certainly shared some of Shaw's social optimism—found him impossibly ideological and ill-disposed toward facts. Yet it was Shaw and Shaw only, says Wilson, who was really making sense, endowing life with purpose, displaying a faith in "government and public spirit against anarchism and selfishness."

Wilson allows that Shaw's own life was unevenly vitalist. He was a late bloomer who coasted purposelessly through his twenties until socialism found him out. Then he had twenty good years culminating in *Major Barbara* (1905), his greatest play, and making him one of the world's two [sic] best dramatists by the time he was fifty. After *Major Barbara*, however, he lapsed badly for a decade or so into a "cul-de-sac" lasting until after World War I.

Wilson obviously has few complaints about Shaw, but the war years he finds a dead loss. Shaw was busy making badly timed pronouncements against the British, and also suffering from the discovery that reason was not in charge of things. Only after the war, with the writing of *Heartbreak House* and *Back to Methuselah*, did he become again a force for life rather than death. And in these postwar plays it was primarily as a thinker, not as a dramatist, that he distinguished himself. It is as a thinker anyway that Wilson finds Shaw preeminent among his fellow artists. Unlike Shakespeare, a chap of "complete intellectual sterility" (Shaw's phrase), Shaw was that rare thing, a *serious* artist, because he thought.

Wilson's argument becomes hard to follow here, and may not be worth following. Shaw was a great thinker, and yet he "was not, in the strictest sense of the word, a thinker." Similarly, Wilson describes Shaw as a romantic but also as an anti-romantic romantic and a classicist. What's that again? Shaw is admittedly a tough nut to classify, but he was also himself a great classifier; he might have found sport in putting Wilson in one of the many circles of hell he had for those who do not see clearly.

After reading the Wilson biography I went back and reread *Heartbreak House*, and a bit of *Major Barbara,* to straighten out my own thoughts about Shaw as a thinker. I could sympathize with Wilson's effort to find some niche for the man between romanticism and whatever its opposite is. The charm of the plays is partly derived from the unexpected combination of practicality and Rube Goldberg fantasy that Shaw enjoyed concocting. The combination is a whole genre, and Shaw's very own, which may be one reason for Shaw's unpopularity among his contemporaries: nobody else could do it. But Shaw's talent here is, I think, a talent for a genre, a dramatic mode, a manner, rather than a talent—which in any event we would not see displayed in the plays—for actually starting socialist-capitalist dream factories or running countries. The Fabians had, we are always told, enormous influence upon early British socialism, and even produced some of its best leaders; but Shaw was not one of them. Shaw was a statesman's bedside reading, a businessman's Halloween guide, not himself a Caesar or Undershaft.

Wilson would hate my contention. I am in effect denying Shaw the seriousness Wilson attributes to him; for while Wilson acknowledges the staginess of Shaw—and has some good things to say about it—he is anxious to get Shaw offstage in order to *assert* his stature. Shaw is the "first philosopher since Plato" to approach the idea of the philosopher king "with any consistency." Shaw is "the most important European since Dante," and so on. I regret I can't agree.

I have run across many Shavians in the past, and even for a time subscribed to a Shavian newsletter; but Wilson's intensity is new to me. I suspect it would have been new to Shaw, too, for essentially the intensity is the intensity of a heady young mystic. There is a fine façade of rationality, and much praise for thought; but the real interest is in the drive behind the thought. In his last chapter, entitled "My Own Part in the Matter," Wilson abandons Shaw in favor of his own thoughts and becomes directly programmatic. He is selling, it seems, a new kind of "evolutionary psychology." He wants us to search out the upper five percent. He wants these talented persons to develop their instinctive powers—which for Wilson means participating with animals in some sort of universal radar—and by these efforts grease the wheels of evolution.

Many literary biographies in recent years have been criticized for their academic attention to small facts in their subjects' lives, and consequent neglect of the significant properties of genius. With Wilson's book we seem to have reached the other extreme: Wilson is obsessed with thesis. Though he is knowledgeable about Shaw, the knowledge is consistently bent to the programmatic occasion. The bending may please evolutionary psychologists, but rationalists of a different school may wonder what the name of reason has come to.

Notes on a Cowardly Lion: The Biography of Bert Lahr, by John Lahr. New Republic, December 20, 1969.

Bert Lahr spent most of his career in the theater. It's especially significant, then, that the title of his biography refers to one of his relatively few film roles. (A social comment in itself.) As a theater-and-film critic, I therefore get the chance to discuss *Notes on a Cowardly Lion* (Knopf, 394 pp.) from two perspectives.

John Lahr had the good luck to be his father's son, something that many thousands of us keenly envy him for. The outstanding quality of his book is that he appreciates his luck: his affection for his father is immediately clear, and it glows throughout the nearly four hundred (big) pages. Also, John Lahr is aware—though on a modest level of perception—of the large cultural transitions through which his father lived, as they were manifested in the theater. Bert Lahr, born in New York of German-Jewish parents in 1895, broke into show business in 1910 when burlesque and vaudeville were bubbling and constantly demanded new materials. As the author says, it was a seller's market. When the comedian began, he used a "station-house" German accent and frequently played in schoolroom sketches, in which various accents were used—a direct response to the experience of the immigrant audiences. Toward the end of his life, Bert Lahr was in the first American production of *Waiting for Godot*. En route he encountered films and, as they were invented, radio and television. His career was a distillation of change.

His son is somewhat overimpressed by the contrast between the public clown and the private worrier. *Pagliacci* aside, this contrast is a commonplace of the theater. One of the oldest theater jokes is about the great clown Grimaldi. A man goes to a doctor because he feels depressed. The doctor examines him and says, "Sir, I can find nothing physically wrong with you. You just need cheering up. Go to see Grimaldi." The patient says, "But, doctor, I *am* Grimaldi." John Lahr's closeness and concern have produced a certain naïveté in him on this point—not for reporting the truth but for losing perspective on it. (I mean the perennial worries of the clown. His father's early marital trouble is a different, terrible story.)

He does well in two regards. He shows the evolution both of his father's ambitions and his changes in style—from knockabout clown to comic commentator. And he underscores the sheer theatrical instinct that enabled Bert Lahr to recognize quality even in the strange. When the comedian read the screenplay of *The Wizard of Oz*, a relatively daring undertaking in its day, he thought it was beautiful and wanted to do it. Much more extraordinary, when he read *Waiting for Godot*—long before the critics had kosherized Beckett—he responded with a fine performer's instincts. The author records a telephone conversation in which Bert Lahr speaks to his agent after reading *Godot* and says: "It's not like anything that's been done . . . Yes, but it's funny . . . I know, Lester, I know it's supposed to be tragic, but there are lots of gags . . . I'm not sure, but the writer's no phony. How many weeks do you think I could get with it?"

Affection, information, color—the book has plenty of them. Nevertheless, the reader has to fight to finish it because it is so very badly written. The net impression is that the author is afraid of the English language, is sweating clammily as he wrestles with it, and loses. There is neither space nor reason to document the struggle completely, but here are some fair samples:

> *Stuff-and-stuffing*. On the day of Bert Lahr's birth, his father goes up on the roof to read his newspaper. "Jacob felt comfortable in the summer air. To the east was the river, muddy and strangely turbulent . . ." Etc.

> *Corn.* "[DeSylva] combined the discipline of a writer with a sense of phrase and romance that made his songs as scintillating as the decade in which they were written." Or: "To the world, [Lahr] was a success; privately, the specter of failure haunted him."

> *Malapropisms.* "Ziegfeld was cut from a more cosmopolitan mold." ("Cast in" a mold, perhaps?) When Mrs. Lahr calls up to her husband's dressing room: "A falsetto voice echoes up the stairwell." (A "female" voice?)

> *Wretched writing.* Just one sample out of dozens: "Later, smaller-scale revues . . . found admiring audiences on Broadway by offering not only more acerbic satire, but also an economic format that counterbalanced spiraling Broadway costs." Aside from the fact that spirals can go either up or down, this sentence says that audiences admired these new shows not only because the satire was harsher but because producers invested less money in them.

There are also grammatical and (numerous) typographical errors. In his acknowledgments, the author thanks his publishing house's president, editor, and copy editor. What for?

In the rather special field of filial theater-biography, *Notes on a Cowardly Lion* is not remotely as accomplished a piece of work as Daphne du Maurier's *Gerald* or Frances Donaldson's *Freddy* (the life of Frederick Lonsdale). But if the reader grits his teeth and bears with John Lahr's barbarisms and banalities, the boisterous, sad warmth of Bert Lahr will come through.

The Autobiography of Joseph Jefferson. New Republic, May 6, 1972.

I have a recording so old that it begins with an announcer's voice. He says: "Mountain Scene from *Rip Van Winkle* by Joseph Jefferson. Columbia Record." Then we hear Rip in the Catskills, meeting the queer little man (whom we don't hear) with the keg of schnapps. The voice is a light baritone with little upward breaks for intimacy and fun, the accent a friendly stage German. On the other side is the Return Scene, twenty years later, between Rip and his daughter (whom we don't hear), with the sentiment as sure and unabashed and therefore effective as in a Chaplin film.

What an eerie, fascinating feeling to put down the autobiography of a man born in 1829 and then hear his voice, a man who knew such actors as Forrest, Macready, Cushman, and Booth, who met Holmes and Longfellow and Stowe, Trollope and Browning. The record supports the central impression of the book: that it is a strand of cultural history leading from a very remote age—more than 140 years in effect, if not in time—to the beginnings of the present. Jefferson's autobiography (originally published in 1890 and now available from Harvard University Press, 363 pp.) is one of the few "classics" among lives of actors, which term I would define as biographies that can be read for pleasure, even by general readers. On the evidence Jefferson was a wonderful one-part actor. He played numerous other roles besides Rip, but several good critics wrote that he was Rip, and wonderful, in all of them. His book lives, not as a memorial of a great artist, which he never claims, but as a picture of an intensely active theater, a compendium of observations on acting, a sketchbook of a changing nation, and a journal of an open-eyed traveler abroad.

Jefferson, who died in 1905, was the son and grandson of actors. So far as his autobiography or his editor, the late Alan Downer, tells us, he had very scanty formal education, so the writing, which is competent Victorianese, is especially remarkable. He started it at the instigation of William Dean Howells, who may have helped, and also had help from Richard Watson Gilder, the editor of *The Century Magazine*, which serialized it before book publication; but their help, whatever it was, was unintrusive because the tone is personal and consistent.

Jefferson's parents were poor and may not have been very good actors: their engagements were usually short and they spent most of their time as strolling players. He was born in Philadelphia but had no fixed residence until much later in life. He made his début in Washington at the age of four in blackface, doing a Jim Crow song. (Among other matters, his book reflects current prejudices against blacks, Jews, and Indians, all points of etiquette, even in a good-hearted man, during Jefferson's lifetime.) His childhood included a tour through the Erie Canal to the new town of Chicago (population 2,000); travel by open wagon and sleigh down to Springfield, where the company was aided by a young lawyer named (but it's *true*) Lincoln; literal barn-storming in Mississippi. His youth included a tour following the American army into Mexico in 1846, where he had his first romantic encounter. About sex and love and marriage—he was twice married—he is reticent. Modern readers are conditioned to supply what he leaves out.

He leaves out a good deal, in fact. The book skips many transitions and, of course, does not conclude his career. He lived and worked for fifteen years more (and got honorary degrees from Yale and Harvard). It is a chronological collection of memoirs, rather than a seamless account.

For instance, in 1856 he made a trip to London and Paris—"not the Paris of today [!], with its gilded domes and modern grandeur, but the old, quaint, dirty, gay, strange city in the early days of the Second Empire, with its high, toppling buildings, narrow streets, and lively people." He says he wanted to see France because his mother's family had come from there, but it still seems an unusual and unusually expensive jaunt for a quite modestly successful actor of twenty-seven to make with his family in those days. In 1861 he went to Australia, without any reason given. Downer says that Jefferson was not in good health and that, after the death of his first wife in that year, he needed to travel. But he stayed in Australia and New Zealand four years, acting much of the time. Is it mere coincidence that his exile was precisely during the years of the Civil War? He does not say; but his book reveals great affection for the South—in later years he had a home in Louisiana, as well as Massachusetts—and one can speculate that he had northern affiliations but southern sympathies and used his wife's death as an excuse to avoid decision.

There are dozens of general anecdotes, mostly vivid (including a murder he witnessed in his youth), but the book's uniqueness is in its view of a nation and a time from a life in the theater of the day. Here, as un-selfconscious cultural history, one can discern four principal themes.

First, the American theater was dominated by English or Irish actors until well along in the nineteenth century. Downer's annotation tells us that the vast majority of the actors whom Jefferson knew were born in the British Isles and often returned there. (And as Francis Hodge says in *Yankee Theatre*, the authors of Jefferson's two big "Yankee" hits, *The Octoroon* and *Our American Cousin*, were an Irishman, Dion Boucicault, and an Englishman, Tom Taylor.) Imagine the mixture of accents in a performance. Jefferson himself says of his first appearance with Laura Keene in 1857 on the "western side" of New York: "It was looked upon as a kind of presumption in those days for an American actor to intrude himself into a Broadway theater; the domestic article seldom aspired to anything higher than the Bowery."

Second, there was, in the sociological sense, a society of actors. Actors lived everywhere, figuratively speaking, because there were companies everywhere, as well as strolling troupes that played "in between" and stars who traveled to the resident companies. In 1868 Jefferson was one of the first stars to employ a "combination," a company of actors who traveled with him, instead of appearing with a local company who supported him; and he feels it necessary to justify this startling innovation at length. There are now some dozens of resident theaters in the United States but they do not yet constitute such a society, because they are not a natural, inevitable product of our culture, they are an attempt to counteract some of its centralizing, polarizing impetus. All hopes for their success; but they make quite a different case from Jefferson's going to Boston or Philadelphia or Louisville or St. Louis and finding old actor-friends living and working there, getting their satisfactions or dissatisfactions where they were.

Third, connected with this, was the status of theater as popular culture. Film critics and historians tend to think that the glamor and mythologizing of actors began with film, but when the only performing idols available were live actors, *they* were mythologized. Instead of, say, Jimmy Stewart's being available in every city simultaneously, every city had an actor doing Jimmy Stewart roles. On a South American visit, Jefferson ran into an American who recognized him and pumped him with questions about actors back home, name after name after name. "They seem like old friends to me," says this theatergoer. He sounds like a modern movie buff.

Fourth is Jefferson's discovery that through the years, the audience was getting impatient with words and was more interested in visual effects:

> Why should this be? Is not the audience of today as intelligent as that of a hundred years ago? This may be so, but by degrees it has been accustomed to a supply of entertainments for the eye, rather than the ear....

This supports the thesis of A. Nicholas Vardac in *Stage to Screen* that the nineteenth-century popular theater was unconsciously moving toward film, that its audience unconsciously demanded the invention of film. (Vardac also notes that in 1896 Jefferson filmed a few minutes of *Rip*.)

Forty years ago, when I first read *The Autobiography of Joseph Jefferson*, I was filled with regret for an era I had missed. Now I'm more suspicious. Great as the best actors probably were, most of the productions, as ensemble work, must have been horrible by our standards. Still, to read the book now is to see a theater that, tackiness and all, had one quality at its height that our theater must regain: it was essential. Outside of religious bigots, very few nineteenth-century Americans would have dreamed of *not* going to the theater.

Obviously it was more widely available, proportionately, than now, and it satisfied appetites that are now satisfied by most films and almost all television. But one definition of the challenge to our theater today is that it must find a way of being necessary without being popular, since the pop hunger, which is in all of us, is fed otherwise. Not hard-breathing "relevance" or preening "uplift" but essentiality, is what our theater needs; and the task is complicated because today's audience is more experienced, more wooed, more selective than earlier ones. Yet there are recurrent occasions—a new play here, a new production there—to believe that the theater can still be a certification, an enlargement, of our existence, unduplicated elsewhere. When those occasions can reasonably be hoped for by a prospective audience, the theater becomes essential. Jefferson's book is no blueprint, but it describes a desirable norm: a time when a theater and its audience depended on one another.

A paperbound edition of the book ought to be available. For theater people, for American Studies people, for everyone.

McGraw-Hill Encyclopedia of World Drama *and Others.* New Republic, *October 21, 1972.*

Fine art, said Bernard Shaw, is either easy or impossible. So is the reviewing of encyclopedias. One can sample but cannot really read an encyclopedia—certainly not with consistent competence. Yet when a four-volume, 2126-page work comes along that is destined for many library shelves and some private ones, surely some comment is needed. I have both read and sampled. I read the first volume of the *McGraw-Hill Encyclopedia*, all 515 double-columned pages, with a better knowledge of some subjects than others; and I turned all the other pages, spot-checking where subjects were familiar or arresting. As a result, I'm (rather reluctantly) obliged to recommend the work because it contains much useful material, some of it not available elsewhere in English, but I recommend it with uneasiness.

First, the title is misleading. This is not an encyclopedia of world drama. Except for a touch of Japan, it's European and American drama; and even so, I saw no Icelandic or Latin American dramatist. The editors, of whom there were thirteen, headed by Bernard Dukore (not to mention sixty-eight contributing editors and a platoon of publisher's editors), say that one criterion for including a writer was whether he was a national of a country with a reasonably long history of drama. Indian drama is much older than Romanian, still there is no Kalidasa here and there are a number of Romanians.

Second, the arrangement. No national histories, some articles on terms like Tragedy, but the bulk of the book consists of articles about dramatists. The lesser ones are handled in conventional manner. Each major one gets a biography (never "complete," as the introduction claims); then a critique; then synopses of his outstanding works; then a list of all his plays in chronological order; then two selective bibliographies, one of his plays and the other of books about him. The advantage of this grouping is that when one is in the A section reading about Aeschylus, one doesn't have to turn to L for the synopsis of *The Libation Bearers*. The disadvantage is that the plays are summarized briefly for discussion in the critique and then a page or two later are summarized again in more detail. With the critique and the synopses so close together, I wonder why the former couldn't have leaned on the latter to a greater degree.

The play lists represent immense research, and each of them will probably be useful some time to someone, but the plan does seem to have gripped the editors by the nape and forced them arbitrarily into disproportions of space. The article on the Alvarez Quinteros, for instance, runs less than two pages; their play list, in smaller type, runs four pages. For Hans Sachs, it's a proportion of two to five, and you can imagine what it's like for Lope de Vega and Eugène Scribe. After a brief article on Ede Szigligeti (no, I had never heard of him, either), his play list runs two pages—and not one of the plays is available in English.

Beyond all this, there are four chief reasons for my unease: style, opinion, fact, and pictures (of which there are many). Here are some instances in each department.

Style. Most of the entries that I read are written in barely passable encyclopediaese. Occasionally there is an article better than that, such as the ones on Cibber and Cocteau and Granville-Barker and Racine. None is as good as, for instance, Irving Wardle's articles on contemporary British dramatists in *The Reader's Encyclopedia of World Drama* (Crowell, 1969).

Sometimes the writing is ludicrous. Of Andreyev: "Although he later remarried, feelings of gloom and emptiness persisted. . . ." "In all, Aristophanes wrote forty authentic plays; four others are spurious." Which, as put, says that, after writing forty authentic plays, Aristophanes wrote four spurious plays. Of Corneille: "Although his plays contain brilliant poetry, his contemporaries found his conversation dull, and though he wrote about heroes, he was known as a shy man." Of D'Annunzio's elopement: "They had three sons before his ardor cooled and a separation was arranged." And from the barrel-bottom: "Although Ibsen's life of embattled exile and uncompromising artistic dedication profoundly influenced such like-minded admirers as James Joyce, it has been largely his work—twenty-six plays written over fifty years—that has affected subsequent drama so decisively as to earn him the title 'father of the modern theatre.'" That clears *that* up, in case you thought he got the title for his lifestyle and not his works.

Opinion. How many would agree that Edward Albee's *Tiny Alice* is a "realistic play with metaphysical overtones"? John Arden is considered a lesser writer and gets much inferior treatment to, say, S. N. Behrman. Is it true that Jean Anouilh "is probably without a contemporary peer in his mastery of stagecraft"? Coward and Rattigan and De Filippo are not equally skillful? Is Arthur Miller's *The Crucible* accurately described as an allegory, in the same breath with Max Frisch's *The Chinese Wall*? Is Carson McCullers "surpassed only by Tennessee Williams and Truman Capote as an exponent of the Southern school of modern American letters"? So much for Eudora Welty and Flannery O'Connor, then. (Faulkner is not considered "modern," I guess.) About Courteline we are told that "in his native France his popularity and reputation as a comic dramatist are second only to those of Molière"; about Feydeau we are told that "recently some critics have tended to call him France's greatest comic dramatist after Molière."

Fact. Maxwell Anderson's *Elizabeth the Queen* (1930) is called "the first successful verse drama presented on the American stage." Obviously the writer means "first successful American verse drama," but even this is inaccurate. It disregards, among others, George Henry Boker's *Francesca da Rimini*, first done in 1855 and recurrently revived with success during the next fifty years. J. M. Barrie, a fervent Scot, would have curdled at being called an "English dramatist," as he is labeled here. Georg Büchner's *Lenz* is not "a novel"; it is not even inarguably an unfinished novel. It is a twenty-five-page piece of prose fiction. *Commedia dell'arte* is inadequately translated as "comedy of 'artists'"; the term was used to distinguish professional, improvised theater from *commedia erudite*, the amateur and literary theater of the Italian court and academy. D'Annunzio may have "reserved" *The Dead City* for Bernhardt—he did indeed offer it to her first—but it was Duse who made the play famous. The lovers in the Davis-Wharton *Ethan Frome* are injured in a sled crash, not a car crash. Hecht and MacArthur's *Twentieth Century* is about theater people, not movie people. In *Hedda Gabler*, Thea and George agree to reconstruct Eilert's manuscript before Hedda shoots herself, not afterward. Shaw's remark about Oscar Wilde's playwriting ability is badly misquoted.

Pictures. An extraordinary number of them are of the Asolo Theater Company of Sarasota, Florida. Odd. For Thomas Dekker's *The Shoemaker's Holiday*, two photos of the Guthrie Theater production are used, none of the most celebrated U.S. production—by the Mercury Theater in 1938. Judith Anderson as Medea should surely be under Robinson Jeffers, not Euripides, since she played the distinctive Jeffers version. Couldn't one of this encyclopedia's thirteen editors have identified Margaret Anglin in the photo of the Berkeley production of *Iphigenia in Aulis*? Or John Barrymore in Tolstoy's *Redemption*? (No mention here that *Redemption* was Broadway's title for *The Living Corpse*.) Or Gustav Gründgens in the German production of Cocteau's *Bacchus*? Couldn't one of the thirteen have known that George Alexander was not "an American Faust"? (He was British—and was in Henry Irving's production.)

I underscore that all the points raised above come from a reader with little knowledge of most of the Spanish and Italian and German dramatists treated and with no knowledge of any of the Romanian and Portuguese and Hungarian ones (except Molnár). If one may take part for the whole, which seems reasonable in a work of this kind, I would expect a good many more dubious opinions and plain mistakes to be found by those with other interests and backgrounds. Hence, despite some useful data, my uneasiness.

The Reader's Encyclopedia of World Drama, mentioned above, was edited by the late John Gassner and Edward Quinn and is skimpier on biographies, pictures, play synopses, play lists, and bibliographies than the new work. (Only fifteen lines on Szigligeti.) But where a play is included, the synopsis is usually fuller than in *McGraw-Hill*. There are many national histories, from all continents, and the articles are generally better written and more critically intelligent. (I have been dipping in it since 1969.) Also, it has an appendix called Basic Documents in Dramatic Theory, an anthology from Aristotle to Dürrenmatt of about 100,000 words. One volume, 1,030 pages, $15—around one-eighth the price of *McGraw-Hill* ($119.50) and almost half its length.

I have scant space to do justice to another encyclopedia, published this summer, a shorter book than the above but a much more prodigious job: *Modern World Drama*, 855 double-columned pages written by *one man*, Myron Matlaw (Dutton; $25). There are also a twenty-five-page character index and a seventy-four-page general index. The book covers the years from Ibsen to the present, contains histories of eighty countries' national drama (only six lines on Szigligeti!), hundreds of biographical-critical articles on individual dramatists with bibliographies, and hundreds of play synopses, many of them long enough to treat the play act by act. I have read the A section of this book and have sampled heavily throughout, and it shows an eminently respectable level of discourse and opinion. I've spotted very few errors. (Walter Hasenclever did not write the film version of *Anna Christie* for Garbo; he may possibly have worked on the translation for the German version she did at the same time.) But this encyclopedia can be recommended without uneasiness. There are numerous illustrations, well captioned.

The Letters of Anton Chekhov, translated by Avrahm Yarmolinsky, Simon Karlinsky, & Michael Henry Heim. *Saturday Review*, **July 17, 1973.**

Riches. It's been eighteen years since publication of the last edition of Chekhov's letters, which was inadequate. Now, almost simultaneously, we get two new editions. Each has assets, and although discrete productions, they are complementary in some ways.

I'm not going to spend time "evaluating" Chekhov himself. Anyone who doesn't feel that Chekhov is one of the relatively rare excuses for the existence of the human race starts from a base in this matter different from my own. And I won't quote at length from the letters to support my view. Just two examples of two kinds of pleasure. First, wry humor carrying considerable insight. Chekhov was asked what he thought of the work of two contemporary painters. He replied: "They're nice, they're talented, you're delighted by them, but at the same time you can't forget your desire for a smoke." Second, a glimpse of the company one keeps in these letters. He writes to a friend from Yalta: "If you intend to come, drop me a line. Tolstoy is here and Gorky is here, so you won't be bored, I hope."

Both of these new editions are drawn from the complete edition of Chekhov letters published only in Russian. One editor (Yarmolinsky) says there are 4,200 items in that edition, the other (Karlinsky) says there are more than 5,000. The Viking edition (490 pp.) contains more than 500 letters (not all of them complete), selected, edited, translated, and annotated by Avrahm Yarmolinsky, who has been writing on Russian authors and translating and teaching Russian literature since 1917. The Harper & Row edition (494 pp.) contains 185 letters, each one complete, selected and annotated by Simon Karlinsky of the University of California at Berkeley, translated by Michael Henry Heim of UCLA in collaboration with Karlinsky. For brevity I'll refer to the first edition as Y and the second as KH, and I'll compare them on specific points.

Translation: No contest. KH is better. I assume, on the reputations of all three men, that the translations are equally faithful and sympathetic; but the English in KH is much more flexible and live. Hundreds of examples could be given; I'll choose one. Here is the first line of the first letter in Y, written by the nineteen-year-old Chekhov to his brother, compared with the same line in KH:

> I received your letter when my terrible boredom was at its peak, I sat yawning beside the gate, and hence you can judge how very welcome your huge missive was. (Y)

> I got your letter while sitting around yawning by the gate at the height of a horrible fit of boredom, so you can imagine how perfectly timed it seemed—and so enormous, too. (KH)

The first is quite acceptable, but no one would ever take it for anything but a translation. The second sounds as if it had been written originally in English.

Selection: There are many more letters in Y than in KH, which would seem to give Y a clear advantage; but I have to note some reservations. Y abridges many of its letters, KH abridges none. Where the same letter is included in both books, abridged in Y, one can see that Y's deletions are often unimportant, sometimes valuable, and sometimes very important. An instance of the valuable: Y cuts the long opening paragraph of the letter of March 11, 1892, in which Chekhov gives details of running his estate at Melikhovo and which extends our sense of his range of abilities. An instance of the very important: In the letter of November 2, 1903, to Nemirovich-Danchenko of the Moscow Art Theater, Y cuts the long, detailed instructions for the casting and playing of *The Cherry Orchard*.

On the other hand, Y includes many of the letters to Lidya Mizinova, a beautiful girl ten years younger than Chekhov, letters full of flirtatious-avuncular charm, appealing in themselves and especially relevant because Mizinova's character and life are "partially reflected" in Nina of *The Sea Gull*. And Y includes a great many more of the letters to Olga Knipper, both before and after her marriage to Chekhov, which help to explain why the ailing writer chose to marry. He knew he was in bad shape (he and Olga spent their honeymoon in a sanitorium!); one infers that he married primarily to leave a child behind him. Olga had a miscarriage in 1902, and Chekhov, forced to stay in the warm south, kept writing to his actress-wife, working in Moscow, about meeting so that they could have their child. September 10, 1902: "Has [the doctor] allowed you to have children? Now or later? Ah, my darling, darling, time is passing." Time passed—he died less than two years later—without a child.

KH concentrates more on the "literary, social, and scientific" Chekhov. This means the inclusion of such letters, omitted by Y, as a fascinating critique of *The Lower Depths* for Gorky (July 29, 1902), a letter to a priest about the troubles of a teacher in the Yalta Municipal School (May 27, 1904), and the draft of a project for a biological research center that he supplied to a friend (May 24, 1902).

Annotation: Y provides just enough notes, but barely—identification of correspondents and principal references, but not much more. KH is very different. First, there is a substantial introduction, more than twice as long as Y's introduction. Second, KH divides the letters into fifteen sections, each one titled, and provides a short, biographical-historical-analytical introduction to each section. Third, many of the letters in KH are followed by substantial commentary.

But this is the most important difference: The KH comments and notes are much more than explanation. In my view, it's not too strong to say that KH is a book with a thesis, a revisionist aim: that, in addition to being a (good) edition of some of the letters, KH is in effect a collaboration between Chekhov and the editors on Chekhov's behalf—an attempt to use the letters and commentary to correct mistakes, small and large, and to alter misconceptions.

Example of a small correction: In that very first letter I quoted, the Russian word *dubanos* occurs, translated by KH as "the hawfinch." A note says that this word has proved a curious stumbling block to previous translators: Constance Garnett omitted the sentence containing the word and S. S. Koteliansky thought *dubanos* must be the name of a dog. Evidently Y shares the Koteliansky impression, because Y renders the line; "Dubanos, whom I promised you, has run away..."

On a larger scale, there are at least four prime misconceptions that KH is out to nail, by means of letters and commentary. First, the image of Chekhov as pale, sickly, melancholic. This Chekhov existed, but only in the very last years. Most of his life he was a big, vigorous, life-savoring man. (One source KH doesn't quote: Nemirovich-Danchenko, in his autobiography, wonders that "a human being with such a fund of cheerfulness and humor" could have written stories and plays of "such infinite sadness.") And through almost all his life he was, one may say, an enthusiast of sex. Instance: On his return from Sakhalin, the Russian penal colony off Siberia that he visited in 1890, he traveled by sea, touching at Ceylon. He wrote to a friend (December 9, 1890):

> Here in paradise I traveled more than 100 versts by train and had my fill of palm groves and bronze women. When I have children [!], I'll say to them, not without pride: "Why, you sons of bitches, I've had relations in my day with a black-eyed Hindu girl, and guess where? In a coconut grove, on a moonlit night!"

Not exactly a tone of pallid resignation.

Second, KH attacks the idea that Chekhov was only *pro forma* a doctor. We are shown how seriously he took his medical work. And he went to Sakhalin and wrote his famous report, not for any romantic or self-martyrizing reason, but because he had not finished the dissertation required for his medical degree and hoped that this report would be accepted in lieu of a dissertation. (Compare Robert Payne in his introduction to the edition of the report published in the U.S. in 1967: "Chekhov himself scarcely knew why he was going there; he knew only that he had to go there, that some impulse stronger than himself was driving him to it.") Chekhov often referred to medicine as his wife and literature as his mistress. Like other civilized men, he was devoted to both.

Third, KH shows that the dominant moods of the four theater masterworks of his last years by no means dominated all his previous writing, that Chekhov responded to a succession of temperamental, social, and aesthetic stimuli. And fourth, KH attacks accepted ideas about the plays and about Chekhov's relations with the Moscow Art Theater, pointing out that the *sole* source of these ideas was Stanislavsky's *My Life in Art*, which, despite merit in other regards, "is the source of more distortions, misconceptions, and historical inaccuracies about Chekhov's person and his plays than any other work ever published." Some of these errors are: that *The Sea Gull* was rescued from obscurity by the Moscow Art after its dismal premiere (it was being played throughout Russia); that Chekhov had a hard time finding a title for *The Cherry Orchard* after he finished it and asked Stanislavsky's help (he mentions the title in a letter before he *started* the play); and that he considered *The Three Sisters* a comedy (letters to people other than Stanislavsky contradict this).

Not all of the excellent notes in KH are necessary; I can't see the reason for the full page about the Tatars. And not all of the notes are excellent; the one on Alla Nazimova is inadequate. But in sum this is an extraordinary piece of work. How often can one call a job of editing "dynamic"?

The reader will assume, I hope, that I've omitted dozens of subjects on which both Y and KH inform us—to name only two, Chekhov's attitude toward the student riots of his day and his contradictory attitudes toward Jews, further complicated by his fierce pro-Dreyfus stand when he was in France. But even to list every topic covered here, every person mentioned, would in a real sense leave matters incomplete, because there are some thousands of letters still untranslated. While American university presses grind out the multivolumed correspondence of every assistant secretary of the interior through history, Chekhov's complete correspondence is ignored.

Between these two new editions, which to recommend? KH is better translated, its letters are unabridged, its commentary much more helpful. But then there are those numerous other letters in Y, adequately translated and annotated. For less than the price of a smart pair of shoes, be a literary sultan. Get both.

Theatres: An Architectural and Cultural History, by Simon Tidworth. *New Republic*, September 29, 1973.

Praeger has just published *Theatres: An Architectural and Cultural History*, by Simon Tidworth, an English art historian. There are 188 illustrations in the 224 good-size pages, which one would expect for the price ($18.50). Less expectable are the authority and wit of the concise text. Speaking of the high acoustic quality in ancient Greek theaters, Tidworth says that this "seems largely the result of accident ... Greek engineers had no way of understanding this. The science of acoustics is still fifty percent guesswork, as some unhappy modern experiments are enough to prove." Speaking of eighteenth-century England's achievements in theater building: "Some of the nobility had cultural ambitions, but their achievements were meager—the little theatre added by [Jeffry] Wyattville to the Duke of Devonshire's Chatsworth in the early nineteenth century is practically all that patriotism can point to."

The architectural view of theater history, incorporating (as time went on) scene design and lighting, is especially fruitful because, as Tidworth says, "In a general way ... the form of drama has determined the form of theater. But in any particular instance it is clear that the form of theater has normally conditioned the form of drama." He deals comfortably with developments from Athens to America—there's even an expedition to Sydney—but he seems most at ease, most expansive, when writing about opera houses. The section on the Paris Opéra is particularly good.

My only real quarrel is with the second half of his subtitle: he's weak on the cultural history, on connective motivations. He doesn't even speculate, for instance, on why the early pure Greek theater form developed as it did into its Hellenistic and Roman forms. At the present-day end of the chronicle he accepts a bit too credulously that productions like Barrault's *Rabelais* and Ronconi's *Orlando Furioso* "have had a revolutionary effect on our ideas of what the theater can do." But he follows his fascinating story with a generally keen eye for inspiration, pomp, silliness, and beauty. Inevitably some of the pictures are familiar but all of them are valuable—and rightly placed in the text.

The Federal Theatre, 1935-1939: Plays, Relief, and Politics, by Jane DeHart Mathews. American Scholar, Winter 1967-1968; & Stage Left, by Jay Williams. New York Times "Book Review," March 10, 1974.

"The brief story of the Federal Theatre was as dramatic as any play it staged." The formulation is pat, the comparison of life and art is naïve, but this opening sentence of Mathews' summary chapter suggests the basic quality of the Federal Theatre's career. In 1940 Hallie Flanagan, who had been National Director of the project, published *Arena*, her impassioned and invaluable account of the Federal Theatre's hectic four-year life. Mathews rightly felt that a view in longer perspective was needed, and this study, *The Federal Theatre, 1935-1939: Plays, Relief, and Politics* (Princeton University Press, 364 pp.)—which "grew from a seminar paper into a book"—is sympathetic and informative. The good feeling and hard work in the book make its lapses all the more regrettable.

Mathews is a historian. Historian, without adjective, means, of course, political historian. She has perceived (her subtitle underscores it) that the Federal Theatre was both a political creation and an anomaly in our political history. Of all the arts projects under the W.P.A. (Works Progress Administration) in the thirties, the theater was inevitably the most troublesome to the government. (Flanagan said in 1938: "Giving apoplexy to people who consider it radical for a government-sponsored theatre to produce plays on subjects vitally concerning the governed is one function of the theatre.") Mathews has seen her subject basically, but not entirely, from a political view. She has seen that the Federal Theatre was not primarily a cultural effort, that it was created by government to help some of the governed in a time of economic stress, and that a three-way conflict—among the concepts of art, politics, and relief—was the venture's curse from its birth. After putting together nine hundred and twenty-four productions in four years—from Shakespeare to vaudeville—and employing an average of nine thousand people a year, the project was killed by Congress: because of the "apoplexy" Flanagan described, because the project was smeared by Red-baiters and by reactionaries averse to this kind of government spending, because the high tide of enthusiasm for the New Deal had receded, and because troubles in Europe began to crowd the American political scene.

Besides its well-articulated account of the political environment of the Federal Theatre, one of the book's chief virtues is its portrait of Hallie Flanagan. In this woman's own book, her clarity of vision, her energy and courage, were, naturally, not emphasized; here they get the memorial they deserve. Very much of the Federal Theatre's work was artistically poor; but, first, Flanagan usually knew this before she was told and, second, she did as well as was humanly—superhumanly—possible. She organized regional theater projects around the country in a matter of months; overcame objections from the very professionals she was trying to help because the project smacked of charity; confronted the Broadway Establishment's worries about unfair competition; battled harassment from the reactionary press and from headline-hungry congressmen; found plays and designers and directors and actors and theater buildings; traveled frequently around the country (in the pre-jet age); and never lost sight of the hope that this project born in philanthropy might shuck its beginnings and emerge as a national *theater*. If Mathews' book did nothing else, its account of Flanagan's wonderful four-year fight would make it valuable—not as a lace valentine, but as hard history.

But there are serious imperfections in the work. Mathews is not a theater specialist, and she does not ask all the questions of her material that a theatrical reader wants answered. Many, many important details are missing: biographical information on major figures, dates and places of important productions, lengths of run, casts, sometimes even the authors of new plays. If she can tell us that *It Can't Happen Here* got seventy-eight thousand lines of publicity before it opened, she might at least have told us who was in it—at least in New York. The production record in the appendix of *Arena*, incomplete though it is, should have been included here, and might have been expanded.

Mathews writes in what might be called the post-pedantic style. She is anxious not to be dry, but her anxiety is sometimes apparent. "Hallie Flanagan toyed with the problem..." "Hallie Flanagan gradually hammered out a plan..." "Hallie Flanagan worked frantically in her stifling, Washington cubicle ..." Besides the *Time*-style diction, the repeated use of Flanagan's full name (the only person created that way) gives that lady's story a touch of late Hemingway.

In the matter of value judgments, Mathews, like all historians of the ephemeral arts, must rely on contemporary criticism and comment. Occasionally the quotation marks get washed away by her enthusiasm, and she offers judgments as statements. That I saw many of the Federal Theatre productions in

New York and disagree with many of the opinions entered here is not important, perhaps; but I could not suppress a slight shiver at the demonstration before my eyes of an ancient axiom: Historians do not record history, they create it.

Nevertheless I venture two small corrections before this creation gets firmly fixed. The role of Faustus in Marlowe's play was not Orson Welles's "first major acting role." He had previously played Marchbanks in Katharine Cornell's touring production of Shaw's *Candida* and had played the leading role in Sidney Kingsley's *Ten Million Ghosts* on Broadway. And this statement, derived though it may be from the *New York Times*, is arrant nonsense: "*The Cradle Will Rock* would one day become to America what Kurt Weill's [sic] *Dreigroschenoper* is to Germany." What cultivated German could not whistle Weill's tunes? How many Americans could whistle three notes of Marc Blitzstein?

Still, faults and all, Mathews has caught such fire from her subject that she has lifted her book above most academic expeditions into art. The work also has a particular timeliness. This country is beginning to demolish the barriers between government subsidy and art. In August 1967 the National Council on the Arts, itself a milestone of progress, sent recommendations to Congress for an appropriation next year of $139 million—and developed these recommendations at Congress's request. The Federal Theatre thirty years ago was a huge precedent step in the, I think, necessary evolution toward subsidized American theaters. Complemented by *Arena*, Jane DeHart Mathews' book helps to illuminate part of that torturous American social evolution, the movement toward formal responsibility for American culture.

A book related to Matthews', and similarly flawed, is *Stage Left* (Scribner's, 278 pp.), by Jay Williams. Williams, now known as a novelist, was an actor and stage manager in the radical theater of the 1930s. Five years ago, in London, he saw a series of performances by (very differently) radical groups and talked to many of the actors. These conversations afflicted him with *déjà vu*: "Thirty-five years before, but in another country . . . I had been a member of a group something like these, and we had used much the same language in describing what we were doing."

Williams decided to write this short history because the fervors and fevers and, especially, the lasting influences of that American era have been forgotten. The one previous book devoted to the predominantly theatrical aspects of the period is mostly concerned with the attempts and failure of the Communists to take over Broadway. (He doesn't name the book in his text, though it's cited in his notes: Morgan Y. Himelstein's *Drama Was a Weapon*, from 1963.) Much more was involved, much more signified. "After us, the American theater was never the same again." Williams remembers the period from the inside, which means from the inside of communal lodgings, scavengings for grub, freezing lofts, and high excitement—excitement not just because he and his fellows were young and committed but because they felt that they were at "the hub of change."

To a considerable degree, he does what he set out to do. *Stage Left* gives us the era as no mere researcher could reconstruct it. Williams' book is not nearly in the class of *The Fervent Years*, Harold Clurman's history of the Group Theater, which is one of the best accounts of theatrical enterprise that I know; but Clurman, by definition, concentrated on the Group. Williams is out to cover the whole field of radical theater, and, instead of treating each important venture separately, he interweaves their stories into one chronicle, to provide a conspectus of ferment and eventual frustration. He doesn't skimp the subject matter of those plays, but his emphasis is on theatrical aspects: how groups were formed, how they rehearsed and played, what their artistic sources were, and, most important, what they bequeathed to the American theater that followed.

First, he exposes the fallacy of the idea that the radical theater was a product of the Depression. The New Playwrights' Theater, whose founders were mostly avowed Communists, was started in 1926—and was backed by financier Otto H. Kahn! (Clurman remembers attending their first rehearsal, where the director announced that this was a theater of the left, then said, "Don't ask me what that means, but let it go at that.") Or course, after the Crash, as conditions worsened, radicalism grew. One of the first agit-prop theaters in the United States was the *Prolet-Bühne*, which played in German—a last vestige of the immense German-language culture that had flourished in New York in the latter half of the nineteenth century.

Other radical groups soon appeared throughout the country. Soon there was a League of Workers' Theatres with national conferences and festivals. There were union theaters, dozens of them, one of whose last manifestations was the I.L.G.W.U.'s revue *Pins and Needles* (1937). And there were the major companies: the Group, the Theater Union, and the Federal Theatre Project (which absorbed some of the workers' theaters). Williams also notes the influence of radicals on some of the commercial producers of the day. In fact, the Theatre Guild, in 1937, apologized to its subscribers for the social consciousness of some of its plays.

All this would be only statistically or sociologically interesting except that, as Williams stresses, the political impact of the radical movement was small, the artistic impact large. These enterprises in sum fostered expressionism in the United States, introduced the teachings of Stanislavsky, promulgated such ideas as street theater and non-proscenium staging, and nurtured numerous talents among directors, designers, and actors. (One Theatre of Action play in 1936 had four future directors in the cast: Elia Kazan, Norman Lloyd, Nicholas Ray, and Martin Ritt.) In short the radical movement, political in origin, was a chief factor in cracking the artistic provincialism of the American theater and seeding its future.

An important point to make, surely; still Williams' book is faulty. He says at the outset that he cannot promise accuracy, and he certainly keeps his non-word. He states that the Provincetown Players produced O'Neill's *Beyond the Horizon*; they didn't. He calls the pre-eminent German playwright Georg Kaiser a "relatively obscure" American playwright. (And misspells his first name—just as several times he renders Doris Humphrey as "Humphries.") He attributes a Victor Hugo play to Molière.

Williams' writing—generally breezy, though sometimes doggedly so—is blotched with barbarisms like the "growing rise" of Fascism and the "objective detachment" of Brecht. And, intellectually, he skates. His exegesis of expressionism is painfully inadequate. He gives the back of his hand to E. E. Cummings *Him*. (What better American play was written in the 1920s?) His analysis of the reasons for the end of the radical movement underestimates, I think, the shift of attention from domestic problems to that "growing rise" of Fascism and the iron fact of World War II.

One unintended point, still urgent, that the book makes for this reader is the risk of founding purportedly permanent theaters to produce new plays. Any such theater must live *ad hoc* even if, when it opens, it has on hand (which none of them has ever had) a dozen masterpieces. No playwrights' theater can really afford long-range policy statements. After two or three or seven years the manifestoes make bitter reading. Theaters, if they aim to be permanent, have to live on what exists, as do opera houses, with more openness to new works than most opera houses.

A pity that this book can't be wholeheartedly recommended. It's juicy, it's firsthand, it tries to fill a gap that really needs filling. But it's just insufficiently reliable and deep.

The Last Days of Mankind, by Karl Kraus. *New Republic*, May 4, 1974.

I first heard of Karl Kraus in 1967 when I read the chapter about him in Max Spalter's *Brecht's Tradition*. I felt less ashamed of my lateness in coming to the subject when, the next year in Walter Benjamin's *Illuminations*, I read the note by the editor (Hannah Arendt) saying that she had omitted Benjamin's essay on Kraus because he was "practically unknown in English-speaking countries." Since then, Kraus's name has kept popping up. W. H. Auden's *A Certain World: A Commonplace Book* is sprinkled with apothegms from Kraus. Last year *Wittgenstein's Vienna*, by Allan Janik and Stephen Toulmin, described the great influence that Kraus had on the intellectual development of Wittgenstein as well as on the music of Arnold Schönberg and the architecture of Adolf Loos.

Who was Kraus? His dates are 1874 to 1936. He was born of Jewish parents in Moravia but spent most of his life in Vienna, most of it as a Catholic. His chief work was as editor of a journal called *Die Fackel* (*The Torch*) that he founded in 1899 and edited until his death. During its first twelve years the contributors included Strindberg, Wedekind, Wilde, and Trakl; from 1911 until the end Kraus wrote all of every issue himself. In that writing, in every possible rigorous and fruitful sense of the term, Kraus was a critic—of art, politics, and society. He was (I take this at second-hand) strong, keen, angry. Berthold Viertel, the theater and film director, said of his own departure from Vienna, "When I fled from Karl Kraus, I was actually fleeing from the most acute mirror-image of an era and its humanity."

Kraus's principal passion, the foundation for all his other concerns including politics, was language. (In this he antedated and outscorched Orwell.) He founded a Theater of Poetry that consisted mostly of his own readings. He wrote poetry. Auden quotes Kraus's reflection on the mystery of words: "I have drawn from the well of language many a thought that I do not have and that I could not put into words."

All this is introduction to the reason for his appearance in my own writings. Kraus's major work outside his magazine was a drama called *The Last Days of Mankind*, which is in five acts and 259 scenes and fills 800 pages in the original German. Kraus says in his preface: "The performance of this drama, whose scope of time by earthly measure would comprise about ten evenings, is intended for a theater on Mars." Perhaps Mars because its subject is war—World War I. The drama was first published in *Die Fackel* of 1918-19, and the fact that

Kraus escaped lynching is one of the few tributes to sanity that I know of during this period.

Now an abridged version of the drama is published in English by Frederick Ungar (263 pp.), who did it, he says in a pleasant introduction, to help pay his emotional and intellectual debt to Kraus, whose readings he used to attend. The translation is by the late Alexander Gode and Sue Ellen Wright and is at least in more flexible English than that of the few scenes translated by Max Spalter in 1967. A helpful concluding essay by Franz H. Mautner fills in the general shape of the drama. This Ungar edition contains about a third of the original; between this condensation and Mautner's essay one gets a good feeling of the texture and a clear idea of the design.

The immediate reference point for readers of English is Thomas Hardy's *The Dynasts*, but Hardy's Napoleonic drama, though comparable in several sorts of size, is intended as an epic of the spirit of history, an *"Iliad* of Europe" with attendant bands of Spirits marking the onward journey of mankind. Nothing could be further from Kraus's tone or intent; he is writing a *Menschendämmerung*—the human race sliding inexorably into the pit that it has dug for itself. He saw the First World War as a steaming stew, started by Austrian stupidities, thickened by German brutalities, compounded by international greed and ego and profit-hunger and sloganeering and blindness. We watch through this work the gestation of the spirit that was coming to mate with Hitler—which has an added irony because Kraus, the ex-Jew, has some bitter things to say about Judaicized Christianity and Jewish capitalists. One would-be apologist has argued that Kraus attacks Jews because they have the greatest moral tradition to live up to. Well ... possibly. He is not the only Germanic ex-Jew to note the shortcomings of Jews, as he saw them, with special bitterness. And, further, I think Kraus made sure not to spare the Jews his lash lest he be accused of partiality and to be certain that *nobody* could claim him as champion.

This drama is continental, immense. Each act begins on a corner of central Vienna with four inane army officers, and each of the five acts deals with events of one of the five calendar years of the war. Ungar calls it a documentary drama, and indeed Kraus does get much of his effect simply from quoting and juxtaposing speeches and editorials and news reports; still, the *ways* he uses them, the manner in which he builds on them, are work of poetic imagination. For example, during the play there is the boastful report of the sinking of an enemy ship carrying 1,200 horses. Near the end the 1,200 horses emerge from the waves and chant a poignant chorus as they trot across the stage. One very brief scene has an army company marching past a garden gate just so that the Crown Prince, in tennis clothes, can speak one line of commendation; another scene has a crowd of 500 people waiting at a railroad station. In contrast to this profligacy there is a choric sequence of scenes between two people: the Optimist and the Grumbler (who is obviously Kraus himself). At one point the Grumbler has an eleven-page monologue. Generals, war correspondents, psychiatrists, victims, the Pope himself, all appear.

At first the individual scenes seem pungent or less pungent cabaret sketches, dealing often with satirical points now fairly familiar. But the work pours on with such grandeur of loathing, such prodigality of disgust, such mordant anguish that the deficiencies fade in the glare of a large Spenglerian fire. One easy and, I think, false modem view of such a drama is to say that it might be practicable as film. But Kraus clearly wanted his work to be *im*practicable. That is his last intrinsic gesture of disdain: civilization can't even perform this drama about its own incapacities.

Kraus, to whom language was the holy of holies, can never really exist outside his own language. (One detail: Mautner says Kraus used a dozen dialects in this play, impossible to render.) But Ungar has done us a benefit by at least bringing us a bit closer to this sharp-eyed, angry, prickly, brilliant lover-hater of mankind.

Black Theater USA: 45 Plays by Black Americans, 1847-1974, edited by James V. Hatch. *New Republic*, June 22, 1974.

The last few years have brought several anthologies of black plays. The ones that I have seen were contemporary. Now we have a much-needed historical anthology, *Black Theater USA: 45 Plays by Black Americans 1847-1974*, edited by James V. Hatch with Ted Shine as consultant. The Free Press publishes it at $19.95 (which, as anyone can see, is less than $20). It's not an unfair price these days, considering that the book has 886 large double-columned pages and that there were many permission fees to pay.

Hatch has done some good research, though his notes are hardly exemplary writing. The level of the plays doesn't vary much: some of them are good, but most of them are mostly interesting for cultural-historical reasons. Still, that's also true of most anthologies of plays by white Americans. How many first-rate American plays *are* there? The point of this book is to help illuminate a neglected aspect of our theater culture, which it does.

The first play is by that (apparent) genius of acting, Ira Aldridge, who had to go to Europe to have a career. *The Black Doctor*, which he adapted for his own use from a French original in 1847, is a romantic melodrama about the title character, a West Indian, who marries a Frenchwoman and gives his life to save her from the consequences. Not exactly the tone or subject of the last play, a kind of chant-celebration by Val Ferdinand of the Free Southern Theater. In between are names I happily expect like Adrienne Kennedy and Langston Hughes, names I not quite so happily expect like Ed Bullins and James Baldwin, names I dread like Lorraine Hansberry and (in his playwriting guise) Douglas Turner Ward, and many names previously unknown to me.

One point: Hatch notes that Paul Green, "a white dramatist," collaborated with Richard Wright on the dramatization of *Native Son*, included herein. In his preface to the next play, *District of Columbia*, Hatch says that the author, Stanley Richards, is the only white dramatist in the anthology.

But this is a bountiful book, nicely produced, essential for the American drama shelf.

Meyerhold: The Art of Conscious Theater, by Marjorie L. Hoover. *New Republic*, January 25, 1975.

Marjorie L. Hoover, who teaches Russian and German at Oberlin, has done a fine and necessary piece of theater scholarship in *Meyerhold: The Art of Conscious Theater* (University of Massachusetts Press). It's an expensive book but worth the price: 349 large double-column pages, many illustrations, four long and helpful appendices, a chronology, a glossary, and a biographical index. Most important, it's a thoroughly researched, sympathetic account of the work of the Russian director-genius—not a biography so much as an artistic history.

Material in English on Meyerhold is relatively skimpy. The best previous book is a collection of his writings, *Meyerhold on Theatre*, translated and edited by Edward Braun (Hill & Wang, 1969). Hoover attempts to reconstruct his career. This means, in theater history, an attempt to reconstruct the ephemeral, by means of illustrations, interviews, documents, Meyerhold's own writings, and contextual material from other arts and disciplines. For me she has been entirely successful, making clear the genesis of his ideas, the flavor of his personality, his seminal effect on other artists (including Sergei Eisenstein), the increase of energy after the revolution in those astoundingly vital early days of Soviet art, and his inevitable doom. (He was arrested in 1939 and died in prison the following year in a manner still unknown.)

Meyerhold was a member of the Moscow Art Theater from 1898 to 1902 and played in their productions of Chekhov's *The Sea Gull* and *The Three Sisters*, but he soon differed with Stanislavsky and branched out on his own. If the theories and work of two complicated men can be summarized, let me use Hoover's phrases for the job: "Stanislavsky took his departure from a hatred of theater and a love of truth ... Meyerhold, on the other hand [was fascinated] with the theater as art, as the very lie Stanislavsky abjured; indeed, it was the art of the theater that Meyerhold tried to develop in every way, deriving it from traditions of other times and places." Hoover's subtitle thus is perfect, for Meyerhold was a formalist, Stanislavsky a realist. Stanislavsky was virtually apolitical; Meyerhold, when the revolution came, devoted all his artistic being to it. And it was Meyerhold whom Stalin wiped out.

Note: One of Hoover's illustrations is Eisenstein's ingenious design for Meyerhold's production of Ludwig Tieck's *Puss-in-Boots*, written in 1796. This is not a fairy tale but a play about the performance of a fairy tale. It has recently been translated by Gerald Gillespie, very readably, and is published by the University of Texas Press, cooperating with the University of Edinburgh, in their smartly designed Edinburgh Bilingual Library (paperbound, $3.45; all these books have facing pages of German and English). Tieck's play is further evidence of the extraordinary anti-realist, socially satirical strain in German playwriting that runs from Lenz and Grabbe—with one twelve-year gap—to the present.

The Theatrical Event, by David Cole. *New Republic*, August 16-23, 1975.

"We live between two kinds of truth ... Imaginative truth and present truth each provide what the other lacks, but only at the expense of lacking what the other provides ... Theater, and theater alone of human activities, provides an opportunity of experiencing imaginative truth as present truth."

This is the credo of David Cole's fascinating book *The Theatrical Event* (Wesleyan University Press, 177 pp.). He begins with a recognition that "our experience of theater lies in fragments" and "we are not even sure what they are fragments of." His short and intense work, full of feeling and thought, tries to supply the means to help correct this situation. Cole, who has taught in Yale College, is not out to tell us yet again what is wrong with the theater, although he does point out conceptual errors; nor is his primary purpose to tell us what to do about it, although he makes some provocative suggestions. His basic point is to say what the theater *is*: essentially to restate, in terms aided by new knowledges, some old forgotten truths, so that the restatement may be a kind of purging and enabling—and a touchstone.

The historical origins of the theater being what they are, it's only fitting that Cole's principal terms come from comparative religion. The key phrase of his discourse is a concept of many religions, *illud tempus* ("that time"—the time of origins, which is not only the time when the religion began but that time as it continues to exist and which can be made *present* at any moment by ritual. (The relevance of Jung is not lost on Cole.) The play-script is the site of the *illud tempus* for the theater, the site of those forces beneath and around our lives that govern and can clarify them. The actor's function is to journey to that *illud tempus* and bring it back to us, make it present.

In doing this, the actor takes on the functions of two universally known religious agents, the *shaman* and the *hungan*. The *shaman* makes the journey to the *illud tempus*; the *hungan* himself becomes "the 'way back' of the *illud tempus* toward us." The actor has the responsibility and power of both functions. The moment of reversal, when the actor passes from one function to the other, Cole calls the "rounding." For him it is the "defining characteristic of theatrical performance. It is in the moment of the rounding that the theater, as an event, is born."

Two others terms are basic to his views. He uses "Image" instead of character or role because he wants to emphasize "that the beings whom actors (and through them, audiences) encounter are numinous dwellers in an eternal imaginative *illud tempus*, not just an assortment of persons who happen to be imaginary." And he takes the term "hierophany" from Mircea Eliade, probably his most-used source, to signify "the manifestation of a numinous presence" in and through physical things other than an actor's body—such as scenery and tight.

Some of Cole's corroborative quotations from theater writings are surprising—Max Reinhardt, for instance. Most of them come from expected, essential sources like Stanislavsky and Grotowski. Stanislavsky's concept of the subtext is of a source beneath the text that produces the words and the actions, the source to which the actor must journey and return. Grotowski's central concept is of the "holy actor" whose task is to penetrate to his own sacred essence and bring it forth. Cole's main work has been to provide a philosophical distillation that both supports and is supported by many of the best theater minds.

To do that would have been helpful enough; but then Cole goes on to apply his quintessence to various elements of theater practice and to make clear why we have been uneasy about some of them. For instance, in the chapter on The Audience, he explains why many of us have felt uncomfortable with the idea of "audience participation" (as practiced, let's say, by the Living Theater). He makes clear that the groping and grabbing of us by actors, far from joining us closer to them in contrast to the often torpid conventional theater, actually destroys the actors' *shamanic* powers, destroys the requisite mystic "distance," destroys the "dread" of rounding that "is the sure, joyful sign that some measure of susceptibility to [the theater's] Images has survived in us."

In the chapter on The Scenic Means, where the idea of hierophany figures beautifully, he uses his special vocabulary to explain why the "thrust" stage is not necessarily the solution to all our staging ills, why the proscenium stage, too, assists hierophany. And writing on Language, Cole compares passages from different plays to determine whether the writing manifests what is beneath the writing. "Does it move with consciousness?" is his only criterion. Pirandello, I add, called dialogue "spoken action" and wrote an essay with that title in which he developed ideas cognate to Cole's.

A recurrent small weakness in the book blossoms into a full-scale defect in the last chapter. Occasionally he extrapolates a subjective state of his own into universal law. For example, Cole says that when a friend puts on a mask or an actress comes offstage after a splendid performance, "we" are not comfortable —and then he builds theory from that questionable generalization. Then in the last chapter, "Interpretation" (his quotation marks), he argues that directorial concepts imposed on plays constitute a refusal of "an offer of participation in a universal—or at any rate, a larger than personal—way of seeing," an interference with the actor's journey to the *illud tempus* and his bringing of it to us.

As one who has suffered through many deformed "concept" productions, my immediate impulse is to agree with Cole here, but the danger for both of us is, again, this extension of the personal into the absolute—the implication that there exists a platonically ideal performance of (say) *Hamlet*, that we know what it is, and that any deviation from it is a refusal of the play's *illud tempus*. I despise the director who begins by asking himself, "What can I do to this production to put my imprint on it?" There are clear-cut cases of directorial distortion that, like actors' audience-groping, leave no doubt of their failure. But I have seen highly individualized "concept" productions that were not my ideas of those plays but that still seemed attempts to reach the *illa tempora*. Can Cole rule absolutely? I can't.

Further, his concentration on the *shamanic-hunganic* function of the actor leads to such statements as: "Historical period and social class count for nothing in determining how a theater character may speak ... The only limit on a character's ability to manifest consciousness is whatever limits there may be on his consciousness itself." This seems to move his principles from the spiritual-archetypal into the merely mediumistic. The power of Cole's rediscoveries for me is that he crystallizes a force for the deepest manifestations of human diversity, not an undifferentiated electric current that will light up a lot of identical light bulbs.

And I offer one difference with Cole, not a criticism. Except for a few passing references, he makes no mention of film. (I think one of those references is wrong. He says that in contrast to film and television, the theater is the place where the eye "chooses for itself when to zoom, where to pan, what to watch." Only in bad theater productions; in good ones, the eye has very little more choice than at a film.) I believe that almost every power that Cole attributes to the theater is possible to film—and film has some that are denied to the theater. The physical presence of imagined truth takes place, except for the literal-minded, in film as well as theater. The director of film takes on some of the *shamanic-hunganic* attributes that the theater director does not have, but I cannot see why such films as *Persona*, *A Man Escaped*, *8½*, *Grand Illusion*, and *The Gold Rush* are not exalting experiences of an *illud tempus* made present.

Cole ends his book with a two page "set of propositions" that fix much of what he has been saying. He calls them "half-truths." So do I. He knows that no one book or set of views is a prescription for perfection. But his book, the product of insight and fervor and reflection, is very valuable.

"The Ride Across Lake Constance" and Other Plays, by Peter Handke. New Republic, November 20, 1976.

The marvelous line of Germanic dramatists continues today with several writers, pre-eminent among them Peter Handke, who is Austrian. Here is his second collection of plays, *"The Ride Across Lake Constance" and Other Plays* (Farrar, Straus, & Giroux, 258 pp.); his first was *"Kaspar" and Other Plays*. Since then American publishers have brought out two of his novels, a unique memoir of his mother, and two books of poetry, none of them less than exceptional. He is thirty-four years old.

I reviewed the title play in this new book when it was produced at Lincoln Center in 1972. A re-reading prompts further thoughts, but space-limits press me to the newer parts of the book. There are four short plays (one of them, *My Foot My Tutor*, was produced by Chelsea Theater Center), each of slender but sure interest. The longest play in the book, and the prize, is *They Are Dying Out*, a work of beauty and power. (I'm told that when it was produced at the Schaubühne in Berlin, the leading role was played by Bruno Ganz, who is the Count in Rohmer's film of *The Marquise of O . . .*—and who has also played the hero in Kleist's *The Prince of Homburg* at the Schaubühne. Michael Roloff, who translated most of this book alone, had the help of Karl Weber on this play, and the result is very actable English.

Not only is Handke in the line that includes Kleist, *They Are Dying Out* is itself related, I think, to *The Prince of Homburg*. This new play deals with the motions of dailiness—in big business now, not in military exploit—carried out by a man who *sees* his life as he lives it, who speaks the usually private strophes of longing and loveliness under the thousand trifles of the day, who feels the veil of dream around the motion.

The two acts are about two meetings of capitalist chiefs, one woman among them. Oversimplifying, we can say that Kleist is Schiller, plus (a poetry of doubt and immediacy). Similarly, we can say that Handke is Bertolt Brecht and Ernst Toller, plus. This play would be a quasi-expressionist satire of capitalist maneuver, strong but only one more such, except that Handke keeps "zooming in" for secrets. With the spoken, he has braided the usually unspoken, two consciousnesses equally present on the plane of the theatrical present. It's a new style for the protean Handke, poignant, truthful, fine.

At the moment I don't know of a forthcoming American production. I hope there will be one—many—soon, with more to be said then.

Wilhelm Meister's Apprenticeship, by Johann Wolfgang von Goethe. New Republic, August 26-September 2, 1978.

"Apprenticeship" is concise but not exact: *Lehrjahre* literally means "years that teach." Georg Lukács said that the theme of this novel "is the reconciliation of the problematic individual, guided by his lived experience of the ideal, with concrete social reality . . . a reconciliation between interiority and reality . . . sought in hard struggles and dangerous adventures." The word "apprenticeship" doesn't fully convey "lived experience." And it's also important to note that the hero is called William Master—that's what a German sees when he reads the name, and it ought to be in our minds too when we read this story of a young man seeking various kinds of mastery.

I first read the book when I was a drama student because I had heard that it was about a young man who goes into the theater. (Since then, I've kept in touch with it only through occasional snatches of Ambroise Thomas's *Mignon*, which is based on the book.) I've now reread it for precisely my original reason and want to discuss it only from that aspect: the theater. Its structure, which combines strategical plan with tactical patchiness; its characterization, which is superficial except for the coquette Philina; the English of this translation (Dutton, 336 pp.)—someone once said that Thomas Carlyle's style is like hearing a load of coal being delivered next door—all these are not my business. (There are subsequent translations, possibly better but not available in Italy, where I'm writing this.) What fascinates is what Goethe has to say about the theater, its practice and its possibilities.

Goethe wrote a first version, *Wilhelm Meister's Theatrical Mission*, in 1777, when he was twenty-eight; a manuscript was discovered early in this century. He published the present book in 1795, four years after he had been made director of the Court Theater in Weimar. He published a sequel, *Wilhelm Meister's Travels*, thirty-four years later—a gap that is greater than the one between the two parts of *Faust*.

The Apprenticeship, our subject here, begins with the young Wilhelm having an affair with an actress in his hometown. It's Germany but we don't know where—there are no place names in the book. He discovers that his beloved is having an affair with another man. Two things are important about this discovery. First, it's accomplished by a device that is theatrical in the most vernacular sense, as if Goethe meant to weave the stuff of popular theater into the texture of his novel about the theater. Second, very much later, Wilhelm learns that he was mistaken about the betrayal: this is one of the many presentations of "fact" that are subsequently shown in other lights, like glimpses backstage to show us the reality behind the appearance.

Disconsolate, Wilhelm goes on a journey to collect debts for his merchant father. In another town he meets a company of actors and eventually joins them. In time he plays nothing less than Hamlet. (Much has been made of Goethe's infatuation with Shakespeare, particularly with *Hamlet*: we often see the quotation about Hamlet as "an oak-tree planted in a costly jar." What is not often noted is that Wilhelm revises the play for his company.) When the novel is about two-thirds through, Wilhelm fairly suddenly leaves the company. The change, like many of the sharp turns in the mazy plot, is thinly motivated. Goethe strategically needs his hero to move on, so tactically he more or less wills it. "On looking back upon the period which I passed in their society," says Wilhelm of the actors, "it seems as if I looked into an endless void; nothing of it has remained with me." This in a novel from an author who was then running a theater, writing plays, and devising new methods of production!

But before Wilhelm's change of heart, Goethe, through him, sheds some light on what he thought about and experienced in the theater. He gives us veristic details of actors' chat, along with technical details of contemporary stage machinery. He voices what we may have thought a recent opinion that "it was easier to write or represent a tragedy than to attain proficiency in comedy." He asserts the primacy of the actor over production: "A good actor makes us very soon forget the awkwardness and meanness of paltry decorations; but a splendid theater is the very thing that first makes us truly feel the want of proper actors." And more than a century before Stanislavsky wrote, he says that not many actors know

> [how] to seize with vivacity what the author's feeling was in writing; what portion of your individual qualities you must cast off in order to do justice to a part; how by your own conviction you are to become another man.

And he pleads with actors for "that internal strength of soul, by which alone deception can be brought about; that lying truth, without which nothing will affect us rightly."

Equally astounding are the ideas about directing that run through the theater episodes. Directing was then hardly a profession in the theater—it wasn't fully established even in 1824 when Carlyle did the translation, yet he uses the word "director." Some of Goethe's ideas are usually thought to have come into theatrical theory much later. For instance, the use of improvisation in rehearsal. The actors do an extempore play while traveling on a boat, just for fun; then one of the group says, "It should be a custom with every troop of players to practice in this manner." Wilhelm, when he becomes a director, puts forth principles, still fresh in that era, of careful rehearsal and balanced interpretation: "What advances we should make if . . . we ceased to confine our attention to mere learning by heart . . . Can anything be more shocking than to slur over our rehearsal, and in our acting to depend on good luck, or the capricious chance of the moment?" And: "A common error is to form a judgment of a drama from a single part in it . . . not in its connection with the whole."

Goethe doesn't mention Lessing's *Hamburg Dramaturgy*, which had been written almost thirty years before. (Lessing's *Emilia Galotti*, however, is the last play in which Wilhelm appears.) But it seems reasonable to infer that Lessing's central themes were in Goethe's mind: the need for a true and truly German theater, both for its intrinsic benefits and as a unifying, elevating national force. The many references to a feeling of high occasion make an American reader think, despite the fact that Goethe is writing about a comparatively ancient country, of Walt Whitman's call, in *Democratic Vistas*, for a new drama that would fit the new America.

This sense of a new age, new choices, is heightened by the recurrent counterpointing of commerce with the hero's realistic-spiritual quest. Wilhelm's father is a rich merchant, and Wilhelm's prospective brother-in-law Werner, of whom he is fond, will have a business career. Werner is contrasted throughout to Wilhelm but with no facile mockery, with the feeling that it is a new age for the bourgeoisie as well. "Where then," says Werner early in the story, "will you find more honest acquisitions, juster conquests, than those of trade? . . . May we not embrace with joy the opportunity of levying tax and toll, by *our* activity, on those commodities that the real or imaginary wants of men have rendered indispensable? I can promise you, if you would rightly apply your poetic view, my goddess might be represented as an invincible, victorious queen, and boldly opposed to yours." There is never any possibility that Wilhelm will share Werner's (historically important) enthusiasm, yet he starts his journey into the world on a commercial assignment, and when he has to do business, he does it well. In reply to a report of his, Werner writes: "Highly as I thought of thy powers, I did not reckon such attention and diligence among the number. Thy journal shows us with what profit thou art traveling. The description of the iron and copper forges is exquisite; it evinces a complete knowledge of the subject."

The praise is counterproductive. Wilhelm turns his back on this business talent, on a career that his brother-in-law finds inspiring, to become an actor. It has long been in his mind. An earlier passage: "He beheld in himself the embryo of a great actor: the future founder of that national theater for which he heard so much and various sighing on every side." Eventually this dream fades for him; he must seek a different "reconciliation between interiority and reality." Nevertheless, most of the book and its strongest strokes are about the theater. Wilhelm's avowals ring clearer than his disavowals. Even when he later rails against the theater, a friend of his laughs and says, "Do you know, my friend, that you have been describing, not the playhouse but the world . . .?" The theater has prefigured the world for Wilhelm, has been the chief instrumentality in his "apprenticeship" to life.

But, in this revulsion of Wilhelm's against what had attracted him, Goethe conveys, I think, something other than that the theater is one step in a life's journey. Put Wilhelm's rejection of the theater against the fact that this book is by a man whom Gordon Craig called "in many ways one of the greatest of stage directors," and we can envision that Goethe is giving us one point in a *cycle* of feeling about the theater, a still-recurrent cycle. He is very possibly making us privy to the recurring doubts that he himself had to, and did, deal with. On the threshold of the modern age he sees the theater as what, in our culture, it has become: an art so marvelous with promise and so ridden with debasement that disillusion must always attack, but whose attraction persists because, for one reason (as Wilhelm's friend says), it epitomizes the world.

Because the world itself persists, we continue, despite our knowledges, to hope in the world. Because the theater persists—the world intensified in dream and dross—we continue, despite our knowledges, to hope in the theater. Seeing theater-director Goethe in the act of writing this novel, we can take him to be saying that the theater, with its "lying truth," is at last no worse than the world; that "lying truth" is better—much better—than none at all.

The House of Barrymore, by Margot Peters. *New Republic*, January 28, 1991.

One day in July 1933, when I was a drama student, I spent the entire afternoon and evening at the Capitol Theater in New York. The Capitol used to show a new film and a bill of vaudeville. The vaudeville bill that week was Ethel Barrymore in Barrie's one-act play *The Twelve-Pound Look*. I saw the whole program at the first showing. When the film came on again, I went out into the ornate lounge with a book I had brought, returning three times to see Barrymore's performance a total of four times—in one day. What a treat.

The four performances were perceptibly different. The first, around 1 PM, was the work of someone who wasn't quite awake yet. The second improved, and the third was the best; the fourth seemed an effort to repeat the third. Somewhat later I learned that a little whiskey might have cheered the day for Barrymore as she went along and, by the last performance, might have overcheered it slightly.

Yet each time I was sharply aware that I was seeing a kind of annunciation. A woman came in who was irresistible, dominant in the very split second of appearance, and before she had been there half a minute she had told us that she was both the woman she was playing and the woman who was playing her. As great actors will, she presented herself as well as her role, and her ability to do that, without either scanting the character or parading her self, was her fundamental gift to us.

I was also aware, even then, that I was seeing one of the last of a line. This was a matter of style, but style rooted in etiology. Barrymore had been born into and brought up in a theater in which the actor was prime, was the reason for the theater's existence. She had survived into an age when the playwright was prime and the director was coming to share that primacy. I felt lucky to have arrived in time to see this scion of an actor's theater.

Her heritage is amply chronicled in Margot Peters' biography of a family, *The House of Barrymore* (Knopf, 612 pp.). Peters tells us early of the extraordinary woman who was Ethel's grandmother, Mrs. John Drew. She managed the Arch Street Theater in Philadelphia for thirty-one years, acted constantly (forty-two roles in her first year there), and bore three children. When Mrs. Drew came to retire in 1892, she said in her last curtain speech, "To hear these walls resound with applause for simply acting and nothing more, the acting of an old comedy, merely acting, is something to make an actor's heart almost burst with joy." It was this woman's granddaughter whom I was seeing at the Capitol.

Peters' book is, as far as I know, the second on its subject. There have been numerous books about Barrymores, including autobiographies, but only Hollis Alpert has previously attempted a history of the entire family. *The House of Barrymore* is much fuller, more thoroughly researched and annotated, than Alpert's book. In one way this history presents a special difficulty: when the author arrives at a certain point, the narrative becomes less a chronicle of succession than an account of three simultaneously crowned and reigning monarchs. Most of the book deals, quite rightly, with Lionel, Ethel, and John Barrymore, whose careers were quite separate almost all the time. Peters drives this troika well, keeping the three lives chronologically abreast with minimal jarring as she turns from one to another.

Mrs. Drew, born in London and brought to America as a child, was the matriarch of the line. Her husband, born in Dublin and brought here as a child, died in 1862 and doesn't figure in the story. She was a vivid influence on both her children and her grandchildren. (When John was dying in Hollywood in 1942, he kept murmuring her family nickname, "Mummum.") All of them became successful actors. The best-known of her own children was John Drew the younger—I can remember the ads for his last appearance in New York in 1927—but Georgiana would possibly have been equally successful if she hadn't died of tuberculosis at age thirty-seven.

Georgiana was the mother of the trio we know best. Her husband was an English actor born Herbert Blythe who called himself Maurice Barrymore. Handsome, dissolute (he died insane, of paresis), he added to the Drew legacy not only his own talent, but a canted view of sobriety and discipline that addled the other strain, especially in John's case. This, to use a worn but terribly apt term, was tragic, because Maurice's three children were gifted even beyond their most celebrated forebears. Ethel was the steadiest of the three and, in the truest sense, the most successful, but even she, racked by various personal problems, did not fulfill herself as, say, Charlotte Cushman did.

Part of the trouble was that these three were overgifted—so much so that initially they weren't even greatly drawn to acting. Ethel was a pianist of some ability. Lionel could paint and etch and compose; after his first marriage, he spent the years from 1906 to 1909 in Paris, studying art. John had notable ability as an illustrator. But all were inducted early into acting by the family. Subsequently, for differing reasons, they returned to it.

Very soon in their acting lives, a new phenomenon crossed their paths: film. Not long after Lionel came back from Paris, he was the first to venture into the new medium (as it happens, in a building that stood about a hundred yards from where I'm writing this), although he also continued to work in the theater until 1927. All through their lives, Peters tells us, film existed as a golden trap or a golden refuge for these three theater figures. John said once, "I was a bridge between two periods, and my period has passed," a statement that marks him as a native of the era of film's arrival. Actors today, born into a world in which film and theater have long co-existed, have—or can have—quite different attitudes.

The three Barrymores never appeared in the same play, though once, in 1905, all three of them were involved in different parts of a double bill. (The only time all three acted together was in the film *Rasputin and the Empress*, 1932. It's also worth noting that all three of them appeared together several years ago on a twenty-cent U.S. postage stamp.) During the Broadway season of 1919-20, each of the three starred in his or her own play. In 1917 and 1919 John and Lionel did plays together, *Peter Ibbetson* and *The Jest*.

John, after making a reputation as a light comedian, had done Galsworthy's somber *Justice* with great success; after the two plays with his brother, he moved on to Shakespeare, *Richard III* and *Hamlet*. (He also did the latter in London.) Lionel then felt constrained to try Shakespeare, and he used John's designer, Robert Edmond Jones, for a production of *Macbeth*. It failed badly. Lionel did some plays after that, but four years later, in 1925, he left permanently for Hollywood. Ethel, great though she certainly was, didn't prove it in the classics. In her sixty-year theater career, she appeared in only three Shakespearean roles, Juliet, Ophelia, and Portia, and then only when she was getting too old for them. She did Ibsen once and Sheridan once. Her reputation was made in new plays, good and less good.

Each of the trio had personal peculiarities. Prominent among Ethel's was her slowness in ending a dreadful marriage. (She had turned down a number of quite eligible suitors—including, during some young years in London, Winston Churchill.) True, the Barrymores were Catholic, but her husband was a vicious wife-beater. After eleven years and three children she consulted the then cardinal in New York, and he agreed to let her divorce if she promised not to remarry. Possibly her fondness for drink began with this marriage; it certainly didn't end with the divorce.

Lionel, no stranger to alcohol, was introduced to cocaine by his second wife, whom he adored. Cocaine and all, he adored her so much that when she died in 1936, he moved out of their house and preserved it as a shrine to her. In the spring of 1939 he began to feel guilt about that empty house. Says Peters:

> On inspiration he wrote the great Richard Strauss that if he should decide to come to America, he would turn over his house and staff to him and his family. To his astonishment the composer he worshiped replied that he had made reservations on the *Queen Mary*.

Lionel was then supposed to swear out an affidavit so that Strauss could get an immigration visa, which is when his lawyer stepped in and dissuaded him, reminding him that Strauss had been photographed with Goering and Goebbels. "On reflection Lionel decided that it might be difficult to explain to Louis B. Mayer [the head of MGM, his employer] that he was sheltering a Nazi." (Shrine though it was, the house eventually went to settle some income tax difficulties that beset Lionel.)

In his later years Lionel's wheelchair became world-famous, but his reason for needing it is still unclear. He denied that he had arthritis or rheumatism, and at different times said his knee trouble was the result of an old gym injury or a fall in the bathtub. His manager believed that Lionel's joints had been affected by syphilis. But neither Lionel nor Ethel could compare in wildness with John. First, and far, far beyond his four marriages, was *amour*. He said he was introduced to sex at fifteen by his father's second wife. After that, he never looked back or, one might say figuratively, up. He was not a tall man, but he was perfectly built, had a face that was beautiful beyond belief, a voice that he could play like several instruments, and a Byronic spirit that he could use as an aphrodisiac. In addition—which, strangely, was part of his attraction for some— he drank. That one verb scarcely covers the subject.

His drinking and his attraction for women would not greatly distinguish him from some others in his profession, including his father. But John had genius. He combined his wildness with an amount of work that, considering his personal life and his many physical breakdowns, is another astonishment, especially since much of that work was fine and some of it wonderful. Opinions on his Shakespeare differ, but from his few phonograph records and film clips, we can gather that at the very least his Richard and his Hamlet were unforgettable. Bernard Shaw criticized him for cutting the text of Hamlet sharply and presenting more of Barrymore's acting than Shakespeare's writing. But Laurence Olivier, who saw the production when he was seventeen, said later that in his own performance of Hamlet, he "emulated" John.

I saw John on stage only once, the only time it was possible for me, when he came to New York in 1940 in a piece of claptrap called *My Dear Children*. He played an aging Shakespearean star, and this permitted him to do snatches of Shakespeare. By then, with his drinking, his breakdowns, his amorous broils, he had become something of a national joke, and he seemed almost to enjoy this status. During the pre-Broadway tour, newspapers were full of his ad-libs during performances. The night I saw the play, when he took a drink, he said, "Christ, how I wish this was real." The production had been directed by Otto Preminger, but he could hardly be held responsible for all that happened on stage.

After that play, as Peters aptly says, "Jack had nothing to sell . . . but his own degradation." But in *My Dear Children* the degradation was not yet complete. Brooks Atkinson wrote truly: "He can still act like a man who knows the art. . . . Although he has recklessly played the fool for a number of years, he is nobody's fool in *My Dear Children*, but a superbly gifted actor on a tired holiday." I've never seen an American actor like him. Marlon Brando and George C. Scott have touches of his quality; Christopher Plummer (to include a Canadian) is his equal in technique. But none of them conveys the full effect of John Barrymore.

In a way he was an exemplum of our existence: we saw the marvels he was giving us, and we could infer the marvels that were beyond his grasp. His gifts and his failure to make the most of them were like a highly intensified summary of human powers and impotence. He could have done anything, we felt. When he spoke, when he gestured, his voice and his movement were marvels in themselves, quite apart from the role he was playing; and as he displayed his powers, there seemed in him almost a counterpoint of regret that he had betrayed those powers. That, in this trumpery play, was tragedy—a tragedy familiar, in lower key, to many mortals.

To sample John's quality, see three of the best films he made: *Reunion in Vienna*, *The Great Man Votes*, and, above all, *Twentieth Century*. In the last, he plays a theater director-producer based on David Belasco and plays him with a knowledge of nineteenth-century acting virtuosity that enables him to embroider the performance delightfully. Two of Ethel's better films are *The Paradine Case* and *None But the Lonely Heart*. Quite different in each, she is an Athenian figure in both. But they are not Ethel at her best, as she was, for instance, on stage in *The Corn Is Green* (1940). Lionel made the most films of the trio—at one point he also directed—and can easily be sampled. His performance of Duval *père* in Garbo's *Camille* might be cited. Lionel and John can be seen together, entertainingly, in *Arsène Lupin*.

A word about Barrymore descendants. Of Ethel's three children, one, her daughter, had some success as a singer. John also had three children, two of whom, Diana and John Jr., were actors, with quite mixed results. The best-known of the family today is the teenaged Drew Barrymore, granddaughter of John, who charmed in *E.T.* and has had troubles since.

Margot Peters has written four previous books, one of which, *Bernard Shaw and the Actresses*, I have read and admired. The writing in this new book is not so firmly controlled. It seems often to strain for snappy effect, particularly at the ends of sections and chapters. ("He was hooked. Death was the only escape. Well, he was trying.") Her references to minor persons in the story are sometimes inadequate. Here's her complete description of Kenneth Macgowan: "the former Broadway critic gone Hollywood." True, but it doesn't quite characterize the man who ran the Provincetown Playhouse with Robert Edmond Jones and Eugene O'Neill, who was an early producer of O'Neill and a considerable influence on him. Occasionally Peters slips into sorry critical cliché: "One could argue that Olivier acted Hamlet, Barrymore *was* Hamlet."

But she has made this long and complex story completely fascinating—horrendously so at times—even to someone who thought he knew a bit on the subject. The bibliographical notes themselves, done in narrative form, are interesting, full of meat. Most important, she has understood the basic truth in her material: not only is it humanly gripping, it is a considerable fragment of a cultural history in transition.

Tragic Muse: Rachel of the Comédie-Française, by Rachel M. Brownstein. Salmagundi, Fall 1993.

Most theater biographies are not read by the general reader. This is as it should be: only the specialist would want or need to plow through the curtain speeches, the teapot-tempests, the dusty scandals that clog the usual chronicles of even major theater artists. Exceptions exist: *The Autobiography of Joseph Jefferson* is a hickory-smoked slab of nineteenth-century Americana; Giles Playfair's *Kean* links Edmund Kean's stylistic innovations with those in other arts of the Romantic era. (Keats said: "One of my ambitions is to make as great a revolution in dramatic writing as Kean has done in acting.") But most such books, recent and past, are insubstantial pageants faded that leave not a rack behind.

Rachel M. Brownstein's *Tragic Muse* (Knopf, 344 pp.) is another exception, a glowing one. Her biography, subtitled *Rachel of the Comédie-Française*, establishes its uniqueness at once with the jacket photograph that is also its frontispiece of Rachel thumbing her nose with both hands. This picture swiftly renders the title oxymoronic, complex. Brownstein's non-hagiographic, exploratory intent is clearly signaled by her juxtaposing of that photograph with the Jamesian title.

Rachel, born Elisa-Rachel Félix in 1821, the second daughter of itinerant Jewish peddlers, died thirty-seven years later, very rich and astoundingly celebrated. Her success in the theater, even in so short a life, has parallels, but her effect on distinguished people was extraordinary. Her devotees included many of the French literary figures of her day, Dumas *père*, Gautier, and Musset among them; equally struck were such non-French figures as Queen Victoria, Disraeli, Emerson, Alexander Herzen, Carl Schurz, and Czar Nicholas. Charlotte Brontë modeled the Vashti in *Villette* on Rachel. Matthew Arnold followed her to Paris after seeing her perform in an Edinburgh theater and remained there two months to see her again and again. He wrote three sonnets after her death, and, says Lionel Trilling, "It is Rachel dying whom the three sonnets make a symbol of modern Europe." In one of them Arnold wrote:

> Ah, not the radiant spirit of Greece alone
> She had—one power, which made her breast its home!
> In her, like us, there clashed contending powers,
>
> Germany, France, Christ, Moses, Athens, Rome.
> The strife, the mixture in her soul, are ours;
> Her genius and her glory are her own.

Brownstein, a professor of English at the City University of New York, says that it was Brontë's absorption with Rachel that impelled her reading about the actress, but Arnold's poems must have fueled that interest.

In these times the word "actress" needs attention. Brownstein, who writes quite distinctly as a woman about a woman, says:

I deliberately use the word "actress" rather than "actor," the term that many women players prefer: I like the fact that it marks the importance of gender. The interplay of gender, race, and class informed Rachel's life and people's perception of her.

Brownstein never uses the term "Jewess" (though Rachel was called *une juive*), probably because the term is now thoroughly outmoded in English and in any case lacks the erotic suggestion of "actress." What Brownstein seeks in Rachel is the woman—the peddler's child, the Jew, the French classical genius, yes, all these certainly, but supremely the woman.

Rachel began performing as a child, singing and dancing with her older sister in the streets of Lyons. Her father, who was her lifelong personal manager (and who outlived her), thought that Paris was essential to her future. There she was enrolled at a school for a while, but, like most people in those days, especially women, her education was scanty, which makes her letters and her taste all the more remarkable. Through one of her teachers, she was recommended to a member of the Comédie-Française who ran a minor theater of his own. By him Rachel was versed in the formalities of French classical acting, though this teacher was also accounted a progressive, intent on developing a student's natural bent.

At this minor theater she made her début. Edwin Forrest, generally accounted the first native American star, happened to be in Paris at the time and went to that theater to see a particular actor of whom he had heard. For that actor he didn't care, but he wrote to a friend about another member of the company, "that Jewish-looking girl, that little bag of bones with the marble face and the flaming eyes—there is demoniacal power in her. If she lives and does not burn out too soon, she will become something wonderful." Rachel was then thirteen years old at the time.

She moved on to a better theater and to some of the best acting teachers of the time. In April 1838 she was signed by the Comédie-Française—her father had to co-sign because she was still a minor of seventeen—and in June she made her début there, as Camille in Corneille's *Horace*. There were five customers in the orchestra. The dominant critic of the time, Jules Janin, returned in August from a holiday, saw Rachel, responded, and launched her into empyrean success.

Two factors, contradictory, need emphasis. First, she was physically slight. Gautier said that her diadem could serve as her belt. She was the precise opposite of the *grande dame* we may imagine as the archetype of French tragedy. It was her fire and voice—the immanent suggestion that she was slender because her fire was consuming her body—that overcame audiences. Second, she did not step into a flourishing line of French classical tragedy. Such a line had indeed existed, but it had been derailed by the irruption of romanticism. Victor Hugo, the chief opponent of classicism, struck it a wounding blow with *Hernani* in 1830; romantic drama, thus romantic acting, was central in the French theater when Rachel appeared. This slim child, by the nature of her gifts and her ambition for the highest tragedy, returned the French audience to Corneille and Racine.

Says Brownstein: "Romantic women performers . . . were praised for expressing with their bodies something beyond and more basic than words. Rachel, in contrast, spoke Racine's rhymed lines as if they were her own thoughts: she was *his* voice, some writers said." Apparently she fulfilled her first teacher's instruction: to revere the classical yet make it personal. She herself wrote in one of her copies of Racine: "Oh, my sweet Racine, it is in your masterpieces that I recognize the heart of woman! I shape my own to your noble poetry." If this reads like something to be left carelessly about for a visitor to read, it nonetheless expresses the fusion that many thought she accomplished between her small self and the majesty of Racine and Corneille.

The trajectory of her career need not be detailed here. She went from peak to peak, sometimes in new plays but mostly in French classics, capping those roles with Phèdre, which she put off playing until 1843 when she was a mature twenty-two! (The English critic George Henry Lewes said, "Whoever saw Rachel play Phèdre may be pardoned if he doubts whether he will ever see such acting again.") She toured—to many of the cities of Western Europe and eastward to Russia, whither she had been invited by the czar. She arrived in Moscow just as France and Russia broke off diplomatic relations on the eve of the Crimean War, but harsh politics did not diminish her wild reception or lessen the gifts that Czar Nicholas presented. In 1855 she traveled to America, played in the big cities of the eastern seaboard, then in Charleston, South Carolina, where a considerable French colony resided. There she collapsed on stage. She went to Cuba for a holiday, after which she returned home. She never acted again. It was believed that she had caught a chill on an unheated train from New York to Boston, the chill had progressed to a fever, and that this fever had aggravated the consumption of which she had already shown signs. She died two and a half years later. Her active life was cruelly shorter than even the death date signifies.

Brownstein, as she says in her introduction, has not attempted a sequential narrative: her book is a study of the paradoxes that Rachel presented. The basic one was in her profession. Acting was one of the few fields open to women, along with painting and writing (though some women writers thought they needed male names, like the two Georges, Sand and Eliot). But acting was the only one in which sexual availability was assumed, no matter what the degree of talent. The reason is obvious: the theater, not least in classic form, deals in sex and violence, often heatedly. One of the reasons why, for centuries, prostitutes patrolled theaters was to catch the stimulated. The female performer of the erotic was taken to be skilled in eroticism and therefore, by male logic, more compliant than other women.

The oddity about Rachel is that, far front resenting the assumptions of this paradox, she exploited them. She had very many lovers, from many of whom she accepted, imperiously asked for, mountains of jewelry, along with other expensive gifts. She made a fortune on her own, and she could have lived as chastely as she chose. But she reveled in lovers and she reveled in gifts—and all this while practicing a difficult art at its most difficult level.

It is as if she accepted the social role that male society assigned to her profession as part of Rachel-in-the-world. Brownstein underscores the truth that Rachel played Rachel; and Virginia Woolf—*there's* a far end of the temperament spectrum—reviewing a biography of Rachel in 1911, said: "The truth seems to be that one does not stop acting or painting or writing just because one happens to be dining or driving in the Park." The woman who went to the theater at night and made magnificence was Rachel, and was Rachel before and after. Lovers, whatever else they meant to her, whether they were genuinely loved or not, were part of the Rachel performance-in-large.

A curiosity about nineteenth-century theater eroticism is the costuming of women. Breeches parts existed, with women in male dress, and there were burlettas and ballets. But most of the serious acting by women was done in contemporary heavy Victorian dress, modified perhaps with a specific touch for a role, like an Oriental bangle. All the paintings and drawings of Rachel in Brownstein's book, done by men and to some extent exercises of male fantasy, show her in moderately revealing Greek or Roman dress. All the photographs of her in her actual costumes show her corseted and upholstered. The eroticism certainly didn't come from display in her case, which makes one admire her genius all the more.

About the multiple lovers, one notable fact. Though many of them were the writers and artists one would expect, six of them were connected to Napoleon, sometimes by blood. One of them was the man who eventually became Napoleon III. One of the others was Count Walewski, the emperor's illegitimate son, who fathered the elder of Rachel's two sons: thus she was the mother of Napoleon's grandson. Her other son was fathered by the son of a Napoleonic general.

By now it's a commonplace that the Victorian era, once thought monolithically puritanical, was not. Pietism certainly and strangulatingly existed, but the exceptions were many. G. H. Lewes, cited above, is less well-known today for his writings than because he was the paramour of George Eliot (herself fascinated by Rachel's art). Giuseppe Verdi's second wife, whom he revered, had borne two illegitimate children before he met her. Rachel's two sons grew up to enjoy successful careers in the French diplomatic service and the navy. Their mother, long dead by then, might have relished the way the world of men looked after its own and the way she, seemingly exploited, had used it—even to the advantage of her sons.

One of Brownstein's salient themes is that "the women stars of the nineteenth-century fascinated men and women by being self-contradictory images of womanly power and its containment." On her very first page she addresses self-contradiction and doubleness:

> Stars are remarkable for doubleness above all.... They seem to be both singular and reminiscent, simultaneously false and true. As such they reflect, reveal, and focus a problem that has preoccupied Western culture for at least two hundred years: the shape and depth of individual character, the outlines of the integral, coherent self, the relation between the substance of a self—sometimes called character—and appearances, self-presentations, temporary roles.

Brownstein doesn't much explore why this problem is today connected with many actors who are not stars or why this problem, dating from about the time of *Rameau's Nephew* and treated in recent times by (among others) Erving Goffman and Trilling, is now so much a part of our beings that it is no longer a problem: it is a given circumstance. Bruce Wilshire says that there is "a particle of fictionality within the very actuality of human life" and that this particle "must be formed by a kind of 'performance' for 'the appropriate audience.'" All the world was a stage long before Shakespeare said so, but in the last two hundred years, in a process fiercely heated in this century by film, each of us actors has seemed, to himself or herself, under-rehearsed, ill-prepared, prematurely thrust before the spotlights of the world-stage, with more consciousness of performing than ability in it. By now this influence of theater-film functions simply because those arts exist more than through the effect of any one performer.

But Brownstein is convincing in her argument that the appearance of the star—the term dates from the early nineteenth century—intensified the problem because, for both the men and women in the audience, adoration was added to art. When the star was a woman, this perception—of the double self in everyone—was sharpened by sexual fantasy and sexual fear in men, by envy and it kind of sororal pride in women. In our day this doubleness has been so ingrained that we can, if need be, get along without stars. Still, we hunger for them. In fact, one of the sterilities of the current American theater, besides substantial artistic problems, is that it no longer feeds this hunger, no longer creates stars.

In Rachel's case, her stardom was all the more strange, more triumphant, because she was Jewish. Judaism as such was not a major force in her life, but, despite rumors otherwise, she never wished to convert to Christianity. When she lay dying in the south of France, her sister sent for Grand Rabbi Isidore of Paris, who hurried there and who subsequently conducted the funeral service in Paris. (Two of the biographies of Rachel are in Yiddish, one of them by the American novelist Abraham Cahan.)

Jewishness, in Rachel's time, was both a usual and an unusual matter. It was usual because, in France, partly spurred by Napoleon's interest in the integration of Jews, many Jewish men had become prominent in business and the professions and a number of Jewish men and women were in the theater. (The next French woman star after Rachel, at her level, was also Jewish—Sarah Bernhardt.) Yet Jewishness was sufficiently exceptional among prominent people, among all people, that it never escaped notice. Partly this came from a social fact: latent prejudice. It would have been no kind of indictment that every non-Jew of the day had in him or her a latent yet arousable anti-Semitism. What non-Jew would have done the indicting? (Beethoven, the embracer of all mankind in a gigantic symphony, complained of a music publisher who had irritated him that he had "played me a Jewish trick.")

This latent anti-Semitism, as well as the active sort of course, flared in the case of Rachel, sometimes stoked by admiration itself. To some, it seemed a bit anomalous, if not impertinent, for a Jew to have so much artistic power. Lewes, in an enthusiastic review, said, "It will ever remain a curious problem how this little Jewess, this *enfant du peuple*, should, from the first moments of her appearance on the stage, have adopted—or rather let us say exhibited—the imperial grace and majesty which no one but herself could reach." It was a "problem" because, deep in Lewes as in so many others, was a fear of someone not exactly like himself, a fear exacerbated by his admiring response to her, including surely an erotic response. This binary reaction was still another paradox in a life that flamed so brightly yet so briefly.

This matter of influence leads to what Brownstein, in her last chapter, calls Rachel's "after lives," her effect on writers. Brontë and Arnold are among those discussed, along with the thematic influence on Eliot in *Daniel Deronda* and the inferable influence on James in *The Tragic Muse*. (In an earlier chapter she discusses Disraeli's *Coningsby* in the light of Rachel.) Brownstein pursues the search through the years to Sylvia Townsend *Warner's Summer Will Show* and Rachel Field's costume romance *All This, and Heaven Too*. This is the one chapter that seems a bit strained, especially when Brownstein tries to establish a connection between Rachel and Willa Cather's *The Song of the Lark* because Cather's heroine is an opera singer who chooses a career over love; and between Rachel and Virginia Woolf's *The Voyage Out* because it was written in 1911, the year that Woolf reviewed the Rachel biography and because her own heroine's name is, in the English pronunciation, Rachel. (Anyway, John Lehmann indicates that Woolf had begun the novel some years earlier.)

In a sense, however, the afterlife begins with the first chapter of Brownstein's book. She opens with Rachel's funeral on 11 January 1858 when "in spite of a cold wet fog over Paris, crowds began to gather in the Place Royale as early as eight in the morning." (The Palace Royale is now the Place des Vosges.) This opening is no facile narrative hook: Brownstein begins with the funeral in order to tell us that she means to consider Rachel's life as a whole, almost like an object she can turn in her hand, not to narrate it as a conventional story. "I call Rachel a cultural construct and read her as if she were a text..." And from the way in which Brownstein "reads" the funeral—as an event in France's cultural-political-social history—we know we are in for a treat, the sort of analysis for which Walter Benjamin's work is prototypical.

Some cynics said later that the funeral had been "orchestrated" as a kind of final appearance to reinstate her in the public mind after her (enforced) retirement in her last two and a half years. If so, whoever orchestrated it did a superb job. Rachel had died in the south of France, and at many stations along the funeral train's way, there had been some sort of service. On the way to Père Lachaise Cemetery in Paris, the hearse, drawn by six horses, was preceded by several dozen brilliantly uniformed municipal guardsmen, some of them mounted. Behind the hearse walked the Grand Rabbi with members of the family, followed by luminaries of the literary and art and theater worlds. They were followed by six hundred carriages and thirty to forty thousand people on foot.

Huge funeral processions were part of European life; see the photographs of Hugo's funeral in Paris or Verdi's in Milan when almost frightening oceans of people flooded the streets. Such funerals had become more than rituals of form, more than outpourings of grief. They had become a species of self-honoring by a city, a state, a nation. "We produced this person," says the immense crowd of mourners. "This person, by art or courage or statecraft or intellect, proved our rightness of belief, of being. Our presence here today is our final chance to approve, to participate in, this life that our society produced." The funeral thus became a species of national rejoicing. In this case the nation was France. It was Rachel's last classical act: her funeral took its place in a line of great national celebrations.

As for her afterlife, Brownstein of course omits its latest manifestation, this book. She calls the book "a postmodern biography... I pay more attention to how she was seen than I do to her own subjectivity.... I think the best way to know what she was and what she meant is to look at her through other people's eyes." Well, few biographies, except those of writers, can do otherwise unless they rely more heavily on letters and journals than apparently were available here; and "other people's eyes" are, in any event, the most appropriate way to look at a life that existed a good deal in the public view.

As for postmodernism, it certainly has a large commitment to doubleness, which is a feature of Brownstein's treatment throughout. But postmodernism implies a dispassion that this book disregards. Brownstein cannot conceal the fervent affection that she feels for the skinny, vulgar, libidinous, ultra-French, immutably Jewish, epoch-making genius who is her subject. Happily for us. Her strong feeling for Rachel touches every page of this attractively written, finely intelligent book.

Postscript: "A Dream of Fair Theaters." *Theater*, Winter-Spring 1995.

My Utopian dream for American theaters is simple, familiar, difficult. Every memorable theater of the last century or so, from Antoine and Stanislavsky and Copeau to Strehler and Grotowski and Mnouchkine, has been rooted in a social and cultural base. The debilitation that now besets American theaters is the skimpiness of that social and cultural base. This is not, preponderantly, a defect in the society and the culture. (If it were, all might be lost; but it isn't.) The defects are in our theaters.

I won't dwell here on the subject of good new plays in themselves. We always hope for them. But it seems more to the point to speculate about the present American forms of theater practice, of which, broadly speaking, there are two.

First, traditional theaters. These theaters exist, primarily though not exclusively, to nourish the present with the vitalities of the past. But these days, instead of glorying in that wonderful mission, traditional theaters worry. They strain to keep themselves from seeming old-fashioned, as if fashion were relevant; they cosmeticize themselves with bizarre physical productions and intrusive concepts to prove that they are up-to-date. Thus they often alienate their best audiences by obfuscating classic texts. Those audiences would presumably be interested in what made those texts survive: the language, designs, and perceptions of their authors. Instead, audiences get the careerism and/or nervousness of directors. Result: social and cultural disconnection.

Then there are contemporary theaters. Serious contemporary theaters consist substantially of partisan and polemical groups dedicated to dramatizing the history and condition of minorities—some not so minor—that have long been slighted, injured, ignored. From the start, there were ready audiences for these theaters. But, as it seems to me, those audiences have deepened in many ways while those theaters have not grown sufficiently. Their audiences have become more complex and comprehending while, to some degree, those theaters are still much concerned with revenge. Result: social and cultural disconnection.

Clearly, Utopian dreams for this multifarious country must be multifarious. There is no place any more for aspiration toward one great national theater, an American *Comédie Française* or even several of them. No such theater, or group of such theaters, can, by itself or themselves, fulfill our complex country's needs. In a harsh way, it helps us to be rid of that now—hollow *Comédie Française* aspiration. Theatrically (because socially) the American motto "e pluribus unum" now becomes: out of the many, many.

But, in itself, that is not enough. To keep connected with their audiences, the variegated theaters cannot merely exult in variety. They must (as they now show signs of doing) outgrow revanchism and become truly secure—which means to become questioning, ambiguous, and subtle, as interested in art as they are in ideas. By this enrichment, they can continue to lead audiences that might otherwise outgrow them. Alongside them, traditional theaters may thrive more fruitfully not by trying to compete with contemporary theaters but by attending committedly to their own business.

These divisions of artistic labor, drawn from social reality, may paradoxically be a road to mutual help. Audiences for the traditional theaters may then feel that the other theaters have more to offer them than polemics.

Audiences for those other theaters can attend traditional theaters, confident that, whatever the traditional theaters may present, their own concerns are being well-tended in their own theaters. (Museum directors have said that good museums for minorities increase the attendance of minorities at general museums.)

I must specify that none of the above is an argument for racial or any other kind of segregation. It is a hope for parity, without regard for anything but artistic quality. (I began arguing, in print, for color-blind casting in 1966.)

Utopia time is by definition dream time: cogent plans are not required. But theater people must do their dreaming for their best audiences, not for themselves. Self-absorption is an old theatrical curse. The way to move theaters from the periphery, where they now are, to the center is not by self-centered manifestoes, however noble. It is by building subscription—in the old theological sense.

Stanley Kauffmann Bibliography

Non-Fiction

A World on Film: Film Criticism and Comment (1966)
Figures of Light: Film Criticism and Comment (1971)
American Film Criticism: From the Beginnings to Citizen Kane (1972)
Living Images: Film Criticism and Comment (1975)
Persons of the Drama: Theater Criticism and Comment (1976)
Before My Eyes: Film Criticism and Comment (1980)
Albums of Early Life (memoirs, 1980)
Theater Criticisms (1983)
Field of View: Film Criticism and Comment (1986)
Distinguishing Features: Film Criticism and Comment (1994)
Regarding Film: Film Criticism and Comment (2001)
Conversations with Stanley Kauffmann (2003)
Albums of a Life (memoirs, 2007)
About the Theater (2010)
Ten Great Films (2012)
Film Critic Talks: Interviews with Stanley Kauffmann, 1972-2012 (2013)
The Millennial Critic: Stanley Kauffmann on Film, 1999-2009 (2015)
The World Screened: Stanley Kauffmann on the Cinema (2016)

Fiction

The King of Proxy Street (1941; *The Bad Samaritan*, U.K.)
This Time Forever (1945)
The Hidden Hero (1949)
The Tightrope (1952; *The Philanderer*, U.K.)
A Change of Climate (1954; a.k.a. *A New Desire*)
Showdown Creek (1955, under the pseudonym Lucas Todd; filmed in 1957 as
    Fury at Showdown, starring John Derek)
Man of the World (1956; *The Very Man*, U.K.)
If It Be Love (1960)

Drama

The Red-Handkerchief Man (three acts, 1933)
The Mayor's Hose (one-act, 1934); *The Prince Who Shouldn't Have Shaved: A Frolic*
    (one-act, 1934)
How She Managed Her Marriage (one-act, 1935); *The Singer in Search of a King*
    (one-act, 1935); *The True Adventure* (three acts, 1935)
Altogether Reformed (three acts, 1936); *Father Spills the Beans* (three acts, 1936);
    A Million Stars (one-act, 1936)
Cyrano of the Long Nose (one-act, 1937); *The Marooning of Marilla* (one-act,
    1937); *A Word from the Wise, for Three Women* (1937); *Come Again: A
    South Seas Vignette* (one-act, 1937); *Coming of Age* (one-act, 1937);

Eleanor on the Hill: A Fantasia (one-act, 1937); *His First Wife* (one-act, 1937)
The Cow Was in the Parlor (one-act, 1938); *Mr. Flemington Sits Down* (one-act, 1938); *Right under Her Nose* (one-act, 1938)
The More the Merrier (one-act, 1939); *Consider Lily* (1939)
Overhead (one-act, 1940); *Play Ball!* (1940); *Close Courting* (one-act, 1940); *The Salvation of Mr. Song* (one-act, 1940); *The Victors* (1940)
Bobino, His Adventures (two-act children's play, 1941)
The Bayfield Picture (one-act, 1942); *Pig of My Dreams* (one-act, 1942)
Cupid's Bow (one-act, 1943)
Food for Freedom (one-act children's play, 1944)

Index

Abbott, George, 71
Abel, Walter, 66
About the Theater, 9, 11, 215
Absurd Person Singular, 91
Absurdism, 11, 51, 156
The Academy, 145
Ackerman, Robert Allen, 84
Acting, 11, 170-172
Actors' Equity,
Actors' Studio (New York), 11, 88
Adams, Brooke, 90
Adelphi University (New York), 2
Adler, Edward, 157
The Admirable Bashville, 144
"The Adventures of the Black Girl in Her Search for God" (Shaw), 144
Aeschylus, 182
After the Fall, 7, 16-17
Agitations, 140, 145
Ahmanson Theater (Los Angeles), 40
Albee, Edward, 11, 17-19, 29, 53, 62, 78, 156, 183
Albert, Allan, 65
Aldredge, Theoni V., 38, 95
Aldridge, Ira, 194
Alexander, George, 184
Algerian War, 19, 112
Alienation Effect (*Verfremdungseffekt*), 114, 116
All for Love, 78-80
All My Sons, 16
All This, and Heaven Too, 211
Allen, Rae, 55
All's Well That Ends Well, 11, 37-38, 169
Alpert, Hollis, 202
America Hurrah, 55, 65
American Repertory Theater (New York), 132
American Scholar, xi, 1
Anatol, 109
And They Put Handcuffs on Flowers, 7, 51
And Things That Go Bump in the Night, 55

Anderson, Judith, 170, 183
Anderson, Maxwell, 21-22, 136, 183
Anderson, Paul, 102
Anderson, Robert, 12
Andrew, Stella, 153
Andreyev, Leonid, 182
Androcles and the Lion, 124, 163
Anglin, Margaret, 170, 183
Anglophilia, 7
Anna Christie, 76-77, 184
Annals of the New York Stage, 172
Anouilh, Jean, 156, 183
Ansky, S. (Shloyme Zanvl Rappoport), 7, 13, 80-82
Anspacher Theater (New York), 54, 60
ANTA (American National Theatre and Academy), 85
Antigone, 64
Anti-Semitism: see "Judaism"
Antoine, André, 213
Antonioni, Michelangelo, 90, 119, 156
Antony and Cleopatra, 7, 78-80
Antoon, A. J., 66
A.P.A. (Association of Producing Artists, N.Y.), 70
Apu trilogy (Ray), 156
Arch Street Theater (Philadelphia), 202
Archer, William, 5, 122, 131-132, 143
Arden, John, 27-29, 183
Arena, 188, 190
Arena Theater (Washington, D.C.), 27
Arendt, Hannah, 192
Aristophanes, 182
Aristotelianism, 42
Aristotle, 184
Armstrong's Last Good Night, 27
Arnold, Jeanne, 49
Arnold, Matthew, 206, 210
Aronson, Boris, 47
Around Theatres, 10, 175

Arrabal, Fernando, 7, 13, 51
Arsène Lupin, 205
Artaud, Antonin, 45
"The Art of Film" (Kauffmann, PBS-TV), 2
As You Like It, 111
Asolo Theater Company (Sarasota, Fla.), 183
Association for Theater in Higher Education, 2
Astor Place Riot, 173
Atheneum Publishers, 64
Atherton, William, 69
Atkinson, Brooks, 205
Auden, W. H., 139, 165, 192
The Autobiography of Joseph Jefferson, 179-181, 206
Avant-gardism, 5, 41, 51, 65, 96, 113
Ayckbourn, Alan, 91

Babe, Thomas, 13, 83-84
Babel, Isaac, 159-160
Bacall, Lauren, 47
The Bacchae, 7, 86-88
Bacchus, 183
Back to Methuselah, 176
Badel, Alan, 154
Bain, Conrad, 36
Baker, Elliott, 110, 175
Baker, George Pierce, 98
Baker, Lenny, 71
Baldwin, James, 112, 194
Ball, Lucille, 85, 157
Ball, Robert Hamilton, 164
Ballads and Songs of Brittany, 140
Ballantine Books, 1
Ballantyne, Paul, 35
Ballroom, 85-86
Bambara, Toni Cade, 58
Bantam Books (New York), 1
Baranski, Christine, 89
Bardach, Emilie, 48
Barefoot in the Park, 29, 110-111, 138
Barnes, Clive, 6, 58
Baroque, 98
Barrault, Jean-Louis, 188
Barrett (Browning), Elizabeth, 170

Barrie, Barbara, 38
Barrie, J. M., 183, 201
Barry, Gene, 94
Barry, Philip,
Barrymore, Diana, 12
Barrymore, Drew, 12, 205
Barrymore, Ethel, 12, 201-206
Barrymore, John, 6, 12, 74, 183, 201-206
Barrymore, Jr., John, 12
Barrymore, Lionel, 12, 201-206
Barrymore, Maurice, 12, 203
Barth, John, 110
Bartlett, Bonnie, 43
The Basic Training of Pavlo Hummel, 13, 54
Bassermann, Albert, 108
Bat Masterson, 94
Battleship Potemkin, 156
Bauer, Richard, 81
Bayer, Gary, 85
Bayreuth Festival (Germany), 141
Beach, Sylvia, 144
Beatty, John Lee, 63
The Beaux' Stratagem, 40
Beck, Julian, 117
Beckett, Samuel, 4, 11, 13, 45, 81, 119, 156, 178
Bedford, Patrick, 25
Beecham, Thomas, 151
Beerbohm, Max, 5, 10, 121, 165, 174-175
Beethoven, Ludwig van, 156, 210
The Beggar's Opera, 11, 49-50
Behrman, S. N., 183
Belasco, David, 171, 205
Benchley, Robert, 7
Bell, Neal, 84
Bellow, Saul, 160
Benchley, Robert, 7
Benjamin, Walter, 192, 211
Bennett, Michael, 62, 85-86
Bentley, Eric, 5, 8-11, 24, 30, 146, 174
Bergman, Ingmar, 76, 156, 158
Bergman, Ingrid, 62
Berkeley, Busby, 85
Berliner Ensemble (Germany), 102

Bernard Shaw and the Actresses, 205
Bernard Shaw and Gabriel Pascal, 161-163
Bernard Shaw: A Reassessment, 175-177
Bernhardt, Melvin, 90-91
Bernhardt, Sarah, 183, 210
The Best Man, 157
Between Two Worlds: see *The Dybukk*
"Beyond Bourgeois Theater" (Sartre), 115
Beyond the Fringe, 78
Beyond the Horizon, 191
Beyond Therapy, 89
Billion Dollar Baby, 85
Billy Liar, 25, 78
Billy Rose Theatre (New York), 25
A Biographical History of Philosophy, 140
Birch, John, 112
Birdbath, 31
Birmingham Film Festival (U.K.), 2
The Birthday Party, 45
The Black Doctor, 194
Black Theater USA, 194
The Blacks, 156
Blau, Herbert, 19, 21, 28, 113-114
Bleckner, Jeff, 55
Blithe Spirit, 153
Blitzstein, Marc, 190
Block, Larry, 89
The Blood Knot, 39
Bloom, Claire, 153-154
Blossom, Roberts, 68-69
Blum, Mark, 90
Blythe, Herbert: see "Barrymore, Maurice"
Boccaccio, Giovanni, 37
Bogart, Humphrey, 85
Bohemianism, 118
Boker, George Henry, 183
Bonaparte, Louis-Napoléon (Napoleon III), 209
Bonaparte, Napoleon, 209
Bond, Edward, 11, 48-49, 146
Booth, Edwin, 2, 171, 179
Bosco, Philip, 52

Boston Museum, 131
Boucicault, Dion, 72, 130, 180
Boy Meets Girl, 70-72
Brahms, Johannes, 149
Branagh, Kenneth, 166-168
Brando, Marlon, 205
Brasseur, Pierre, 109
Braun, Edward, 195
Breathless, 157
Brecht, Bertolt, 6, 11, 28-31, 48-49, 100-103, 114-116, 148, 191, 198
Brecht's Tradition, 192
Brenton, Howard, 146-148
Bridges, Beau, 27
British Information Service, 126
British National Theatre: see "National Theatre"
Broadhurst Theatre (New York), 73, 75
Broadway, 98
Broadway (New York), 4-5, 11, 14, 28, 33, 36, 38, 43, 46-47, 59, 62, 69-72, 75, 79, 82, 90, 95-96, 98, 101-102, 110-111, 116, 118, 133, 135-139, 146, 178, 180, 183, 189-190, 203-205
Brontë, Charlotte, 206, 210
Brook, Peter, 40, 50, 102, 120
Brooklyn Academy of Music (New York), 49, 67
Brooklyn Eagle, 173
Brooks, Albert, 90
Brooks, Jeremy, 52
Brown, Arvin, 57-58
Brown, Ivor, 127
Brown, Lewis, 36
Brown, Pamela, 151
Browning, Robert, 179
The Browning Version, 61
Brownstein, Rachel M., 206-212
Brueghel, Pieter, 30
Brustein, Robert, 5, 10-12
Bruzzichelli, Aldo, 159
Bucharest Yiddish State Theater (Romania), 81
Büchner, Georg, 30, 113, 148, 183
Budberg, Moura, 42
Bullins, Ed, 59, 194
Bunyan, John, 144

Burdick, Jacques, 128
Burge, Stuart, 28-29
Buried Child, 90
Burlesque, 49, 85, 174, 177
Burlesque, 98
Burlingame, Lloyd, 25
Burnett, Carol, 85
Burns, Catherine, 84
Burns, Ralph, 99
Burrows, Abe, 110
Burton, Richard, 151
Butley, 78
Byron, George Gordon (Lord), 21, 105-106, 204

Cabaret, 54, 100
Cacoyannis, Michael, 86-88
Cactus Flower, 110
Caesar, Adolph, 92
Caesar, Gaius Julius, 176
Caesar, Octavius, 79
Caesar, Sid, 85
Caesar and Cleopatra, 121, 162
Café La Mama: see "La MaMa Experimental Theatre Club"
Caffé Cino, 117
Cage, John, 45
La Cage aux Folles, 93-96
Cagney, James, 71, 85
Cahan, Abraham, 210
Caignez, L. C., 173
Calderon, Ian, 66
Calderón de la Barca, Pedro, 80
Caldwell, L. Scott, 93
Caldwell, Zoe, 43
Caligula, 21
The Cambridge Companion to Shakespeare on Film, 164
Cambridge University (U.K.), 27, 147
Camille, 205
Camillo, Marvin Felix, 60
Camino Real, 101
Cammarano, Salvadore, 109
Campbell, Douglas, 33-35
Campbell, Mrs. Patrick (Beatrice Stella Tanner), 161
Camus, Albert, 21, 112
Candida, 122, 190

Candide, 19
Cannon, J. D., 38
Capitalism, 37, 176, 198
Capitol Theater (New York), 201
Capone, Al, 99
Capote, Truman, 183
Captain Brassbound's Conversion, 162
The Caretaker, 45
Carey, Ann, 103
Carey, Henry, 103
Cariou, Len, 34
Carlyle, Thomas, 199-200
Carné, Marcel, 109
Carter, Mrs. Leslie, 171
Casablanca, 85
Casson, Lewis, 154
Castellani, Renato, 165
Castro, Fidel, 114
Cather, Willa, 211
Catholicism, 77, 192, 203
The Caucasian Chalk Circle, 6, 29-31, 114, 116
The Cenci, 106
Center Stage (Baltimore), 160
The Century Magazine, 179
A Certain World: A Commonplace Book, 192
Chaikin, Joseph, 64-65, 80, 85
Chambers, David, 85
Chambers, Mary, 104
Chaplin, Charles, 154-156, 179
Charba, Marie-Claire, 31-32
Charley's Aunt, 109, 165
Chayevsky, Paddy, 156
Chekhov, Anton, 6-7, 11, 40-42, 51-52, 79, 91, 118-120, 184-187, 195
Chelsea Theater Center (New York), 5, 49, 67, 198
Cherry Lane Theater (New York), 93, 116
The Cherry Orchard, 120, 185, 187
Chicago, 32-33, 98-100
Children of a Lesser God, 136
The Chili Widow, 12
The Chinese Wall, 160-161, 183
Chips with Everything, 37
A Chorus Line, 65, 85, 137-138
Christianity, 48, 128, 193, 210

Christie, John, 147
Christie in Love, 147
Churchill, Caryl, 146
Churchill, Winston, 147, 203
The Churchill Play, 147
Cibber, Colley, 182
The Cid, 23
Cioran, E. M., 45
Circle in the Square Theatre (New York), 70, 86
Circle Repertory Company (New York), 63
Citizen Kane, 85, 158
City Center Theater (New York), 23
City University of New York, 1-2, 206
Civic Repertory Theater (New York), 132
Civil War (American), 84, 180
Clair, René, 155
Clark, Bryan, 85
Classicism, 11, 13, 23-24, 45, 50, 66, 79, 87-88, 101, 107, 112, 124, 148, 152, 170, 176, 179, 207-208, 211, 213
Claudel, Paul, 112
Clayton, Jack, 156
Clurman, Harold, 27, 190-191
Coates, Carolyn, 21, 113
Cochren, Felix E., 93
Cocteau, Jean, 112, 182-183
Coghlan, Charles, 108
Cole, David, 195-198
Coleridge, Samuel Taylor, 106
Colicos, John, 28
The Collected Screenplays of Bernard Shaw, 161
Collins, Pat, 87
Colored People's Time, 92-93
Colton, Jacque Lynn, 31
Columbia Records, 179
Columbia University, 11
Comden, Betty, 85
Comédie Française (Paris), 12, 23, 206-213
Comedy, 11, 18, 26-27, 32, 38, 44-46, 61-62, 69, 71, 74-75, 77, 89-91, 98, 108, 110-112, 117-118, 138, 143, 151-153, 157, 159-160, 166, 170, 172-173, 183, 187, 200, 202
Coming Attractions, 88-89
Comma: see *Anna Christie*
Commedia dell'arte, 183
Commedia erudita, 183
Commentary, 1
Communism, 16, 41, 115, 148, 191
Company, 47
Complicité Theatre (London), 101
Compton-Burnett, Ivy, 46
Comte, Auguste, 140
The Condemned of Altona, 19-21, 31, 112, 114
Congreve, William, 61, 70-71
Coningsby, 210
Conklin, John, 87
The Connection, 5, 36, 156
Connell, Gordon, 49
Conolly, F. V., 143
The Constant Prince, 80
Constructivism, 47, 81
Conversations with Stanley Kauffmann, 215
Converse, Frank, 57
Cook, Barbara, 52
Cooke, George Frederick, 106, 129
Copeau, Jacques, 213
Coriolanus, 105
The Corn Is Green, 205
Corneille, Pierre, 23, 182, 207-208
Cornell, Katharine, 170
Cornell University Press, 146
Cotsworth, Staats, 38
Coulouris, George, 19-21, 113
The Country Wife, 19, 30
Court Theater (Weimar), 199
Court Theatre (London), 141
Courteline, Georges, 183
Courtenay, Tom, 78
Covent Garden Theatre (London), 104, 107
Coward, Noël, 64, 77, 183
Cowen, Ron, 55
Cowles, Matthew, 18
The Cradle Will Rock, 190
Craig, Edward Gordon, 201
Craven, Robin, 153
Crimean War, 208

Crimes of the Heart, 90-92
The Criminal Prisons of London, 140
Crimmins, Alice, 84
Criticism, 1-15, 27, 34, 43-44, 54-57, 59-60, 64, 72, 78, 113, 117, 135, 137, 140, 156, 158, 161, 163, 170-172, 174, 189, 197
Crowell, Thomas Y., 182
Crowl, Samuel, 166
The Crucible, 183
Cruikshank, Andrew, 152
Cugat, Xavier, 99
Cummings, E. E., 191
Curran, Paul, 42
Cushman, Charlotte, 171, 173, 179, 203

Dallas, 137
Dallas Theater Center (Texas), 13, 72
Daly, Augustin, 130
Dana, Barbara, 27
The Dance of Death, 6, 34-36
Dangerous Corner, 82
Daniel Deronda, 210
D'Annunzio, Gabriele, 183
Dante (Dante Alighieri), 176
Danton's Death, 19, 30, 113, 148
Dassin, Jules, 156-157
Davis, Donald,
Davis, Geri, 24
Davis, Ossie, 58
Davis, Owen, 183
Day of Absence, 111
The Day of the Locust, 69
Days of Heaven, 90
de Broca, Philippe, 156
de Courcy, Frédéric, 109
De Filippo, Eduardo, 183
de Lambert, Marie-Emmanuel (Guillaume Marguerite Théaulon), 108
De Munn, Jeffrey, 84
De Sica, Vittorio, 155-156
The Dead City, 183
Dean, Phillip Hayes, 59
DeAnda, Peter, 36
Death of a Salesman, 16
The Death of Tintagiles, 117

Decca Records, 151
The Defiant Ones, 157
Deiber, Paul-Emile, 23
Dekker, Thomas, 183
DeKoven, Roger, 68
Delacorte Theater (New York), 37
Democratic Vistas, 200
Denker, Henry, 157
Derek, John, 215
DeSylva, George Gard ("Buddy"), 178
Dewhurst, Colleen, 39
DeWitt Clinton High School (New York), 1
Dexter, John, 64
"Di provenza il mar" ("The Sea of Provence," Verdi), 38
Dillon, Mia, 91
The Dining Room, 92
Dirty Hands, 112-113
Dishy, Bob, 75
Disraeli, Benjamin, 206, 210
District of Columbia, 194
Dix, Richard, 71
Doctor Faustus, 143, 190
The Doctor's Dilemma, 70, 122, 162
Documentary, 2, 37, 67, 117, 193
Does a Tiger Wear a Necktie?, 101
A Doll's House, 76
Don Giovanni, 109
Don Juan de Maraña, 108
Don Quixote, 168
Donaldson, Frances, 178
Donen, Stanley, 158
Donizetti, Gaetano, 174
Donleavy, J. P., 110
Donley, Robert, 76
Donnelly, Donal, 25
Dorst, Tankred, 13, 66-69
Dostoevsky, Fyodor, 159
Douglas, Lord Alfred, 161
Downer, Alan, 179-180
Doyle, Arthur Conan, 163
Doyle, Patrick, 167
Dr. Dolittle, 61
Dr. Kheal, 82
Drake, Alfred, 107, 109
The Drama Observed, 4

"Drama on the *Times*" (Kauffmann), 137
Drama Was a Weapon, 190
Draper, Anne, 23
"A Dream of Fair Theaters" (Kauffmann), 213-214
Dreamgirls, 95
Die Dreigroschenoper, 190
Drew, John, 202
Drew, Mrs. John, 202
Dreyfus, Alfred, 187
Drummond, Alice, 18
Drury Lane Theatre (London), 104-105
Dryden, John, 78-80
du Maurier, Daphne, 178
du Maurier, Gerald, 178
Duff-MacCormick, Cara, 54
Duke of Saxe-Meiningen (Georg II), 13, 148-150
Duke Theater (New York), 148
Dukore, Bernard F., 161-163, 182
Dumas, Alexandre, 103, 107-109, 113, 206
Dumas, Alexandre *père*: see "Dumas, Alexandre"
Dunne, Griffin, 89
Dunnock, Mildred, 23
Durang, Christopher, 13, 85, 89
Durning, Charles, 38, 43
Durrell, Michael, 23
Dürrenmatt, Friedrich, 70, 184
Duse, Eleonora, 183
Dutton, E. P., 184, 199
The Dybbuk, 7, 80-82
The Dynasts, 193

Eastman, Arthur M., 121
Ebb, Fred, 98-100
Ebert, Joyce, 57-58
Eddison, Robert, 64
Edinburgh Bilingual Library, 195
Edinburgh Festival (U.K.), 78-79
Edison, Thomas Alva, 164
Edwardianism, 131
Edwards, Ben, 26, 73
Edwards, Christine, 171
Edwards, Hilton, 25
Edwards, Ryan, 49-50

The Effect of Gamma Rays on Man-in-the-Moon Marigolds, 55
8½, 197
81st Street Theater (New York), 159-160
Einstein, Albert, 96-97
Einstein on the Beach, 96-97
Eisenstein, Sergei, 155-156, 195
Electra, 86
Elektra, 150
Eliade, Mircea, 196
Eliot, George, 208-209
Eliot, T. S., 175, 210
Elizabeth the Queen, 183
Elizabethanism, 78, 102, 123, 140, 166
Elizondo, Hector, 75
Ellington, Edward Kennedy ("Duke"), 156
Elliott, Patricia, 36
Ellmann, Richard, 145
Emerson, Ralph Waldo, 206
Emilia Galotti, 200
Emmons, Beverly, 81, 96
Emmy Awards, 2
Enemies, 51-53
Les Enfants du Paradis, 109
English Stage Company (London), 27, 122
Enlightenment, 172
Enters, Warren,
Erby, Morris, 36
Eriksson, P. S., 66
Ernotte, André, 89
Ernst, Max, 45
Eroticism, 207-210
Ervine, St. John, 125
Esslin, Martin, 101-102
Establishment Theater Company (New York), 27
E.T., 205
Ethan Frome, 183
Euripides, 7, 23, 50, 86-88, 183
Evans, Edith, 153
Evans, Maurice, 153
The Exemplary Theatre, 125
Existentialism, 115
Expressionism, 54, 191, 198

Faber, Ron, 51
Fabian Society, 124, 140
Fabianism, 175-176
A Fable, 64-65
Die Fackel (*The Torch*), 192
The Facts of Life, 157
Fairbanks, Douglas, 164
Falstaff, 168
Fantasio, 118
A Far Country, 157
Farce, 61, 70-72, 75, 93, 110-111, 116, 156, 160, 174
Farewell to the Theatre, 127
Farquhar, George, 40
Farrar, Straus, & Giroux Publishers, 198
Fascism, 191
Faulkner, William, 65, 183
Faust, 148, 184, 199
The Federal Theatre, 1935-1939: Plays, Relief, and Politics, 172, 188-192
Federal Theatre Project, 11, 188-192
Fefu and Her Friends, 82-83
Feiffer, Jules, 110
Feingold, Michael, 100
Feist, Gene, 48
Feldman, Jack, 89
Fellini, Federico, 156
Ferdinand, Val, 194
Ferguson, Otis, 158
Fergusson, Francis, 11, 41
Ferrer, José, 75
The Fervent Years, 190
Feydeau, Georges, 23, 75, 183
Field, Betty, 26
Field, Rachel, 211
Fielding, Henry, 142
Fierstein, Harvey, 93-96
"Film Culture: Past and Present" (Kauffmann), 2
Film noir, 166
Finch, Peter, 154
The First Man, 76
First World War: see "World War I"
Fisher, Clara, 170
Fitzgerald, F. Scott, 14
Fitzgerald, Geraldine, 57

Flambeau, James, 140
Flanagan, Hallie, 188-189
Flanagan, William, 17
Flanders, Ed, 34
A Flea in Her Ear, 61
The Flies, 112
Follies, 46-47
Fontanne, Lynn, 162
Fonteyn, Margot, 153
For the Love of Movies: The Story of American Film Criticism, 2
Forbes-Robertson, Johnston, 164
Ford Foundation, 2, 132
Formalism, 22, 195
Forman, Milos, 69
Fornés, María Irene, 82-83
Forrest, Edwin, 170, 173, 179, 207
Forrest, George, 109
Forsythe, Henderson, 74
The Fortnightly Review, 140
Fosse, Bob, 98-100
Foster, Paul, 33
Fowler, H. W., 89
Fowlie, Wallace, 112
Foxy, 75
Framing Shakespeare on Film, 167
France, Anatole, 124
Francesca da Rimini, 183
Franco, Francisco, 51
Frank, Josef, 148
Freddy, 178
Free Press, 194
Free Southern Theater (Mississippi), 194
Freud, Sigmund, 44, 142, 157
Freudenberger, Daniel, 71-72
Freudianism, 38, 87
Friedman, Bruce Jay, 110
Friel, Brian, 24-25
Frings, Ketti, 56
Frisch, Max, 160, 183
The Front Page, 98
Fry, Christopher, 13, 151
Fry, Ray, 30
Frye, Northrop, 12
Fugard, Athol, 7, 38-40
Fuller, Charles, 13, 92-93
Fuller, Hoyt, 58-59

A Funny Thing Happened on the Way to the Forum, 75, 111
Fury at Showdown, 215

Gable, June, 89
Gagnon, Roland, 49-50
Gaines, Sonny Jim, 59
Galileo: see *Life of Galileo*
Gallicism, 108
Galsworthy, John, 142
Ganz, Arthur, 141
Ganz, Bruno, 198
Garbo, Greta, 76, 184, 205
Gardenia, Vincent, 62, 86
Garner, Jay, 94
Garnett, Constance, 186
Garson, Barbara, 55
Gassman, Vittorio, 109
Gassner, John, 184
Gautier, Théophile, 206-207
Gay, John, 49-50
Gayle, Addison, 58
Gazzo, Michael V., 157
Geer, Ellen, 34
Gelbart, Larry, 13, 75
Gelber, Jack, 5, 36-37, 156
Genet, Jean, 49, 51, 113, 156
Gerald, 178
German Life and Manners, 140
Getting Married, 141
Ghelderode, Michel de, 139
Ghosts, 5
Gibbs, Wolcott, 7
Gibran, Khalil, 65
Gide, André, 112
Gideon, 156
Gielgud, John, 119, 121, 126, 151, 169
A Gift of Time, 157
Gilder, Richard Watson, 179
Gilford, Jack, 75
Gill, Brendan, 7
Gillespie, Gerald, 195
Gillette, Anita, 69
Gillette, William, 70-72
Gilliam, Bryan, 149-150
Gilman, Richard, 5, 10-11
Gilroy, Frank D., 56
The Ginger Man, 110

The Gingham Dog, 43
Ginsburg, Mirra, 160
Ginsbury, Norman, 35
Gish, Lillian, 85
Glass, Philip, 96
Glengarry Glen Ross, 136
Glenville, Peter, 54
Globe Theatre (London), 148
Godard, Jean-Luc, 157
Gode, Alexander, 193
The Godfather, 49, 101
God's Favorite, 62
Goebbels, Joseph, 204
Goering, Hermann, 204
Goethe, Johann Wolfgang von, 140, 148, 198-201
Goffman, Erving, 209
The Gold Rush, 197
Goldberg, Rube, 176
Goldenberg, Billy,
Goldman, James, 47
Gordone, Charles, 56
Gorky, Maxim, 11, 51-53, 120, 185
Gothicism, 33
Gould, Lois, 83
Gower, Sir William, 107
Gozzoli, Benozzo, 121
Grabbe, Christian Dietrich, 195
Grand Illusion, 156, 197
Grand Rabbi Isidore (Isidore Loeb), 210
Granger, Michael, 30
Granville-Barker, Harley, 13, 120-127, 131-132, 161, 182
The Grass is Greener, 158
Gray, Simon, 77-78
Great Depression, 191
The Great Gatsby, 68
The Great Man Votes, 205
Green, Adolph, 85
Green, Guy, 157
Green, Paul, 194
Greene, Graham, 165
Greene, Loretta, 59
Greenwich Mews Theater (New York), 23-24
Greenwood, Jane, 76
Grey, Joel, 100
Griffith, D. W., 74, 174

Grimaldi, Joseph, 177
Grimsted, David, 172-174
Grotesque, 30, 33, 91, 102, 135
Grotowski, Jerzy, 65, 80, 138, 196, 213
Group Theater (New York), 190-191
Gründgens, Gustav, 183
Guare, John, 55, 69, 84
Guggenheim Fellowships, 2
Guinness, Alec, 163
Guitry, Lucien, 108
Guntner, J. Lawrence, 166
Guntram, 150
Gurney, A. R., 13, 92
Guthrie, Tyrone, 70, 81
Guthrie Theater: see "Tyrone Guthrie Theater"
Gutiérrez, Antonio García, 109
Guys and Dolls, 138
Gwynne, Fred, 73

Hack, Keith, 98
Hadary, Jonathan, 89
Hall, Peter, 45
Hallelujah, Baby!, 94
Hambleton, T. Edward, 70
Hamburg Dramaturgy, 200
Hamlet, 6, 39, 86, 103, 164, 166-168, 197-199, 203-205
Hamsun, Knut, 66-69
Handel, George Frideric, 107, 144, 154
Handke, Peter, 11, 49, 198
Hansberry, Lorraine, 157, 194
Happy Ending, 111
Hardy, Thomas, 193
Hare, David, 46, 146
Harper & Row Publishers, 80, 185
Harrington, Margaret, 83
Harris, Barbara, 111
Harris, Baxter, 73
Harris, Julie, 61
Harris, Rosemary, 45, 111
Harrison, Rex, 61, 78
Harrison, Tony, 63
Hart, Moss, 70, 89
Hart-Davis, Rupert, 174
Harte, Bret, 172

Hartman Theatre (Stamford, Conn.), 72
Harvard University, 11, 126, 180
Harvard University Press, 179
Hasenclever, Walter, 184
Hatch, James V., 194
A Hatful of Rain, 157
Hattaway, Michael, 166-167
Hauptmann, Gerhart, 77, 122
Hauser, Frank, 79
Hayes, Helen, 170
Haymarket Theatre (London), 104
Hays, Michael, 138
Hazlitt, William, 105, 107
He Who Must Die, 156
Hearn, George, 94
Heartbreak House, 141, 176
Hecht, Ben, 183
Hecht, Paul, 38
Hedda Gabler, 11, 152, 183
Heffernan, John, 18
Hegel, G. W. F., 11
Heijermans, Herman, 77
Heim, Michael Henry, 185
Helen Hayes Theater (New York), 24
Heller, Joseph, 110
Hellenism, 188
Hellman, Lillian, 4, 156
Hello and Goodbye, 6, 38-40
Hello, Dolly!, 94
Helm, Michael Henry, 184-187
Hemingway, Ernest, 189
Henley, Beth, 13, 90-92
Henry, Sam Haigler, 23
Henry V, 42, 166-168
Henry Irving's Waterloo, 163
Herman, Jerry, 94
Hernani, 207
Hertzler, John Noah, 87-88
Herzen, Alexander, 206
High Street, 89
Hill & Wang Publishers, 195
Hill Street Blues, 137
Hiller, Wendy, 58
Him, 191
Himelstein, Morgan Y., 190
The Hindenburg, 69
Hindy, Joseph, 22

Hippolytus, 23
His Majesty, 126
A History of American Acting, 170-172
A History of the American Film, 85
Hitler, Adolf, 66, 68, 101-103
Hodge, Francis, 180
Hoffman, William, 31-32
Hofmannsthal, Hugo von, 143
Hollywood, 62, 70, 85, 111, 118, 133, 155, 161, 202, 205
Holmes, Oliver Wendell, 179
Home Before Dark, 158
Home of the Brave, 94
The Homecoming, 44, 46, 133
Hooks, Robert, 26
Hoover, Marjorie L., 194-195
Hope, Bob, 157
Hopkins, Anthony, 147
Horace, 207
Horizon, xi, 1, 103-110, 120-135
Horovitz, Israel, 55
The Hot l Baltimore, 55, 63
The Hot Rock, 69
Hotton, Donald,
The House of Barrymore, 201-206
The House of Blue Leaves, 55, 69
Howard, Alan, 52
Howard, Peter, 99
Howard, Trevor, 58
Howe, Irving, 70
Howells, William Dean, 179
Howlett, Kathy M., 167-168
Huddle, Elizabeth, 30
Hughes, Langston, 194
Hugo, Victor, 10, 191, 207, 211
Humanism, 115
Humphrey, Doris, 191
Huneker, James, Gibbon, 7
Hunt, Leigh, 107
Hunter-Blair, Kitty, 52
Hunter College (New York), 2
Huntington, Helen, 124
Hurst, David, 160
Hurt, Mary Beth, 66, 71, 91
The Hustler, 157
Hutchinson Publishers (London), 175
Hynes, Samuel, 140

Ibsen, Henrik, 4-5, 7, 38, 48, 52, 122, 152, 148-149, 203
Ice Age, 66-69
Ice Capades, 96
The Iceman Cometh, 77, 97
Ikiru (To Live), 157
I.L.G.W.U. (International Ladies' Garment Workers' Union), 191
The Iliad, 193
Illuminations, 192
Imagism, 32
The Importance of Being Earnest, 11, 79, 152-153, 175
In Praise of Love, 61-62
Inadmissible Evidence, 27
The Indian Wants the Bronx, 55, 101
Indiana University Press, 170
Inge, William, 4, 25-27, 74
The Innocents, 78
Institute for Advanced Studies in Theater Arts (IASTA), 24
The Internationale, 41
Internet, 14
Intolerance, 85
Ionesco, Eugène, 13, 119, 156
Iphigenia in Aulis, 86
Irony, 3, 11, 21, 61, 77, 110-111, 125, 193
Irving Henry, 143, 149, 184
Irving, Jules, 19, 30
Isn't It Romantic, 90
It Can't Happen Here, 189
Ivanov, 119

Jackness, Andrew, 89
Jackson, Glenda, 98
Jackson, Robert, 36
Jackson, Russell, 164-165
Jacobi, Derek, 79, 166
James, Henry, 66, 210
Jan Hus Theater (New York), 21
Janik, Allan, 192
Janin, Jules, 207
Japan Foundation (New York), 2
Jarrell, Randall, 42
J.B., 5, 62
Jeffers, Robinson, 183
Jefferson, Joseph, 172, 179-181

Jefford, Barbara, 79
Jellicoe, Ann, 25
Jenkins, David, 58
The Jest, 203
John Bull's Other Island, 122
Johnson, Celia, 169
Johnson, Samuel, 80, 175
Jones, David, 51-52
Jones, LeRoi, 112
Jones, Preston, 13, 72-75
Jones, Robert Edmond, 203, 205
Jonson, Ben, 75
Jordan, Richard, 38
Joslyn, Allan, 71
The Journey of the Fifth Horse, 55
Joyce, James, 144-145
Joyce, Stephen, 72
Judaism, 13, 62, 69, 80-82, 92, 102-103, 159-160, 177, 192-193, 206-212
Judson Memorial Church (New York), 117
Jung, Carl Gustav, 195
Justice, 203

Kabatchnik, Amnon, 22
Kabbalism, 81
Kahn, Otto H., 191
Kaiser, Georg, 191
Kalegi, Sylvia, 24
Kalidasa (India), 182
Kander, John, 98-100
Kanin, Garson, 4, 157
Karlinsky, Simon, 184-187
Kaspar, 198
Kass, Jerome, 85
Kauffmann, Stanley, ii, 1-15, 215-216
Kaufman, George S., 36, 70, 89, 111-112
Kazan, Elia, 191
Kazin, Alfred, 172
Keach, Stacy, 6
Kean, 107, 113, 206
Kean, Edmund, 13, 103-110, 113, 206
Kean, Moses, 103
Kean, ou désordre et génie, 108
Keats, John, 106, 175, 206

Keene, Laura, 180
Kellman, Barnet, 90
Kelly, Eamon, 25
Kemble, John Philip, 107
Kennedy, Adrienne, 194
Kennedy Center (Washington, D.C.), 73
Kenny, Sean, 41
Kenyon Review, 1
Kerensky, Alexander, 11
Kerr, Jean, 157
Kerr, Walter, 5, 11
Kesey, Ken, 51
Key Exchange, 89-90
Keyishian, Harry, 166
Kid Champion, 84
Kim, Willa, 17
King, W. D., 163
King Lear, 21, 40, 86, 105, 126, 167
The King of the United States, 65
Kingsley, Sidney, 190
The Kitchen, 36-37
Kleist, Heinrich von, 143, 149, 198
Klotz, Florence, 47
The Knack, 25
Knipper, Olga, 185
Knopf, Alfred A., 1, 202, 206
Knox, John, 78
Kopit, Arthur, 55
Koteliansky, S. S.,
Krafft-Ebing, Richard von, 31
Kramer, John, 36
Kramer, Stanley, 157
Krasna, Norman, 4
Kraus, Karl, 13, 192-194
Krupp, Friedrich, 19
Krutch, Joseph Wood, 8
Kumonso-djo: see *Throne of Blood*
Kurnitz, Harry, 4
Kurosawa, Akira, 157, 164-165, 167
Kurtz, Marcia Jean, 81
Kurtz, Swoosie, 85

L.A. Civic Center (Calif.), 40
La Mama Experimental Theatre Club (New York), 31-33, 50-51, 86, 117
Labour Party (U.K.), 140
Lacy, Tom, 52

Ladd, Diane, 73
Lady Hamilton, Emma (Amy Lyon), 103
The Lady's Not for Burning, 151
Lahr, Bert, 75, 177-178
Lahr, John, 177-178
Lamb, Charles, 163
Lamb, Mary, 163
Landscape, 46
Landscape of the Body, 84
Lapine, James, 92
The Last Analysis, 160-161
The Last Days of Mankind, 192-194
The Last Meeting of the Knights of the White Magnolia, 73-74
Last Summer, 84
Last Theatres, 15, 175
Laurence, Dan H., 139-145, 161
Laurents, Arthur, 94
Lawrence, D. H., 57-58
Le Gallienne, Eva, 132, 152
Leach, Wilford, 83
The Leader, 140
League of Nations, 142
League of Workers' Theatres (New York), 191
Lee, Leslie, 13, 92-93
Lee, Ming Cho, 38
Lee, Will, 52
Lehmann, John, 211
Leibman, Ron, 69
Lemaître, Frédérick, 108-109
Lemon Sky, 43
Lenin, Vladimir, 11
Lenz, 183
Lenz, Jakob Michael Reinhold, 195
Leoncavallo, Ruggero, 109
LeRoy, Mervyn, 158
Lesser, Gene, 49
Lessing, G. E., 200
The Letters of Anton Chekhov, 184-187
Levene, Sam, 160
Lewes, George Henry, 140, 208-209
Lewis, Clunn, 142
Lewis, David, 152
The Libation Bearers, 182
Das Liebesverbot (*The Ban on Love*), 168

The Life and Times of Joseph Stalin, 96
Life of Galileo, 148
Life of Richard Strauss, 149
Limelight, 154
Lincoln, Abraham, 179
Lincoln Center (New York), 11, 13, 40, 51, 53, 58, 101, 113-114
Lincoln Center Repertory Company (New York), 16-17, 19, 21, 29-31, 112
Lindner, Albert, 149
The Lion in Winter, 47
The Lion King, 5
Lipari, Victor, 31
Lithgow, John, 66, 71
Little, Cleavdon, 49
Little Theatre (New York), 72
Live Like Pigs, 27
The Living Corpse: see *Redemption*
Living Theater (New York), 11, 117, 196
Lloyd, Norman, 191
The Local Stigmatic, 101
London Assurance, 72
London Labour and the London Poor, 140
The Loneliness of the Long Distance Runner, 78
Long Day's Journey into Night, 35, 77, 90, 97, 156
Long Wharf Theatre (New Haven, Conn.), 57-58
Longfellow, Henry Wadsworth, 179
Lonsdale, Frederick, 178
Loos, Adolf, 192
Loot, 91
Lope de Vega (Félix Lope de Vega y Carpio), 182
Loquasto, Santo, 58
Loren, Sophia, 158
Loudon, Dorothy, 86
Lowell, Robert, 24
The Lower Depths, 52, 186
Lu Ann Hampton Laverty Oberlander, 73-74
Lucia di Lammermoor, 81
Luckinbill, Laurence, 84
Lukács, Georg, 198

Lumet, Sidney, 70
Lumière, Auguste, 164
Lumière, Louis, 164
Lunt, Alfred, 162
Luv, 110
Lyceum Theatre (New York), 112

MacArthur, Charles, 183
Macbeth, 164-165, 168, 203
MacBird!, 55
Macgowan, Kenneth, 205
Machiavelli, Niccolò, 83
MacKay, Lizbeth, 91
Mackintosh, Woods, 81
MacLeish, Archibald, 5, 62
Macmillan Publishers, 42
Macready, William Charles, 107, 127, 173, 179
Macy, R. H., 83
The Mad Show, 111
The Madras House, 123
Maeterlinck, Maurice, 117, 162
The Magnificent Ambersons, 164
Magritte, René, 45
Majestic Theatre (New York), 85
Major Barbara, 10, 122, 162, 176
Makeham, Eliot, 151
Malcolm, 17-19
Malina, Judith, 117
Maloney, Peter, 51
Mame, 47, 94
Mammen, Edward, 129, 131
Man and Superman, 122, 142
A Man Escaped, 197
The Man Who Married a Dumb Wife, 124
Mandragola, 83
Manhattan Theater Club (New York), 72
Manheim, Ralph, 101
Mann, Thomas, 102, 143
Mannheim School (Germany), 140
Mantell, Robert, 170
Manvell, Roger, 165
Marat/Sade, 65
Marchand, Nancy, 52
Marivaux, Pierre de, 49
The Mark, 157
Marlowe, Christopher, 190

Marowitz, Charles, 91
The Marquise of O..., 198
The Marriage of Figaro, 173
The Marrying of Ann Leete, 122
Marshall, Herbert, 162
Martinique Theatre (New York), 31, 116-117
Marty, 85
Marvin, Mel, 85
Marx, Groucho, 75
Marx, Karl, 11
Marxism, 115-116
Mary, Mary, 157
Mary Stuart, 70, 80
Masefield, John, 122
"M*A*S*H" (CBS-TV), 75
Mason, Richard, 157
Massinger, Philip, 105
The Master Builder, 7, 48
Masters, Ben, 90
Mastroianni, Marcello, 158
Mathews, Carmen, 152
Mathews, Jane DeHart, 172, 188-192
Matlaw, Myron, 184
Mauriac, François, 112
Mautner, Franz H., 193-194
Maxwell, Roberta, 46
Mayer, Louis B., 204
Mayhew, Henry, 140
Mazursky, Paul, 83
McBurney, Simon, 100-103
McCarthy, Lillah, 122, 124-125
McCarthy, Mary, 10
McCarty, Mary, 47, 76
McCowen, Alec, 64, 79
McCullers, Carson, 63, 183
McElroy, Evie, 34
McGrath, Leueen, 65, 153
McGraw-Hill Encyclopedia of World Drama, 181-184
McNally, Terrence, 55
Measure for Measure, 37, 168
Medea, 11, 50
Meiningen Theater (Germany), 148-150
Meininger (Meiningen Company, Germany), 148-150
Melfi, Leonard, 31

Mellers, Wilfrid, 172
Melodrama, 20, 29, 59, 71-72, 109-110, 113, 116, 157, 172-174, 194
Melodrama Unveiled: American Theater and Culture, 172-174
Memorial Theatre (Stratford-on-Avon, U.K.): see "Royal Shakespeare Company"
Mercer Arts Center (New York), 51
The Merchant of Venice, 105, 144, 203
Mercury Theater (New York), 183
Merivale, John, 153
Method acting, 170
Methodism, 147
Metropolitan Opera (New York), 171
Meyer, Michael, 48
Meyerhold, Vsevelod, 11
Meyerhold: The Art of Conscious Theater, 194-195
Meyerhold on Theatre, 195
MGM Studios (Metro-Goldwyn-Mayer), 204
Midnight Cowboy, 43
A Midsummer Night's Dream, 102, 120, 124, 152, 163
A Midwinter's Tale, 167-168
Mielziner, Jo, 53, 62
Mifune, Toshiro, 158
Mignon, 199
Milgrim, Lynn, 78
Miller, Arthur, 7, 16-17, 156, 183
Miller, Jason, 55
Milner, Ron, 13, 58-60
Minneapolis Theater Company, 33-34
The Misanthrope, 11, 63-64, 79
The Miss Firecracker Contest, 91
Mitchell, David, 61, 66, 95
Mizinova, Lidya, 185
Mnouchkine, Ariane, 213
Modern Romance, 90
Modern Times, 156
Modern World Drama, 184
Modernism, 68, 145
Modjeska, Helen, 171
Moiseiwitsch, Tanya, 33

Molière (Jean-Baptiste Poquelin), 63-64, 70, 79, 183, 191
Molnár, Ferenc, 184
Monroe, Marilyn, 16-17, 157-158
Montgomery, Earl, 30
Montgomery, Robert, 56
Montherlant, Henry de, 23, 112
A Moon for the Misbegotten, 77
Morality plays, 75
More Theatres, 174-175
Morgan, Debbi, 93
Morning Chronicle (London), 105
Morse College: see "Yale University"
Moscow Art Theater (Russia), 41, 185, 187, 195
Mosel, Tad, 56
Mostel, Josh, 74
The Mound Builders, 63
Mourning Becomes Electra, 55
Mozart, Wolfgang Amadeus, 109, 140, 173
Mozhukhin, Ivan, 109
Mr. Hulot's Holiday, 158
Mrs. Dally Has a Lover, 18
MTV (Music Television), 138
Much Ado about Nothing, 66, 168
Mumford, Lewis, 172
Munday, Penelope, 151
Murdoch, Rupert, 147
Murray, Gilbert, 122, 141
Music in a New Found Land, 172
Musser, Tharon, 17, 47
Musset, Alfred de, 118, 206
Mutual Broadcasting Company, 1
The Mutation Show, 65, 85
Muzeeka, 69
My Dear Children, 204-205
My Fair Lady, 138, 163
My Foot, My Tutor, 198
My Life in Art, 187
My Own Private Idaho, 167
Myers, Bruce, 81

Napoleonism, 193, 209-210
Narrow Road to the Deep North, 48-49
Nathan, George Jean, 2, 4-5, 8, 11, 77

National Actors' Theater (NAT, U.S.A.), 100-103
National Book Awards, 2
National Council on the Arts, 190
National Endowment for the Arts, 2, 132
The National Review, 10
National Society of Film Critics (New York), 2
National Theatre (London), 27, 40, 42, 63, 131, 148
Native Son, 194
Naturalism, 20, 36-37, 58, 174
Natwick, Mildred, 153
Naughton, James, 100
Nazimova, Alla, 187
Nazism, 20, 68, 102-103, 113, 204
Nefertiti, Neferneferuaten, 117
Negro Ensemble Company (New York), 13, 92-93
Nelson, Barry, 110
Nelson, Gene, 47
Nelson, Horatio, 103
Nelson, Richard, 30
Nelson, Ruth, 33
Nemirovich-Danchenko, Vladimir, 185-186
Neoclassicism, 23-24, 79
Neuwirth, Bebe, 100
Never on Sunday, 157
Nevis Mountain Dew, 93
New American Review, 7, 137
New Deal, 189
New 81st Street Theater (New York), 36
New Left, 112
New Playwrights' Theater (New York), 191
New Republic, xi, 1, 38-86, 140, 172-184, 187-188, 192-206
New Statesman, 109, 140
New Theater (New York), 111
New Theater Workshop (New York), 27
"The New Theology" (Shaw), 145
A New Way to Pay Old Debts, 105
New York (magazine), 10
New York Institute for the Humanities, 2
New York Shakespeare Festival, 13, 37
New York State Council on the Arts, 2
New York State Theater, 40
New York Times, xi, 1, 3, 5-7, 11, 17-38, 55-56, 58-59, 62, 110-120, 137, 146-148, 159-161, 170-172, 188-192
New York Tribune, 171
New York University, 1
New Yorker, 7, 139
Newman, Paul, 158
Newman, Stephen D., 49
Newman Theater (New York), 69, 80
Next Stop, Greenwich Village, 71
Nicholas II, Czar of Russia, 206, 208
Nichols, Mike, 29, 62, 110, 138
'night, Mother, 9, 136
No Exit, 112-113
No Love for Johnnie, 157
No, No, Nanette, 47
Nobel Prize (Literature), 69
None But the Lonely Heart, 205
Noonan, John Ford, 56, 69
Norman, Marsha, 9
Northeastern University, 167
Notes on a Cowardly Lion, 177-178
Notes on Shakespeare, 165
Novelli, Ermete, 108
Nuyorican Poets Café (New York), 13

Oberlin College (Ohio), 67, 194
O'Brien, Edna, 24
O'Brien, Justin, 21
O'Brien, Pat, 71
O'Connor, Flannery, 13, 183
O'Connor, Frank, 24
O'Connor, Kevin, 31-33, 117
The Octoroon, 180
The Odd Couple, 62, 110
Odell, George C. D., 172
Odets, Clifford, 39
Oedipalism, 57
Oedipus the King, 22, 42, 61, 138, 141
Oedipus Rex: see *Oedipus the King*

Off-Broadway (New York), 14, 18, 23, 27-28, 31, 36, 38-39, 48, 51, 82, 89, 93, 95, 111, 116-117, 133, 138
Off-Off Broadway (New York), 14, 50, 82, 85, 89, 95, 116-118
Oh Dad, Poor Dad, Mamma's Hung You in the Closet and I'm Feelin' So Sad, 55
Oh! What a Lovely War, 42
O'Hara, Jill, 48
Ohio University Press, 167
O'Horgan, Tom, 31-33, 117
Oklahoma!, 138
Old Phantoms, 93
The Old Stock Company School of Acting, 129
Old Times, 7, 43-46, 133
Old Vic Theatre (London), 41, 131, 153
Older People, 56, 69
The Oldest Living Graduate, 73-74
Olivier, Laurence, 14, 41-42, 79, 138, 166, 169, 204-205
Olympic Theatre (London), 104-105
"On the Marionette Theater" (Kleist), 143
On Native Grounds, 172
On Overgrown Paths, 66
On the Rocks, 144
Once in a Lifetime, 70, 85, 89
One Flew Over the Cuckoo's Nest, 51
O'Neill, Eugene, 5, 35, 39, 55, 76-77, 90, 97-98, 156, 191, 205
O'Neill, James, 76
Open Theater (New York), 5, 64-65, 80, 117
Oresteia, 55, 112
The Organizer, 164
Orlando Furioso, 188
The Orphan, 54-57
Orton, Joe, 91
Orwell, George, 192
Osborne, John, 27, 122, 156
Ostend Interviews, 139
Ostrovsky, Alexander, 40
O'Sullivan, Mairin D., 25
Otello, 168

Othello, 42, 105, 107-109, 129, 165, 203
Otherwise Engaged, 77-78
Otho the Great, 106
Our American Cousin, 180
Our Theatres in the Nineties, 3-4
Our Town, 31
Outcry, 53-54
Oxford English Dictionary, 128
Ozzie and Harriet, 54

Pabst, G. W., 168
Pace University, 101
Pacino, Al, 14, 84, 100, 103
Packard, William, 24
Pagliacci, 109, 177
Pal Joey, 138
Palace Theatre (New York), 93
Papas, Irene, 87
Papp, Joseph, 13, 37-39, 58, 60, 66, 69, 83-84, 101
Pappas, Theodore, 89
The Paradine Case, 205
Paris Opéra, 139, 188
Parker, Carolyn, 33
Parody, 91, 95, 141
Parry, Idris, 143
Parsifal, 19, 141-142
Parsons, Estelle, 18
Pascal, Gabriel, 13, 161-163
Pastene, Robert, 35-36
Pathos, 51
Patterson, Charles H., 93
Paul, 147
Payne, Robert, 187
Peaslee, Richard, 65
The Pelican, 117
Pendleton, Austin, 72
Penn, Arthur, 75
The Penny Wars, 175
Percy, Walker, 157
Père Lachaise Cemetery (Paris), 211
Performing Arts Journal, xi, 10, 82, 135-146
Persona, 197
Persons of the Drama, 8-9, 11, 141, 215
Peter Ibbetson, 81, 203

233

Peters, Brock, 30
Peters, Margot, 201-206
Phaedra, 6, 23-24, 208
Phèdre: see *Phaedra*
Philadelphia, Here I Come!, 24-25
Philistinism, 11, 19
Phoenix Theater (New York), 70, 72
Piave, Francesco Maria, 109
Picasso, Pablo, 160
Pickford, Mary, 162, 164
Pickup, Ronald, 42
Picture Post, 144
Pietism, 209
Pilhofer, Herbert, 36
Pinero, Arthur Wing, 71
Piñero, Miguel, 13, 60-61, 66, 75, 107
Pins and Needles, 191
Pinter, Harold, 7, 18, 43-46, 78, 119
Pirandello, Luigi, 11, 53, 70-71, 197
The Pirates of Penzance, 70
Plato, 143, 176
Playfair, Giles, 103, 206
Playhouse Theatre (New York), 70
Playwrights' Horizons (New York), 89, 92
Plummer, Christopher, 102, 205
Pointer, Priscilla, 21
Polk, George, 2
Pollard, Percival, 7
Pop art, 26
The Pope's Wedding, 48
Post-impressionism, 124
Postmodernism, 5, 211-212
Pound, Ezra, 67, 175
Powell, Michael Warren, 31-32
Praeger Publishers, 187
Pravda: A Fleet Street Comedy, 147
A Prayer for My Daughter, 83-84
Prefaces to Shakespeare, 120
Preminger, Otto, 205
Prendergast, Shirley, 93
The Presence of the Actor, 64
Price, Reynolds, 157
Priestly, J. B., 82, 121
The Prince of Homburg, 198
Princess Ida, 47
Princeton University, 126
Princeton University Press, 188

Pritchett, James, 24
Problems of Life and Mind, 140
Prokofiev, Sergei, 41
Prolet-Bühne Theater (New York), 191
Promenade, 82
Propaganda, 116
The Proposition, 51
Provincetown Players, 191
Provincetown Playhouse (New York), 39, 205
The Public and Performance, 138
Public Broadcasting Service (PBS, N.Y.), 76
Public Theater (New York), 46, 51, 54, 60, 66, 80, 83, 101
Pulitzer Prize (Drama), 55, 90, 92
Punch, 140
Purdom, C. B., 120, 124, 126
Purdy, James, 17-18
Puritanism, 7
Purnell, Louise, 42
Puss-in-Boots, 195
Pygmalion, 162

Quinn, Edward, 184
Quintero, José, 76
Quinteros, Alvarez, 182
Quisling, Vidkun, 68

Rabb, Ellis, 52, 70
Rabe, David, 13, 54-57
Rabelais, 188
Rabelais, François, 30
Rachel (Elisa-Rachel Félix), 206-212
Racine, Jean, 6, 11, 23-24, 182, 207-208
The Racket, 98
Rafalowicz, Mira, 80
Rains, Claude, 162-163
A Raisin in the Sun, 59, 157
Rameau's Nephew, 209
Ran (Chaos), 167
Randall, Tony, 100-103
Rasputin and the Empress, 203
Rattigan, Terence, 61-62, 183
Rawlins, Lester, 22
Ray, Nicholas, 191

Ray, Satyajit, 156
RCA Victor Records, 153
Read, Herbert, 12
The Reader's Encyclopedia of World Drama, 182, 184
Reagan, Ronald, 71
The Real Thing, 136
Realism, 11, 20, 23, 31, 39, 41, 43, 53, 66, 74, 76, 104, 145, 148, 160, 166, 174, 183, 195, 200
Rebel Women, 84
The Recluse, 33
Red Gloves: see *Dirty Hands*
Redemption, 183
Redgrave, Michael, 41
Reinhardt, Max, 196
Reinking, Ann, 99
Reisz, Karel, 156
Renaissance, 128, 139, 157
Renoir, Jean, 156
Repertory theater, 127-135
Resistance: see "World War II"
The Resistible Rise of Arturo Ui, 11, 100-103
Resnais, Alain, 117
The Respectful Prostitute, 112
Restoration (U.K.), 44, 79, 118
Reunion in Vienna, 205
Revenge, 148
Ribman, Ronald, 55
Rice, Elmer, 36, 59, 136
Rich, Christopher, 88
Rich and Famous, 69
Richard III, 37, 42, 69, 101, 105-106, 169, 203
Richards, Stanley, 194
Richardson, Jack, 156
Richardson, Lee,
Richardson, Tony, 102
Richler, Mordecai, 110
The Ride Across Lake Constance, 198
"The Ride Across Lake Constance" *and Other Plays*, 198
Riefenstahl, Leni, 67
Rienzi, 97
Rigg, Diana, 64
Rigoletto, 105
Rip Van Winkle, 179, 181

Ritman, William, 17, 39
Ritt, Martin, 191
The River Niger, 59
Robbins, Rex, 58
Robertson, Toby, 79
Robespierre, Maximilien, 52
Robinson, Andy, 49
Rockefeller Fellowships, 2
Rodgers, Richard, 4
Roe, Patricia, 73
Rogan, Peter, 36
Rogoff, Gordon, 11
Rohmer, Eric, 198
Roloff, Michael, 198
The Romans in Britain, 147
Romanticism, 47, 55, 66, 103, 107, 109, 166, 175-176, 194, 206-207
Romeo and Juliet, 11, 143, 153-154, 165, 171, 203
Ronan, Richard, 38
Ronconi, Luca, 188
Room at the Top, 156
Roseland Ballroom (New York), 85
Der Rosenkavalier (*The Knight of the Rose*), 150
Rosenthal, Raymond, 160
Rosina Meadows, 173
Rosqui, Tom, 21, 113
Rossen, Robert, 157
Rossini, Gioachino, 162
Roth, Wolfgang, 68
Roundabout Theatre Company (New York), 10, 48
Roxie Hart, 99
Royal Academy of Dramatic Art (U.K.), 140
The Royal Box, 108
Royal Court Theatre (London), 122-123
The Royal Family, 70
Royal Shakespeare Company (London), 51-53, 72, 120, 131, 133, 148
Rudy, Martin, 159
The Runner Stumbles, 72
Rutman, Leo, 117
Ruy Blas, 10

Sabella, David, 100

Sacco, Nicola, 21
Sachs, Hans, 182
Sackler, Howard, 56
Saint Joan, 153
Salmagundi, xi, 1, 206-212
Salmon, Scott, 94
Salomé, 101
San Francisco Actors' Workshop, 27
Sand, George, 208
Sander, August, 78
Sanders, Peter, 67
Sandrow, Nahma, 80
Saroyan, William, 84
Sartre, Jean-Paul, 11, 19-21, 30, 103, 107-109, 112-115
Satire, 46, 49, 85, 88-89, 111, 137, 178, 193, 195, 198
Saturday Night and Sunday Morning, 156
Saturday Review, xi, 1, 3, 86-98, 151-154, 174-175, 184-187
Saved, 48
Savoy Theatre (London), 120, 124
Scenes From a Marriage, 76
Schaubühne Theater (Berlin), 198
Schell, Maximilian, 21
Scheme and Estimates for a National Theatre, 122, 131
Schiller, Friedrich, 70, 149, 198
Schnabel, Stefan, 52
Schneider, Alan, 18, 73
Schnitzler, Arthur, 109, 122
Schönberg, Arnold, 192
Schubert Theatre (New York), 17, 119
Schull, Rebecca, 83
Schultz, Michael, 59
Schurz, Carl, 206
Scott, George C., 75, 205
Scott, Robert Falcon, 89
The Screens, 49
Scribe, Eugène, 182
Scribner, Charles, 190
The Sea Gull, 65, 82, 120, 185, 187, 195
Seale, Douglas, 160-161
Second (French) Empire, 180
The Second Shepherds' Play, 57
Second World War: see "World War II"
The Secret Life, 125
Secret Service, 70-72
Selected Correspondence of Bernard Shaw, 161
Seneca, Lucius Annaeus, 50
Sentimentalism, 11, 26, 37, 54, 59, 73, 85, 171, 179
Separate Tables, 61
Serban, Andrei, 50, 86
Serjeant Musgrave's Dance, 11, 27-29
The Serpent, 65
Seyler, Athene, 154
Shakes versus Shav, 143
Shakespeare, William, 7, 30, 37-38, 43, 61, 66, 69, 78-80, 86, 102-103, 106, 123-124, 127, 140, 149, 153-154, 157, 163-169, 172-173, 175-176, 189, 199, 203-204, 209
Shakespeare and the Film, 165
Shakespeare Institute (University of Birmingham, U.K.), 164
Shakespeare on Silent Film: A Strange Eventful History, 164
Shakespeare on the Stage, 120
Shannon, George, 51
Shapiro, Lou, 85
Shapiro, Mel, 69, 85
Shavianism, 97
Shaw (journal), 8
Shaw, Charlotte, 124, 126
Shaw, George Bernard, 3-5, 8, 10-11, 38, 57, 61, 78, 121-125, 139-145, 147, 150, 152, 161-163, 175, 181, 183, 190, 204
Shaw, Robert, 45
Shaw and the Doctors, 161
Shaw on Dickens, 161
Shaw on the London Art Scene, 161
Shaw on Shakespeare, 161
Shawhan, April, 85
Shaw's Moral Vision: The Self and Salvation, 146
Shaw's Music, 161
Shawn, Wallace, 83
Sheen, Martin, 39
Shelley, Percy Bysshe, 106, 148

Shelton, Reid, 49
Shepard, Sam, 32-33, 56, 90, 117
Sheridan, Richard Brinsley, 61, 203
Sherman, George, 160
Sherman, Hiram, 25-26, 38
Sherman, William Tecumseh, 84
Sherwood, Robert E., 136
Shine, Ted, 194
The Shoemaker's Holiday, 183
Short Eyes, 60-61
A Short History of Shakespearean Criticism, 121
Shubert Theatre (New York), 119
Shute, Nevil, 96
Silence, 46
Simmons, Jean, 158
Simon, Barney, 39
Simon, John, 10
Simon, Neil, 29, 62
Simon, Roger Hendricks, 46
Simpson, O. J., 99
Sinden, Donald, 61
Six Characters in Search of an Author, 70
"60 Minutes" (CBS-TV), 88
Skelton, Red, 85
The Skin of Our Teeth, 11, 33-35
Skladanowsky, Emil, 164
Skladanowsky, Max, 164
Slag, 46
Slapstick, 117
A Slight Ache, 18
Sly Fox, 75
Small Craft Warnings, 53
Smith, Alexis, 47
Smith, J. P., 161
Smith, Maggie, 42
Smith, Priscilla, 50
Socialism, 36-37, 124, 144, 147, 176
Sokol, Marilyn, 49
A Soldier's Play, 92-93
Some Like It Hot, 156-157
Sommer, Josef, 52
Sondheim, Stephen, 46-47
The Song of the Lark, 211
"Sonnets of Love and Opposition" (Brenton), 148
Sons and Lovers, 57-58
Sontag, Susan, 10, 82, 146, 148

Sore Throats, 146, 148
Southern, Terry, 111
Spalter, Max, 192
Sparer, Paul, 48
Speaight, Robert, 120
Spengler, Oswald, 193
Spewack, Bella, 70-72
Spewack, Sam, 70-72
St. James Theatre (New York), 63
Stage Design Throughout the World Since 1950, 41
Stage Directions, 126
Stage Left, 190
Stage to Screen, 181
Staley, James, 73
Stanislavsky, Konstantin, 113, 149, 187, 191, 195-196, 199, 213
The Stanislavsky Heritage, 171
Stearns, James Hart, 30
Stephens, Robert, 42
Sternhagen, Frances, 52
Stewart, Jimmy, 181
Sticks and Bones, 13, 54
Sticks and Stones, 172
Stitt, Milan, 13, 72
Stone, Peter, 107, 109
Stoppard, Tom, 9, 78
Storey, David, 57
The Storm, 40
A Story of Waterloo, 163
Stowe, Harriet Beecher, 170, 179
Straight, Beatrice, 23
Strange Interlude, 11, 97-98
Strasberg, John, 63
Strasberg, Lee, 63
Strauss, Richard, 149-150, 204
Streamers, 13
Streep, Meryl, 66, 71
Strehler, Giorgio, 213
Strick, Joseph, 79
Strickler, Dan, 89
Strindberg, August, 6, 16, 34-36, 97, 117, 192
Stritch, Elaine, 85
Studio des Ursulines (Paris), 109
Subject to Fits, 56
The Subject Was Roses, 39
Subotnick, Morton, 30
Sullivan Dan, 48-49

Summertree, 55
Sunset, 159
The Sunshine Boys, 62
Surrealism, 45
Sussman, Bruce, 89
Sutherland, Joan, 33
Svoboda, Josef, 40-41
Swados, Elizabeth, 50, 86
Swan Lake, 153
Sweet, Blanche, 76
Sweet Bird of Youth, 157
Symbolism, 53, 83
Symonds, Robert, 30, 48-49
Szigligeti, Ede, 184

Table Settings, 92
Tabori, George, 102
Taking Off, 69
Tales from Shakespeare, 163
Tally, Ted, 13, 88-89
The Taming of the Shrew, 116, 164
Tango Palace, 82
Tanguy, Yves, 45
Taplinger Publishers, 175
Tarkington, Booth, 154
Tati, Jacques, 158
Tatspaugh, Patricia, 165
Taylor, Horacena J., 93
Taylor, Sam, 164
Taylor, Tom, 140, 180
Taymor, Julie, 5
Teatro la Fenice (Venice), 109
Teer, Barbara Ann, 26
Telluride Film Festival (Colorado), 2
Ten Million Ghosts, 190
Terra Nova, 89
Terry, Ellen, 161
Terry, Megan, 65
A Texas Trilogy, 72-75
Thank You, Miss Victoria, 31
That Championship Season, 55
Theater (magazine), xi, 1, 100-103, 161-169, 213-214
Theater architecture (American), 213-214
Theater Criticisms, 9, 11, 215
Theater de Lys (New York), 27
Theater East (New York), 31, 116

Theater for a New Audience (New York), 146
Theater of Dionysus (Greece), 93
Theater of the Living Arts (Philadelphia), 160
Theater of Poetry, 192
Theater of the Riverside Church (New York), 60
"Theater Space as Cultural Paradigm" (Hays), 138
Theater Union (New York), 191
Theater vs. Film, 155-169
Theatre Arts, xi, 155-159
Theatre Arts Books (New York), 41
Théâtre des Variétés (Paris), 108
Theatre Guild (New York), 75, 191
Theatre of Action (New York), 191
Theatre Masterworks, 152-153
Theatres: An Architectural and Cultural History, 187-188
The Theatrical Event, 195-198
Theatrics, 161
Théaulon: see "de Lambert, Marie Emmanuel (Guillaume Marguerite Théaulon)"
They Are Dying Out, 198
They Got Jack, 117
This Is the Rill Speaking, 31
Thomas, Ambroise, 199
Thomas, Ralph, 157
Thompson, Emma, 166
Thompson, Eric, 91
The Three Sisters, 7, 40-42, 79, 119-120, 187, 195
The Threepenny Opera, 29, 49
Throne of Blood, 164-165
Thyssen, Fritz, 20
Tidswell, Charlotte, 103
Tidworth, Simon, 187-188
Tieck, Ludwig, 195
Tilton, James, 72
Time, 189
The Time of the Cuckoo, 94
The Times (London), 106, 140
Tiny Alice, 18-19, 183
Toller, Ernst, 198
Tolstoy, Leo, 19, 145, 183, 185
Tom Sawyer, 76
Tony Awards, 95

Tootsie, 13
Torch Song Trilogy, 95
Torn, Rip, 36
Tosca, 84
Toscanini, Arturo, 121, 151, 162
A Touch of the Poet, 77, 97, 156
Toulmin, Stephen, 192
Townsend, Sylvia, 211
Toys in the Attic, 156
Tracy, Lee, 71
Tragedy, 11, 17, 21-24, 34, 57, 63, 77, 79, 86-88, 107, 109-110, 120-121, 127, 146, 154, 157, 165-166, 171, 173, 178, 182, 200, 203, 205-207, 210
The Tragic Muse (James), 210
Tragic Muse: Rachel of the Comédie-Française, 206-212
Trainer, David, 92
Trakl, Georg, 192
Travesties, 9
La Traviata (*The Fallen Woman*), 38
Trebitsch, Siegfried, 161
Tree, Herbert Beerbohm, 165
Trelawny of the "Wells", 66, 107
Trilling, Lionel, 12, 14, 206, 209
Tristan and Isolde, 97
Triumph of the Will, 67
The Trojan Women, 86
Trollope, Anthony, 179
Trotsky, Leon, 11, 58
El Trovador (*The Troubadour*), 109
Il Trovatore (*The Troubadour*), 109
Tucker, Michael, 66
Tumarin, Boris, 30
Turco, Jr., Alfred, 146
Turgenev, Ivan, 52
Turman, Glynn, 59
Turner, John, 79
Tutin, Dorothy, 79
Twain, Mark, 75, 172
Twelfth Night, 52, 103, 124
The Twelve-Pound Look, 201
Twentieth Century, 183, 205
The Two-Character Play, 53
Two Gentlemen of Verona, 69, 124
Two Small Bodies, 84
Two Women, 156

Tyler, Jim, 94
Tynan, Kenneth, 10
Tyrone Guthrie Theater (Minneapolis), 33-35, 183

UCLA (University of California at Los Angeles), 185
Ullmann, Liv, 76
Ulysses, 79, 144-145
Uncle Vanya, 41, 119-120
Undset, Sigrid, 67
Ungar, Frederick, 140, 193-194
University of California at Berkeley, 170
University of California Press, 163, 185
University of Chicago Press, 172
University of Edinburgh, 27
University of London, 140
University of Massachusetts Press, 194
University of Texas Press, 195
University of Toronto Press, 161
Ure, Mary, 45
The Use of the Drama, 126

Vagabond Stars, 80
van Itallie, Jean-Claude, 32-33, 55, 64-65
Van Peebles, Melvin, 59
Van Sant, Gus, 167
Vanzetti, Bartolomeo, 21
Vardac, A. Nicholas, 181
Vaudeville, 25, 73, 99, 157, 174, 177, 189, 201
Vedrenne, J. E., 122
Verdi, Giuseppe, 38, 109, 168-169, 174, 209, 211
Verism, 76, 200
Veronica, 111
Victoria, 66
Victoria, Queen (U.K.), 206
Victorianism, 32, 66, 99, 179, 209
The Victors, 112
Vidal, Gore, 157
Viertel, Berthold, 192
Viet Rock, 65
Vietnam War, 13, 54-55, 89
Victorianism, 99, 127, 139-145

Vidal, Gore, 157
Viertel, Berthold, 192
Viking Press (New York), 52, 140, 185
Village Voice, 11, 100
Villette, 206
Vilna Troupe (Lithuania), 80
The Virgin Spring, 158
Vivian Beaumont Theater (New York), 19, 29-30, 48-49, 52-53, 66, 70, 76, 101, 114
The Voice of Nature, 173
Voight, Jon, 43
Volkov, Alexander, 109
Volpone, 75
Voltaire (François-Marie Arouet), 144
von Bülow, Hans, 149
von Heldburg, Frau (Ellen Franz), 150
von Hofmannsthal, Hugo, 143
von Sydow, Max, 158
The Voyage Out, 211
The Voysey Inheritance, 123
Vye, Murvyn, 30

Wade, Kevin, 13, 89-90
Wagner, Richard, 97, 142, 149, 168
Wagner, Robin, 21
Waiting for Godot, 4-5, 156, 177-178
The Wake of Jamey Foster, 91
Wakefield Master, 57
Walewski, Count (Alexandre Florian Joseph, Count Colonna-Walewski), 209
Walken, Christopher, 43, 88
Wallace, Ronald, 58
War, 32
Ward, Douglas Turner, 111, 194
Wardle, Irving, 182
Waring, Richard, 152
Warner's Summer Will Show, 211
Warren, William, 172
Washington Square Players (New York), 1
Wasserman, Alan, 89
Wasserstein, Wendy, 90
Waste, 127

The Waters of Babylon, 27
Watkins, Maurice, 98
Watson, Lucile, 153
Watts, Jeanne, 42
Way Down East, 74, 174
Weapons of Happiness, 148
The Weather-hen, 121
Weaver, Fritz, 70
Weber, Karl, 198
Webster, Margaret, 152-153
Wedekind, Frank, 192
Weill, Kurt, 49, 190
Weiner, John, 94
Welk, Lawrence, 99
Welles, Orson, 158, 165-166, 190
Wells, H. G., 161, 175
Welty, Eudora, 13, 183
Wesker, Arnold, 36-37, 39
Wesley, John, 147
Wesleyan University Press, 195
West, Jennifer, 18
West End (London), 137
West Side Story, 94
Westbeth Theater Center (New York), 64
Wharton, Edith, 66, 99, 183
What the Wine-Sellers Buy, 13, 58-60
Where's Daddy?, 25-27
Where's Poppa?, 69
White, Ruth, 18
Whitebait, William, 109
Whiteside, Walker, 108
Whitman, Walt, 173-174, 200
Who's Afraid of Virginia Woolf?, 19
Wickwire, Nancy, 34-35
Widdoes, Kathleen, 49
The Widowing of Mrs. Holroyd, 57-58
Wilde, Oscar, 152-153, 192
Wilder, Billy, 156
Wilder, Thornton, 33-34, 43
Wilhelm Meister's Apprenticeship, 198-201
Wilhelm Meister's Theatrical Mission, 199
Wilhelm Meister's Travels, 199
Willems, Michele, 165
Willett, John, 101

Williams, Dick A., 59
Williams, Jay, 190
Williams, John, 153
Williams, Tennessee, 11, 13, 53-54, 63, 91, 156-157, 183
Wilshire, Bruce, 209
Wilson, Colin, 175-177
Wilson, Edmund, 12
Wilson, Garff B., 170-172
Wilson, Lanford, 13, 31, 43, 63, 89, 116-117
Wilson, Robert, 96-97
Wilson Library Bulletin, xi, 16-17
Wind, Edgar, 12
The Winslow Boy, 61
Winter, Edward, 30
Winter, William, 171
The Winter's Tale, 38, 124
Winterset, 21-22
Wiseman, Joseph, 52
Wittgenstein's Vienna, 192
The Wizard of Oz, 178
WNET-TV (New York), 1-2
Wood, John, 52
Woolf, Virginia, 208, 211
Woollcott, Alexander, 7
Working Girl, 13
The World of Suzie Wong, 157
World War I, 73, 97-98, 142, 162, 175-176, 192-193
World War II, 8, 29, 41, 47, 62, 92-93, 109, 112, 126, 131, 191
Worth, Irene, 70

W.P.A. (Works Progress Administration), 89, 188
W.P.A. Theater (New York), 89
Wright, Richard, 194
Wright, Robert, 109
Wright, Sue Ellen, 193
Wyattville, Jeffry, 188
Wycherley, William, 30

Yale College, 195
Yale Review, 1
Yale School of Drama, 13, 89
Yale/Theatre, 8
Yale University, 1-2, 11, 126, 180
Yankee Theatre, 180
Yarmolinsky, Avrahm, 184-187
Yeats, W. B., 122, 175
Yiddish Art Theater (New York), 70
York, Michael, 54
York College: see "City University of New York"
You Can't Take It With You, 112
Young, Stark, 5, 8

Zakkai, Jamil, 50, 81
Zaslove, Arne, 68
Zeffirelli, Franco, 166-168
Ziegfeld, Florenz, 47, 96, 178
Zindel, Paul, 55-56
Zomina, Sonia, 81
Zweig, Stefan, 75

James R. Russo is an independent researcher who holds graduate degrees, including the doctorate, from Louisiana State University and the University of Richmond. He has taught at those schools as well as Tulane. Russo's primary scholarly interests are the cinema and comparative literature.

Among other works, he has edited or authored the following books: *The Bookman: William Troy on Literature and Criticism, 1927-1950* (2021); *Drama According to Alexander Bakshy, 1916-1946* (2021); *Pillars of Society: Ibsen, Shaw, Brecht; Essays in Dramatic Criticism* (2022); *Open Hatch: The Theater Criticism of Robert Hatch, 1950-1970* (2022); *Understanding Adaptation: Drama, Fiction, Film; A Casebook* (2022); and *"Film Culture" on Film Art: Interviews and Statements, 1955-1971*.

www.ingramcontent.com/pod-product-compliance
Lightning Source LLC
Chambersburg PA
CBHW062157080426
42734CB00010B/1729